To Edie
with very best
wishes.
Sue Herdman.

Happy Birthday My Darling

Susan Uebel

This edition published in Great Britain in 2015 by
Farthings Publishing
8 Christine House
1 Avenue Victoria
SCARBOROUGH
YO11 2QB
UK

http://www.Farthings-Publishing.com
E-mail: queries@farthings.org.uk

ISBN: 978-1-291- 92699-6
January 2015 (q)

DEDICATION

To my dear Father, CHARLES HENRY UEBEL

Also to St. Paul's Girls' School, members of its teaching and administrative staff and Governors, for the many productive years I spent there as a senior member of staff and for the support I received from teachers, pupils and Governors when I was building up the new Drama department to a level which attracted high acclaim.

I also thank the numerous Paulinas who passed through my care, many of whom contacted me on my retirement. I wish them all well and hope that each prospered in whatever field they chose to follow.

My thanks extend to members of the present Governing body for their acknowledgement and response in the writing of this book.

ACKNOWLEDGEMENTS

My grateful thanks for their professional guidance and kindness to DAVID FOWLER of Farthings Publishing, and ROBERT ENGLAND.

I should like to thank those who, through their friendship, support and expertise have made a contribution to this book:

ROBERT JOHNSON: for his tireless patience, humour and loyalty when explaining the intricacies of computer science.

STEVE JONES: who gave me such confidence in the early days of e-mails, Word Processing and the mysteries of machinery.

My close and dear friends who have remained faithful and true. I could not have told my story and Ronnie's without their unfailing belief:

MORAGH GEE

ALESSANDRA RICHARDS

LINDA LAWRENCE

NICOLAS DAKIN

PETER & TERESA BLACKETT

I have been very grateful for the help I received from:

JOHN FENWICK (Retired Chairman of the Governors of St. Paul's Girls' School) and PAT GEATER (Retired Bursar of St Paul's Girls' School)

***

CONTENTS

'The moving finger writes and, having writ, moves on;
nor all thy piety nor wit shall lure it back to cancel half
a line'

OMAR KHAYYAM

PART 1

T H E N

THEATRE IN THE ROUND, SCARBOROUGH
1979

Ronnie remembered our first meeting. I found that memory vague and uncertain. He said I appeared to be careworn, pensive and sad. He was quick to add 'Until you smiled'.

I had gone to the Wardrobe Department for a costume fitting. I was to play Rebecca Nurse in 'The Crucible'. She was eighty-five, so I suppose it was an accurate description. I was thirty-nine. It was my first show with Alan Ayckbourn and the job was important. I hoped to be invited back for a further season. I was, however, at the start of a nervous breakdown.

The Wardrobe staff was frantic, trying to get the play ready for opening. Two men were in charge, one very tall and angular with not much to say: the other was short, thickset and busy. Both were very competent and it was reassuring to be moved about, pinned and arranged, but my tremulous feelings and thoughts brought about a disturbing anxiety and I wanted to bolt. Escape is welcome to people who are troubled, agitated, lonely and frightened. Ronnie, the busy one, spoke with pins in his mouth and said I was done. I recall nothing more...

Rebecca Nurse did not appear often, so my rehearsal calls were brief and spasmodic. I had taken a flat in the town, but was too anxious to stay there. Instead, I borrowed a car and commuted to my family home in

Beverley. The journeys were disquieting for I was petrified, afraid of driving over the cliff on the coast road. I didn't.

I was in a strange, dazed state: on some days I was alert and capable: others found me unable to marshal any feeling of normality. I managed to camouflage...I rehearsed, I performed and I functioned.

My family was worried. A search for help was becoming more and more urgent.

Some time ago, my brother had been introduced to an unusual and compelling man. He was a Parapsychologist. It was suggested that I meet him. By then, I was beyond caring and agreed. The man was unusual; he was compelling. He cured me. How he helped me is irrelevant; suffice it to say that past influences, trials and unhappy episodes had played their part in engendering this painful instability. He unravelled the mess.

Before, my professional life had been a success. In 1960, I trained at the Guildhall School of Music & Drama, went on to teach Drama for eight years, gained an Honours degree in Drama at Hull University, and then, at the age of thirty-five became an actor. I completed ten promising years in provincial Theatre Repertories before my illness began. Superficially, I must have seemed confident, vivacious and talented.

The therapy months taught me to be emotionally strong, independent and focused. I worked hard. I learned about cause and effect. Once origins of unrest were clear and I was secure in knowing the reasons for my despair, incentive and motivation replaced the turmoil and I was set to heal myself. Slowly, the confusion and strife ceased and I found myself on the brink of a new, affecting and accomplished life. And....Ronnie....

Rebecca saw me through the first, faltering stint at the Stephen Joseph Theatre. The following year, I was invited to join the company for a full season.

The first play was to be Priestley's 'Time and The Conways' and directed by Alan Ayckbourn. Initially, he rehearsed the play in what turned out to be a Godforsaken church hall in Parsons Green, London and then the National Theatre where he was supervising the opening of one of his blockbusters. Trudging down to London, finding digs and travelling was a nuisance, but I luxuriated in being well again and working. Rehearsals were daunting and a test for my new-found confidence. No one knew it was new-found...

There was much to throw me, not least a young American trainee who trailed after Mr. Ayckbourn wittering about his 'awesome' technique. Her presence in the rehearsal room put me on edge. My scenes - I was playing Madge - were complicated and I could do without her rustling script and mirthless titter. I found that some of the leading players knew one another, some were friendly, and some were distant and careful. It was a lonely time, but I had travelled far.

Ronnie appeared towards the end of the rehearsal period. We had stopped for tea. Suddenly, the Wardrobe man came through the door. Of course there was no recognition of me, so I was able to observe him. I wondered why he was there. He looked different. I suppose the occasion was different for he was not fitting costumes, pins in mouth. He was interesting, quirky. Someone said, 'Oh Ronnie, it's good to see you' and laughter began. He had newspaper cuttings, reviews from a play. I watched. He had brought them for the Company. It was generous, for his journey had been specially made. 'Typical of Ronnie', someone said. I weighed him up. First, my attention was drawn to a large brass safety-pin attached to his leather belt - on it hung a bunch of keys. Extraordinary. He was wearing twill trousers with myriad pockets. Ronnie was popular and...funny. He was entertaining a very receptive group. He had curly hair and a fetching, disarming smile. The brass safety-pin now hangs on the wall of my kitchen....

We returned to our Scarborough base, the Westwood building situated on Valley Bridge Parade. While in London, I had made friends with an actress also in the play. Tess was outgoing, great fun and much younger than me. It didn't seem to matter. We heard of a theatrical house in town which was to let and we decided to share. It was an apt arrangement for we had a lot in common and many opportunities to discuss our work, the theatre and its atmosphere.

Soon, we were approaching the opening night of 'The Conways'. Costume fittings were frequent and it became an exciting time. The play had a huge time-span, popular with Priestley. The characters were considerably older in the second act and then in the final one reverted to the youth of the first. Madge, a complex woman, had become an embittered schoolteacher in the middle of the play. Our designer had captured her mood effectively in his costumes. My 'young' creation was of dark brown silk enhanced with cream lace collar; my middle-aged 'embittered' one was precise in its harsh, masculine simplicity. Ronnie Herdman, I discovered, knew all about it. Once more, he materialised in the Wardrobe Department, and appeared to be very satisfied with the unprepossessing, gingery tweed suit he had taken great pains to find. Quite carried away, he produced a trilby hat, brogues and lisle stockings to complete the gear.

Ronnie was a perfectionist when working in the Wardrobe. He was skilled. Not only did he have an eye for the finished product and the impact it would make, he was able to visualise costume as part of the whole. More importantly, he made it his business to generate comfort for actors. His work was an adjunct. It completed the characterisation.

I went along to the Wardrobe for my final fitting before the Technical and Dress Rehearsals. I admired myself in the long looking-glass. A figure appeared behind me in the reflection. Ronnie was appraising the tweed suit, hat and outrageous shoes. 'Mmn,' he remarked, 'a real bull dyke'.

I had discovered that the other man in the Wardrobe was Philip. He and Ronnie worked together, but as far as frocks were concerned, Ronnie seemed very much in charge. Philip chuckled loudly and trembled. I reckon he was as edgy as me...I liked him.

I was nervous, very nervous on the First Night. As always, all my insecurities vanished on first entrance, and from then on, until the play came down, I was Madge: centred, confident and able, technically and creatively, to express every nuance of her personality.

The Company changed quickly, eager to get into the Bar. The American assistant, who had, thankfully, kept a low profile during later rehearsals, appeared beside me. 'Jeez', said she, 'you come up on the night!' I suppressed a contented giggle...

Ronnie was in the bar, and wearing a very classy shirt. Philip was downing a pint beside him. I knew at once. They were partners, not just Wardrobe assistants. They were partners. Both praised my performance. The tweed suit was to be remembered with affection for many years to come.

I had got off to a good start. Shared digs were easy-going and companionable. It was a sound, reassuring three-week run of 'The Conways'.

Soon after its opening, rehearsals began for the next play in repertoire and we were introduced to an Associate Director. It was a new play by a new writer. Much to my amazement, Ronnie Herdman's name appeared on the cast list. He was to play a leading part. What a surprise...

We attended for the read-through. Tess, together with another young actress and actor, made up the small, resourceful company. The camaraderie was robust from the start. No wary glances or guarded behaviour crept into the overall ambience. Contact was open, friendly; there was no contention or vying for supremacy. Our Director was easy and uncomplicated while, at the same time, being encouraging and firm. He knew where he was going...indeed he needed to, for the play was awful. Nevertheless, the characters were well-rounded and presented excellent opportunities for an inventive cast.

Ronnie was a superb actor. He was playing an arrogant, pushy Business Director, who was quite unscrupulous in his dealings with others. Ronnie was not type-cast.

I watched him in rehearsal. He was not sure of himself. He would look at me...then smile. Like me, he was not a quick study and lines often eluded him. Remarkably, Ronnie could improvise until the correct dialogue returned. Not only did he contrive and fabricate. He could ad-lib, vamp, and wing the script; in so doing the words sounded as if they were the words he was supposed to be saying. It was skilful, but hell for those working with him. Ronnie was an instinctive actor, applying pure common sense to any unforeseen development or issue. There was charisma. Charm and warmth shone through his character's bluster and insensitivity. Consequently, the person became oddly attractive....very attractive. Ronnie was attractive...

A friendship was beginning between us. Ronnie and I were in tune. This affinity served the company well and we became a strong, capable unit.

When Ronnie was not involved in scenes, he would sit at the side of the rehearsal room, crocheting. He did not look at the wool. He watched as we worked. The crochet hook seemed to have a mind of its own, for below it, would appear a garment of such beauty one wondered from where it came....sleeves, collars, delicate traceries in every hue imaginable. I noticed the hands moving effortlessly; noticed the nails bitten to the quick.

Ronnie was generous. Everyone admired his self-taught craft and he would spend fruitless hours trying to teach us how to accomplish the simplest of stitches.

One morning, he arrived toting a prodigious carrier-bag. After delving inside, he produced two dazzlingly beautiful crocheted coats. Both were decorated with spangles, beads and brilliants. A brown one was given to Tess, and the other, lavender and blue, trimmed with lapis lazuli beads, was given to me. 'For you', Ronnie said, 'to match those eyes'. I wore it until, many years later, it was threadbare...and others had taken its place...

Ronnie's gifts were renowned. He and Philip lived in a large Victorian house in Scarborough. In the walled garden at the rear, there was an Edwardian greenhouse. That was where Ronnie cultivated a grapevine. Gravely, he would appear in the Green Room with bunches of his grapes wrapped in tissue. They would then be decanted into a large dish and left for famished actors to sample. I often wondered why, at the end of the day, they would be hanging fire. Apparently, these bonne bouche were so sour as to be inedible...poor Ronnie.

We would often find ourselves chatting in the Green Room, Ronnie and me. That was how I found out about West Bank and the house where he lived. I heard about Jessie, the cross Border Collie Lurcher, who belonged to Philip and I listened to the description of Ronnie's garden.

I enjoyed teasing Ronnie. He was fun. His fun was infectious. His jokes would be boyish and daft; he was vulgar, yet refined; sophisticated yet simple. Ronnie was the common man, able to blend in anywhere. As I grew to know him, I realised how fragile he was beneath the façade of bonhomie. We had much to share. We understood our frailties, lack of confidence and self-esteem. These interludes became light-hearted, focal points in our days.

The awful play opened and - was a huge success! Audiences can be mystifying, but what matter as long as they come and enjoy us. We were a tight ensemble, playing off each other with gusto. Ronnie's memory played tricks on him; also, on his fellow actors! He extricated himself from the most aggravating scrapes with sheer wit and expertise. Sometimes, the young members of the cast on the receiving end of his wriggling, were left reeling and uncertain....alas, no one could be cross with Ronnie. Except, perhaps....for me...

One night, his bravura ran away with him. He goosed me quite boldly while we were awaiting a cue. I was so astonished, all I could say was: 'I thought you were gay!' This met with rampant gaiety. I did, however, get my own back. I waited until other cast members were around and then tackled Ronnie. He thought I was about to engage him in serious conversation, but instead I said: 'Ronnie, if you ever goose me like that again, I will grab your bits, so much so that you may be out of action at a crucial moment'. He was alarmed. He blushed. He grinned. His eyes were wide. 'Is that a promise?' he replied.

In performance, Ronnie was innovative. Although professional and adept, he was not hidebound by stringent rule or restriction. He approached each night differently, waiting to see what the audience brought to the play. Whatever it was, he reacted to it.

A champagne scene in the middle of the piece had presented problems from time to time; bottles with faulty corks; corkscrews that did not screw, and so on. Inevitably, the unforeseen happened. All were centre stage, Ronnie poised with bottle in hand, when the aforementioned cork exploded sending fake fizz forcibly down my decollete. With the adroitness of a practised conjuror, Ronnie produced an overly large white handkerchief from his breast pocket and proceeded, in ostentatious and animated fashion, to mop my bosom. Audience response was guaranteed. In the uproar that ensued, Ronnie was heard to whisper audibly, but fortunately only in my hearing: 'You don't get many of those to the pound!'

I never regarded Ronnie's saucy behaviour as objectionable or offensive. It was part of a beguiling package. Besides, double entendre or disreputable comment has always appealed to my dubious sense of humour.

Once the play was up and running, our attentions were then turned to Lunchtime shows and the anticipation of Alan's new play.

In the meantime, Tess and I had been invited to lunch at West Bank. We got on very well. We were at home in our little house where late-night liberal gin n' tonics oiled the wheels of conversation.

Tess, also, had grown fond of Ronnie and Philip. We were looking forward to our Sunday outing. Tess spent most weekends in Scarborough. I would often travel to Beverley to see family and keep in close touch with my Doctor. Therapies as such had finished, but I still made regular phone calls. Occasional visits were reassuring and all helped to bolster my growing self-reliance. Tess knew of my past difficulties. So did Ronnie...he listened with great interest.

West Bank was situated near to town. It was a leafy street which opened out into a park at the far end. No 17 was part of a terrace and rose to three floors. It was different from any other house I had known. The homes in which I had spent my childhood and early adult life had been built in the thirties. West Bank dated back to 1890.

Ronnie was framed in the doorway as we approached. He beamed and wiped his hands on a capacious, navy striped apron which almost reached the floor. Jessie dashed in and out and then dashed back in again as Philip called her. The hallway was dark; in fact the whole house seemed dark. We followed Ronnie. The kitchen was a bright, shining, sunny place furnished with antique pine dressers and two unusual pine settles. These faced each other: there was a table between.

We were shown into the back-yard which was a sun-trap. It was furnished with wrought iron wheels and ornaments, all painted white and fixed to the brickwork.

A huge iron bench, very ornamental, was ready with colourful cushions invitingly placed. All was absorbing and Tess explored, her eyes becoming wider and wider as she became more enamoured with the collection of treasures.

Philip was in charge of drinks. Hefty goblets were produced, accompanied by a ship's decanter brimming with white wine. Three glasses later, we climbed the yard steps and entered the house once more. I had not noticed the Aga in the kitchen. It seemed that Ronnie was very attached to it. Philip, however, was doing most of the cooking and his comments were droll: 'Ronnie Herdman, you're not going to serve that are you?' or 'Ronnie Herdman, just get out of the way!' It was all so good-natured and comical; reminiscent of listening to a married couple who knew each other so very well and were supremely comfortable together.

The top of the Aga was covered with bubbling saucepans and delicious smells were left behind as we were taken into the front room of the house where a table was set. Momentarily, one reeled with shock...the walls were painted chocolate brown! I, a girl reared on magnolia or white, stifled a gasp.

The dining-table and handsome, brass-handled sideboard were dark polished oak. The table setting was memorable - more goblets, this time the size of Sundae glasses and table mats decorated with sepia photographs of Scarborough. Softly-lit table lamps, some Art Deco, picked up the glow of brass and silver. The curtains, of lighter fabric, a William Morris design, were tethered on either side of the bay window by two brass elephant heads.

A cupboard, probably once a bookcase and filled with glassware of every description, stood by the wall near the door. Perhaps most impressive of all, was the mahogany floor-to-ceiling shelf unit which dominated one corner of the room, beside the fireplace. It displayed a varied collection of china - Clarice Cliff, egg-shell and Old Chelsea. I was not familiar with names then. Ronnie had not enlightened me about the wonders of antiques.

Philip appeared in the doorway. He ran nicotine-stained fingers through his hair.

'Oh dear,' he said lazily, 'my glass seems to be empty' and disappeared. Tess and I were left to wonder at it all, while frenzied conversation continued down the hall-way and into the kitchen. Then...it came into being...lunch...or rather...a banquet. Tastefully-arranged flower arrangement was set aside and in came the plates. Earthenware dishes, steaming with every known vegetable, were placed beside us. Cauliflower cheese and roast lamb quickly followed.

Our hosts gave us a most delectable Sunday lunch in lush, enticing surroundings. We went on to learn that the vegetables had been grown on an allotment at the top of the hill. Philip went on to tell of a goat, a rather disagreeable one, which was secured and shackled near to the entrance of the plot. Apparently, Ronnie had fallen foul of it. Philip had not gone to his rescue in time. Before anything could be done, the goat had wound its rope round and round poor Ronnie until he was powerless to move. All his carefully-gathered new potatoes fell from his grip and rolled down the hill. Of course the incident was absurd, farcical and ludicrous. The image of a hapless Ronnie was laughable, but somewhere in the story, was a hint of the vulnerability within Ronnie. It was a tender image.

We had been told of the Secret Garden and the Edwardian glasshouse, but that day, we did not have time to see them. We said our goodbyes at the gate, and, as I turned to wave, I looked up at the house again. One day, it would no longer be someone else's house...it would become my home...my beloved West Bank...

Lunchtime shows were popular at the Westwood Theatre. Alan devised musicals that were intricate and challenging. Fortunately for us, in the Summer of 1980, Ronnie and I were cast together in 'Second Helping'. The rest of the Company were engaged in 'First Course'.

Rehearsals operated in the cramped confines of the Theatre Bar. Performances were presented on a mini platform stage at one end of the Theatre Restaurant. Members of the audience, seated at small tables, enjoyed the intimate, Continental atmosphere of café culture.

Stage wing space was restricted. There was much pressing of bodies, smothered giggles and the probability of missed cues. Ronnie and I found ourselves cheek by jowl. There was holding of hands, arms around shoulders and provocative talk...all in the name of close friendship. Why did I find this vaguely disturbing, exciting? Such fleeting thoughts were crushed. He is gay, I reflected...

I looked forward to the backstage moments spent with Ronnie, the searching glances and his prevailing, potent presence. Did others notice the chemistry between us?

Once the lunchtime shows were running, the thrill of Alan's new play was rippling through the Company.

Tess and I planned a party at our house in Castle Road. Ronnie and Philip had agreed to help with the food. Ronnie appeared on the doorstep at 2.00 p.m. clad in red and gold brocade jacket and evening trousers! Philip was in the pub. We were busy. Ronnie was laying into the sherry as he, along with my mother who had taken a bus trip in order to lend a hand, turned out dish after dish of party fare. Suddenly, he disappeared. We laboured on. Eventually, I went in search of Ronnie. I found him in one of the bedrooms. He had removed his trousers and was standing before me in underpants and brocade jacket. 'I've 'ad it' he declared weakly, then got into bed and fell asleep. When Philip turned up, somewhat worse for wear, he testified: 'Oh yes, love, he's always pissed before the guests arrive.'

I remember being dimly disappointed. Was Ronnie going to be around for the party? Two hours later, there he was, ready and organised. In the years to come, I grew to know that Ronnie would always be there... and ready...

Alan's new play was late. In fact so late that we had only ten days to rehearse before opening. We were told that the play's arrival was imminent and everyone waited in the Bar after the evening show. This happened night after night with monotonous regularity. The process was customary to all who had worked for Alan before, but for me it was untried and trying. In due course, HE arrived carrying a weighty armful of scripts. Each was ceremoniously handed out. Inside the cover, one found a hand-written missive from Alan. Mine read: 'Sue, I'd like you to play Phyllis in 'Season's Greetings'. She's the silliest woman I have ever written'.

Ronnie had discovered he was to play Bernard; the ill-starred Doctor and my husband.

Rehearsals began at once. The play was taxing, but a formidable, uphill delight.

Ronnie's character was a brilliant but overwhelming tour de force. Bernard's traditional, Christmas offering was a puppet show. 'Fuck', announced Ronnie, 'all that and the lines as well!' Mmn...

Phyllis, his wife...me...was a drunk! Left to prepare the Christmas Eve meal, she knocks back an inordinate amount of Harveys, remindful of Ronnie at our party, and appears at the close of Act I completely blotto.

Rehearsals were riveting, intensive and, for me - scary - in fact, almost a disaster. I could not find the key to Phyllis, try as I might. I leaned on the obvious and played her as a giggly, predictable inebriate. Alan, I discovered, was not an intrusive Director, nor did he impose interpretation. I was adrift and only a few days to the First Night....

Ronnie was, as usual, having trouble with the onerous task of learning lines. We spent many frantic hours in the Green Room drilling each other with words. One tearful encounter in the Dressing-Room brought about my salvation. Like a spectre, wholly unannounced, Alan appeared in the doorway. Alan was a shy man. He was also solicitous. ' When you're drunk, Sue, do you take life very seriously? Sometimes one's conversation becomes studied and careful'. He turned and left. All at once, I began to examine my own drunken conduct. Had he watched me in the Bar? Shock, horror! Alan had, however, provided the turning point. At the next rehearsal, Phyllis became intensely serious and my problem was solved.

Ronnie, too, had mastered his puppets - and - the lines. His was a gifted, intuitive, evocative and timeless performance which possessed all the innate qualities of Ronnie himself.

Once again, Ronnie had been on hand to assist Philip in the Wardrobe. He trod a very frequent path to a nearly-new shop, Fishermen's' Wives, foraging for play clothes. My dress for Phyllis came from this imposing emporium. He also knew of some swanky boutiques on Bar Street. One morning, he came to rehearsal armed with a shoe box. 'For you,' he said, blushing, 'I thought you might like these'. Inside, wrapped in tissue, I found the most exquisite pair of scarlet high-heeled shoes. I could not speak. These were the first of many such presents. Ronnie never returned empty-handed. There would be nail polish, perfume, flowers, or a vintage dress.

'Season's Greetings' opened. It was a success and became my mother's favourite play. After its initial spell at the Westwood Theatre, it was to transfer to London's Roundhouse for a limited run. Before I moved to Town, my Doctor and his wife came to see the play. Afterwards, we had supper at Medi's, a bistro very popular with the Company. On arrival, a waiter came to our table with a package, saying, 'This was left for you Madam'. I opened the parcel and inside found a crocheted, black mohair hat which was decorated with an outlandish black feather held in place with a Jet ornament. There was a note: 'With all my love'. He was never far away. He has never been far away....

Philip was in the Bar after evening shows. Ronnie would sometimes leave without him to return home. His parting shot would be 'What would you like for supper, Philip?' Often, the reply would be non-committal or slightly offhand. Why, I thought, should I notice these things? In a curious way, I found myself feeling a little jealous for there was an intimacy there, a part of Ronnie's domestic life which I had witnessed. I would dismiss the thought - and, have another gin n' tonic. I was fond of Philip. He, like Ronnie, watched over me.

Philip drank - a lot. Then, so did I in those days. After the show was my time and when I returned home to visit my mother, she and I were drinking companions. Philip and I ignored health risk and warnings. We smoked and we drank. Then, one attached little importance to danger. Theatre life embraced both vices. They were accepted foibles. Dear Ronnie did not indulge in either weakness. He partook of a dash of alcohol, except on party nights when he succumbed to being under the influence on half a bottle of sherry. He did not smoke. Except, he told me, for puffing his way through twenty Capstan Full Strength cigarettes at a New Year celebration 'just to see what it was like'...

In view of all this, Ronnie was remarkably tolerant. At that time, the effects of passive smoking were either unknown or ignored....

Those rehearsal days, before The Premiere and eventual decampment to the Roundhouse, were frenetic, but there was time to get to know Ronnie. We often stole an hour or two to wander the streets of Scarborough where we would haunt the charity shops. Ronnie seemed to know every proprietor. Our conversations could be searching; descriptions of feelings and past scares. I discovered that Ronnie had endured three breakdowns. His symptoms had been upsetting, unsettling and full of anguish. In turn, I confided in him and told of my troubles. We laughed and took comfort from knowing that each other had walked a similar path.

Although... I had not upholstered a three-piece suite while suffering...nor had I found myself hopelessly lost on a familiar beach when walking Jessie. Then, taken three long, desolate hours to reach home.

Now, Ronnie appeared to have recovered. Our chats were positive and his attitude upbeat and amusing. I told him that I still saw my uncommon, phenomenal Doctor. He was interested, especially when I confided that with the help of this man's ingenuity and finesse, my life had been renewed, changed and rejuvenated. I was aware of Ronnie's insecurity, his nervousness and uncertainty. He was unhappy, I was sure. One day, I gave him my Doctor's address. It was not mentioned again...

We arrived at the Roundhouse Theatre. I was sharing accommodation with Tess. Ronnie lived at his agent's house when working in London. He had known the family for years.

Audiences were reasonably good and shows ran smoothly, except for a ghastly attack of food poisoning for me. Buckets were left at every exit and entrance in case I was overcome.

Once 'Seasons' was playing, we began rehearsals for 'The Importance of Being Earnest'. Ronnie was to be Dr. Chasuble and I was cast as Miss Prism. We had great rapport both on and off stage, so the pairing was perfect. Ronnie went to Philip's aid again and together they produced some sovereign designs.

Our scenes coincided, so Ronnie and I were called for rehearsal at the same time. When free, we made use of countless opportunities to explore Camden Market and the Chalk Farm Road. Often, we would find ourselves outside furniture shops; reactions were interesting. We exchanged our ideas on taste and preferences. There was much suggestive chat when looking at beds; fleeting, indefinable comment. Our hands would clasp, be squeezed and then returned hastily to pockets or bags.

Our laughter would herald re-entry to the rehearsal room. The others seemed happy for us, enjoyed the carefree relationship we shared. We were just good friends...

During this London stay, I had caught glimpses of Ronnie's agent and family. Those early impressions of raucous shrieks, a clique of theatrical allies and some rather minor hangers-on. Ronnie was swept along quite happily it seemed...none of my business, just part of the picture.

Our evening performances of 'Seasons' were a treat, a romp. I found myself flirting quite audaciously with Ronnie when waiting in the wings. I suppose I told myself it was all quite harmless, the bottom-pinching, his reactions and my own reborn joy of being able to give and respond once more. Most of all, I knew I was safe. Ronnie was gay. It was just a bit of fun.

Ronnie was mesmerised. I remember his eyes, so clearly. The expression was bewildered yet awakened. I did not realise then that he would not have known how to deal with this barrage of sexual innuendo. He was, nevertheless, where he wanted to be and so was I.

Our return to Scarborough was a relief. It was good to be back on home turf, while preparing for 'Importance'. Dear Philip had done wonders with the costumes and the set was captivating, complete with stream and miniature bridge. The trysts between Chasuble and Prism were enhanced by this romantic vision. Mmn....

School matinees were a challenge, so often being a call to combat for actors.

True to form, poor Ronnie was having traumas with memory. Chasuble speeches were burdened with great hunks of ecclesiastical terminology. I would find him in the Green Room, crochet-hook in hand, sweating profusely before entrances. He was also inclined to be overweight which made him breathless when fearful or uneasy. He had dried quite spectacularly one afternoon when the theatre was crammed with restless school children. Again, his singular talent for substituting words which were astoundingly similar to those he should have been saying came into play. For some seconds, or was it minutes, he ad-libbed. The reckoning came on the following afternoon, when, while waiting in the wings, Ronnie announced: 'I say, wouldn't it be funny if I dried in exactly the same place'.

Of course, he had tempted providence, and he did dry in exactly the same place. Fortunately, I was not engaged in dialogue with Ronnie at that time, for it would have been impossible for me to do so. I was quite out of control and so was everyone else on stage. In fact, we were so weak with effort to muffle giggles that poor Ronnie was abandoned; left to rely on his own devices. Yet again, he hauled himself out of the mire. He saved himself from disaster, but much panic-stricken stuttering went on. I was full of admiration for Ronnie. He was a master of ingenuity and intuition. After the curtain call, however, it was noticeable that Ronnie was in a state. This time the whole experience had been an ordeal. He was very white and cold perspiration beaded his face. His hands were shaking. I wanted to hold him close. So I did. He said, 'Let's go for a cup of tea'.

Unforeseen circumstances were round the corner. While happily enjoying being together, we had not taken into consideration the possibility that this accord could come to an end. We had presumed, very unwise in the precarious ways of the theatre, that we would continue being together in the forthcoming Autumn Season.

In due course, Alan's Cast Lists went up. Alan had written a musical 'Suburban Strains' and the late-night show was to be Michael Frayn's 'Clouds'. Ronnie was cast in both and the musical was bound for London. I was to be in the Christmas show 'Simple Simon' - in Scarborough. We were to be separated. I knew I would miss Ronnie, but that was that.

The present Season had not come to an end, and, in the time between, we had parties. There were invitations to West Bank, where Ronnie and Philip arranged magnificent curry suppers for the Company. This enabled Tess and I to view a little more of this intriguing house.

At night, it was as enthralling, as eye-catching, as it was by day. An upstairs sitting-room had a real coal fire, surrounded by brass canopy and marble hearth. Philip heaved buckets of fuel and logs up two flights of stairs to reach it. Indian rugs covered the floor and a three-piece moss-green uncut-moquette suite furnished the room. I was very impressed with this upstairs sitting-room, but the thing that drew my attention was an elephant's foot over in the corner! It was a footstool. I was repulsed, but mortified all at once. I mentioned it to Ronnie.

'Oh, that came from my Uncle Sandy; he used to work on the dust in Hampstead, and he'd save a few things for me. Do you like it?' explained Ronnie. I was speechless. I did, however, meet Uncle Sandy years later and long after the demise of the elephant's foot.

Ronnie seemed full of energy. We didn't talk much about our future work. What happened next came as a bolt from the blue. 'Importance' finished and rehearsals began for the Christmas show. Tess was in 'Suburban

Strains' and burst into the dressing-room one day to announce that Ronnie Herdman had come out of the show and also, 'Clouds'. He had left the Company. I was very troubled and decided to see Philip in Wardrobe. Apparently, Ronnie was ill again. I had visions of yet another three-piece suite being covered. I sent him my love.

That night, there was to be a party in the Restaurant. I was astounded to find Ronnie there. He was buoyant, amusing and, seemingly, well. We danced, joked and flirted. It was a joyous evening. Ronnie's behaviour must have seemed odd to the bystander, for it transpired that his reason for giving notice was ill health. Those who are ignorant of breakdown symptoms would not know about the highs and lows of depression, its erratic symptoms or the unpredictability of mood.

Ronnie confided to me that he could not bear the thought of working on 'Clouds'. He hated the play and the initial rehearsal for it had brought on more harrowing panic attacks. Nor could Ronnie envisage moving to London for the musical. He concluded with 'I would miss you.'

There was to be another interesting development. I had not been offered work beyond 'Simple Simon'. By chance, an availability enquiry came for me from the White Rose Theatre in Harrogate. The Artistic Director there hoped to offer me a contract for three plays, one being Ayckbourn's 'Joking Apart'. This would begin in January 1981, after the Christmas show finished. In those days, the Stephen Joseph Theatre was dark for the early months of the year, so it would mean at least three month's work. I was free to accept. It was exciting. Everyone was very pleased for me, and I think the idea appealed to Alan because I was to do one of his plays, but be directed by someone else. Ronnie, too, was pleased but quiet about any commitments he may have had. I knew I would miss him...

I acquired very comfortable digs in Harrogate. The Yorkshire Ripper had not been caught at that time. Ronnie's parting shot was 'Make sure you go straight home!'

My rehearsals began in earnest once my ties with Alan's theatre ceased.

Letters, cards and phone calls came from Ronnie. Loving and humorous cards - some romantic, some vulgar and many with strange captions and quotes. One in particular sticks in my memory. It was a quote from Longfellow and beneath was written 'From a Shortfellow'...

Soon afterwards, Ronnie phoned to let me know that he was going to work in London, for the BBC Radio Repertory Company. I was delighted for him. I knew how much he enjoyed Radio work. His vocal versatility and flexible, proficient handling of dialect lent themselves particularly well to broadcasting. Also, he would meet many old friends. Ronnie seemed well and happily looking forward to the work. As usual, he planned to room at his agent's house.

I became very immersed in my work at Harrogate. It was a friendly Company and rehearsals were stimulating. It took a while to accustom myself to a different Director. After all, it was Alan's play, but without Alan. I did miss his verbal shorthand and unassuming manner. Yet, it was a valuable experience.

I had settled well into my accommodation. The large house was light, airy and welcoming. The family I lived with was homely and down-to-earth. The owner of the house was the son of a greengrocer; he seemed obsessed with consuming large quantities of good fruit! What a relief it was to be staying in clean surroundings. Actors can encounter appalling conditions when renting rooms.

I was contented and happy in my work.

I learned that the other two plays were to be Priestley's 'When We Are Married' and 'Arsenic and Old Lace'. Both were favourites. I was cast as Annie in the first and, needless to say, one of the old ladies in the second...

First Night cards, flowers and phone calls from Ronnie continued to flow into my life. Then, silence for quite some time....Then, a phone call...He rang just before the Half-hour Call on the second night of 'Arsenic'. 'Guess what?' he said excitedly, 'I'm coming over to see you! Can you put me up?' I was sure that he would be able to stay for one night at my digs, so we arranged to meet in the Bar after the Friday show. I so looked forward to seeing him. We hadn't met for over three months.

I did a good performance that night and the atmosphere in the Dressing Room which I shared with a young actress, Penny, was very genial, impudent and eager. We were dressing for a night out...Fridays were popular for relaxation. Saturday mornings, free from rehearsal, promised a lie-in. I looked for Ronnie in the Bar, but there was no sign of him. Drinks were being ordered, when I heard my name called. I turned, and there was Ronnie walking towards me. He was smiling and arms were outstretched as he waited to hug me.

Ronnie was different. He was casually, tastefully dressed. His hair was shorter. He had lost a lot of weight. He was confident and very attractive, as always, but now he was changed and I did not know why. We talked, shared jokes and I introduced him to friends in the Company. Soon, we were to be alone. 'I've been to see your Doctor' said Ronnie.

We were then whisked away for supper and a nightclub. We danced, teased and philandered as usual, but...there was a transformation. Our contact was different for nothing was in the way. Ronnie and I were able to express so many of the things that until that magical night had been secret.

We returned to the digs. I had explained that Ronnie was a dear friend, but would be sleeping on the sofa! Everyone congregated in the kitchen for more drinks, cigarettes and pasta. I found sleeping difficult that night. My thoughts kept straying to Ronnie tucked up downstairs and also, to the news that was still to come...

The following morning, we walked to the town centre. As we strolled, Ronnie told me of his visit to my Doctor. His panic attacks had increased and a decision needed to be made. He asked for help. After, he attended for therapy every week whenever he could manage to travel to Hull on leave from the BBC.

The outcome had been astounding. In the course of therapy, Ronnie discovered that it was very unlikely that he was homosexual, but instead, a victim of circumstances which had led him along a different path. He had been attracted to women, but was confused and unable to act upon his feelings. The years went by and he accepted the status quo. 'Then,' said Ronnie, 'I met you. How do you know where to begin at the age of forty-eight?'

His therapy had included regression. He had been taken through many teenage experiences. In the safe environment of a clinic; in the care of a sympathetic, enlightened and dynamic Doctor, he had been set free from the sad, lonely existence he had known for most of his life.

It was some time later that Ronnie decided to keep a journal. I think it would be appropriate to include his words here:

RONNIE'S STORY

'Ever since I was interfered with in a cinema at the age of thirteen, I have lived in a confused world. I had two girlfriends though and fell madly in love with a student teacher before I went off to do my National Service. A kiss and a cuddle was as far as I went with any of them. I always ran away. I suppose the memory of my one encounter was too strong.

Some peace came for me when I joined the RAF. I supposed I was gay and I liked it - that, as far as I was concerned, was that.

I went into the Theatre and I was very happy. In all, I suppose I've had three big affairs in my life and they all lasted a long time. Philip was my last and longest affair - eighteen years - but for the final five or six years I had become very unhappy. I was promiscuous and made Philip unhappy too. Things were not good in the Theatre. I was busy, but on two occasions I was unable to deliver the work and had to leave plays before they were even rehearsed. I was very anxious and the GP prescribed Valium, and forbade me to work.

At the beginning of 1980, I started to work for Alan Ayckbourn in Scarborough. I was to play a big part and desperately wanted to be in the Company. I suppose I was still anxious because I began to learn the part over Christmas 1979 ready for its production in May. It was in 1979 at the Scarborough Theatre that I first met Susan Uebel. She was to play a large part in my recovery.

Susan was also in the Season of 1980 and it made a huge difference to me. We were a happy Company and the weeks flew by. I discovered I was very attached to Sue.

*The Season ended but we all stayed on for the Winter that followed. (*Here, Ronnie lists the plays I mentioned earlier*) I was tired and during performances of 'Importance' I started to shake. My fingernails, always bitten down, were getting worse. Sue was a great help, but I was chalky white most days and needed more than to be comforted. To make matters worse, Sue was leaving to do a short Season in Harrogate. 'Clouds' was hell to rehearse. I loathed it and was getting withdrawal symptoms. I couldn't work with the other actors or learn lines. Another play was looming and I was afraid to carry on. I knew I had to get out, to leave the Company while I was still able to do so. In fact, before I had a breakdown. The symptoms were already with me.*

After leaving, I was feeling a fraud. I felt released, happy and started looking well, until a week later. I took my dog for a walk along the beach and met an old friend. I talked to her and suddenly began to tremble. I was talking nonsense, babbling on about houses I wanted to buy and was angry with Philip because he wouldn't agree. My friend left me, and on a beautiful day I felt as if someone had placed a glass tube over me. I could not connect with the outside world, but started back home. The journey took me three and a half hours.

I then rang Sue's doctor. I think it was a Monday, when after a bath and clean clothes, I took the train to Hull and made my way to the appointment. I was very down and wasn't sure what could be done for a nail-biting, depressed and anxiety-torn practising homosexual of twenty-eight years. I felt ashamed but did not know what to do to help myself.

I had met the Doctor and his wife when they had come to the Theatre as Sue's guests. I was greeted with great friendliness. Notes were taken as I began to talk about myself and my problems. I seemed to talk for hours, pouring everything out - my fears, my hopes and my desolation.

As I drew to a close, my Doctor spoke. I was astounded and overjoyed for I was told that there was a possibility that I was predominantly heterosexual but living as a homosexual. The confusion had brought about acute anxiety which in turn presented as physical symptoms - panic, guilt and intolerable stress. I was asked what I wished to do about it.

I wasn't shattered. I was elated. I had been told what I secretly wanted to hear, what I had been missing all these years and what I had not had the courage to face up to. I remember saying: 'I don't know what Philip will say, but I think I owe it to myself to try and live the rest of my life as I was meant to live it and if I know Philip, he will help me.

After eighteen years, if nothing else, we are very good friends and, whatever happens, we still love each other.'

This was to be a huge decision. It would mean months of therapy and patient understanding. I hoped that it would not be a selfish decision but one which was to prove greatly satisfying and right. I was to find myself. I was ready. I told Philip. He said, 'It's your life Ronnie. You carry on.'

I remember my first therapy so well. I was shown the beauty of the female body. Everything was explained to me. How misled I'd been, basing my knowledge on what men had told me. How wrong they had been.

In due course, my Doctor helped me to explore many imaginary situations together. The Role Plays were searching and intimate, but I was progressing. For the first time, I began to feel mentally strong, stronger than I can ever remember. I was secure in the knowledge that I was doing the right thing.

It was about this time that I realised I was in love with Sue. It was something I had known for some time, but bewildered I was unable to do anything about it. Half way through my therapies, I travelled to Harrogate to see her. I knew I was changing. I felt more masculine. I even walked differently. I wanted to wear well-cut trousers and look smart...'

That glorious morning in Harrogate, when Ronnie told me of those early therapies and his true happiness, has remained as one of my most unwavering, abiding memories.

We called at my Dressing-Room at the Theatre. There, dear Ronnie wanted to kiss me for the first time. I suppose I was thinking of these impressionable, sensitive circumstances; Ronnie was in the process of learning so much about himself and now I was the one who did not know how to handle things...

I steered him gently in another direction - to Betty's Café down the road! We looked at each other across the table - no words, just looks. We did not need to speak of love. Ronnie knew and I knew.

Ronnie picked up a restaurant napkin. He wrote on it 'Ronnie' and underneath, his Islington phone number. That serviette is still in my handbag wallet, a little worn over the years, but like the memory, intact...

I walked with Ronnie to the coach station. He climbed on to the bus and into his seat. I looked up at him. By then, he had put on his unspeakable flat checked cap. As the bus moved off, he wound down the window and called 'One day, I'm going to make you feel like the Queen of Sheba!' I averted my eyes from the disbelieving glances of innocent passers-by.

I walked back. The show did not start for several hours. I think I had always known that I was in love with Ronnie, but until then had not been able to acknowledge it. Suddenly, I was filled with such euphoria, such intense rapture and was, at last, able to say to myself 'I love you Ronnie'.

My time at Harrogate was coming to an end. I did not have any further work in the offing. My days were free; there were only the evening shows and remaining matinees.

I was very happy and my thoughts were occupied with my Ronnie. I spoke to him frequently on the phone and there were letters. We did not, however, speak of our love for each other. I was uncertain what to do. I contacted our Doctor. He would know how to guide this wonderful, but complex situation.

I combined a visit to the Stephen Joseph Theatre with another to our Doctor. It was good to talk to old friends still working in Scarborough and fun to see dear Philip again. Philip and I did not probe into Ronnie's new life. Philip was busy, as usual, and interspersing costume design for the forthcoming Spring/Summer Season with long, liquid lunches at the pub. Everyone seemed surprised that I had not had word from Alan about the next plays; it was taken for granted that I would join the Company once more.

Advice from our Doctor was reassuring, sensible and cautious. I knew I needed counsel if my fledgling relationship with Ronnie was to unfold and be nurtured in the right way. I was a novice. How was I to cope with Ronnie's lack of knowledge and tentative beginnings? I was told to take everything a day at a time. Slowly, patiently we were to lovingly explore the wonder of such a pure, true partnership. I was also advised to keep in constant touch. We were now being shepherded together.

Before I met Ronnie and began working for Alan Ayckbourn I had been fretting about the need to buy a house of my own. These thoughts and finding the money to fund them had long been shelved. As my Doctor's meeting came to a close and I turned to wave at the garden gate, his farewell prediction stunned me - ...'and don't try to buy any property. You won't need to'.

The content and progress of Ronnie's therapies were his secret. There had been no betrayal of confidence. It was up to him to share this private affair in his own words:

RONNIE'S STORY (continued)

I remember my trip to Harrogate and wanting to kiss Sue but being the good 'therapist' she is, a peck was all I was to have. I was deeply aroused by Sue.

Somehow I was changing. My Role Play therapies were a revelation. My growing knowledge of the female anatomy in relation to my own body was a most amazing discovery. I was in awe, fascinated. In one of my first Role Plays, a clinical helper and I acted out a first meeting when we were thirteen years old. We were trembling, very nervous, but soon we had a wonderful rapport. I found it all such a relief. We were discovering all about each other, shyly as youngsters do. It all had great humour. I remember telling her about my Dad's pigeons in the back garden. I felt that first crude sexual experience with a man in the cinema being overwhelmed by the innocence of this new realization and my first meaningful encounter with a woman.

I also noticed in the course of my treatment that I did not need fantasy any more, for I had the real thing to focus on - Sue. Most of the time, sexual focus in a clinical atmosphere is almost impossible. I suppose the truth was that because I was in love with Sue, even though we had not kissed as I wanted to, I refused to obey any signals from another source! The subconscious plays havoc with the male anatomy!

After only five double sessions of two to three hours each, I was fit and already quite changed. I was able to diet quite easily. I felt incredibly well. When a Theatre job came along - 'Storky and Co.', a television series - and I knew I was to be in London for some time, my Doctor suggested Hypnotism enabling me to relax and form a strong link with him. I had thought Hypnotism was quite different. I did not expect to be conscious and remember all that was said. I did, very clearly. I was told that I would be more relaxed than I had ever been and that learning lines would be easier. Also, I would enjoy my own company without being lonely again; not a word about biting my fingernails which was something I had done since childhood. It gave me great discomfort and shame. I would hide my hands when attending interviews; sure it was a part of my being inferior.'

I had an invitation from Alan Ayckbourn to join the Summer Season beginning April 1981. I was delighted for the plays sounded exciting. There was to be a revival of 'Season's Greetings', 'The Conservatory', 'Me, Myself and I' - a musical lunchtime show - and lastly, a new Ayckbourn play. No doubt Alan would be 'on nights' for some time. I envisaged another tense interlude in the Bar waiting for the script. That was very distant.

In the meantime, I had been in touch with Tess. She was now based in London, but we both looked forward to her joining the Company again and, more importantly, sharing a house once more. Actors never learn…Fate took a hand and Tess was offered a television role in 'The Bell'. It was the leading part and an offer she could not refuse.

So, on my return to Scarborough, I was, yet again, looking for accommodation. I told Ronnie the tale. He immediately announced: 'Oh you must live with Philip. He'll be thrilled!' I hoped that Philip would be thrilled, but did not know how much he would welcome the intrusion. Ronnie continued to stay with his agent while working in London. He seemed to get on very well with the family and was close to all. His association did not depend entirely on business and work.

Philip was a kind, caring, humorous and easy-going landlord. My bedroom was cosily furnished; the bed made up with embroidered linen sheets! Even a portable television had been installed. Jessie enjoyed having another companion. She had been used to spending most of the days alone while Philip was at the Theatre, so having someone else to talk to was a rare treat.

The house at West Bank was a comfortable refuge from the frantic workload of the Theatre. Like Jessie, I did spend time alone there. We wandered through the rooms together and often ventured into the Secret Garden at the back. It was vast. The land consisted of a double plot - much to Ronnie's joy - surrounded by walls, climbing roses and clematis. Our next-door neighbours, Bob and Dorothy, had only a yard. No one seemed to know why, other than that the deeds proved the extra-large space was ours. Ronnie had bought the house in 1975 for £7,000 and paid off the mortgage in record time. The garden was filled with rare treasures and around every corner there was a new discovery - primroses, pansies, snowdrops, tulips and daffodils. In the summer months, cascades of roses hung down over taller trees. At that time, the old Edwardian glasshouse was still standing. Inside, was the largest fuschia I had ever seen and its fronds burst through the dilapidated roof. An equally massive Fatsia Japonica fought for notice. Here, Ronnie reared his grapes - the sour ones....

The garden was neglected while Ronnie was away. It became overgrown and rather sad. I remember, in those early days of knowing him, he would return from London and go to explore each new shoot. He could not hide his sorrow if plants were struggling. He had already bid farewell to his beloved allotment. Gardens need constant love, care and hard work. He could not be there.

'Season's Greetings' got the Season off to a good start. How strange it seemed having another actor take over Ronnie's affectionate interpretation. Rehearsals soon moved into 'The Conservatory'. The play was new and out of the ordinary. I was at ease with the work and strolling home with Philip after our session in the Bar after the show was fun. We had long conversations which invariably continued into the night at West Bank. Philip would cook 'a spud or two' and feed the faithful Jessie while I sat at the kitchen settle downing a convivial gin. Of course our talks included Ronnie and we would laugh long and oft about his market flings, house-hunting and multiplicity of antiques.

I learned that Ronnie would be drawn to houses for the most whimsical reasons. It was important for the house of his choice to have an ingenious feature: a winding staircase, stained-glass window, or, most essentially - a conservatory. Apparently it mattered not if the rest of the dwelling was falling down, Ronnie would be prepared to take it on. I concluded that these things had been the source of argument for Ronnie and Philip. Perhaps it had been another manifestation of Ronnie's anxiety as he searched for order in his life. Philip was practical, far-seeing and settled. Why would he wish to move? I sensed Ronnie's restlessness, and yet, I was aware of how very difficult the turn of events must have been for Philip. He knew of the change that was coming and he also knew that that change would mean change for him. Philip accepted my presence in Ronnie's life. He seemed to enjoy the friendship. It did not shut him out. Philip was gathered in from the beginning...

I spent time at my family home when there were gaps in the schedule. My mother was pleased to share my theatrical life. She was a regular visitor to the Theatre-in-the-Round and had met Ronnie and Philip several times. She liked them and was in praise of how well they looked after her. Her knowledge of the gay world was limited, shutting her eyes to what she did not wish to see, but insisted that she was worldly-wise and full of understanding...Mmn...

Ronnie's First Night flowers arrived aplenty at the Stage Door, but often these would be delivered in person when he would appear unexpectedly from nowhere. He revelled in surprise. Many years into the future, when out shopping, I would be irritated when I couldn't find him, fearful for his safety. His apparition would then appear from behind a display cabinet, smiling and unrepentant.

The cards I received from Ronnie - bawdy, blue and naughty - could hardly take their place in the Dressing Room, to be displayed over mirrors and surfaces. Two of these were irresistible and may I be forgiven for including them here. Of course, they were visual and so much glee is lost in words.

One had the caption: DID YOU HEAR ABOUT THE O.A.P. WHO STREAKED AT THE FLOWER SHOW? Underneath was a grotesque caricature of a naked gentleman, pipe in mouth, arms outstretched as he runs toward a female pensioner, her hat flying off in fright and astonishment. Inside was the inscription: HE WON FIRST PRIZE FOR HIS DRIED FLOWER ARRANGEMENT!

The second card also won much admiration and mirth. It depicted a rosy-faced, perspiring female harpist, her instrument firmly placed between knees, her hands moving fervently over the strings, notes of music reverberating around her. The caption: HOW TO HAVE SEX IN PUBLIC WITHOUT BEING NOTICED!

Laughter and merriment was central to Ronnie's outlook on life. This was infectious. The constant communication of love, wit and generosity was forever present and gloomy days were rare.

I learned of Ronnie's work. He was thrilled to be in his television play and still found time to read countless books to help the cognitive process of his new life. He studied and scrutinized new thoughts and ideas.

Life at his agent's house was also described and I realised what an integral part Ronnie played in that life. It appeared to be a social and domestic role. It was one that Ronnie clearly embraced. He was enthralled with his joy of re-discovery. I knew he would not be able to resist sharing every facet of this new development. He was ecstatic. When in such a jubilant state, we do not realise that others do not move at the same rate. I wanted to caution him....

RONNIE'S STORY (continued)

'Yes, I did start to write - poems, letters, cards and my journal. A thing I have not done before! Within weeks I was aware that my fingernails were growing! A miracle! I was able to have my first manicure - needless to say, I had proof that all was going well. I was staying away from my usual haunts and didn't see any of my gay friends, except socially. I found I was standing outside myself, relieved that I no longer felt prey to disappointment and torment - the sort of guilt that makes you feel sullied and an outcast.

It was on one of my trips home that I took Sue and Philip to dinner at the Royal Hotel. It was fun and I had missed Sue and Philip. We had a lovely meal and perhaps a little too much to drink! Sue and I decided to take a taxi home as a storm had blown up. Philip couldn't be persuaded to join us, he wanted walk. We arrived home first, let Jessie out into the yard and stood hand in hand on the step watching the storm. We kissed for the very first time and everything was in tune, the right signals you see. It was lovely! We were really in love! I was now desperate to have my first ever full experience with Sue, but the timing had to be right. I was still undergoing therapy and my Doctor's word was law. He was very sympathetic, but insisted that we confided in Philip for it was right for him to know. Secrecy was forbidden. Truth was of paramount importance, for when honesty rules, fear of misunderstanding or distortion disappears. Philip's feelings had to be considered.

Afterwards, my Doctor suggested that Sue became involved with extra healing to speed my recovery. She agreed and additional gentle help began. We discussed the plan with Philip and his reply touched us both very deeply: 'It's your life, Ronnie - you both must do whatever is the greatest help'.

I was more than ever convinced that I had found the real me and that all would be well. My little therapist was delighted with my progress and after each meeting a report was sent to our Doctor.'

Ronnie and I knew that we loved each other. Our time in Harrogate put a seal on our feelings. In retrospect, it is easy to see that perhaps we had been deeply in love for very much longer. Our tentative closeness when walking on the Chalk Farm Road so many months before had been a prelude, an initiation.

While Ronnie continued in therapy, this love was not spoken of. He was reminded that he was at the start of a new way of life; his awakening could be part of early adolescent exploration, so making a commitment to me was too early.

I, too, governed still by past influences and doctrines, was cautious. I had been a fifties juvenile, hidebound by strict codes of behaviour, double standards and some sexual bigotry. The effects had lived with me well into adulthood. Although my hang-ups were different from Ronnie's, they were still inhibiting. We were learning together. Ronnie remarked: 'It's not easy being 40 and 48 is it?'

Our therapies together were kind, loving and searching. We observed the rules and did not move too quickly. There was much laughter and recognition of our frailties. Ronnie was so eager, hungry for more knowledge. He devoured countless volumes and articles on sexual expertise! He regarded Nancy Friday as a household name! To watchers and observers in the agent's home this pattern must have seemed somewhat disturbing... Ronnie paid no heed to that. His happiness was palpable.

It was not until Ronnie's treatment was drawing to a close, that our love was finally consummated, with, I might add - much fun, much passion and accompanying cries of seagulls taking off from the roof!

RONNIE'S STORY (continued)

There were still things to sort out. I attended for four or five more sessions of therapy. Then, I was free! No Valium! No pills!

I've read so many books about women and their problems, about homosexuality, about men. I wish I had learned earlier about the mysteries of life, most of all, the wonderful relationship a man can have with a woman. All youngsters should learn about it. Deviation then can become a matter of choice not ignorance.

Our Doctor counselled us together on several occasions. He explained how vitally important it was to include Philip in our lives. Also, my mother needed to be introduced gently to the new relationships. All this promised to be honourable, open and sincere, but not without its difficulties. We were warned that this change would be met with suspicion by some and benevolence by others. Integrity was vital for our peace of mind and our future together. We were reassured that help was at hand. Therapies were ending, but association with our Doctor was not. Ronnie and I were ready to begin...

I carried on with my work at the Theatre and Philip and I continued to enjoy our warm friendship. Ronnie returned to West Bank frequently and gradually our love affair was noticed. Very few comments were made and the attitude of most members of the Company seemed to be unaltered. As I look back, I suppose we were often the topic of conversation and gossip - all quite natural. What was happening was unusual and dramatic. Ronnie and I, happy and insulated in our world of unison and love, were totally unaware of spite, cruelty or unkindness which may have been lurking. Fortunately, it was many years later when some ugly truths surfaced...ignorance was bliss...

My mother's reaction was understandable, upsetting as it was for us to deal with. She was bewildered in that she, too, knew of Ronnie and Philip as a partnership. It was hard for her to contemplate such a relationship now reverting to Ronnie and her daughter. Also, she was concerned about the possibility of my making a second mistake; I had had a previous short-lived and disastrous marriage. Perhaps all was put into proportion when Alan Ayckbourn's mother snared her in the Theatre Bar and observed: 'Oh, never mind, she could have gone off with a murderer!'

Like Philip, my mother and brother, were not neglected or left out. They were loved, cherished and protected

Ronnie and I were living separate lives from then on; he in London and me busy with Alan's new play 'Way Upstream'. Rehearsals were complicated for action centred round a motor-cruiser moored on a 'flooded' Theatre in the Round. Technology was a continual nightmare; the fire-brigade occupied the Theatre as often as the audience. My character, Mrs. Hatfield, appeared intermittently through the First Half of the production. I was relieved to be placed on the river bank. Watching from afar made for compulsive viewing. Lunch-time shows took up much of the remaining itinerary.

When future programmes were announced, I found that I was to miss a forthcoming presentation of 'Twelfth Night', but take part in another musical, 'Making Tracks'. I was cast in a cameo again; a rather baffling charlady who made an incomprehensible musical contribution somewhere in the First Act.

While all this was going on, I received almost daily letters from Ronnie telling of his life in London. He divided his spare time between looking after his agent's mother and helping out domestically at a house in Golders Green. There, he went to the aid of Margaret, a disabled eighty-six year old lady. Margaret, who lived alone and suffered miserably from rheumatoid arthritis, was the sister of an actress friend of his.

Another enterprise of Ronnie's was upholstery. This time, it did not go hand-in-hand with the symptoms of a nervous breakdown, but rather in order to supplement his earnings. Rod, a long-time pal and accomplished soft-furnishing specialist, put some creative assignments Ronnie's way. So, life was busy for him and this varied activity made for enthralling news for me.

Throughout these appealing, entertaining letters ran the thread of pure happiness. Ronnie delighted in being well again. His words conveyed the thrill of a new reality. Also, I was overjoyed to realise how much he loved me. Perpetually, he tried to find different words and means to express his feelings, almost always ending with 'You're just a little Magnet'! 'Magnet' became a special word, our word.

Many of the letters were scorchingly passionate, so much so that I concealed them before the paper burst into flames! One such missive ended: 'Make sure you destroy these letters - I wouldn't want Jessie to read them and escape over the garden gate again!'

For an interval, my work at the Theatre ended. A hiatus followed and provided a welcome break. I was happy to spend a few days with my Mother. Before that, a meeting was called for the existing Company. Alan broached a plan to travel to Houston, USA, as part of an exchange of productions. This was proposed for January 1982. The chosen plays were to be 'Way Upstream' and a revival of 'Absent Friends'. Of course this was an exciting turn of events and an important opportunity for most. I was torn betwixt thoughts of career prospects, what this chance may mean and the unthinkable anticipation of leaving my beloved Ronnie, even for a matter of weeks...

I told Ronnie what was to happen. He was thrilled for me and instantly began planning my wardrobe for all the social events to which he was sure I would be invited. In a few days, the dust had settled over this development and Ronnie was planning once more; this time, for me to visit London. My Birthday was approaching in the Autumn and Ronnie thought it would be a romantic idea for us to spend a few days there - 'I'd love to show you London'. My mother warily expressed doubt and disapproval. Mmn...

Arrangements were made. I was to stay with Ronnie at his agent's house. All manner of treats were in store. Ronnie regaled me with detail and features of the jaunt and rang off with 'I'll have to give you a ring.'

My train would be arriving at King's Cross at 3.30 p.m. I knew Ronnie would be there. He had booked leave from the BBC where he had been working for several weeks. I could hardly wait to see him. There he was, running towards me on the platform, arms outstretched ready to hug. I felt a surge of expectancy and love for him. As the years went by, that promise did not dim or waver...its fervour grew; it became a power, a force of gladness to nourish and uphold.

I was led along the platform and propelled towards the King's Cross grubby cafeteria. It was, however, a rapturous brief encounter. We sat at a small, awkward table, sharing it with two elderly ladies eating doughnuts. Neither seemed pleased to have their conversation overheard or interrupted. Ronnie brought tea and we looked at each other. It was as if we had become one and all those around us had receded to nothingness. The moment diluted long enough for Ronnie to search his pocket for - a tiny, leather box. He opened it and there was the ring he had said he must give to me: three opals, my birth stones, surrounded by diamonds. The two ladies, halfway through jam and cream beamed and whispered congratulations as Ronnie slipped the engagement ring on my finger. By this time, the surrounding tables were waiting for the magic words: 'Will you marry me?' I had said 'yes' before the question was complete.

Hand in hand, we left the Buffet and made our way to the Tube. It seemed as if we walked in an abstract, quixotic faraway land.

I was looking forward to meeting the agent and her family. The townhouse was in the centre of an imposing terrace and rose to three floors. Apparently, most of the domestic activity took place in the basement where the open-plan kitchen was positioned. There, I was first introduced to the agent's mother who seemed pleasant enough, of few words, but ready to offer a lukewarm welcome. I was so eager to show her my ring and could hardly contain my happiness. There was little or no response. In fact, I would describe her reaction as shock. The moment was crushed. Ronnie quickly took the initiative showing me to the top of the house where we were to sleep. This was Ronnie's room. An appropriate reunion took place....

The following day was to be a feast of theatregoing. We saw the original cast in 'Cats' and spent a starry-eyed, glamorous afternoon tea-dancing at the Waldorf Hotel.

Love can be blind and being middle-aged does not necessarily make one more primed for reaction and mood. Therefore, Ronnie and I believed that everyone was happy for us. We had misjudged the state of affairs entirely.

For me, the house atmosphere was unnerving. The family consisted of the agent, her sister, a divorced sister, the mother and a young nephew. Ronnie was affectionate, almost dutiful to the mother and seemed almost like a surrogate son. He had, on occasion, looked after both parents before the father died and acted as carer for them when the rest of the family took a holiday abroad. He shopped, cleaned and when his time allowed, he was caretaker. Ronnie was obviously an important ingredient. I discovered that the family had frequently taken holidays at West Bank where Philip was also a valued entertainer. There was no doubt that Ronnie and Philip were held in very high esteem. So, I had not realised that I would be regarded as an interloper. I am sure that Ronnie had not envisaged this either. We two were on a cloud of optimism and exalted carelessness. Who would dream of being unkind to us? We were soon to find out...

The family was preparing for a Sunday lunch party. The meal was timed for four o'clock. Several friends and acquaintances had been invited. Ronnie and I were happy to join the group and celebrate our engagement with people who would wish us well. The kitchen was buzzing and wine was liberal. I was uncomfortable, for, although Ronnie was central to the banter and sociability, I was ignored. How thankful I was to feel his hand squeeze mine. It was consolidating and a comfort.

The food was excellent and, at first, the family friends were warm and hospitable. Quite soon into the meal, I could feel the mood change and become scathing. Jokes about gays were exchanged and eventually humorous attacks were directed at Ronnie. We had hoped for congratulations and good wishes, but instead we were on the receiving end of intimidation and insult. We felt nothing but sadness and humiliation. The guests, mostly clients of Ronnie's agent, were corroborative. We tried to join in, to laugh, but it proved to be impossible. We were left feeling out of place and alone. A conversational let-up spared us further unease and discomfort. We excused ourselves thankful for the moment to shun the crude crowd.

Our first reaction was to get out of the house. We took Emily the dog for her constitutional. We walked in silence, stunned into silence. I then became angry. In defence of Ronnie I began to criticise and judge. Ronnie, perhaps embarrassed for his friends, or confused, was evasive and flailing for an excuse. We were terribly hurt, lost and attempting to deal with an unexpected development. Our Doctor's wise words and warnings came flooding back.

We spent a restless and unhappy night. The following morning found us despondent and shaky. We had planned a visit to Covent Garden and in the evening a trip to a new nightclub, Heaven, was arranged. The previous day's events were still indelibly printed on our minds. We reached Covent Garden, but instead of wandering around the various stalls and boutiques, we found ourselves sitting at a table, drinking tasteless coffee, and contemplating a frightening future. Ronnie was very much on edge. His sunny, debonair nature was flattened and dispirited. I tested him with questions and eventually uttered the unwise words, 'Ronnie, are you unsure? Unsure about us marrying?' and he replied with the devastating 'Yes'.

I was numb and reacted very badly. Instead of reassuring poor Ronnie, I thought only of myself and damaged pride. I should have known so much better. I rushed headlong into a plan of action. I would leave. I would return to the bosom of my family again. The family who was sure that I had made a mistake. I told Ronnie to take me to King's Cross, buy my ticket and say goodbye. He said, 'Come with me to Heaven tonight'. What a fool I was to refuse. What lack of understanding and kindness. Had I learned nothing?

We found ourselves at the station, wordless and desolate. I boarded the train, found my seat and Ronnie turned to leave. I allowed him to. I didn't rush to stop him. I remember being swamped by my own emotions. The feeling of being let down obliterated the words I should have spoken, the comfort I should have given to the man I loved so much. So long after, now, I can still visualise him walking away from me down the platform, his red cardigan getting further and further away. He did not turn but continued to fade until he was out of sight. I took my seat and began to smoke until I was nearly sick.

The young girl sitting opposite me, across the table, watched. Even in my dazed brown study, occasional glances made me realise that she was peering, inquisitive about my solitude. I was numb, impervious to all outside influence. In happier circumstances, I would have chatted and perhaps made a new acquaintance. Instead, I willed the train to travel faster while I, desperate, in disorder and upheaval, longed for Ronnie.

I phoned our Doctor. As soon as the train pulled in to Hull Station, I phoned. His words were a lifeline: 'Come straight here, I will put you together again'. I needed only our Doctor. I had not fled to the family home. There, I would have been sucked into defeat and finality. All would have been lost.

Our Doctor urged me to make an immediate phone call to Ronnie. I was to accept full responsibility and blame for our break. Ronnie needed to have my love and strength to drag himself up from the hopelessness he must be perceiving at that moment. His voice, so far away, sounded frail and perplexed. I cannot begin to explain how I felt. I would have done anything to inspirit, to convince him of the depth of my love. He was so defenceless and unguarded, so exposed and so new to all the strange yet fine feelings which were affecting him. I told him of my sorrow. I told him of so many things....I asked him to forgive me. His voice became stronger. He listened. He was comforted. Then came the glorious words: 'I'm coming to Scarborough tomorrow'. Once again, we had been rescued....

I did return to the family home that night. The reaction was tight-lipped for I had not sought advice there. I was silent and preoccupied with anticipation of the following day. The day when I would be on Scarborough platform...waiting....

Many years later, I heard about reactions at the agent's house. There had been some ill-concealed rejoicing culminating in, 'It wasn't right for you Ronnie' and 'You'll be able to go to the market and stock up our fridge again'.

Our meeting at the station was subdued, but strong, sound and binding. We were together again and naught else mattered or impinged. Our place was fortified and built on a love so powerful that we felt impregnable.

Ronnie said, 'Let's have a cup of tea'. That cup of tea, sipped in the warmth and solace of West Bank kitchen with Jessie at our feet, was nectar. After, walking around our dear, loved, Secret Garden in the pouring rain has been one of the most abiding keepsakes of my life with Ronnie. I re-live it now as if it was only a moment ago....

Rehearsals for the weird 'Making Tracks' was about to get underway. I say weird for I failed to see why my character, Mrs. Witts, was there. Consequently, I found motivation for her somewhat threadbare. I tried to get in tune, but to this day, I remember feeling wholly redundant in that part.

Ronnie returned to London. Although unsettled at his agent's house, he was happy to be doing the Radio work he so loved. We were secure once more. All else remained on the periphery of life. Except, that is, for wearing my beautiful opal engagement ring. I half expected that there would be some reaction. The Company, Front-of-House staff and many others knew we were engaged but very few remarks were made. I was embarrassed when I mentioned it to a long-standing programme-selling friend of Ronnie's. She said, 'Oh, I thought I saw something glittering'. After that, I did not look forward to felicitations. I expect no one knew what to say, especially as Philip was propping up the Bar with me on most nights. No wonder they were stumped. Perhaps it was thought we were a threesome! I have giggled about that being the source of tittle-tattle...ah well, if so, while they prattled about us they were leaving someone else alone...

Ronnie arrived for the Opening Night of 'Making Tracks'. I was so pleased that he was as bamboozled as me about the extraneous presence of Mrs. Witts.

Ronnie had brought a large collection of clothes from London. He had been to numerous Red Cross centres, Nearly-New shops, Dejas-Vu (leaves much to the imagination), Help-the-Aged marts and Vintage Evening Wear costumiers. There he had shopped for my Houston wardrobe. His taste was impeccable. He had thought through probable American occasions: dinners, luncheon parties, first nights and receptions.

The trying-on stints in the workroom of West Bank were something to behold. The workroom was striking in itself. Shelves covered three walls and all held rolls and bales of material; some cloths that, now, would be unusual and scarce. Fabrics such as barathea, gaberdine, crepes, chenille and crepe de chine all made up a designer's venerated trove of riches. Other shelves had room for tin boxes filled with period buttons and buckles.

Sewing machines and dress-making tools occupied tops and mantelpiece. The book collection took up any spare space. I was particularly taken with 'A History of Women's Underwear'! I became acquainted with a stitch-ripper and a leather needle. Dear Ronnie...

I was a tailor's dummy. I tried on Susan Small dinner dresses, Horrokses cotton sun-dresses, and, most spectacular of all, a heavenly crushed velvet black Twenties supper gown - 'cut on the cross' said Ronnie. He maintained that as there was not enough money for appropriate American haute couture, then my costume would have to be second-hand. We were enthralled, fascinated. Philip would be summoned now and again to offer comment. He would offer it most enthusiastically, then disappear muttering, 'Oh God, my glass seems to be empty'.

'Making Tracks' ran until after the Christmas of 1981. The last play of the season was to be 'Butley'. I had an interesting part. For once I was not a 'character'. It was a change to play straight.

There were numerous meetings for the imminent Texas launching. We were to leave early in the New Year and Company groundwork was ongoing. Then, Alan called an extraordinary general meeting. The agenda took everyone by surprise and the disclosed data was met with some consternation. Apparently, a few days before, the Artistic Director of the Alley Theatre, Houston, had been murdered in the car-park. It was a shock and certainly put the damper on eager anticipation. My mother, as usual, expected me to return to the family home for the couple of days Christmas break. Needless to say, I hated leaving Ronnie, who, in turn, hated leaving Philip. So, we were the ones who ended up being apart...we accepted this with good grace; after all, there would be many more Festive years to look forward to.

'Butley' opened in the New Year of 1982. Rehearsals were stimulating, the cast small and the Director humorous, affable and without artifice. My fellow actor, Malcolm Hebden and somewhat unknown to me then, was a thoughtful, clever and talented professional, so I looked forward to the working days.

Ronnie managed to be in Scarborough frequently and the time we spent together was valued and dear.

Time for the American departure drew near and Airline arrangements were made. Ronnie planned to travel with me to Gatwick. We were to take the coach to Victoria, stay overnight there and then make our way to the Airport. An actress friend, met during the run of 'Conservatory' and I hoped to fly together, share American accommodation and on the whole, keep each other company. The whole process left me nervous and twitchy. My flying career had been practically zero.

In the meantime, 'Butley' would close and I had to consider the tearful goodbyes of my mother and brother. I knew that would not be easy. They did not hide their fearful feelings and unfortunately, I found this unsettling and negative, especially as I was doing my utmost to be bright and breezy.

My family came over to Scarborough for a day on the weekend before I started out on my journey. As I had predicted there were disorientated farewells. Ronnie and Philip saved the day and once again Sundae glasses of wine eased the passage of time... but, by evening, stress had manifested itself and I developed an appalling stomach-ache, which incidentally, did not clear until I was seated on the plane!

Ronnie and I clung to those valued, dearest days. Soon, the case containing its priceless cargo of dresses was packed and we were ready to leave. Philip hoisted Jessie to wave us off and I remember thinking of how relieved he would be to have the house to himself. 'Little-Miss-Make-A-Job' (Ronnie's epithet) would no longer blight and make his life a misery with Domestos bottle and duster.

The coach journey South offered much scope for reflection. Ronnie and I were quiet. Hand-in-hand, we looked out over the fields and endless motorway, mulling over the two months to be spent apart.

Earlier, Ronnie had surprised me with the news of a two-week holiday he had booked to spend with me in Houston. We would live for that time...

Our work would always make the demands of parting. We had found each other and to be alone again was akin to a physical wound. The greatest recompense was that we **had** found each other. No obstacle that life could throw at us was insurmountable.

The Victoria Hotel was clean, reasonably comfortable and basic. Our room was minute, but more than adequate for us to love each other. Sleep came in snatches, desultory and erratic. Dawn brought with it the sinking sensation of something painful to be done. Our original hope, to say goodbye at Gatwick, was thwarted at the last minute by a BBC call for Ronnie to report for work at 9.00 a.m. We looked at each other in dismay. We would part at Victoria Station. Each second was eked out until I was seated at the rear of the Gatwick-bound coach. Ronnie was standing motionless, waiting for the moment that had to come.

Slowly, I was moving away and my darling became smaller and smaller. The waving hand remained until all was out of sight and I was forsaken...

As the plane skirted London on the first leg of its protracted flight, I scoured the landscape looking for landmarks that would point out the roof-space of the BBC. I knew he would be standing there....how foolish we are when so terribly in love.

How foolish and yet, how ecstatic, how blissfully full of heartening promise knowing that your love is returned so perfectly, from beginning to end...

***

PART ONE
THEN

HOUSTON 1982

I had expected Houston to be different. The approach to the City was dull and nondescript. I had had concepts of wealth and majesty in the shape of momentous sky-scrapers and visionary architecture. That did exist, but at this stage when I was jet-lagged and despondent, all seemed strange, bleak and lacklustre. In truth, I was homesick for Ronnie...

We were deposited at Houston House. This was a well-appointed apartment building where the Company was to be housed during our stay. On arrival, my one thought was accessing the nearest telephone. It was off-putting to discover that we were to be feted, wined and dined by the Production Staff and Technical Crew. It was now approximately midnight British time and I needed to call home before it was too late. More time elapsed before I could at last phone Ronnie. The two minutes we had to transmit our love over ocean depths was exhilarating and glad. I also set the family mind at rest, but...it was the link with Ronnie that stayed and remained suspended in the air....

As I replaced the receiver, I was removed, aloof and lonely. The days and weeks stretched endlessly in front; I longed for the letters that I knew would come....

Our apartment was luxurious and we had every comfort. My friend and I settled into a round of rehearsals, receptions and the generosity of Texans. Our first production was 'Way Upstream'. The outlandish set raised exclamation, but the inclusion of nudity did not go down terribly well in this Bible belt of America. Outraged members of the audience who did not take kindly to this new venture of Alan's, met us at the Stage Door: 'How long has Mr. Ayckbourn being doing these kind of plays!'

Again, the project was handicapped by technological problems; even Hollywood wizards of technical expertise could not fathom let alone solve the entanglements of a boat on deluged stage, supplemented by real rain which took on the persona of flash flooding on an off night. I was relieved to be operating on the river bank. That is, once I had fought my way down a treacherously long grass pathway and, in tight pencil skirt, scrambled over a very mean-looking stile. The round of applause was worth it... Meantime, my actor mates, enclosed within the vessel's cabin, found themselves incarcerated with electrical wiring and innumerable hazards that were the foes of water!

After shows, we were marshalled into coaches and cars bound for Houston House. Allegedly, the City after dark was inclined to be deserted and dangerous.

Amid warnings to be careful, we were astonished to see red-bereted vigilante groups on patrol. The demise of the Theatre's Artistic Director was an unremitting reminder of menace. During the day, we were occupied with rehearsals for 'Absent Friends'. I was playing Marge. It was a large, consuming part. This was fortunate, for the time passed more quickly and there was the steady challenge of trying to give life to one of Alan's irresistible, compelling people.

Rehearsals for 'Absent Friends' were awkward. There was an intangible aura of distraction; some actors were ill at ease and I heard whispering. I could not get to the bottom of it, but rested assured that this time I was not the butt of irony. As always, however, I would rather face fidgety coach parties in a packed house on Saturday afternoon matinees, than a rehearsal room full of watching, analytical actors. I was confident with my interpretation of Marge, although in the early days her suburban accent had thrown me. At that time, I was not overly familiar with the precincts of London. My saviour had been the proprietor of a small drapers shop on Falsgrave in Scarborough.

Sometime before our departure for America, Philip had asked me to call in; tights were needed for the Wardrobe. I found myself ear-wigging as the lady behind the counter was deep in conversation with one of her regulars. There and then, I had found my suburban Southern cadence, but deep in the heart of Yorkshire! I told her of my predicament. Peg suggested that I bring in a tape recorder. In the course of conversation, I learned that Peg hailed from Walthamstow. I also pinched some of her very individual, appropriate ideas for dress. Her hair was 'up' and tethered at the back with a large, black velvet bow. Her smart costume, not suit, completed the total effect. We struck up quite a friendship, Peg and I. Complimentary tickets were bestowed and we were both enriched by the experience.

So, once my lines were surely grasped, I was happy with what Marge was doing. Alan's notes were encouraging. Others were not so assured and there was unrest. What was causing this undercurrent of misgiving? I deduced that come what may, this was not an issue of mine. The mood culminated in a very cringe-worthy moment when the leading lady collapsed in despair and floods of tears. I was glad to be on the perimeter.

Ronnie's letters arrived. What a joy it was to see the customary Airmail Blue. Often, they were opened in the Dressing Room. I was consumed with suspense and powerless to save them until a more fitting time in the day. Some were numbered, some were not. I read them feverishly, hungry for news and hungry for contact. I wrote as many in return. I knew that Ronnie too would be waiting by the letterbox.

Ronnie was lonely. Although very occupied with absorbing Radio Drama, I soon realised how empty his spare time had become. Margaret, in Golders Green, was being a stalwart friend and rallied, with her kindness and affection, Ronnie's certainty and nerve. Also, he was busy looking for flats. We had spoken of setting up home together in London, although West Bank would always be our permanent buttress and bolt-hole.

Poor Ronnie was very disillusioned. The hunt for a London harbour was proving to be exhausting and - very expensive. Added to that, we had become inseparable and the severance was agonising. Ronnie soothed himself with visits to the Airline Booking Office where he could see his flight to Houston flash up on the screen...He was counting the days. So was I.

It seemed that life at the agent's house was also disagreeable. I realised that Ronnie was now very unsettled and itching to find another retreat. His letters, although never complaining, were plaintive and full of longing. Yet, there was abiding humour and indestructible fortitude.

Ronnie and I would have been loving, devoted parents. Had we been younger, parenthood would have brought us great pleasure and satisfaction. We decided that advancing years and irregular, spattered earnings was not a satisfying foundation for bringing up children. Then came the dilemma of how to prevent this. We had been bored and frustrated with numerous so-called solutions. The matter then hung somewhere between risk and limbo!

Once I was out of the way in America, it seems Ronnie had taken the business into his own hands. I received a letter which was, as usual, filled with love and yearning. Towards its conclusion, came these words: 'Oh, by the way, I went along to the Marie Stopes Clinic this afternoon and had a vasectomy. Then, although I felt like a plucked (did I say 'plucked'?) chicken, I caught the bus home. So, my darling, you won't have to worry any more...won't it be fun!'

I laughed - but - I cried. I marvelled at his courage, his lonely day of such self-sacrifice, and most of all, I wept in gratitude for the love we shared.

I saved every cent in preparation for Ronnie's arrival. I had flagged places to visit and restaurants in which to sample those Texan steaks.

In a recent letter, Ronnie said, 'Why don't we get married in America? I've got the rings!' I was rapt, gladdened and elated, but, characteristically, I was mindful of family being unable to attend. Foolishly perhaps, I put that first. My mother must have been aware of Ronnie's plan; I knew he phoned her regularly. Forever caring, he knew how much she would be missing me. I was stunned to read in one of her letters that if we did decide to marry in Houston, we were to be sure to take plenty of snaps. Wonders never cease!

At last the day dawned for Ronnie's arrival. I was in rehearsal, so the Production Manager met him at the Airport. He appeared: dishevelled, jet-lagged and exalted! We were together again! We joined my flat-mate at the apartment where Ronnie promptly gave way to inert, somnolent state. His body clock was totally out of kilter and at 3.00 a.m. he was on the lookout for bacon and eggs!

'Absent Friends' was now running and the Company freed up to take full advantage of the many invitations the Alley Theatre League Ladies' offered. As luck would have it, these coincided with Ronnie's holiday visit. Also, there were receptions and book signings for Alan. The League occupied a formidable stance in the Theatre's hierarchy. We had already sampled hospitality provided by the women who were uppermost in its organisation. It was impressive to say the least and Houston's wealth and generosity was amply represented.

One such occasion presented itself during the second week of Ronnie's stay. It was to be a sumptuous evening hosted by Theatre 'Angels'; a prominent and affluent couple ('old money', someone ungraciously volunteered). Inevitably, out came the black, crushed velvet, 'cut-on-the-cross' dinner gown. This was rounded off by a turban - also crushed velvet - trimmed with a black ostrich feather. Ronnie (of course!) oversaw the dressing and then appeared himself, beaming in evening dress and a somewhat crooked bow-tie. The whole Company had been invited. We were ferried in a convoy of limousines to the mansion which was situated on River Drive. In the distance, the approaching view was reminiscent of 'Dallas'.

The cars drew up before the front entrance. I fear 'Tara' was foremost in everyone's mind. Instead of clapping eyes on Scarlett, we could see two figures standing between the gigantic pillars which framed the doorway to the house.

Mr. & Mrs. Harris-Masterson were in late middle-age and extravagantly dressed. Mr. H.M. wore evening dress and a large, very large solid gold chain around his neck. That was remarkable enough, but one's gaze was drawn to the conspicuous, startling wig which had slithered to one side, partly obscuring his left eye. His wife was clad from head to foot in grotto blue chiffon. This vogue, this dernier cri was set off by a parur of diamonds and sapphire: necklace, bracelet, ring and a substantial clip which was anchored to her ample bosom.

Enquiries were made for Mr. Ayckbourn'. We had been led to believe that he was secretly holed up in a Downtown Houston apartment. Apparently, our hosts had been advised otherwise and to all intents and purposes, he was at that time aboard a helicopter on his way to an unavoidable business trip. We knew that certain social entanglements were not his metier.

The residence was colossal. The entrance vestibule contained display cabinets groaning with Meissen china. We were ushered to reception areas and plied with champagne flutes. From then on we perambulated through conservatories, balconies, dining-rooms, snugs and drawing-rooms. Tables set with fine glass, china and cutlery were at the ready. One balustraded platform looked down over the central indoor courtyard. Here was the top table, lavishly decorated and waiting for its VIP guest. Alas, he was not there.

In the meantime, Ronnie was straying from the main party and scouting at will. He reappeared from time to time from behind an ornamental palm or titanic flower arrangement; his bow-tie even more crooked with the thrill of it all.

My black velvet had caused quite a stir and many Houston grand dames were making enquiries about my British designer. I promised an introduction to my betrothed later in the evening.

We were seated, then served with beef stew, accompanied by a simple selection of vegetables: Mr. Ayckbourn's favourite dish. My actress friend had visited the Rest Room. She returned, flushed and hardly able to contain herself. The Rest Room walls were adorned with what she thought to be genuine El Greco paintings!

Coffee was to be served in the Ballroom. By then, alcohol had flowed; everyone was quite well oiled. The Ballroom was Herculean in size. A white grand-piano was standing in the corner waiting to be coaxed into life. One of our gathering, a somewhat intoxicated leading man, was suddenly and relentlessly pursued by Mrs. H.M. In due course, they spent the remainder of the evening smashed and exchanging confidences side-by-side on the piano stool.

Mr. H.M. sauntered over to us. We were sitting upon a very tempting chaise-longue, sipping coffee from minute china vessels. He was very charming and soon we were deep in conversation about his family. We found it rather sad that he and his wife, we were told, often took coffee in the Ballroom, but, all alone. Ronnie, eager to make some contribution to the talk, said: 'Are those real El Greco's in the rest Room? Mr. H.M. replied: 'I dunno, son, but we sure paid an El Greco price for 'em!'

Ronnie and I made several close friends in Houston. Many of them remain so to this day....it was a memorable time....

Soon, the day dawned for Ronnie's return to London. I was to remain for a further ten days. Also, my room-mate was preparing to leave; her contract was ending. The days that followed were very lonely and I spent much time in Houston House, by the apartment window, watching helicopters flocking to and fro like taxis. Days were free and trips to San Antonio and Galveston were arranged. All was very pleasurable, but since Ronnie's departure, the light had gone out of Houston.

Within a few days, I received the last American letter from Ronnie. It was very upbeat and cheerful and signed off with 'See you at the Airport!'

I had not given much thought to our plans after Houston. I assumed that a further contract would be upcoming from Alan; surely Scarborough would beckon once more. We were approaching the final performance of 'Absent Friends'. Alan was calling in to all the Dressing-Rooms, giving thanks and going through the goodbye process. He was also delivering an indisputable blow. How foolish it is to presuppose any theatrical arrangement. Nothing is ever a forgone conclusion.

Each Dressing-Room was given identical news. Our contracts were being terminated. Only two actors would be returning to the Stephen Joseph Theatre. Alan had written a two-hander and everyone else was surplus to requirements.

'Intimate Exchanges' was to run for the entire Summer. I wonder, thought I, if the earlier whispering I had noticed was linked to this prospective strategy...trust me to be in the dark...

So, when the time came for me to board the plane for London, I was professionally adrift. What awaited me three thousand miles away was far more important...Ronnie.

On American First Nights, I had received cards from our Doctor and his family. All contained good wishes and affectionate messages. At the beginning of the stay, a greeting bearing an illustration of Dick Whittington arrived. Inside was an inscription: 'Your life will follow a similar path...'

As the plane was taxiing for takeoff, I thought of the prediction....where was I going? What lay ahead?

We landed mid-morning. Yes, there was Ronnie. I was home at last. After frustration with baggage and Airport formalities, we boarded the train for Town. I did not think beyond being with my Ronnie. When he turned to look at me, I realised that he was agitated. He was worried. Then came the explanation. Circumstances had come to a head at the agent's house. The story, if in another context, could have been amusing, but...no...'I've had a terrible week' said Ronnie.

Ronnie was known to be fond of aftershave and toiletries. A favourite was Penhaligon's Bluebell. Often, it was applied rather liberally. The previous week, he had returned from the BBC to discover that his lotion had gone; in its place, was a raw onion. Ronnie had been angry, deeply hurt and unable to find an excuse for what had happened. There and then he struggled to find somewhere else to live. At last, he had managed to find one room, shabby but furnished in a fashion, for £30 per week. In 1982 that was expensive.

Poor Ronnie had been thrown into panic, knowing that the bed-sitter was sordid and depressing. Elderly Margaret had risen to the occasion and provided kitchen utensils and basic necessities for him to set up a meagre, scant home. So, we were bound for Gloucester Road, Finsbury Park.

I resolved to call my family, for they needed to know that I was safely home. The news that I would be staying with Ronnie for a few days did not go down very kindly. I had been expected to return to the North.

***

PART ONE
THEN

GLOUCESTER ROAD, FINSBURY PARK 1982

We reached Gloucester Road. The street was pleasant enough. It was light and trees flanked the pavements. The room was at the rear of a large Victorian house. The entrance was dark, grubby; cooking smells hung in the air. I was apprehensive as I followed Ronnie down the corridor until we reached a door on the right. He fumbled for the key and all at once we were on the threshold of what was to be our first home.

Ronnie did not speak - nor did I. My gaze took in the humble dwelling. I saw, in an instant, all that Ronnie had done to welcome me: saw the strain he had had to make the run-down surroundings comfortable.

There was a double bed, a Thirties kitchen dresser with drop-leaf front and glass-panelled storage above. The far wall boasted an old-fashioned brown wood cupboard and to the right were French doors opening on to what appeared to be waste land. Perhaps it had been a garden, but now, after years of neglect, it was decayed and forgotten.

Heartbreakingly, in the centre of this sad, tired room was a table. There, a lace cloth was spread and upon it rested a cake and lovingly-placed cut-glass vase of Spring flowers. I felt the tears, but knew I must conceal them. I thought, in those fleeting moments, of Ronnie's solitary hours. I thought of him hurrying to make a shelter for me. My love for him spilled as he held me in his arms and said: 'Lovely Margaret helped me....'

The tawdriness of our environs paled into insignificance that night. We were swept away with our love - a suite at the Savoy could not have complimented such ecstasy...

The days that followed were taken up with practical considerations: where was the lavatory? Where was the bathroom? Where was the vacuum cleaner?

Behold, the toilet was on the first floor. It was quite disgusting, but then understandable, when we discovered that three Irish navvies occupied a room beside it which was directly above our abode.

Incidentally, those Irish navvies turned out to be the most obliging, courteous, helpful and funniest men I had met for a long time. They hated the absentee landlady and sabotaged the lavatory flush by attaching the 'pull' in a fixed position thus making it impossible for it to function unless the jinxed occupant climbed up to free it at cistern level!

All this information transpired at a later date and was imparted by Betty, a lady of the night who lived in the ground floor front room.

We decided that it was going to be hell using the house lavatory in the middle of the night, so, we requisitioned an unusually large mixing bowl from Margaret's house. I hasten to add that she had finished with it! It's regrettable to say that it became our interim emergency amenity and was regarded with hilarity, relief and fondness.

The bathroom was positioned at the top of this - er - imposing building and was three floors up! Baths became slightly more infrequent for several reasons. Money needed to be put into the meter at least an hour before ablutions, thus allowing the paltry amount of water to heat. While this was happening, there was scope to clean the bath; Irish navvies come to mind again. Preparedness happened well in advance, for the whole modus operandi involved the transference of much equipment. To add insult to injury, the bath was mega - to use today's parlance - and required superabundant amounts of hot water to make the campaign worthwhile. Ronnie and I solved that teaser. I would climb in closely followed by my beloved. As a consequence, the water level rose to half way...this malarkey was not conducive to passion, but we were certainly clean.

I was hell-bent on getting our little sanctuary spotless, so, as the landlady seemed to find the vacuum cleaner request inscrutable, Ronnie found a second hand appliance shop round the corner and bought one for £2. If only dearest Scarborough had been in closer proximity. All we desired resided nearly three hundred miles away...

In the midst of this reorganisation of our lives, relations with my Mother were tense. I found her attitude puzzling for she had seen the likelihood of us marrying in America. Why was she unkind about us settling in London?

I spoke to her almost every day from an ancient, unreliable Payphone near the front door, within full earshot of the Irishmen tinkering with their equally ancient, unreliable truck. At fixed intervals, they would nod sympathetically as my conversation became more exasperating. In the end, I would be resigned to peace-making; the promise and reassurance of a visit to the North. This tenor cast a gloom. It was frustrating, for we had done our best to do the right things.

Ronnie's few days leave from the BBC was over and I knew that being out of work offered me a chance to practise a new life, a life of liberty. For the first time, I was my own woman, with my own home, my own choices and options.

It was April and the sun shone every day. Our little room began to take on a homely, cosy element. I became attached to it. We acquired domestic needs for the time being and that was that.

One Sunday morning, Ronnie was called to work early. I remained at home, happily engaged in chores. Then came the sound of chanting, wailing and the ringing of bells. I went to the open French windows. In the adjoining garden, Indian men were dancing around what appeared to be a Maypole. In the air, hung an exotic aroma which was wafting over the broken-down fence. Women's lamentation was coming from the house interior. Entranced and a trifle alarmed, I closed the window and remained cooped up for most of the day. Ronnie thought my induction to Eastern custom and culture was side-splitting, but did expand upon its significance. Years ago, while on an Arts Council tour, he had been smitten with India. One measure of his admiration was to adopt the Lungi instead of pyjamas. I found this, when first faced with Ronnie in a skirt, as zany as Eastern men dancing in a Finsbury Park back garden. That was my forerunner to a very different way of life...one that was to take an important place in our future...

We kept in regular touch with Philip. He seemed happy to spend leisure hours in his favourite haunts. We made sure that he did not find himself in financial difficulty. Previously, Ronnie had paid household bills, insurances and the like. We were careful to maintain this arrangement, while, at the same time, trying to be sensitive to Philip's feelings. Jokes and a light-hearted repartee preserved the delicate balance. We never lost sight of the fact that West Bank was Philip's home and providing he could always say, 'Oh God, my glass appears to be empty', then all would be well.

We did experience financial hassle. I was not working, but 'signed on' in a nerve-wracking dole queue in Finsbury Park. Iron grills separated those seeking benefit from the smug individuals handing it out. I witnessed heated exchange and violent shakings of the grating. My first assessment meeting had taken place in a different venue. I reported at the appointed time and was asked to sit in a vacant cubicle until my interrogator appeared. Obediently, I waited...as I did so, my gaze fell upon the desk in front. There, some unfortunate had carved the following: 'Ring the bell and some cunt will come'.

The resulting allowance was not a king's ransom, but it served as an adequate contribution to the pot. Dear, generous Ronnie announced: 'Now, I'm going to give you £40 a week for housekeeping...don't spend it all at once'.

Armed with my cache and clad in Fifties sundress from my American collection, I set out along the Blackstock Road in search of provisions. These were absorbing forays and I covered quite a distance while sussing out the neighbourhood and in the meantime, gaining a subtle suntan.

The afternoons were spent getting ready to meet Ronnie from the station, or, more often than not, journeying to the BBC to surprise him. Sometimes, he would manage an afternoon off and we would roam through the West End, gawping at Old Bond Street goodies, oohing and aahing at all the things we could not afford. Ronnie showed off all his best-loved stamping grounds and, when exhausted, having flopped into pavement café chairs, we held hands and smiled. A glass of wine, perhaps a cigarette for me - it was our timeless time...

Those were the days; those poignant, evocative, unforgettable days...the early memory days....

Ronnie worked hard behind the scenes to get me noticed in television. He had many contacts and several small jobs came my way. Obtaining an agent was more tricky and when I did, he was ineffectual. It was a disenchanting time. I had grown accustomed to working without interruption in Northern Repertory Theatres for seven years. The thought-provoking thing was that, apart from the monetary insecurity, I did not mind. My life revolved around Ronnie.

I conceded that I should visit my Mother sooner or later. I was loathe to leave London, but Ronnie had a good suggestion to make. We knew that my family would be seeing a show at the Stephen Joseph Theatre. What a surprise it would be for them if I appeared unexpectedly. How thrilled they would be, broached Ronnie.

The plan was that I would stay at West Bank, then emerge in the Theatre foyer before the performance. Ronnie had taken me on a shopping sally a few days before, resulting in a very fetching white linen two-piece which impacted on my deepening tan. Philip was most appreciative. He sent me off with 'You look lovely'. I knew he would join us later. I waited in anticipation by the ticket booth. At last, my family entered and I stepped forward, waiting for the cries of joy. They did not come and I was ignored. My Mother looked at me and then looked away. I suppose I did look different. Perhaps I had not been recognised? So, I had to stop her and impose myself. I should have turned and left. I should have gone back to West Bank and Philip. What I did not know was that Philip was there and saw all. He did not forget or forgive...

Two miserable days later, I walked along Gloucester Road with a spring in my step. I was home. I had come home. I had had plenty of time to think on the train from Hull. My Mother's reaction and behaviour was not strange to me. For many years, she had governed my emotional development. My continual search for approval had been suffocating and debilitating. Relationships had fallen by the wayside. My Brother, caught in an identical trap, mirrored my state. Yet, my Mother loved me. Possessive love crushes and, as the years go by, it imprisons and destroys. As the train pulled in to King's Cross, I thought of Ronnie's wisdom. Instead of allowing unhappiness to colour my disposition, I thought of him. Whenever my despondency surfaced, Ronnie would soothe with the words 'We have each other and all that love. We can spare some of it for your Mother, Nick and Philip'.

I loved my new life in London. We continued to make additions to our scanty home. By this time, the room was 'sparklin'. Here, I quote Betty of the ground floor. We had met from time to time, usually by the front door as she returned from her twilight excursions. She joined me for coffee one morning and was full of admiration for the miniature plate-rack which Ronnie had hauled home on the Tube! 'Oh Sue,' said she in Belfast tones, 'sparklin'. Betty was a warm, vibrant woman and I enjoyed her company, especially when she regaled me with scandalous stories about 'the awld fella' who seemed to reinforce her earnings!

Soon, Ronnie and I realised that the time was drawing near for us to move. Gloucester Road was a stop-gap. We had known that, but some roots had been set down. The first of many foundations in years to come and never to be forgotten.

Flat-hunting was aggravating. Many rental properties were way beyond our financial reach. One sunlit morning Ronnie sent me along to the Jenny Jones Flat Agency near Carnaby Street. I was interviewed and then shown brochures. Not one stirred any spontaneous reaction. As the propitious young lady was drawing the search to a close, she mentioned a likely solution which was situated in Alperton. 'Where on earth is that?' said I. It transpired that it was near to Wembley. Unused as I was to geographical detail in London, I had only a faint idea that it was some way out. I was right. It was practically at the end of the Piccadilly Line. My assistant then pointed out that there was a choice of two flats, both self-contained, one ground floor and the other, first. More importantly, both were to let for £30 per week. When I exclaimed, it was pointed out that distance from Town had possibly pronounced the apartments unsuitable for City workers. For us, however, this was a distinct possibility! Plans were set for contact to be made with the landlord and I was assured that an appointment to view would be fixed.

That evening, I told Ronnie of my adventure and he coached me with all the questions I needed to ask when confronted with the owner.

Time elapsed and in the meantime, Ronnie introduced me to the eighty-four-year-old Margaret in Golders Green. From first meeting, I knew that she would be a friend beyond price. Housebound, incapacitated and hamstrung with rheumatoid arthritis, Margaret was dependent on the telephone and Ronnie's visits.

The house, a three-story semi-detached example of Thirties elegance, was much neglected. It was filled with antediluvian furniture and Chinese artefacts. Margaret had started life in China where her father worked. At some point, the family moved to England where her parents and two sisters died, leaving her alone. In younger days, there had been a loving relationship with a Chinese doctor. Then, mixed-race tolerance was thin. The association was brought to an end. Margaret, a professional woman, had worked in Argentina. She became a high flyer in the world of business and enterprise. Now, her conversation was sprinkled with South American phrases and interjections.

My visits became more regular, sometimes when Ronnie was working, and, enthralled with monopolizing tales of a life so different from mine, I wiled away placid hours sitting in a chintz-covered armchair smoking Benson & Hedges Kingsize. These would have been placed on the table, opened, with one cigarette eased from the packet in preparation for my arrival. Fortunately, my companion smoked like a chimney, so guilt was not uppermost in my mind.

Margaret's arthritis was so tortuous, that not only was she housebound, but almost chair bound. Six feet tall, she wore a 'uniform' which consisted of crimpelene skirt ('easily laundered, dear'), loose cardigan, blouse and slippers.

All could be removed smoothly at bedtime and did not hinder her passage to the kitchen where her Meals-on-Wheels delivered lunches three times a week. Ronnie prepared the rest when he was free.

Margaret's sole physical support was a tea-trolley, manoeuvred and laden with requisites for the day: letters, diaries, pills, 'my long-handled pick-up device', cigarettes, Selfridges' shopping lists, and - incoherently - nail varnish! Margaret's fingernails were immaculate; very long and carefully polished with Revlon's Quiet Pink...

Support for Margaret and ourselves was mutual. She was an invaluable source of common sense; her house became a retreat where gentility, refinement and resolute advice proliferated. Her garden, now overgrown and wild with unrestrained shrubs and climbers, still glowed with promise. Here, I learned of Zephrin Druin and Viburnum for the first time. Viburnum was known thereafter as Margaret's tree. It was an important fixture in all the gardens that followed.

Margaret made an indelible impression on us. Now, she is gone...but her memory lives on, most of all, at 5 o'clock in the afternoon when she would announce: 'Ah, sherry time, dear. Would you mind?'

I would then make my way to the kitchen where, among discarded newspapers and detritus of the elderly, I would find a silver salver complete with Edwardian decanter and two sherry glasses.

On return to the drawing-room, I would pour several tots of Concha. By the time Ronnie appeared to collect me, I would need to be supported all the way to the 83 bus.

Jenny Jones Agency contacted us with news. Mr. Rea, the elderly gentleman who owned No 20 Bowrons Avenue,

Alperton, would travel from his home in Marlow to meet me.

As the Tube rattled along the Piccadilly Line, I wondered about my destination. Soon, the train left the tunnel and was out into the sunshine. Alperton was very different from what I had expected. It was light, tree-lined and open.

Bowrons Avenue was not far from the station and on the way, I came by pavement stalls and a variety of shops. It seemed to be a growing Indian community. Heather Bakeries looked enticing...I still correspond with David and Kay, its proprietors. Just beyond, I saw the sign and began searching for No. 20.

It was in a residential neighbourhood and Cherry blossom trees were abundant. Pre-war bay-windowed houses made up the road. No 20 had a hedged garden; the front door boasted a coloured glass panel. My knock was answered by a small, wiry old man in checked sports jacket and corduroys. Behind him, appeared a very tall chap in overalls. This was Mr. Rea of Marlow and his handyman, Ken. Mr. Rea was blustery and said, rather abruptly, 'Which one do you want to look at first?' How different it was then. The Suzy Lamplugh tragedy was still to come.

I was escorted to the first floor. The house had been converted into two flats (I wondered if the industrious Ken had done it) but it was possible to see the charm of the original features, especially the Adam fireplaces which were placed across the corners of rooms. The space was adequate, but I was eager to see what the ground floor had to offer. In layout it was similar, but the kitchen was a minute galley and possessed some hideous cooking pots. The front room was sunny. Its main feature was a floor-to-ceiling oak fireplace across the back corner. The threadbare carpet and equally shabby curtains left much to be desired.

The back room, however, was much more uplifting and opened out through French windows on to a garden. Why were we always faced with a garden that resembled pasture? This one was a tangled mess of Jacob's Ladder weed!

Much to my amazement, the house bathroom had been cobbled together as an extension, but, was tacked on to this rearmost sitting-room! Could it be another of Ken's imprudent brainwaves? Again, the room was enhanced by a white-painted, cross-corner fireplace and a COAL fire! That was a fillip!

Our tour ended. I thanked Mr. Rea who apologised, reluctantly, for the state of his furniture, adding: 'It's a bit tacky, but you'll be able to do something with it'. I took my leave, saying that I would need to talk things over with my Husband. How ridiculous, I thought, thinking that Mr. Rea would look more benevolently on a married couple renting his 'tacky' flats. They were not Utopian. Ah well, decorum at all costs!

I had reached the end of the street when a magnificent Rolls Royce drew near. Seated inside, was Mr. Rea. The doughty Ken was driving.

I reported back to Ronnie with news of No. 20. He was very enthusiastic. When he heard of Adam fireplaces and a stirring garden he was in raptures. 'Sue', he said, 'surely you settled it there and then?' I admitted defeat for I had been dismayed at sight of the shoddy furnishings. Unlike Ronnie, I was quite unable to see light at the end of the tunnel. Determined to take the matter into his own hands, Ronnie made plans for us to view the flat a second time the following evening and our fortune was sealed.

Mr. Rea was not one to be fobbed off with hasty arrangements. We were summoned to his Marlow estate to fix the deal. We resolved to make a day of it and took Southern Railway to Maidenhead where we were assured that the versatile Ken would meet us. I was hoping to flaunt it in the Rolls Royce, but, much to my disappointment, a Morris Minor traveller was drawn up at the station. Ken was ready. We motored through the leafy Berkshire countryside. Ronnie was sitting beside the taciturn driver, but when tired of attempting to instigate conversation, he would turn to me, wink, and say: 'All right in the back there, kidda?' The following facial expression, unspeakably coarse and suggestive, reduced me to a frenzy of choking hysteria!

Eventually, we turned into a very narrow lane. Ken offered no explanation, but soon we could make out a Tudor mansion, immense and very beautiful, taking shape ahead. We alighted and, as we were about to manhandle the gigantic door-knocker, Mr. Rea appeared and waved us into the hall. We followed him into the drawing-room where we were asked to sit on what had been an eye-catching French chaise-longue. The room was brimming with sunlight and monolithic furniture. The vast bay window, complete with window-seat, looked out on to grounds profusely planted with Azalea and Rhododendron bushes.

The air was musty and damp. While we were able to disregard the dust, it was more difficult not to notice the cats. Every surface supported feline occupants. They slumbered on worn Turkish rugs and meandered dangerously across the mantel where heirloom china braced itself for an imminent calamity.

'Now, young man,' said Mr. Rea, 'how are you going to pay my rent?' Ronnie, flattered by the reference to his youth, gave his pledge of certainty that the cheque would be in the post on the appointed date. I wanted to giggle.

Business over, I made some effort to offer social pleasantries and commented upon the allure of the cats. I went on to say that we, too, were animal lovers. Mr. Rea launched into a resume of his affairs, saying, 'I'm not married. There's a few relatives, but they're not getting any of it. It'll all go to the cats'.

Mr. Rea did not provide refreshments, which was something of a relief, for I had illusions of a cat-filled kitchen where hygiene was not of principal importance.

We had been given permission to decorate the flat and the obliging, cordial Mr. Rea agreed to waive the rent until we had moved in. It only remained for us to obtain the keys before life in our new home could begin.

Over the following weeks, our spare time was devoted to the gradual transformation of No. 20. Fortunately, the first floor flat had not been let, so we had the whole house to ourselves. Cleaning materials and painting apparatus was shifted via the 83 Bus. What a blessing a car would have been! Oblivious of hardship, we looked on our task as a labour of love. The ever-faithful Margaret bequeathed a variety of extras, some extremely useful, some useless in that they had been lovingly preserved since the War. Ronnie had been horrified to discover swelling tins in the cupboard-under-the-stairs!

The 83 Bus ran through Golders Green as it wended its way to Finsbury Park, so we were able to drop in on Margaret en route to Gloucester Road. After, fortified with Concha, we dozed on the top deck. I recapture the total happiness of those far-off days and remember them as an inestimable treasure to be taken out of the memory-chest and loved forever.....

Notice had been given to our churlish landlady at Gloucester Road. Our Irish friends and Betty seemed sorry to see us go. We knew, however, that the emergency mixing-bowl would not be called into service again!

Removal day arrived and with it came Eddie and Brian. Friends of Ronnie's, they were, at that time, owners of a Golders Green pet-shop and, some years before, had bought the ground floor flat which had belonged to Ronnie and Philip. Coincidentally, this apartment was situated on the main Golders Green Road and not far from Margaret's. All this was well before West Bank and Scarborough.

Eddie Wilson went on to become Artistic Director of the National Youth Theatre; Brian was his Designer. The friendship had begun many years before in Newcastle. He and Brian were a likeable, amusing couple and, as removal men, they brought hilarity and kindness to what might have been a stressful occasion.

Our possessions were humped into the rear of Brian's station-wagon and weighed down by an accumulation of dusters, bowls, portable electric cooker and 'sparklin' plate-rack. Ronnie and I eased ourselves into the truck and as it rumbled off, the loyal Betty and the three Irish Navvies waved us off. Ronnie looked at me and said, 'That's not a tear in your eye, is it?' I replied, 'That was our first real home together and I loved it.'

***

PART 1

T H E N

NO 20 BOWRONS AVENUE, ALPERTON

1982 - 1990

Ronnie turned the key of No. 20's front door; we passed through, and there began the next eight years of our life. Eddie and Brian left us to it, and, for precious moments, we wandered through the rooms of our new home as if exploring the Ritz.

It was a warm summer evening and one of our first joys was opening the French windows to admire our estate. All at once, a bald head appeared over the wooden fence. Its owner volunteered 'ow d' ye do' and vanished. We ventured into the rampant weeds and looked to the other side. It seemed that we had an Indian family next door. I noticed curtains being tugged, but no one introduced themselves.

As we began the laborious job of unpacking and making up Mr. Rea's seedy double bed (Ronnie, in his wisdom, had bought a luxurious Sanderson's duvet, sheets and pillows which went a long way to salving its tattiness), I opened the one-and-only large cupboard in the bedroom. There, I made a startling discovery. Previous tenants must have been avid boozers for I was faced with a substantial quantity of forgotten bottles of rice wine! Without more ado, Ronnie decided to crack one open. I was cautious. How long had it been there? We could run the risk of severe alcoholic poisoning. Always the optimist, Ronnie went in search of mugs and the dipsomania that followed, made for an apt christening of Bowrons Avenue.

It was not the thumping hangovers which roused us the following morning, but a tentative tapping on the back door. I opened it to reveal a good-looking, graceful young Indian woman standing inside the garden gate. Smiling broadly, she said, 'Hello, I Jasu' and bowed. She then turned and called, 'Bina! Bina!' The gate opened wider and I stared...and stared. There stood a very small, curly-haired two-year-old. I was ricocheted back to when I was twenty-two. I had dreamed of an oval picture. Within the frame was a small, dark, curly-haired child whom I could not place. When I had quizzed my mother about it, she knew nothing of such a child. The dream remained a mystery. I had often dwelt on this, thinking that the delusion may prove to be a part of my future life. When Bina appeared that morning, I knew I had been right. The child of my dream was standing before me. Bina is now thirty-two with a dream-child of her own. When I was told of Anmoi's birth, Bina's inscription on my card read, 'to a dear Grandmother'.

How much of our life is preordained, I wonder? So many extraordinary happenings are credited to coincidence. As our years together progressed, Ronnie and I realised that nothing commonplace had brought us together. There was a purpose.

Bina tapped on the garden gate and went on to spend the lazy days of Summer with us. She 'helped' with the painting, she 'helped' with the shopping and she 'helped' in general. Jasu, her mother, was often to be found engaged in conversation with either Ronnie or me. I say 'conversation', but her sentences were heavily laced with Gudjerat. We, too, picked up never-to-be-forgotten clips of Indian nomenclature such as 'Ronnie-G', or 'cubardier' for the cupboard-under-the-sink. Although Jasu's English was limited, she managed to remark, while convulsed with laughter, 'Ronnie, he very funny man' when she saw him, effulgent in Lungi, eating toast and marmalade in a back garden which was knee-high in grass.

Weeks passed and I was still out of work. I did not care. We pottered and created our haven together; perhaps heaven is the word I should have chosen; a heaven in Alperton.

As the Summer months slipped by, we had no word from Ronnie's agent, in fact very few words from anybody, my family and Philip included. Fortunately, we were self-sufficient and our new life was filled with pleasure, domestic incident and new friends. There was much to find out, new neighbourhoods in which to shop and a rich community was on our doorstep.

Our Doctor still remained an important facet and we shared all our new discoveries with him. He never failed us in his perception, kindness and invigorating advice. It was always positive. He did not remind me of the Dick Whittington prediction, but I found myself reminiscing and being drawn to its enigmatic significance.

After all, a short time ago, I had thought I would be bound for a fresh season in Scarborough. Yet here I was in Alperton. Before, I did not know such a place existed. Nor did I know that Ronnie and I would never work for Alan Ayckbourn again.

On the other side of the fence lived Hester and Reg. Hester, a vibrant, friendly and exuberant Irish lady told us much about their life. Reg was not so forthcoming and mowed his lawn in somewhat belligerent fashion. Hester, looking at him in disgust, would mutter half to herself, half to us: 'He's a dreadful man'! Sadly, she told us of Pamela, their only child, a Downs Syndrome little girl who had lived to be fifteen. It seems her death had driven the couple apart leaving a gaping hole. Devoted to Pamela in their different ways, they could not be consoled. Acceptance of her passing was inconceivable.

Reg channelled his affection into Wilbur, an adopted aged cat. Wilbur's real owner had long since departed and so Reg became devout carer. Wilbur was a sight to behold.

One ear was ragged and disfigured, the other practically non-existent. Reg, in declaring the cat's toothlessness, opened the poor creature's mouth to prove it. Sure enough, two decaying gnashers gleamed from within. Reg concluded: 'e's been a warrior, 'as Wilbur'.

Reg's behaviour was strangely contradictory. One dusky evening, Ronnie was labouring in the garden, attempting to demolish some of the weeds. All at once, the bald head appeared. "ow do you get rid of slugs, Ronnie?' Ronnie volunteered various remedies such as pellets, saucers of beer or Vaseline to smear around pots. Reg gave him an arch look and said: 'Personally, I fink that's crool. I wait till it's dark, then I get the velocipide out, shine the lamp on 'em, then....I run 'em over'.

I phoned my Mother two or three times a week and tried to engender some enthusiasm from her. Even Reg's escapades failed to stimulate much interest. I knew that I would not be forgiven for deserting the sinking ship. That being, subjecting her to an unvisited, unfrequented life without my dutiful companionship between Theatre jobs. Ronnie was equally solicitous, but, all to no avail.

Ronnie was still contracted to the BBC Radio Repertory Company, but there were idyllic days off. Sometimes, these occurred on Fridays, so we set out at an unearthly hour to plunder and ransack the Portobello Road Market (the seamy end), Brick Lane, or Camden. Ronnie had a remarkable eye for labels and designer clothes. In fact, for most of my married life I was kitted out in second hand gear. These campaigns began with our favourite Friday breakfast; a ham and cheese Panini from the Italian bakery. Thus sustained, we went into battle.

On his journey home from the BBC, after a day's work in the Studio, Ronnie's greeting would be: 'I say, look what I've found!' The carrier-bags, bursting with booty, were then emptied and a blithesome trying-on session followed - Bina in attendance. His finds often took in curtains and loose-covers for Mr. Rea's tacky chairs. Ronnie's talents were legion.

One day, we decided to give Bina an outing she would not forget. We were exhausted, but instead of pursuing the usual entertainments, we ended up at Heals on the Tottenham Court Road. There, Bina became obsessed with the water beds and refused to leave! Much cajoling followed and the promise of sipping a Cappucino coffee in a wayside bar saved the day, but was not, however, productive for calm and serenity on the way home.

The garden at No. 20 was an eternal source of activity, pleasure and - expense. It was obvious that plants could not thrive there until steps were taken to obliterate the ferocious Jacob's Ladder Weed. Not being privy to the mysteries horticulture, I jumped in at the deep end. I knew that the rugged Reg possessed a scythe. That was to be the Weed's opponent! One glorious Summer day, when Ronnie was safely off to work, I approached Reg and outlined my plan. He curled his lip in sardonic smile and handed over the terrifying implement. Thus armed, I attacked Jacob's Ladder with unrelenting zeal. I should mention that I was clad in strapless tee-shirt and brief denim shorts. Two hours later, the garden was shorn and I was suffering from sunburn and gnat-bites. The Weed was infested and below were roots that a Titan could not have unearthed. When Ronnie came home, he was horrified at the state of me, but overjoyed at the metamorphosis that was his garden. I was dismayed when he added, 'Perhaps we need a rotavator!' It was then that I eschewed all responsibility...

Ronnie made a good job of the decorations and the flat was beginning to look light and airy. I acted as builder's mate fetching, carrying and brewing brickie's tea. I dare not stray near the tins of magnolia for fear of hindering or having a major catastrophe. Instead, I whispered sweet nothings and made extravagant compliments. Bina put in her two-pennyworth with 'Ronnie busy.'

The tacky furniture took on a new lease of life, for, fortunately for us, the chairs and sofa were old-fashioned, lending themselves well to Ronnie's wizardry with material remnants. No nervous breakdowns this time...

In and around these pursuits we made more friends. From time to time, Ronnie escorted me all over London making introductions to companions he had known for years. I was profoundly touched by his wish to show me off. He was so proud of me and his new life. I was also moved by the obvious affection that others had for Ronnie. Sally, an actress whom he had known for many years and had appeared with him in several plays, summed up her esteem: ' Well Ronnie, at last you've got a dolly to dress'! All these people seemed so happy for Ronnie. We did not encounter unkindness anywhere.

The garden began to resemble a garden and less like disused waste land. The digging over was horrendous, but, albeit with aching joints, we were at last able to sit and admire our handiwork. The bald head surfaced again and 'you got my scythe?' was all the endorsement we needed. Hester always managed to make a warm and constructive observation.

On Saturday mornings, when we were not otherwise engaged with visits to Margaret's or the Portobello, we would take a look at the seething Ealing Road at the top of Bowrons Avenue. The pavements were crowded with fruit and vegetable stalls. Colourful Indian ladies of all shapes and sizes bargained, argued and chattered. The sari shops boiled over on to the street and we would thrill at the sight of exotic chiffons, silks and bejewelled throws. The idea was to make our way into Wembley where there was an English market and thriving open-air plant mart. Before long, the shopping-trolley-on-wheels was loaded with goodies; triumphant, we staggered home peering through the branches of baby Willow and Cherry blossom trees. All the while, we paid no attention to the possibility of a short sojourn at No. 20. We were setting down roots in more ways than one.

On occasion, Ronnie would set forth alone in his search for plants. I would be happily engrossed cleaning, going to the launderette, or making a cake. I was learning to cook and needed practice. Yes, Ronnie was also an inventive, painstaking and proficient chef. How spoiled was I with so many accomplishments! He was also patient and good-hearted when coaching me. I was the one with the short fuse.

On one such lone visit to Wembley, Ronnie had decided to investigate St. John's Road. Here, he had come across an Oxfam shop. He answered a window advertisement for helpers. As if he didn't have enough to do! I was never sure whether Ronnie was intent on having first pickings of all the clothing donations, or if he just wanted to be of service. Perhaps it was a little of both. Apparently, the reception he received from one of the honourable ladies behind the counter was rather unexpected and harsh. Ronnie was taken aback by: 'Well, we're not used to men. I don't like them because they whistle and leave the lavatory seat up!' Interestingly, Ronnie could be held to account for both transgressions... Undeterred, he turned up for work the following week. Of course, he won over Attila, as he dubbed her, and the Herdman charm won the day once more.

Ronnie was very, very happy. I marvelled at the courage he had shown. I marvelled that somehow I had managed to fulfil his yearning for so many things. It was all so new to him. He whistled and sang his way through the days, and in so doing, he blessed others with his gladness. I discovered that, in the past, he had relied on Philip to fix domestic trials, but now, because **I** was reliant on **him** to solve household problems, he relished being in charge. My lack of patience with all things mechanical, provided Ronnie with the chance to be redeemer from all that vexed me.

I was very lucky, for I had the best of both worlds in my lover. I had found a man who not only understood a woman's sensitivity to clothes, shoes and ornament, but also gained much gratification from seeing me wearing them. This same man wallpapered, dug the garden and cooked. Also, Ronnie was prepared to take on a plethora of issues which had not, previously, been within his province. My respect for him was boundless.

Our life was about to encompass a further dimension. Ronnie's weekly tarries to the Oxfam shop brought him into regular contact with other Wembley hives of interest. On returning home one morning, he announced: 'I say, I've found the Spiritualist Church on St. John's Road. Wouldn't it be fun to go this Sunday!' This was a novel development. As Ronnie was so enthusiastic and insistent, we did go, and on that Sunday evening, embarked upon an exceptional and elevating life-change.

The Church was set back from the road and was not an imposing building. Its façade was nondescript. A simple board near the entrance was the only identification. I was very sceptical and, perhaps, reluctant to go any further, but Ronnie, ever the adventurer, had engaged in a very earnest conversation with a feminine member of the congregation. She was a very large black lady, sumptuously dressed and impeccably groomed. Ronnie magnanimously made the introductions and Violet, in the weeks to come, became a firm friend.

We had not attended a Spiritualist Church before. Our only connection with the Movement had been indirectly through our Parapsychological Doctor, his healing and predictions.

The Church interior was not palatial and the furnishings were ancient. A musty fragrance filtered through the inner door. There, we were met by a most friendly helper who provided hymn books and copies of the Psychic News. We came to know her as Hilda. The gathering was noisy and the usual silence which precedes religious services was non-existent. The atmosphere, nevertheless, was uplifting and full of anticipation. Ronnie and I, novices, were welcomed with great warmth and affection. We sat side by side and looked toward the front of the Church. The beaming Violet, sitting forward, kept turning reassuringly, determined to furnish us with the details of spiritual obedience! Our attention was drawn to the platform. Apparatus and furnishings special for the conduct of the programme were placed in readiness. Most noticeable was fresh flowers and numerous water jugs. Ronnie clasped my hand in his, looked at me and winked.

A primitive harmonium stood beside the dais. Perched on its accompanying stool was an equally archaic lady. Violet, keen to oblige, offered information via audible whispering: 'That's Miss Brown, usually called Brownie. She's only got one eye, poor soul, that's why her head is on one side'. All this was relayed in a broad West Indian accent. Sure enough, when Miss Brown turned to smile, the effect was astounding. One eye was permanently closed, but the other was unnerving in its piercing, shrewd gaze. She was clad from head to foot in a lilac, hand-knitted two-piece. Miss Brown was tiny so her skirt almost touched the ground. The notes that she managed to coax from that bygone instrument were nothing short of miraculous. As time went by, Miss Brown became a principled, upright, level-headed friend and confidante. Whenever Ronnie visited her at home, she and her loveable Labrador, Bess, would give him a conducted tour of the striking garden. One day, as he was taking his leave, she called: 'Ronnie, before you go, you must smell my Daphne'. The story of that invitation was disclosed by Ronnie ad infinitum, but in less reverent tones and certainly with some added vulgarity.

The Service on that first evening was a revelation. I suppose I had envisaged some sort of hocus-pocus and, facetiously, looked forward to an element of ridicule and giggling. I was chastened. The simple proceedings and the sincerity of the speakers humbled me. We sang unusual hymns; I had not heard them before. A 'silence' was observed during which we were encouraged to think and pray for all those in need. The sick and lonely were not forgotten. We gave healing thoughts to the Animal Kingdom and all souls looking for reassurance and help. There was a reminder that the teachings of the Spirit are those of love, compassion, gentleness and tolerance; that we get out of life what we put into it, no more, no less. Both Ronnie and I were focused. The teachings were powerful. The theme was unexpected. It made sense to learn that there should be responsibility for one's own evolution; that one could not cheat the natural law of cause and effect.

The conductor of this procedure was introduced as Winifred Smart. Softly spoken, direct and emanating care, she spoke of hope, deliverance and a firm belief in an Afterlife. The ideas were seductive and at no time was there a belittling of traditional religious belief. Jesus was mentioned often, but referred to, intriguingly, as the Nazarene. His promise of an Afterlife and death as a beginning was vouched for. I wanted to learn more, and, as I daydreamed, I thought of the Christian faith being based on resurrection and life after death; likewise, the fundamental truth behind Spiritualist teaching is that there is no death. I deduced that we aim to reach salvation, but follow different pathways.

The Service changed gear. Winifred introduced the guest speaker: a gentleman from the main Spiritualist Centre in Belgrave Square. He was the medium. The remaining section of the Service was devoted to clairvoyance. This is where my scepticism returned and I awaited confirmation of my disbelief.

Ronnie, in the meantime, was gripped. We were given instructions of how to respond if the spokesman came to us. We were to acknowledge with a 'yes' or 'no'. There was a ripple of anticipation in the congregation.

The atmosphere was electric. All were silent, eager and watchful. The man spoke to a woman on the front row. The 'message' was received with tearful gratitude. Apparently, every detail was accurate. Names of loved ones were given and she recognised numerous references to her life and experience. She had her proof, yet still I doubted.

The medium announced that he had a very curious image to describe and wondered if anyone in the church could 'take' it. He laughed as he explained that Spirit often gave inexplicable symbols which were meaningful only to the true recipient. He resumed with: 'Can anyone take a pig?' There was laughter. It was not an unkind reaction but rather a genuine appreciation of how mystical or cryptic Spirit could be. 'The shape of a pig?' he insisted. I began to feel uncomfortable. The gentleman looked directly at me and I squirmed. 'I'd like to come to the lady at the back of the room'. It was me and I did not want it to be me. I was only there as a spectator. Ronnie squeezed my hand. 'I am bringing a Father figure to you and with him comes the pig.' I had no choice but to nod and say 'yes', for I knew only too well that this was evidence for me. I thanked the medium and was left with the glow of remembrance.

My father had been a pork butcher. He kept a shop and delicatessen in Hull and advertised by displaying a neon-lit pig in the window. Even Ronnie did not know of those far-off times, no one could have known, least of all the medium that night. Had our introduction to the Spiritualist Church come about by chance or intention?

My father remained in my thoughts long after that evening. I had been very proud of my father's hard-working occupation. Many years ago, when at Drama school, I remember talking about this quite freely, but was silenced and snubbed when the daughter of a professional man scoffed at lowly trade. Such hurt can heal, but I wonder, did fragments of it remain? Was that why I was reticent, unforthcoming in responding to the medium's enquiry? I had learned a lesson. Truth triumphs and snobbery, scorn or derision pale into insignificance beside it. My loving Father was there and I was warmed by his presence...

In the weeks that followed, we were regular attenders at the Church and we were not disappointed. New friends were made; some remain to this day. It was there where we became acquainted with Yvonne, who in turn knew Michael. He organised a team of wheel-chair dancers. Who made the costumes for this group? Why, Ronnie of course! Together, Ronnie and I entered into a totally unexpected world where Theatre and ambition were of secondary importance. We discovered an enriching outlet for our talents.

A surprise came my way. A theatrical availability call arrived via my ineffectual agent. Alan Ayckbourn's 'Season's Greetings' had been running in Town for several months. Ronnie and I had been to see the production but were not impressed. Perhaps this was because we had appeared in the original Scarborough performances and had seen the magic of true Theatre-in-The-Round as opposed to the London proscenium staging. Or, perhaps we were still smarting from being bypassed when the play was cast for London. Whatever the cause, we had forgotten it.

The upshot of this unheralded turn of events, was that the actress playing the character which I had originated in Scarborough, Phyllis, would be leaving the cast. Presumably, I was the next port of call. Ronnie and I were thrown into a frenzy of excitement. This could be the turning point in my career! Was fate playing a wonderful set of cards which would drive my theatrical destiny? We fantasized about casting agents coming to see the show; of fame and fortune knocking on the door. We waited with bated breath for the telephone call to come. It did, but only to break the news that the play was coming off! It was to close in a matter of weeks...

It was a blow, but...we consoled ourselves with even more trips to the Portobello Road! It was on the way home, on the top deck of the bus, that Ronnie announced: 'Well Alice, we'll get married instead!'

It was August. We planned to make the Big Day on Ronnie's Birthday. That way, he declared, he would never forget his Wedding Anniversary! Enquiries were made at Willesden Registry Office for 18th September, but unfortunately, there was to be an industrial dispute on that day, so would we mind making it the 20th or 22nd?

My Mother's Anniversary was on the 22nd, so the thoughtful Ronnie pondered that if we were to choose that date, she would be so delighted to think that we had wished to honour her on such a memorable day. Not a bit of it. She expressed disapproval and an unmistakable desire to obstruct. So, our Wedding Day was fixed for 20th September 1982.

It would be true to say that darling Ronnie made more preparations for our Wedding than me. I loved Ronnie deeply and could not wait to be his wife. My longing, however, was dogged by an uneasy undercurrent of foreboding. This was caused by my Mother's moroseness. It was very difficult to ignore and my impending happiness was spoiled quite deliberately by my Mother who flatly refused to come to the Wedding. As a consequence, my brother also declined the invitation. Silence followed. A letter from my Mother arrived during the week before our Wedding. It devastated me. I was told that I would be making a colossal mistake and should not go through with the marriage. No holds were barred and I was left distraught and disbelieving.

Ronnie was angry. As always, he did not allow this to impinge on what was to be such a happy time for us. He buoyed me up, stemming the weeping with his resilience and love.

Surprise after surprise flowed into No. 20 that Wedding week. Two cases of champagne appeared and when I said, 'Who's coming?', the reply was, 'Wait and see!' I planned to wear the splendid Susan Small bronze shot-taffeta 50's dress that had been such a hit on the American jaunt. Ronnie decided that it needed a head-dress and set about making one. It would be called a fascinator today...This was a silver grey piece de resistance trimmed with small ostrich feathers...

Ronnie then went on to finish off the flat's upholstery and helped me to arrange the furniture for the Big Day. All the while, my excitement was tinged with sadness. My husband-to-be refused to allow despondency to creep in; instead he engendered optimism and anticipation.

Many of our friends were unable to come. They were working. Two of our dearest ones, Tess and Owen, who were to be our witnesses, were suddenly called away.

This threw our arrangements into disarray until Carol, the pal from my Scarborough season, and her partner, Patrick, kindly agreed to take their place. Philip sent good wishes, but, much to our disappointment, decided to stay away...

The 20th September was a Monday and the weekend before saw our flat, take on the appearance of a Wedding venue. Ronnie spent Saturday in the kitchen, preparing food. I tried to find out who was going to eat it, but was told, 'Wait and see, Alice!' A salmon was cooked and chicken was to accompany a variety of salads. Cards began to arrive and a most lavish, de-luxe bouquet of flowers from Tess was delivered.

We walked to Church on the Sunday evening before our Wedding Morn. It was the time of Harvest Festival and the front platform was bedecked with flowers and fruit. The Service, taken by Winifred Smart, began and the opening hymns seemed to be played with more than the usual gusto by Brownie. Then, Winifred made an announcement: 'Will our Sue and Ronnie come forward?' Ronnie took my hand and led me to stand before the altar. Winfred continued:' Tomorrow, Ronnie and Sue are to be married. Here, we will give them our Blessing'. I was overwhelmingly touched and this absolute kindness dispelled the misery of the preceding days. Here was the unselfish, caring love that I so craved for Ronnie and me. Our real Wedding took place on that evening and the joy of those moments have lived with me ever since. The Blessing was concluded with the gift of a simple bunch of Sweet Peas, tied with ribbon and given to me by Brownie. The card read: 'For our Bride, Sue'. Sweet Peas were my real Wedding bouquet and throughout our life Ronnie found an excuse to find them for me. I discovered later that it was Ronnie who had told Winifred of our Wedding. Together, they had arranged the lasting, memorable solemnization for me. We were truly blessed....

The Wedding cards that came from our Doctor and his family reminded us of the continuing link with him, his unusual healing and the philosophical unfolding world of Spirit. I began to recognise the past crossroads in my life and how, in the sweep of indecision or distress, succour or advice had come my way. Helpmates had appeared, stayed a while until the crisis was over, then disappeared. Intuition had guided me. I spoke of this to Ronnie. 'Well, I knew all along. Why do you think I persuaded you to come to the Church with me?'

Sunshine streamed through the windows of No. 20 on the morning of our Wedding. A Florist arrived. He delivered an Orchid corsage for the Bride and a matching buttonhole for the Groom. It seemed that my loving Ronnie had thought of everything...

The ceremony was booked for late morning. Our friends were to meet us at the Registry Office. Dressed in our finery, we climbed into the taxi. Hester was waving from her window; Bina and Jasu waved from the gate.

Aching regret came over me. The Day would have been so much more special if our loved ones had been there. In that moment, I realised how much Ronnie and I had accomplished on our own. Thoughts of Margaret, our Doctor and loyal friends who, for various reasons, could not be by our side, comforted me. We sped on, hand-in-hand and profoundly in love.

It transpired that our simple ceremony was to take place between Indian and Chinese Weddings! We were met with a packed car-park bursting at the seams with groups of Indian men and dragons being manipulated by exuberant Chinese guests. Carol and Patrick had arrived in good time and were standing, somewhat bewildered, in the centre of this alien, exotic fray. As luck would have it, Patrick had remembered to bring a camera, so waiting time was occupied with photographs. Later, I was sorry that our only record of marrying was a few snaps taken in haste.

We were ushered into the Registry and there we were married. Outside, the lavish Indian ladies gossiped and compared the luxuriance of their saris. The surroundings were recherché and the company bizarre, but all added to the joy of our Day. It was precious and our solemn vows were exchanged with reverent promise.

Carol and Patrick declined our invitation to return home with us. It was a disappointment, but before leaving, they presented us with a cushion cover and a box of Weekend chocolates. Ronnie never forgot that gesture and it was recalled often in our reminiscences!

We returned to our flower-filled flat and were met with neighbours' congratulations. We toasted ourselves and every other person nearby with champagne in plenty. Ronnie then announced that he had invited several old friends of his to join us that evening. This was yet another commemoration and an unexpected present for me. The day progressed with laughter, noise and jubilant phone calls from far-away friends. There was another call - from my Mother. It was a tearful exchange and it saddened me, but the parting words were hopeful and tentative arrangements were made for my family to visit at Christmas.

I turned my attention to the present and looked forward to welcoming our guests - Hester and Reg, Douglas (an Australian actor friend of Ronnie's), Dora and Fred, and the redoubtable Sally who had remarked on Ronnie having a dolly to dress. Dora and Fred were older friends and very dear to Ronnie. It was a charming, heart-warming gathering. Hester and Reg fitted in well, although Reg was his gruff self. Hester, determined to draw a veil over his blunders, became more garrulous with each champagne top-up. Douglas, a very witty, and not a little wicked, gay gentleman seemed to find the choleric Reg somewhat attractive. He confided later that a bit of rough had always appealed to him. Douglas was funny and more than a match for Reg, especially as he was egged on, surreptitiously, by Ronnie. Reg seemed to enjoy himself and made his glowering contribution as supper was served. Dora and Fred were a gentle, loving couple and became loyal friends until their death just a few years later. Unhappily, Sally did not survive critical illness, but the one remaining - Douglas - has been with us all our days. Ours was a joyous Wedding...

Ronnie remained in constant work with the BBC. He was a gifted broadcaster and much in demand. His versatility, command of dialect and every nuance of the spoken word was invaluable for both the World Service and the Radio Repertory Company.

Ronnie proved to be an excellent agent for me and I was cast in several plays as a result of him approaching his many contacts, inveigling them to take me on. To be fair, I was a good actress and so never felt that work came my way as a favour to Ronnie. Perhaps it started out that way!

Films and television also played an important part in Ronnie's working life and for that reason, relations with his agent needed to be kept on an even keel. Nevertheless, a distant slant prevailed and meetings were of a formal nature as opposed to one of social compatibility. From my point of view, the association was diffident and I tried to avoid contact. Whenever this could not be shunned, I was nervous and filled with dread. I made the best of such situations for Ronnie's sake, but they were an ordeal.

Ronnie's calls to work were often irregular depending on the size of part he was playing. This offered opportunities for leisurely days devoted to exploring our surroundings. We walked through the avenues and lanes near home, usually with the diminutive Bina in tow. Much to our astonishment, we found a rambling park at the top of Bowrons Avenue. This was known as One-Tree Hill Park. We were puzzled as to how it got its name, for it was planted with miniature copses and shrubberies. Brent Council obviously took great pride in keeping the recreational area in pristine condition; the grasslands and children's swing space was immaculate. Ronnie was ridiculously overweight for the see-saw, so Bina and I corrected the imbalance by both sitting firmly on the other end.

The main walkway was lined with Poplar trees. The whole perspective was illustrious Summer and Winter alike. I remember taking Bina bramble-picking in the Park. This was on the pretext of making bramble jam. She was very quietly filling the basin with fruit, when she turned and asked: 'Are these Indian brambles?' They certainly made the most delicious Indian jam.

Jasu, Bina's mother, visited often. Also, our kitchens faced one another, so most mornings and evenings we waved across the fence. Sometimes, Ronnie would intervene, making faces and wittering to himself in cod Gujarat. Jasu would smile broadly, then hastily look behind to see if her Mother-in-law was around.

The family was large, packing a quart into a pint pot, consisting of grandmother, grandfather, three older unmarried daughters, Jasu and her husband Vassant, Bina and three of Jasu's step-children from her husband's first marriage!

It was more than I could take in on first introduction. Relationships there were strained and poor Jasu had a thin time of it attempting to assert some kind of stature in this close-knit hierarchy. Needless to say, Grandma ruled the roost. On one tearful occasion, Jasu, sitting in the refuge of our sitting-room (this could be referred to as 'the shitting-room' - but we didn't have the heart to put Jasu straight on this error!) and haltingly outlined her dilemma. Ronnie occupied Bina in the garden. He was showing her how to sow Hollyhock seeds!

Vassant's first wife had upped and left him. Ronnie told me later that this was a most unusual occurrence in Indian culture. I suppose the poor woman had had enough of her in-laws. Whatever had happened, Vassant was carted off to India and there a marriage was arranged with the much younger Jasu. At this point in the story, a soaking Ronnie appeared framed on the other side of the French windows. Bina, bored with Hollyhock seeds, had turned the hose on him. So, the solemnity of Jasu's narrative was interrupted with a frantic dash for towels.

It seems that Jasu's own family was a close and affectionate one. The wrench of parting was painful for her. Young and defenceless in a strange country, Jasu had experienced intense isolation and anguish.

All at once, Jasu reached inside the folds of her sari and produced an envelope. She held it out to me, saying, 'Open'. Inside was a photograph. A young, handsome face smiled at me. 'He my husband,' said Jasu. 'He twenty-one - I twenty-one. We marry. We very happy. He die. I love him much. Like you and Ronnie'. I did not know what to say. Before I could think of how to comfort my new friend, she said, 'You keep'. The photograph has remained in our desk ever since. As the years went by, I asked Jasu if she wished to have it returned.' No' was always the answer. 'You keep,' she would say sadly, 'it safe with you and Ronnie'.

The marriage between Vassant and Jasu was blessed with the winsome, endearing Bina. Jasu had tried to vindicate herself, tried to assume her rightful status as a wife by taking on chores and responsibility in the household. She was, however, confronted with jealousy and spite. Forced to occupy one room at the top of the house, the threesome slept and existed in almost unbearable cramped conditions. Vassant, true to custom, remained loyal to his parents and sisters and so Jasu became ostracized and Bina punished. No 20 had become an oasis of gentleness for them.

Nevertheless, the family were friendly and courteous to Ronnie and me and whenever there was a celebration, a wedding or a feast day, we would be presented with a platter of Indian food and rich hospitality. We took a backseat only when voices were raised across the way and the kitchen door was open wide enough for us to see, alarmingly, Grandma on the warpath yet again, wielding a hefty cleaver and bringing it down on the work surface. Jasu had fallen from grace yet again.

When we were breakfasting in the garden on sunlit days, or enjoying supper at a rickety old table beneath the young Cherry Blossom tree, we would look up and at the window above see two melancholy faces pressed against the glass...wishing...

Bina could see us beckoning and soon little feet clattered on the house stairs. The gate would burst open as impish laughter brought her to sit beside us, 'Bina hungry' was the plaintive cry.

The garden was taking on a true identity. The willow tree at the bottom of the plot was weeping dramatically and many infant shrubs were coming to life. Flowers were abundant and Ronnie introduced strange mobiles and ornaments to complement the effect. Two orange plastic discs swung crazily in the breeze and were the cause of much merriment among our friends. Reg's reaction was one of sheer disbelief. He commented, 'Well, each to 'is own'. Ronnie's apparel was also worthy of annotation. On warm Autumn days, he would rake out the most staggering shorts. One particular pair, of Union Jack design, was a favourite and bound to attract derisory response. These would be worn with thick woollen socks and sandals. Regardless of his extensive varicose veins being on full display, he would remark, 'Oh, perhaps I'll get a tan today'. When the sun became too hot for him, an enormous Mexican straw hat would finish off the outfit - indeed, it almost finished off all who witnessed this unselfconscious show.

A small brick barbecue began to take shape. I mentioned that it was now very Autumnal and would we be able to eat out for very much longer? Undeterred, Ronnie constructed his device. When it came to fuel, Ronnie's ideas ran riot.

Previously, he had dismantled some of Mr. Rea's tacky chairs, and, in their place, had bought me a wondrous Arts and Crafts rocking-chair. The old woodworm-infested remains of the has-been furniture were chopped up and hurled on to Ronnie's barbecue. I might add that, when lit, the aroma of paint blistering and burning must have infused the whole of Alperton. The tandoori chicken, however, cooked upon the embers was nothing short of cordon bleu in its excellence. In fact, Ronnie's tandoori, somewhat magenta in hue, became legendary. Life was delicious, and funny, and so, so happy....

I had not met Ronnie's family. He hailed from Hartlepool, so was just short of being a true Geordie. He could, however, lapse at will into broad dialect. This delighted all who were used to his Queen's English. He preferred to refer to the Queen rather than RP. He said it was more appropriate in his case! Ronnie could execute a brilliant imitation of Her Majesty and I would ask him, repeatedly, to launch into it whenever a good laugh was on the cards. It was quite a performance. He needed to psych himself up vocally in order to reproduce the falsetto tones. 'My husband and I', he would bleat, 'wish to thank the people of the Soviet Union, for this **won**-derful combine harvester!'

Another favourite would be: 'My husband and I take great pleasure - every Friday night!' or, 'Don't do that Philip, it's not nice!' There would follow high-pitched regal cackling. It was a bravura representation.

Ronnie was endowed with a mellifluous speaking voice. No wonder Radio was his forte. I asked him how he came to acquire such impeccable speech, especially as he grew up in the North East, where dialect was rich but thick with distorted vowels and consonants. Ostensibly, as a little boy he had been glued to the Radio, listening to Alvar Lidell, Children's Hour and Uncle Mac. This painted the picture of a lonely child, immersed in a world of make-believe and a home-made minute model Theatre, where he would present his collection of actor prototypes, all clad in costumes made by himself. He had imitated the forties language of BBC Radio presenters. I asked if this had encouraged bullying at school. 'Oh no,' Ronnie replied, 'but Miss Robinson did make me the flower monitor!'

Plans were made for a coach trip to the North. Ronnie's mother lived in sheltered accommodation in Hartlepool and his sisters, Kathy and Violet, both married with families, lived on the outskirts of the city. There was a brother, Ken, who had married a Welsh girl and to all intents and purposes, was now more Welsh than the Welsh.

We had been invited to stay with Kathy. I was looking forward to meeting them and I hoped they would welcome me into the family. I wondered what their reaction would be. First Philip, and now...me... Perhaps explanations are unnecessary.

The journey to Hartlepool by coach was arduous. Kathy met us at the terminal and I was immediately drawn to Ronnie's pretty, friendly younger sister. I was given a generous, affectionate greeting by the whole family. My uncertain feelings had been unwarranted.

Hartlepool proved to be similar to many other cities; a mixture of affluent and disadvantaged areas. Ronnie was eager to point out the house where he was born and Winnie Wawne's Dancing School where he had learned to tap and master the complexities of step-camat. Many years later, I would be entranced and rendered incapable with laughter, as Ronnie reproduced these ludicrous contortions, a la Isadora Duncan, in the West Bank kitchen.

The highlight of our short stay was a visit to Ronnie's mother, Louie Belsham. Ronnie had taken the name of her first husband. Both he and Mr. Belsham were deceased. Louie's sheltered pensioner's flat was situated in pleasant surroundings opposite to the Park. This she loved for, in her youth, gardening had been a passion. Ronnie believed that the term 'sheltered' should be applied to the protection of callers who had the temerity to cross her threshold. Louie was certainly an imposing, dominant woman. In appearance, Ronnie was the absolute image of her. The story goes that, a few years earlier, Louie had paid a visit to West Bank. Friends knew that she was around but had not been told of her departure. Ronnie invited them for supper. Then, dressed in appropriate drag, he descended the stairs meeting with calls of 'Oh Mrs. Belsham, how lovely to meet you'. I wondered at the validity of this yarn!

I think Louie weighed me up with some suspicion on first meeting, and said, 'Where's Philip?' This was quite understandable. Fortunately, Ronnie had told me of her addiction to Mills & Boon, so I made sure I was armed with a good supply. This diluted the atmosphere and we spent a fruitful couple of hours chatting about 'such good books', especially those that had a racy, romantic theme...

Before leaving, Ronnie disappeared into the lavatory and, on returning to the sitting-room, was saluted with 'I 'ope you 'aven't left a banger in there, our Ron!'

This was a show-stopping moment and, once outside, the belly-laughs rivalled those to be heard during a robust second-house in Panto.

Our stopover in Hartlepool came to an end. Kathy accompanied us to the coach station and waved as we pulled away. I had, in such a short time, looked upon her as a sister. Little did I know then that our meetings would be few. Sadly, Kathy died of cancer not long afterwards and I had lost a treasured friend. My lasting memory of Kathy is of her brave, smiling face when we visited her in hospital. We had taken Dior's Diorissimo as a gift. Ronnie opened the package for her and Kathy was elated saying 'Our Ronnie, this is only for high days and holidays!'

Christmas 1982 was fast approaching and Bina was helping yet again! We had made fleeting visits to West Bank, and, as always, returned clutching armfuls of furnishing appendages for the flat. One large bag contained the Decorations! Bina's face was a study. She found paper lanterns, Nativity crib and animals, tinsel and the tree ornaments. Needless to say, we became as preoccupied as Bina for, through her, we relished all the Christmas rituals anew.

My cooking was improving and I ventured to bake The Cake - no mean feat in our galley kitchen. Bina 'helped' with stirring ingredients, licking spoons and bedecking the tree. There was no limit to her exploits and our pleasure.

There was another important consideration. My family did accept our invitation and were to spend the festive time with us. We hoped it would be festive! Ronnie took all in his stride and made lavish preparations for the provisions. The kitchen was a hub of activity and by Christmas Eve the flat resembled Aladdin's Cave. My mother and brother were scheduled to arrive early evening, so Ronnie made one final expedition to Wembley Market, leaving Bina and I to last-minute confections for the table.

Eventually, Ronnie returned - with the turkey. He announced: 'Guess what? I got it cheap. You see, it only has one leg!' With that, Christmas 1982 was clinched. It was a happy Christmas. Dearest Ronnie, who could have been forgiven for reluctance to be sociable towards my family, proved instead his inestimable generosity of spirit. He cooked the one-legged turkey to perfection and later concocted luscious meals throughout the Celebration. My Mother appreciated it all, and, to be fair, many of the circumstances must have seemed very odd. Life in Alperton was indubitably different in both custom and appearance from Yorkshire.

My Mother had never encountered the Indian culture, so a stroll down the Ealing Road was a hazardous enterprise which left her awe-stricken for the rest of the day. We were stunned when Grandma from next door made an unexpected entrance. Having noticed my Mother coming and going and no doubt overhearing Bina's chatter to Jasu, she must have decided to investigate for herself. She stood at the garden gate motioning to my Mother, who looked at Ronnie and me in abject terror. Ronnie guided her and soon, unbelievably, the two old ladies, neither comprehending each other's language, were holding a remarkable signed conversation. Judging from the gesticulations, children are a constant source of torment and aggravation! My brother, dear Nick, was benefiting from an allegiance with Ronnie. Unused to having a male ally in the family, my Father had died some years before, he must have found the support was a release from hassle.

Reg and Hester joined us for a jolly evening. Reg actually smiled. Quite by chance, my Mother brought about this miracle. In the course of conversation, several Northern vowels crept into Mum's speech. Her sense of humour overcame any embarrassment when Reg beseeched her to repeat 'b**U**s', 'b**U**tter' and 'b**A**th'! I think Reg had a secret admiration for my Mother. What would Doug have thought!

New Year came and went and so did my family. It had all been a success and relations were levelling out for the time being. Again, I was left amazed at Ronnie's magnanimity and his ability to let bygones be bygones. I was to learn so much from him and his belief that the past was to be relinquished in favour of the present and the future.

The first months of 1983 were occupied with walks in the Park, shopping in Wembley High Street and entertaining Jasu and Bina. Our bus outings to Margaret and the Portobello Road continued and we wallowed in a swathe of good fortune.

Our sole occupancy of No. 20 came to an end. A young couple, Carol and Michael, became tenants of the upper flat. Michael was a newly graduated Film Editor and his partner, Carol, an Illustrator. They seemed friendly enough and although our paths did not cross often, we made every effort to usher them in. They were invited to join us for drinks in the garden and we were more than willing to share our outdoor sanctuary.

Much to our delight, Philip agreed to spend a few days with us and brought Jessie all the way by train! It was lovely to see them both. Pleasure was marred by Ronnie being confined to bed with gastro-enteritis and Jessie going missing. We were frantic but impotent. Nothing could be done. Philip and I searched the neighbourhood and then, incapacitated, sat up all night in the hopes that our beloved dog would be returned to us. Poor Ronnie was weak and unable to lift his head from the pillow.

We resolved to leave the French windows ajar. By now, it was 5.00 a.m. and exhaustion took over. I lay beside Ronnie unable to sleep. Then - rapturous cries of 'Jessie! Jessie'. She had come back; bedraggled, weary, wet and suffering a cut eye. Disorientated, Jessie must have fled in panic. What had followed remained a puzzle. It was enough to enfold her again...

In the course of our nocturnal tete-a-tete, Philip revealed that he was in serious debt. A credit card was the culprit. This, accompanied by too much congress in the pub. His was a predicament that amounted to sundry hundreds of pounds. I decided to keep this to myself until he was en route back to Scarborough.

We had a happy time and Ronnie recovered with the help of a very bland diet. There was much ribaldry, indelicacy and general coarseness in the summing up of his devitalizing lurgy. I refer to the expose - 'It was like shitting through the eye of a needle!' Thank you Ronnie...

After Philip's leave-taking, I broke the news of his financial fix. It worried us both and there seemed to be little else we could do but try to raise some cash through the sale of surplus West Bank furniture. After much deliberation and some regret, we resolved to part with a handsome, fetching chiffonier which stood in the West Bank hall. Some time before, Ronnie had coveted this stylish cupboard. It had belonged to the elderly couple who lived next door and when they were removed to residential care, Ronnie bought it. We came to the conclusion that its sale was inevitable and procured freedom from anxiety. This was the first of many crises concerning Philip's financial management. Later, it led us to consider seriously the selling of West Bank and releasing half of its value to him. Philip would then be liberated and self-governing. The house belonged to Ronnie, but there was an understanding that half of the property would be consigned to Philip if changes came about. In those circumstances, our problem would be to find a home for ourselves. That would be well-nigh impossible in London when reliant on a limited amount of money. We elected to shelve any decision for the time being.

Ronnie's agent received a call from the Artistic Director of Oldham Coliseum Theatre - would he be free to take part in a play there? It was to be a six-week contract. The Director turned out to be an old friend of Ronnie's. How could he refuse? It was troubling for me to contemplate such a long parting, but work was work. Ronnie was interviewed and came home wreathed in smiles. There was a female role in the offing, and - Ronnie had suggested me!

I read for the character, a feisty woman of my age, met the Director and liked her. I got the part. I reckoned it could be convenient to have husband and wife in the same Company; unproductive for some! We were not, however, to reason why. We could be together and the prospect was exciting. It was late Summer by then. We were due to depart, by coach once more, for the North.

Leaving No. 20 and our settled life there was an upheaval, but our profession can demand nomadic endurance. Now, we had the rare luxury of working together.

Bina cried, Jasu cried, Hester cried - Reg did not! Our bags were packed and we left for Victoria Coach Station.

Finding digs or self-catering accommodation is always an actor's headache. Comfort and security is a priority, but so often elusive. On this occasion we had been fortunate. The friendly Director knew of a terraced cottage, at present rented by the Theatre's Lighting Director, who wished to vacate temporarily as he intended to move in with his girlfriend. We were in luck!

***

PART ONE
THEN

COLISEUM THEATRE, OLDHAM
1983

The journey so far North seemed to take an eternity and we arrived travel-sore and weary. The cottage curtains were drawn and we stood hopefully on the doorstep. The Lighting man responded to our knock and we were admitted. No wonder the curtains were drawn. The room, which opened on to the street, was a sight to behold. I was filled with dismay. It was another domestic disaster area. Dust covered every surface, the carpet was filthy and the kitchen passed muster. At the point of mutual introduction, our landlord had not yet got as far as giving a tour of the first floor. I smiled weakly, dare not look at Ronnie and was relieved when we were at last left alone to make the residence fit for habitation - at least for our first night. 'All I can say is fuck' declared the assiduous Ronnie.

We had noticed a general store nearby. Without pausing for breath, I took it by siege and filled a trolley with every imaginable cleaning material. It turned out to be a very well-stocked shop and run by a most obliging Pakistani gentleman who hijacked his young son into helping me along the street.

In the meantime, Ronnie had found the bedroom and bathroom upstairs...it was providential that we had brought our own sheets! The lavatory stirred memories of Gloucester Road and Irish navvies. Windows and doors were opened and soon a refreshing breeze moved layers of dust from one place to another. As luck would have it, the cottage was small and soon we could see that an impression had been made. The prospect of a spotless temporary home arose somewhere on the horizon. We could see light at the end of the tunnel, but, after a bumpy coach trip, scanty meals and middle-aged debilitation, we were slow to recognise it. The cooker was so repugnant that we draped three No. 20 tea-towels over it and set off to find fish n' chips...

As darkness fell, we snuggled down in what vouched to be a very comfortable bed knowing that, eventually, the cottage would be yet another home. Long after the Oldham days were over, we would muse on how many times we had set down roots. Neither of us could resist the temptation to nest. As the years unfolded, it was from those safe launching pads that we embarked upon all-embracing, evocative tasks.

Rehearsals were interesting. The cast for 'Dear Old Blighty' was amiable and talented. Ronnie was playing a blustering, dominant Northern Mayor and I a wholesome, spirited lass from Manchester. We met Richard, an experienced actor raconteur who had a wealth of Theatrical stories which offered ample slots for name-dropping.

In Act II, he and I had mild, romantic exchanges, one culminating in a mild, loving embrace. Poor Richard was acutely embarrassed at having to practice these scenes in front of the newly-married Ronnie. Ronnie, always one to reassure said: 'I've never been a swinger...but....maybe...'

The play was humorous and much mirth ensued during rehearsals. Line learning presented the usual problems and the resolute Richard found himself labouring beside us at the cottage of an evening. We had imagined that audiences would find 'Blighty' equally entertaining and gag lines were savoured in anticipation. When Opening Night met with almost deathly silence, we were very shaken. Ronnie was uneasy, for he possessed most of the comic interjections. Actors question themselves and Ronnie was no exception. There is a lesson to be learned here. Laughter between actors does not guarantee a similar reaction within an audience.

We soldiered on throughout the three-week run and came to the conclusion that those out front were enjoying the play, but 'listening very intently'. This was a reasoned excuse that performers immemorial have been known to come up with at some juncture in their career.

Blithely, we approached the Last Night. We were quite unprepared for what happened. The final audience was engaged, in tune and gleefully showing its appreciation. We were thrown.

Ronnie entered halfway through the first Act, making some oblique reference to a picture which he had to remove from the wall. In a moment of Thespian innovation, he made to blow dust off the frame. Much to the consternation of all, it flew far and wide, no doubt having accumulated in volume over the play's run.

Poor Ronnie was drastically affected with an acute coughing fit which added to the general melee. I was alarmed, for I noticed Ronnie's white face and accompanying panic. He coped until the scene ended and was able to retire to the wings, where the Stage Manager realised something was very wrong and called for the Theatre Doctor.

In the meantime, Richard and I were left on stage, concerned but compelled to continue until the curtain came down on the Interval. By the time I had reached the Green Room, the Doctor had arrived and was ministering to Ronnie, with, preposterously, a cigarette clamped between his teeth! It remained there for the duration of the consultation, only to be removed when another was required to complete the chain.

Ronnie was ill. He had acute cramps in the chest area and a cough. I feared the worst. He was insistent that all would be well and that it was just a 'do'. The Doctor was non-committal. Ronnie, determined to resume with the

Second Half, claimed that the pain had begun to fade. I was worried. Ronnie, the consummate professional, insisted on performing in the second half. Admittedly, his absence would have brought about momentous difficulty. So, on we went. To say that I gave a competent interpretation would be telling a lie, for nervous tension held me in its vice-like grip. Ronnie seemed to be functioning remarkably well, while the rest of the cast depended heavily on automatic pilot.

The curtain came down on rapturous applause, and, succumbing to fierce relief, we repaired to the Bar. Ronnie was by no means recovered. He was very pale and still complaining of chest pain. Meantime, the bootless Doctor had disappeared. I was anxious to get Ronnie home and to bed but, as usual, he was eager not to make a fuss and we hung on a little longer.

We spent a fitful night. Ronnie was still experiencing pain. The following morning I decided to call the Doctor once more. He was reluctant to come out, so I resorted to threats of an ambulance being called. That did the trick and he surfaced twenty minutes later. On examination, he came to the conclusion that Ronnie may be suffering from inter-costal muscular spasms and recommended a warm bath and painkillers. He then scarpered post haste. On reflection, I am confounded that a further observation was not carried out at A & E.

Ronnie obeyed instructions and the pills gave respite. My fear began to subside and slowly he returned to normality. Nevertheless we had had a scare. The episode left me watchful. Much to my dismay, I was on the lookout for symptoms.

Ronnie was asked to stay on for a further play. This was to be a production of 'The Silver Sword', a children's story and intended as a lead-up to the Coliseum's Christmas programme. There was to be a change of Director, but, much to Ronnie's delight, a BBC Radio actress friend of his, Ann Rye, was also cast. This time, however, there was not a role for Ronnie's spouse! I was not downcast but only too pleased to be on the periphery where I could keep an eye on him. I also planned to have a day or two at No. 20. Weeks had elapsed since we had been home.

Richard was returning to London, so I was grateful for a lift. Leaving Ronnie was always a wrench, but this time apprehension accompanied it. Would he be alright? Would the pain recur? The mood going South was companionable and the nattering relieved me of worrying thoughts. In the silent lapses, my loneliness gushed forth. Ronnie and I were like a pair of gloves. When one was misplaced, the other was ceaselessly looking for its missing fellow.

No. 20 warmed me and, as I opened the door, the sound of the ringing phone filled me with exhilaration and expectancy. I knew who would be calling!

Ronnie's voice has never failed to thrill and comfort me, more so when it came from far away and was our solitary loving link. Now, a marriage and many years later, people ask why it remains on my answer-phone. It is still my loving physical link from very far away....

The first day's rehearsal for 'Silver Sword' had gone fairly well, I was told. Neither Ronnie nor Ann had taken to the new Director - 'an objectionable, cocky little shit' was Ronnie's character assessment. Much to Ronnie and Ann's scepticism, the little shit had insisted on one of their duologues as a married German couple be played entirely in German! Reasonable enough, but to a succession of school matinee audiences? The intention, I tried to convince Ronnie, was probably to encourage language expertise. 'Bollocks!' was Ronnie's cultivated, urbane reply. I could hear Ann's agreement in the background. I had a shrewd suspicion that both of them were furious at the prospect of memorising foreign dialogue and that this was uppermost in mind, rather than any educational benefit the young audiences may acquire.

No. 20 was an empty shell without Ronnie's presence. In those days, I had not learned how to be alone. What I did know was that love lingers in the air and walls. There lies the strength. Little-Miss-Make-A-Job found much to do and by the time came round for the return to Oldham, all was 'sparklin'. I had managed visits to dear Margaret who was hungry for news, baked a cake with Bina's help for Bina and laughed with Hester. The bald head bobbed over the fence and Reg's derisive guffaws followed 'Are you goin' back by b**U**s?'

I returned by train. I had left home and yet I was going home. I pondered, as one does on travels. I thought of Philip and hoped his glass did not seem to be empty; I thought of my family and was glad that there was agreement; I thought of our Doctor, his predictions and wisdom, but, most of all, I thought of Ronnie, my beloved Ronnie. Soon, the gloves would be a pair...

Many rehearsal days had passed while I was away- allegedly, days of frustration and annoyance. The German scene had been galling, taxing and certainly not helped by repeated giggling fits. To make matters worse, the little shit was totally devoid of sense of humour. Consequently, he failed to realise that the helpless laughter was a safety valve. It transpired that the one line that Ronnie could remember without difficulty was 'Wo ist mein Frühstück'? or 'Where is my Breakfast?' Typical of Ronnie - food could never fail to jog his memory. So, whenever a memory lapse occurred, he was wont to utter 'Wo ist mein Frühstück'? Gales of merriment ensued, but instead of joining in, the little shit stamped and raved. While I was being regaled with this news, I was relieved to see how much better Ronnie was. Much of this improvement was due to Ann's calming effect. They were having fun and that would get them through.

The little terraced cottage was now spruce, untarnished and cosy. It was a pleasure to keep house while Ronnie was at work. The Lighting Director arrived unannounced one evening. He needed to discuss rental matters and obligation to his landlord. After all, he was sub-letting. I opened the door, he entered and said: 'Christ!' I ignored the blasphemy and offered tea. I think he found his place of residence completely unrecognisable. Quite right.

'The Silver Sword' ran successfully and the German scene met with unrestrained ridicule. Ronnie and Ann struggled through and 'Wo ist mein Frühstück" became indelibly printed on our memory. It was repeated in time-honoured fashion at breakfast tables up and down the country for many years to come.

'Jack and the Beanstalk' was the chosen Pantomime for the Coliseum, Oldham in 1983. The Artistic Director, Kenneth Alan Taylor, invited Ronnie and me to stay on for it. We were delighted, for this was extra work and a double wage packet was very seductive. At that time, Kenneth was renowned for his traditional Pantos. The scripts were peculiar to him, idiosyncratic and special. Also, his Dames were legendary. This time, however, he was to be Director. It was an exciting prospect.

I had not taken part in Pantomime before so the technique was very new to me. Ronnie was an old hand and could count a number of Dames in his repertoire. We were contracted until mid-January 1984. It would mean Christmas in Oldham and with the guarantee of two shows a day, an exhausting one.

One week of 'Silver Sword' remained before the Pantomime casting and read-over. Our lives were taken over long before then by an unforeseen turn of events.

For some time, Ronnie had been mulling over the fact that my Mother spent a great deal of time alone. In his view, she needed company. A little dog perhaps?

We knew she was very fond of Poodles having reared one many years ago as the family pet. Still, it was a mere notion and no steps were taken either to speak of this to my Mother, or to put such a plan into action. Need I say more?

'Silver Sword' came to an end and the Company was to enjoy an interval of rest before the onslaught of rehearsal. Ronnie had discovered the Oldham open-air market and, if free on Saturday mornings, he would waste no time in inspecting, scrutinising and working over umpteen stalls. My wardrobe swelled and even at that stage, I knew another suitcase would be dragooned into action.

We were on holiday for a few precious days! True to form, Ronnie set out, with his large bag over the shoulder. He was gone for much longer than usual and I began to worry. Eventually, he came into view. I knew a surprise was imminent. Ronnie's face betrayed him. Without exception, he would try to open his Birthday presents the night before his Birthday!

'Look in my bag', he said. I prized open the capacious holdall and was mute. A tiny, blonde, furry face complete with black nose was revealed. Black eyes stared back at me. My mouth opened and shut. 'He's for your Mother,' Ronnie confidently explained. 'He's for Christmas, but we're going to look after him until then and make sure he's had all his injections'.

At last, my vocal apparatus righted itself and I managed to croak, 'Ronnie, this is crazy - if we keep him for weeks, how on earth will we be able to say goodbye when the time comes?' Suddenly, I realised that Ronnie was looking at me in exactly the same soulful way as the puppy had done. 'Yes, I see what you mean,' he replied thoughtfully, 'but what I should tell you, Sue, is that he has a little sister. She's the last one in the litter. Would you like her for Christmas? That way you won't miss him so much when he goes.' It was an unbelievable scenario. I opened Ronnie's bag and drew out the tiny Poodle. Ronnie added, 'The lady said he's an Apricot one'. I held him and, fatally, fell in love. 'Yes,' I said. 'Yes what?' answered my adored husband. 'Yes, I would love to have her for Christmas.'

Ronnie had replied to an advertisement in the Oldham News and set off on that auspicious Saturday morning to walk as far as the other side of town. He had made this decision for my Mother. His tender-heartedness knew no bounds. Yes, he set off yet again, bag over the shoulder, in pursuit of the last of the litter....

Left alone with my charge, the enormity of what we were doing hit me like a sledge-hammer. This was irresponsible. I knew it and yet, anew, I allowed myself to be led along Ronnie's path. All would be well. The little one and I waited excitedly for Ronnie and the addition to our family to return. 'Isn't she lovely?' beamed Ronnie, as he clambered over the doorstep.

The following hours were spent with two puppies to care for. Appointments were made with a local Vet. who advised on a care programme until arrangements could be made for an appointment. A makeshift bed was improvised in the kitchen with a fleece from the market. Innumerable newspaper sheets covered the floor in preparation for countless accidents and the Pakistani shopkeeper provided baby food until we settled on a proper puppy diet. Madness and joy prevailed. Charlie was named after my Father who loved Poodles and Phyllis was bestowed with the name of my 'Seasons Greeting's' character. She was just as blonde and just as dizzy.

Our little family endured a very restless and active first night together. We were earnest in our belief that one must start as one means to go on. The 'babies' - Ronnie's terminology, I hasten to add - were put to bed in the kitchen corner. They watched, in silence, from the depth of their fleece. The house stairs led from the kitchen and, in due course, we made our way to the bedroom. All was quiet. Bliss. Then, Hell broke loose as the yapping and whimpering began. We looked at one another in defeat. Ronnie, a slave to this mode of manipulation, stated: 'They'll have to come up'. After that, it was playtime. The babies raced from one end of the bedroom to the other and refused to be disciplined. In what seemed an eternity they, mercifully, collapsed prostrate and sleep was had by all. We came to, somewhat jaded the next morning and settled on an important conclusion. They would have to be trained.

Ronnie came upon Barbara Woodhouse's tome in the local bookshop. Her instructions baffled us both. We were advised to use one word when house-training, such as 'now' or 'hurry up'. Dutifully, we obeyed, but two puppies were double the trouble. We chose the word 'quickly', chaperoned the babies to the tiny backyard and repeated our word again and again. Charlie and Phyllis looked at us as if we were deranged and promptly ran inside and peed all over the kitchen floor.

Later, when the Northern snows arrived and the yard was heavens high in drifts, our disconsolate, woebegone 'quickly' rang through the frosty air. By then, we had had a grain of success and were able to see where they had 'been', the evidence being a small and steaming amber-coloured plash.

Much of this schooling, or rather drilling, was time-consuming. Soon, we were to begin rehearsals for the Pantomime. This canine education took place in tandem with our preparation for two shows a day! We were extremely gratified when the little ones were able to understand 'bed', 'down' and, most important of all, 'No!'

We had no choice but to leave them to their own devices when we were called for the read-over. I was much more apprehensive than Ronnie, who, true to form, refused to acknowledge the possibility of impending disaster. The kitchen was fortified in a manner appropriate to the circumstances and newspaper became a fitted carpet. The Pakistani newsagent was overjoyed by our patronage.

'Jack and the Beanstalk' was a feast of tradition, inventiveness and drollery. Ronnie was cast in the role of villain - Slurp by name. His costume was to echo this sentiment by being covered in a green slime, 'Rather reminiscent of snot', quoth he. My casting was threesome: The Old Woman with the Beans, the Giant's Wife and the Fairy Godmother. It all professed to be great fun, but wearisome. Audience participation is the stuff of Pantomime, so for me, an apprentice, there was much to learn. Also, while I was learning, my thoughts strayed to the cottage kitchen and to what horrors may be taking place there. In short, I was worried. In the main, this was unnecessary for the babies were content, well fed and nurtured. All we had to contend with were Lilliputian piles of excrement placed at intervals over the carefully-laid newspaper. Whenever we returned, we were greeted with matchless joy. Our lives were enriched by these loveable companions.

Ronnie was not at ease with rehearsals and I could see tension mounting. The Director was the thorn in his side. I sensed a clash of personalities. The working atmosphere was strained and I was torn between caring for Ronnie's peace of mind, reassuring him for I sympathised with his point of view, and keeping on top of my own work.

Sometimes, the babies came with us to the Theatre. We had a ridiculous conceit that they could become Theatre dogs. After all, we knew of many actor friends who had made this work. So, we tried depositing them in the Dressing-Room, but were vanquished when their miserable wails disturbed the Company. The general consensus was that we were insane.

About half-way through the rehearsal period, I became conscious of sharp pain in my groin. I had experienced this once before while playing Nellie the Elephant in the Scarborough Christmas show. I blamed Nellie forthwith!

Then, the excruciating discomfort had taken me to the Doctor who prescribed an extremely nasty injection to get me through. He had an inkling that the pain could be the onset of arthritis. This time, however, I laid the rap at the door of the Giant's Wife. I decided on a fractionally less energetic portrayal and the twinges disappeared.

We were approaching the Panto's Opening. Ronnie was jumpy and on edge. He knew that Oldham audiences acclaimed and gloried in Kenneth Alan Taylor as Dame or principal character. He was fidgety about measuring up to this. I, too, was uneasy for I had the niggling feeling that this nervousness could be a prelude to another bout of indisposition.

At this point, we thought it a good idea to cheer my Mother with news of her impending Christmas present - Charlie! Consumed with excitement, we phoned. Jabbering on about Charlie's attributes, we were slow to gauge reaction. It was not one we expected, but perhaps, one that we had secretly hoped for. My Mother was kindly and appreciative, but adamant in refusal. She could not take on such a responsibility at her age.

Charlie and Phyllis were not to be separated after all! We could not conceal our rapture. Not for one moment did we consider any inconvenience that this may cause, or the enormity of our task. We loved our 'babies' and parting would have left us bleak, forlorn. For many years to come, they would be cherished and held dear; they too had come home.

My fears were realised. Ronnie was taken ill with gastro-enteritis yet again and two days before the Pantomime Dress Rehearsal. Kenneth Alan Taylor came out of Dame retirement and his Slurp reigned supreme. He was good. Fortunately, poor Ronnie was laid so low that he did not witness the rapport that Kenneth had with the people of Oldham. Nor did he see the exposition so alien to his own. Oldham was Kenneth's home town. He had lifted the Coliseum to great heights; he was popular and audiences loved him. He was a hard act to follow...

I was relieved to see that Ronnie appeared to be - relieved. He was poorly, but quite content to remain at home with Charlie and Phyllis until he was well. My relief stemmed from the realisation that this illness was not a recurrence of his previous malady. As always, Ronnie was conscientious and concerned about getting back to work, but did not appear to be overly anxious or desperate to demonstrate undying loyalty to Kenneth Alan Taylor. He recovered and was soon tussling with the thankless Slurp.

The show was arduous. Pantomime, I discovered, is tiring and two shows a day a relentless pursuit of energy. The turn-around between shows was brief, so Charlie and Phyllis were safely established once more in the Dressing-Room.

We had rigged up a playpen contraption at one end of the space where the alarming Slurp costume extravaganzas were hanging. Once settled, the babies looked on entranced and infatuated as we prepared for our two-show marathon. All was well. Not a sound as we made our way for the Beginners call. The matinee started, the Beanstalk began to grow successfully after my Beans Scene, and, as I was hastily doing a quick change into the Giant's Wife's copious Michelin-woman outfit, who should appear in the Wings, but the Stage Manager, her arms full of Charlie and Phyllis, and mouthing: 'Look what I've found!'

My cue was coming up and I could hear my Giant husband roaring, 'Where's my Wife?' I was transfixed, for I knew the babies, despite my gross appearance, had clocked me. At that point, the Giant was supposed to blunder towards the Wings to look out. The difference between wife and husband was that the Giant was balancing on stilts! Charlie looked at him in wide-eyed terror. Then, much to my consternation, intent on protecting his sister, began to create the mother-'n'-father of all commotions. The Giant wobbled alarmingly and 'went', that is, he corpsed. It was a monumental fit of laughter infecting all within earshot.

The audience knew something was amiss, remained in ignorance of the cause, but joined in the catastrophe. I signalled to the Stage Manager to get the babies out of the way before Charlie expired in panic.

This incidental event put the stamp on the Theatre being out of bounds for the babies. The decision did not descend upon us via Theatre bureaucracy, but came about through our own desire to have peace of mind restored before it was lost beyond recovery. This experiment was over and we rearranged our itinerary so that the babies stayed safely at home. Consequently, a frantic dash ensued at tea-time to make sure misfortune had not taken place.

The worst development in our absence was when the adventurous Phyllis had scaled the stairway and was at the summit endeavouring to entice the trusting, naïve Charlie to follow suit. He was faltering, timid, scared and trembling. Undeterred, Phyllis egged him on. Fortuitously, we arrived in the nick of time...

Our friends remarked, perceptively, how dogs can take on characteristics of their owners. What they were trying to say, was that Charlie resembled the gentle, trusting Ronnie, while Phyllis took on the likeness of me, the bossy instigator of mutiny and mischief! Rubbish!

It was a hard Winter that year and soon Christmas was hovering. It was impossible to return to No. 20, so plans were made for an Oldham break. What we had not bargained for was entertaining.

My Mother viewed this Christmas as no different from past ones. Since my childhood, it had been a foregone conclusion that regardless of our own commitments, relationships or wishes, my brother and I would return to the family home. Foolishly, in an effort to overcome an uncomfortable rift and in an attempt to be noble and munificent, I invited my Mother and Brother to spend Christmas Eve and Night in Oldham. This was also to smooth the passage for my Brother who was recovering from a broken marriage. True to form, Ronnie was his selfless self and we looked forward to the festivities, despite the fact that we were very tired and could have done with a rest.

My family's arrival proclaimed bustle and the unloading of equipment; a television set being the foremost encumbrance, demonstrating a determination not to be without Christmas spectaculars. This, to be sure, was a gesture given with the best of intentions, but the intrusion on our simple but hard-working life was almost too much to bear.

Bear it we did with good grace, but the crunch came when we served roast beef for the Dinner instead of my Mother's conventional, fixed choice of turkey. This was not popular. In other words, Mum expected to bring her old established idea of Christmas with her. Ronnie did not take kindly to criticism of his festive fare and showed his displeasure. I was left with the agony of divided loyalty. In the end, there was an unavoidable private confrontation between my Mother and myself. She had the gall to question Ronnie's attitude and I had no choice but to admonish her. Relations were estranged. My family's departure brought immense relief. A prolonged hike with the babies restored us to our loving, peaceful state. The return to work was a reprieve.

The wintry conditions continued and, although the babies were reluctant to brave the back yard and a foot of snow, their 'quickly' times were at last beginning to register. Miss Woodhouse's book became dog-eared with repeated searches for words of wisdom. Nevertheless, we were on the verge of triumph!

We had now been married for over a year and our relationship was deepening. Always a passionate and fulfilling union, our affinity with each other became richer with each passing day. We enjoyed working together, talking together and being together. Charlie, Phyllis and our domestic life enhanced this happy time; we approached each hurdle and accomplishment with equanimity.

Ronnie was a stimulating, unpredictable presence. Every moment presented surprise, humour and an exhilarating, animated recounting of his past life. Much of the gaiety came from his colourful childhood and his observations of life and character. Some impressions remained with him throughout later years. The tale of Mrs. Fredrickson was a prime example.

As mentioned before, Ronnie had suffered gastric trials from time to time, the latest occurring in Oldham. Now, well into the run of Panto we found ourselves dealing with the reverse. Constipation worried Ronnie; he became anxious and fixated. When reasoning with him, he embarked upon a Mrs Fredrickson story which left me shaking with laughter and some sympathy. Ronnie had been affected by eavesdropping on an adult conversation. Ronnie's Mother, an over-the-garden-wall bosom pal and neighbour of Mrs. Fredrickson had been engrossed in dialogue about bowel function. The story goes that Mrs. Fredrickson had been having some difficulty in moving hers and surmised that she was certain of a 'stoppage of the bowel'. Little Ronnie, aghast, realised at this tender age, that eavesdroppers did not always receive news to their advantage. The information had remained in his consciousness like the Sword of Damocles. A dollop of fibrous medication soon shifted Ronnie's cause for alarm.

Another Mrs.Fredrickson narrative was prompted. She seems to have been quite a gal. Ronnie had noted that her preference for button-through dresses was not an observance of fashion, but for convenience. Her husband kept an allotment and retired there for most of his day when not at work. In the meantime, Mrs. F. was free to entertain her gentleman caller. He would know when the coast was clear for Mrs. F. would display an OMO packet in the bay window - Old Man Out!

Oldham, mid-January, was covered in snow. Our cottage was a snug refuge. It was, however, time to make plans for our return to No. 20. We were looking forward to going home and introducing the babies to Bina. We had forewarned everyone at Bowrons Avenue and made animated phone calls to Margaret. She could not conceal her astonishment when told of Charlie and Phyllis. Her retort was 'Oh no, Ronnie, not two!'

There was much to do for the cottage had almost swollen to accommodate the added luggage, dog basket and paraphernalia. The principal topic for debate was transport. The train was out of the question. Ronnie alighted on what seemed to him to be the obvious answer - we would hire a car! I had not envisaged this possibility and indeed would have fought shy of it if I had. Yes, I did drive, but had not driven for some years. Most important of all, I had not had any experience of motorway driving.

Undeterred as usual and persuasive, Ronnie was confident of my expertise. So, without any more ado, a Mini Micra was rented for the day of our departure. Ronnie had absolutely no idea of the excruciating prospect of fast-moving traffic and intimidating heavy-goods vehicles. He was not a driver. Just as well, for if he had ever taken the wheel, he would have had one eye on the road and the other on a wayside antique shop. Our leaving day soared on the horizon and my nerves were taking the upper hand.

The Pantomime came to a close and, although eager to be off, we were sorry to be bidding farewell to the many friends we had made in Oldham; even the Pakistani shopkeeper gave us good wishes. His newspaper sales would certainly be down.

The cottage was 'sparklin', all was ready and the car collection day was nigh. Driving the Mini on trial runs around Oldham and negotiating the ice and snow, proved easier than I had expected. In fact, it was like riding a bike.

Charlie and Phyllis were perplexed. Why was their home thrown into confusion? More importantly, were they included in this derangement? Consolation and reassurance was the order of the day.

Removal Day dawned and brought with it a further blanket of snow. Beneath, was hard, packed ice. Given a choice, I would have declined to make the journey. Ronnie, optimistic as ever, announced that conditions may be much improved going South. Blithely, he loaded the little car until it was stowed to the gills. An oversight was to leave the babies until last. They were distracted by the thought of being left behind.

I made sure that Ronnie was safely settled in the passenger seat, Phyllis on his knee and Charlie gazing loftily from the pinnacle of luggage in the rear. I wanted to have one last look at our little cottage. So different from when we arrived, it was now an inviting retreat - for someone else.

I did not reveal to Ronnie that my legs and hands were a-quiver as I prepared for take-off. It was still snowing! Astoundingly, our little vehicle started first time and, with a shudder, I accelerated. We slithered forth and managed to travel along the now familiar side streets of Oldham. I could see Charlie in the mirror. He was quite unconcerned. Phyllis was in her element, there on Ronnie's lap.

Ronnie was studying the map in extremely professional manner. I just hoped and prayed he knew what he was doing. He did. He navigated superbly. It also seemed that he had been something of a prophet, for the snow was now turning to sleet. Moments before we reached the dreaded motorway, the sun parted the clouds and we knew all would be well. My beloved guiding officer had brought us through.

My stomach pitched and rolled as I waited on the slip road; slipway would have been a more appropriate term, for that is how I viewed the three lanes of throbbing, pulsating traffic, all moving at breakneck speed. I felt as if I was being emptied into an abyss.

'Stay in the slow lane - at first', instructed Ronnie. All too ready to obey, I took courage in both hands and moved forward. 'Keep up with the speed,' urged my non-driving comrade, 'and keep a weather-eye open for the lorries - they're buggers'. I gripped the wheel with a tenacity born of numb, frozen terror. I was somewhat pacified by the sight of Robin Reliant three-wheeler in front of us. Well, thought I, if he dare do it, so dare I.

Ronnie was glowing with satisfaction and testified: 'Well, we're on't roaaad!' How well I came to know that statement. It was forecast, noted and celebrated on all our motoring campaigns for years to come.

The first service station came to us like an oasis in the desert. My body slumped and I wondered if it would rouse sufficiently to complete our travels. Charlie and Phyllis stretched their legs and gambolled as we, or rather I, partially refreshed, made ready to face the rest of our crusade with renewed vigour.

'She's running well', remarked Ronnie knowledgeably. I reminded him that our mode of transport was a modest Micra and not some ocean-going vessel. 'I say,' said Ronnie, 'look at that'. I hastened to point out that I couldn't 'look at that' when driving. He was referring to the fact that Charlie had urinated over a pile of magazines. At that juncture, I abandoned all hope, moved over into the middle lane and increased 'her' speed to over sixty miles an hour...I was ready for the most imposing articulated lorry bearing down upon me. I would not be bullied...

***

PART ONE
THEN

BACK TO BOWRONS
JANUARY 1984

We received a rapt welcome. Everything but the fatted calf awaited us. How glorious it was to be home. The babies were eyed suspiciously by Reg who stood like an effigy in the gateway saying, 'What do you want with two?'

Bina and Jasu were wary and a little nervous. Indian people can be so when in contact with dogs, but both were smiling. Hester could only gush 'Bless! Oh, Bless!' After, we staggered gratefully into our own much loved home and breathed a special sigh of relief.

The next days found us hurriedly setting our belongings in order, introducing the babies to No. 20 and establishing a routine for them with regular walks to One-Tree Hill Park. All activity accompanied by Bina. How we had missed her and how our hearts were gladdened when surrounded by such comfort and rejoicing. 'We could do with a car,' asserted Ronnie. 'Sorry darling,' I replied, 'she goes back tomorrow.' Later, I drew my own conclusions. Ronnie had made a cryptic comment!

The early part of 1984 was devoted to settling back into our contented domestic existence. Life was busy; caring for Charlie and Phyllis made it busier. At the same time, we caught up with our Alperton friends and made frequent visits to the Spiritualist Church. Everyone there was keen to learn about our Oldham adventures and meet the babies. Work and its availability remained somewhere in the distance.

Margaret was over the moon to have us back and thrilled at the probability of our being around for a while. She adored Charlie, but made no bones about showing some disapproval for poor little Phyllis, largely because Phyllis was noisy. I resolved that fear prompted her barking. She was soon consoled if one had a moment to cuddle. Ronnie never failed in that department; he cuddled many a time and oft.

Margaret pointed out that Poodles needed clipping and that this could be expensive. In due course, Ronnie sought the help of Eddie and Brian who were still running the Golders Green pet-shop. Sure enough, they could recommend a specialist dog beautician, by the name of Anthea. So, an appointment was fixed.

Anthea hailed from North London and arrived armed with Poodle clipping equipment. Charlie and Phyllis ogled her with horror, especially when the rather gruesome electric shears emerged from her bag. Anthea was posh. Her opening gambit was, 'Now come along, who's first?' Phyllis shrank. I, too, was nervous. Charlie stood his ground bravely, so inadvertently volunteered himself as a lamb to the slaughter. Phyllis was glued like a limpet to my lap. Anthea tossed a glance in her direction and barked 'Bad luck being a Poodle, isn't it Phyllis?' In spite of Anthea's hearty demeanour, she was skilled and we were intrigued by the whole process. Anthea was charming and garrulous. She told us of her Rottweiler, Thor, who was an habitual farter. Ostensibly, this was so pungent that the mighty one could empty a room of dinner guests in a trice.

The babies behaved impeccably and when their puppy clip was finished, they paraded and posed for all to admire. Anthea's subsequent calls engendered instant respect.

A call came from my ineffectual agent. I had been asked to read for the part of Gracie Fields in a forthcoming production of 'Our Gracie', a musical, to be presented - at Oldham Coliseum! Jack Rosenthal was involved as writer. Alarmingly, the Director was The Little Shit! I predicted another 'Wo ist mein Frühstück'?

Gracie was to be divided into three roles: child, middle years and Gracie between thirty-six and eighty. I was first choice for the old one! Mmn... Needless to say, one should be a singer. I could sing well but rated myself as a singing-actress and not a Diva.

The availability call filled me with dismay. I did not want to leave home. Like Phyllis, I clung to my security. The logistics involved seemed insurmountable. Who would look after the babies? Why must I leave Ronnie? All these thoughts overcame me before I had attended for audition. I half hoped I would not be successful. Ronnie being Ronnie was positive and saw the chance as an exciting breakthrough for my career. I was given every encouragement and I knew he was right, but my consternation and feeling of being cast adrift was consuming.

Yes, I got the part.

Next, came the inevitable search for digs. Then, I remembered Esther and Clifford, the dearest elderly couple who lived in Chadderton, near Oldham. They had gladly received me into their home years ago on a one-play visit to Oldham, long before I met Ronnie. Yes, said they, it would be lovely to see me again. Afterwards, I had the option of renting the cottage for the remainder of the run.

All seemed to fit into place. I should have been excited...The contract was for approximately eight weeks. Ronnie was not working during my rehearsal period so could be at No. 20 with the babies. The plan was for him to bring them up to Oldham in time for the First Night. My days would be free and I could take over their care at the cottage while Ronnie returned to London for TV filming.

All I could anticipate was sheer chaos! Ronnie's equilibrium came to the rescue. 'Twas ever thus!

At first, I was lucky enough to manage weekends at home. I was thankful, for they were the only get away from what proved, in the main, to be a nightmare.

As with all happenings, there are things to revere and remember. It is those instances during my testing third visit to Oldham that echo in my memory.

The Little Shit spent five precious rehearsal days playing games for actors. These proved to be ideal opportunities for the brash to be brash and the vulnerable to be exposed in their sensitivity. I fell into the latter category.

The Middle Gracie oozed confidence. Young, from the Italia Conti School and in possession of a forcible soprano voice - 'I'm a trained singer and I can get up to Top G, which is higher than even Gracie could reach' - she unnerved me.

After losing valuable rehearsal time messing about, we started work. Middle Gracie lost no time in inventing alternative plans for attention seeking. A favourite ploy in the rehearsal room was the changing into practice dress while I strove to master Rochdale lingo and Gracie's distinctive style. To the onlooker, it was tricky engaging with an actress who was giving her all to re-create the eighty-year-old icon when she was in competition with a gyrating figure in bra and pants. I had already given up on The Little Shit. He was transported.

My contralto voice was in good shape and came as a shock to this younger version of Gracie. In her view, this called for further diversion. She chose to practice her considerable vocal range in the Stage Door lavatory just as I had begun, nervously, on 'Sally'. I recall it now with some amusement, but at the time, I was devastatingly unhappy, insecure and certain of failure. Where was Ronnie when I needed him most? Nearly every evening, he was on the other end of the phone renewing rational thinking. The following naff poem (Ronnie's jargon once more) arrived to rescue me. With it came his protective, loving warmth and encouragement:

How sweet you are, how dear you are,
I hear your honey voice afar,
From Oldham town, where we have played
In Panto costume fresh arrayed...
Where you now feel the pressure mounting
The dark days that you are counting.
Think! Just think, do not make a move,
Your own supremacy to prove.
For, on the Night when crowds surround you
You'll know that Gracie's spirit found you.
All will see the heart of you,
The play becoming part of you.
(These awful rhymes aren't doing well,
It just would help if I could spell!)
I think you know what I am saying,
About this part that you are playing.
Look ahead, be not put off
By callow youth who deign to scoff.
I think I mentioned tit-for-tat,
Don't have anything to do with that.
Be sweet and smile, bide your time,
For what she's doing is not a crime.
Head up now, shoulders back,
Soar your voice and let it crack (couldn't think of another   word)
The walls from floor to ceiling!
So, close your eyes to foolishness
Come not up with swift redress
Wait and let the audience judge
By sound of sweet applause.
Like the fountain rich and pure,
You'll come off best if you're demure!

Here was the wisdom and simplicity of Ronnie's thinking, the wacky humour that was so infectious and uplifting. He was right. I did come through and all was made more memorable because I knew that Ronnie, my darling Ronnie, was out Front and a part of me.

The Show was such a success that I thought it a good idea to invite the ineffectual agent. He announced that he considered it a distance too far North, and, as he would feel obliged to take Ronnie and me out for a meal, the whole stopover would be too expensive for him. Mentally, I sacked him there and then.

I made a very great friend while in the show. Judith was an actress who played her scene seated at a startlingly white grand piano. She made the whole Oldham process bearable. Sadly, she died of cancer some years later. Ronnie and I were often at her bedside. She was married in a London hospital days before her death and I remember her, so touchingly, when she looked up into my face close to hers and said, 'Do you still use Clinique make-up?'

I continued to smoke. This did not affect my singing. I was, however, reminded of its possible consequences. While staying with Esher and Clifford, I had a very disturbing dream which, in frightful hallucination, told me of impending illness caused by cigarettes. I ignored it and carried on. It was not until 'Gracie' was over and I had returned to Bowrons Avenue, that the dream recurred. Identical, the illusion this time prompted some concern but not enough alarm to deter me. I ignored it and carried on.

A couple of months later, Ronnie flew to Amsterdam to shoot a commercial film. He returned gripping a large pack of duty-free cigarettes. I smoked greedily over the weekend, but on Monday morning woke to an unusual feeling. I had no inclination to smoke. I did not - ever again. This did not happen without a battle. I had been a habit smoker and there were occasions when the habit nearly won. Eventually, it left me. So, extraordinarily, did the Theatrical profession. My appearance on the Coliseum stage was my last, although I was unaware of it at the time.

***

PART ONE
THEN

BACK TO NO. 20

The Summer of 1984 brought one of the most leisurely and peaceful times of our life together. My work was sparse although, from time to time, there were isolated BBC Drama and World Service broadcasts. Ronnie worked steadily both in Television and Radio.

Our existence at No. 20 was made up of golden days spent in the garden with our adopted Bina and the babies. Meals alfresco became one of our favourite pastimes and Alperton friends congregated often, overlooked by an interested but pugnacious Reg. Remarks such as 'You've got some rowdy friends' emanated from him. Hester loved the company and, of course, so did Charlie, Phyllis and Bina. The garden was an extension of our comfortable, airy flat. Now, the Willow and Cherry blossom trees were moving into adult life and, at the foot of them, were Astilbes, Clematis, and Margaret's tree, the sweet-smelling Viburnum. At that stage, we had not acquired Brownie's Daphne!

Ronnie's whistling and singing among the plants and snatches of 'Salad Days' - 'Timothy's late...Timothy's late...never mind, I'm happy to wait..' - could be heard. Reg's baldness would appear over the fence. 'Timothy a friend of yours?' preceded by a coarse, homophobic-type snort.

Ronnie's renderings interspersed his indoor activities and one would be jolted into consciousness on awakening with 'Oh quick, the French fleet's in the harbour and not a piss-pot emptied!' One of his more louche depictions would be, 'They're changing guard at Buckingham Palace, Christopher Robin went down on Alice!' Ronnie was fully aware of the reception these presentations would receive and came up with ad lib additions from his extensive repository of double entendre. I did not complain, for each day was filled with stimulus, skirmish and non-stop skylarking.

Ronnie never displayed mood-changing demeanour. His was a sunny, carefree disposition; a life full of optimism and grace. He could be stubborn and often prickly, an offshoot perhaps from Louie, but never cantankerous or surly.

On sun-filled mornings, Ronnie would tramp towards the Park with Charlie and Phyllis in convoy; perhaps Bina hanging on to his free hand. It was on such a day that our friends Brian and Grace encountered Ronnie for the first time.

Brian conducted his motor-repair business from home which was halfway down Bowrons Avenue. He was underneath a car at the time, when he noticed a pair of sandalled feet and woollen socks. On emerging into the daylight, he was astonished to behold a figure wearing Union Jack shorts and a large Mexican straw hat. Beside this apparition, were two Poodles. Ronnie then disclosed, 'I'm very good at massage, if your back bothers you. I live just along at No. 20!' Swiftly, Brian retreated beneath the car. The tale has been remembered and held dear ever since.

Betty and Marjorie lived at the Park end of Bowrons. Maiden ladies both, they had known each other since schooldays. As usual, it was Ronnie who first befriended them, wearing, I hasten to add, a more acceptable outfit. Certainly for exchanging the time of day with the refined. When Ronnie was passing, Betty had been pottering in her front garden, and he, always eager to offer advice on plant cultivation, stopped for a word. Betty was a devoted animal lover and so fell for the charms of the babies. Ronnie, never backwards in coming forwards, invited the good lady to visit, saying, 'If ever you fancy doggie-sitting, we would be so grateful!'

I loved my domestic life. I experienced a contentment which was entirely new to me. Caring for my home was not a chore. It was a consummation of all the things I had wished for. I shopped on the Wembley High Street when Ronnie was at work and indulged in choosing and buying. Then there was time to walk Charlie and Phyllis; long leisurely strolls in the Park where I could watch them running freely. I was running freely, for Ronnie had brought me to a place of unfettered delight. I was a happily married woman thriving in the mundane minutiae of launderette, ironing and cooking. Bina and Jasu, after so long spent in loneliness, were companions in my peace.

The phone rang often. Ronnie's voice, in the few minutes we shared talking, never failed to bring a hope, anticipation, a tingle, a flurry and a sense of belonging.

As work time drew to a close, we would watch out for his return, faces at the window, looking, until we could see the loved jaunty gait and the grin. Doors were thrown open and arms outstretched in welcome. Then, out into the garden where Ronnie's opening proclamation would be 'I say, have you noticed - the delphiniums are coming out!' Gin 'n' tonics poured, we could sit and talk over the day...

'Izzy-Swizzy' appeared towards the end of 1984. This nickname was given, inexplicably, by Margaret to a scarlet Volkswagen Beetle car which came our way.

Periodically, Ronnie would set off to explore Bowrons Avenue more closely. These strolls were designed to swoop on the odd skip which might hold riches for Ronnie but junk for others. A recent find had been a very becoming swivel bookcase complete with brass feet. Joyce, from two doors down, thought it an eyesore and so her loss was my husband's gain. It has joined us on every move, polished, restored and the subject of admiration over the years. On passing it in various locations, Ronnie would comment 'Eee, Joyce would be so pleased that I rescued it'.

It was on such an outing that Ronnie encountered the Beetle. I was hustled down the Avenue to look. By now, Ronnie was brimful with excitement. The car was bright red and in immaculate condition. A 'For Sale' notice hung in the window. It was parked very close to Brian's house.

I was cautious. How could we afford it? I sensed a familiar feeling creeping over me. It was very similar to the one I had sensed when Charlie and then Phyllis arrived! The temptation was irresistible. What a difference a car would make.

Then, I noticed something that had completely eluded Ronnie. The car was a left-hand drive. I imparted this information, only to be met with 'Oh it's alright, it can't be that much different from an ordinary car. You've just got to watch for the proper side of the road!' Mmn...

We solicited Brian's help. Did he know who owned the car? We discovered that it belonged to a young German student living in digs across the way. Ronnie, now in full sway, found him, made a price enquiry and, without arranging for an inspection or test drive, clinched the deal. The price paid escapes me, but it must have come vaguely within our scant budget. Ronnie, confident as ever, was certain that all would be well. Needless to say, because he said so, it was so!

The first drive was hair-raising. Phyllis and Charlie, determined to be part of this maiden voyage, scrambled aboard. Phyllis insisted on occupying her usual position on Ronnie's knee. This gave the impression that she was driving. Well she might have been, for I was in an initial state of utter confusion, striving to master the controls. Courage was screwed to the sticking place and blood began to return to every sinew. We were 'on't roaaad'. It was a grand little car, and, as everyone said, it seemed to fit in with our general ambiance - eccentricity would be more apt.

Strangely enough, it was some time before I felt confident enough to drive alone. Ronnie was a tower of strength as passenger and with him beside me, I was ready to face the wrath of London traffic. Margaret and Golders Green seemed to be a suitable goal for one of our initial treks. Lathered in perspiration, I was very relieved to reach our destination. Margaret, standing beside her trolley in the doorway, beamed with satisfaction. 'Izzy-Swizzy!' she exclaimed and that was that.

I need not to have worried about the financial strain of running our car. Margaret generously contributed to petrol costs and maintenance expense. She knew that the transport enabled us to visit much more often; also, there was ample room for provisions and treats for her. Not least, I was able to cart Charlie and Phyllis along to Golders Green. They were quite happy to explore Margaret's long-forgotten rooms while the two of us set the world to rights.

Margaret was a fund of information which included fascinating detail about her South American life. She was craving diversion. Rheumatoid arthritis is relentless in its discomfort and pain. The regular Bell's Whisky order from Selfridges ('they deliver, dear') provided some cessation, and often, oblivion. Margaret's real pleasure was found in our visits and the stories we shared about our daily life. When we were flush, there would be a trip to our favourite restaurant. Later, Margaret would sit enthralled as we detailed the component parts of the menu. Her life of isolation never met with complaint.

So many years later, I think of Margaret and the joy of her friendship, but most of all, I now understand what it means to be solitary and how filled are the hours with thought...

Jobs for me remained elusive. I did not care. My happy life absorbed me. Until: the spiders! The flat was spotless, but, much to my dismay, we seemed to be invaded by the whole arachnid population. The babies were fascinated. Bina, although scared at first was taught by Ronnie to retrieve these creatures by hand and deposit them in the garden. She comforted me with 'Inky-Spinky not hurt, Sue'. I would willingly have crushed Inky-Spinky beneath my foot. Ronnie, however, came up with something of a solution. 'Why don't you write about them? You're out of work, it would be something you'd enjoy and it may get rid of your fear'. I dismissed the idea totally.

In the days that followed, I gave some thought to the Spiders and one fine morning, Bina and I found ourselves in the Ealing Road Library, looking for the Spider shelf. I decided that they needed to be researched. The local Library offered them much space. My fear did evaporate somewhat, for I found that there are thousands of Spiders of every shape and hue. The process of enlightenment became an incredible scheme. All my findings were shared with Ronnie on a nightly basis and he, too, was fired with enthusiasm.

I worked on a plan where my Spiders became a community: all Spider characters introduced were based upon people I knew. As a consequence, this fictional society could become roguish, ribald and often bawdy! Ronnie's imagination ran riot and he supplied outrageous names for Spider folk: Miriam Crammit, Araki Nidd and Dorian Scuttler. Bina and I were constantly entertained by Ronnie's boyish euphoria, but also by his wisdom and perception. His inventive Spider poems became an integral part of this pastime and Bina and I were engaged. His serious and poignant 'Josh the Lonely Spider' poem prompted a chance, rather sad conversation about elements of Ronnie's past. I discovered that his nervousness and fear established itself most when he was embarking on new territory. He confided that, in the past, when faced with a new or unfamiliar Cast, he would retreat alone to a park at rehearsal lunch-break rather than face strangers. Yet outwardly and in contrast, Ronnie demonstrated an old-style confident professionalism, irrepressible glee and a positive, genial outlook - and, rare in the world of Theatre, all without a trace of malice.

So my speculative steps towards the creation of the odd Spider story revealed accidental food for thought. No encounter is ever wasted when it comes to the baring of souls...

We had occasional visits to West Bank and kept regular meetings with family and Philip. There was some social contact with Ronnie's agent - just enough. It was difficult to avoid such gatherings and I was eager to be a friend to the family.

Unfortunately, I did not find it easy to build bridges, for I was ignored and they were rude. I could not understand why this was so. I tried very hard, but ended up feeling an isolated fool and something of a curiosity because I had married Ronnie. I played safe, stopped striving and remained on the fringe. Imagine my shock when I was cornered in the kitchen and given an awkward, discomfiting apology for unkind behaviour in the past. The explanation given was 'we thought he was having another breakdown'. Presumably, that must have been the manner in which they dealt with depressive conditions. Nevertheless, it was a breakthrough and I was gladdened. Life was cordial after this. It was easier, more affable, in view of what had happened, to be friendly. Life can be full of surprises. Ronnie's goodness and altruism brought the best out in everyone.

We were engaged in a very important activity when a call came from my Brother. My Mother was faced with prospect of moving house and, at her age, this was causing some distress.

The very important activity was hair-dyeing. 'Gracie' had necessitated a change in hair colour. There had been a request for me to 'go baby-blonde'. This had been something of a major development, for my hair was dark auburn with premature grey streaks. I remember the Make-up Artists saying, 'Do you realise that women pay the earth for that?' After the Show, however, and the success of baby-blonde, we thought it worth carrying on. Instead of 'paying the earth', we came upon Belle Colour which did the job very successfully. Who executed this delicate formula? Ronnie of course! So, when the call from the North came, we were mid-dye and Ronnie, brush in hand, was telling me the story of Blondie Godiva Haig. This captivating yarn originated in Music Hall where Blondie, a stripper/burlesque artiste appeared on stage with abundant blonde hair concealing her person. On such an occasion, she came to sit upon a bench. Calamity struck, for it seems that Stage Management had neglected to warn her that the seat had been painted recently and not allowed to dry. When Blondie came to rise and turn upstage to exit, her bottom displayed angry paint stripes emerald green in hue.

Arrangements were made to drive North. At least my hair was ready for the trip. Ronnie wangled a few days leave from the BBC and my family were grateful for the offer of practical support. Apprehension hung over me. Whenever unanticipated circumstances came about involving my Mother, I am ashamed to say that I contemplated the possibility of argument, sulks and my dependability being divided once more. It was a force to be reckoned with and, in spite of Ronnie's hopeful mood, I failed to look on the bright side when adjudging the forthcoming state of affairs.

Izzy-Swizzy behaved admirably and although we had set off at the crack of dawn - 'to avoid the lorries', said Ronnie the soothsayer - we made good progress. Conversation was always lively and usually concerned day-to-day plans and tasks. This time, Phyllis was given the once-over. I mentioned that it would soon be necessary to have her spayed. 'Why?' replied the trusting Ronnie. 'Ronnie, for goodness' sake, we don't want litters of puppies!' I almost stalled the Beetle when the reply came. 'Oh, that won't happen: she's his sister'.

All hands were on deck to move my Mother's home. We tried, desperately, to reassure her and all was done to cradle the stress. She responded and, although there was no need for gratitude, she was very appreciative. Ronnie instilled real faith, for to him nothing was impassable. If he could not see a way through, he would find a way round. The climax was when he decided to decorate. With the help of my Brother, he acquired tins of magnolia and set to work. In the space of a couple of days, Mum's new pad was made-over, along with my Mother's opinion of her son-in-law. Ronnie had turned the key.

It had been an exhausting interlude, and, before setting off for the South, we travelled to Scarborough for a few harmonious days at our beloved West Bank. We arrived without giving notice and were dismayed to find the house looking sadly rundown and uncared-for. Jessie had obviously been left unattended for long periods while Philip was at the Theatre. In the past she had been known to have accidents. She spent time alone. We had dealt with this as best we could. Now, we noticed that the house reeked of urine.

Downcast, we introduced Charlie and Phyllis - who growled unsociably - and then embarked on the disagreeable business of heaving the sullied rugs from upstairs into the back yard. 'He's drinking', Ronnie muttered. Dear Ronnie, thrilled to be back beside his prized Aga, happily diverted himself preparing a casserole. It was much later and into the night when Philip returned, worse for wear and annoyed at our disposal of carpets. We had had no choice. Knowing that we were fighting a losing battle for the time being, we planned to leave sooner than intended. We had heavy hearts as we closed the front door behind us.

The situation was uncomfortable. I felt as if I was encroaching upon another life. West Bank belonged to Ronnie and Philip and it would be some years before I could call it my home. Meanwhile, its fate was shelved and Izzy Swizzy was made ready for our return to No. 20.

As 1985 got underway, Colin Cant called Ronnie for interview. He was to direct a television play, 'Who Sir? Me Sir?' and had Ronnie in mind for a leading role. It remained to be seen whether or not Ronnie mentioned me during his meeting, but within days, I was called to audition. Ronnie's character, Reginald Smith, needed a wife and so, conveniently, I was cast as his frosty Mrs. It was a lucky opportunity for me and I looked forward to a television break at last.

I was beset with worry about arrangements for the babies. Twice, we took them along on location and it was precarious, not because Charlie and Phyllis were badly behaved, but because conditions were unfavourable. We were obliged to leave the car in the park allotted and the days were hot. We were back and forth in full make-up and costume to check if all was well. Never again, for this interfered with work and reduced us to nervous wrecks by the time we wrapped.

Ronnie had a brainwave! Betty may come to the rescue...what a coincidence that Ronnie had casually mentioned dog-sitting to her so long ago!

Betty was in seventh heaven and appeared every day at lunchtime - the babies were quite happy to be on their own until then. The good lady passed her time reading and partaking of the appetising snack we left for her. On our return, out came the gin bottle and an early-evening tipple was taken by all.

Betty was about sixty-five and rather like Mrs. Doubtfire in appearance. We learned that before retirement she had been a corsetiere at Harrods. She and her neighbour, Marjorie, remembered Wembley and area in its heyday and we encouraged descriptions of leafy lanes and residential neighbourhoods. Betty became our Mrs. Doubtfire and Charlie and Phyllis adored her. She spoke to them as if they were intelligent children and would not tolerate undue noise or lack of discipline. Their response was exemplary.

Towards the end of shooting, we were disturbed to hear that dear Hester had been diagnosed with cancer. It was dreadful news. She had become so close to us and it seemed inconceivable to visualise the likelihood of life without her.

Hester's illness lurked in the background of our lives and minds. We came upon a pause in work commitments and so were able to spend valuable, transient time with her. Running in tandem with our everyday existence was the knowledge that days were precious.

At the same time, we continued to be closely connected to our Church. Brownie issued an invitation to join her developing Circle. We were to meet with one or two other Brownie prodigies or promising 'sensitives' for an hour on Tuesday evenings. Ronnie was about to implode with a passion and was certain that his future lay alongside such eminent Spiritualists such as Conan Doyle, Ursula Roberts, Bomber Commander 'Stuffy' Dowding and Arthur Findlay. Brownie, a spirited feminist, soon put him straight! He took her put-downs with good-natured optimism and waited patiently for Spirit to make themselves known. The whole observation was interesting and in the silent, meditative atmosphere one felt very close to loved ones. Although sceptical, I admitted that where proof prevailed one was more inclined to accept it. Nervously, on one occasion I had information for a lady in the Circle. She was to benefit from a new life in the North, which included living in a large country house. Of course my confidence was dampened when she had no knowledge of this, nor any hopes of my news coming to fruition. The lady kept in touch and, four years later, she phoned to let me know that she had received a legacy which involved her moving to live on a Northern country estate.

Ronnie's healing became a predominant gift. He joined the Healing Group and there came into contact with many needy, disadvantaged people. His gentle patience calmed and restored injured minds and bodies. When laying on of hands, it was remarkable to notice the intensive heat which transmitted itself through his touch.

Ronnie took his healing round and about. He learned of a gentleman living nearby who was housebound, disabled and lonely. He seemed to have slipped through the hospital's net. Ronnie visited Mac on a regular basis to help with housekeeping, shopping and not least, restoration of confidence. All this was not achieved without some discomfort for Ronnie. Mac was doubly incontinent and his house swamped with urine. It had seeped into carpets and furnishings until the effects were overpowering. Mac was not easily persuaded to welcome any Social Service aid and so it became Ronnie's lot to save the day. This trial lived in his consciousness for years and, well into the future, illness prompted an hysterical visit to Boots in search of male incontinence pads. He said he drew the line at Tenalady!

A lady Chiropodist was also on Ronnie's peripatetic list. This was a useful association, for whenever the need, he was able to 'get his feet done' at the same time as attempting to heal the lady's anxiety. I thought that an anxious Chiropodist was somewhat alarming. One day, I called for Ronnie on my way to shop and he was accompanied to the front door by his podiatrist companion. Her parting shot was, 'Whatever you do, Mr.

Herdman, don't shloak it'! I did not know that she also had a speech impediment!

Hester's condition worsened and eventually she was taken into the Central Middlesex Hospital. We helped Reg as much as possible, but he sank into an impenetrable silence which became difficult to dissolve. Soon it was obvious that Hester would not recover and the times spent at the bedside of our dear friend were sad and disconsolate.

One day, I visited alone and as I was sitting, silently hoping, I began to think 'if Hester cannot get better, please send someone for her'. I looked up after a few moments and saw a tall figure standing at the bed-head. He was young, handsome and dressed in black tunic and trousers. He was looking down at Hester, not at me. Momentarily, I looked away distracted. When I turned once more to speak to him, he had gone. I left the Hospital but could not forget the unknown visitor. I told Ronnie of it at home. I recalled time and time again the young man's presence and remembered it in absolute detail.

After the funeral, there was to be a small reception next door. Many of Hester's Irish family were present. We were invited and introduced. I was talking to relatives when I sensed Ronnie coming near. He held out a photograph, saying 'I think you should see this'. In the centre of the family group, a young man was standing. He was the young man I had seen at the Hospital. I learned that he was Hester's soldier brother who had been killed some years before...

Within a month of Hester's death, Reg had acquired a lady friend...

I came to a crossroads during 1985; a professional crossroads. While blissfully happy with Ronnie, I had not made any serious attempt to further my career and, more importantly, to respond to the constant mental reminders which were harrying me. These came in the form of thoughts and ideas. They were insistent and produced a nagging pressure to take action. I found this unsettling and in an inscrutable way was led to believe that I was being pointed in a predetermined direction. I had often found it puzzling that during my professional life which was divided into two sections - education and acting - I had not applied for my teaching appointments. Unlike Theatre, they had appeared uninvited.

I mentioned this to Ronnie now and again. 'Perhaps you're being pushed...you need pushing!' Mmn...

Two days later, I was preoccupied with the mind-blowing assignment of vacuuming the sitting-room carpet, when my thoughts were interrupted by a very pronounced message: 'Go back into teaching'. It was not what I wanted to hear. This monopolized our conversation when Ronnie returned from work. 'That's what I was trying to tell you' said he, 'when one helps others, the path can become clearer and you know where you're needed'. 'How did you think of that?' I enquired. 'God knows, it just came into my head'. We laughed and carried on making supper.

In the following days, I was seeing to domestic doings....no more thoughts...Theatre work would materialise sooner or later, and we returned to the status quo.

Some weeks later, Ronnie bought a local paper. In the centre pages he found an advertisement for Home Tutors. Brent Council was looking for part-time qualified teachers. Triumphantly, he waved the newspaper in the air, saying, 'Sue, what did I tell you? I knew the answer would come.' 'But Ronnie,' I persisted, 'I'm an actress now. I don't want to go back into teaching.'

Two days later, my application was in the post! Ronnie was full of anticipation and very supportive of this new enterprise. He was eager to find out in more detail what the job entailed. Quite rightly, he had pointed out that while I was out of work this would offer scope both vocationally and financially. True. I had always found teaching to be satisfying, largely because Speech & Drama was my speciality and Educational Drama provided a wealth of expediency for young people to be enthusiastic, confident and, most of all, happy. I was passionate in aiming for a climate where they could develop self-assurance, courtesy and consideration for others.

I was called for interview and thereby No. 20 was a hive of activity in preparation for the big event. Betty was in attendance for the babies and dear Ronnie in charge of suitable attire. Clad in a smart suit and high heels I climbed into Izzy Swizzy. I was nervous. This was new. I had not been inside a classroom for over twelve years and I knew I would be in for searching questions. Ronnie, as was his wont, was seated beside me and constantly offered sound advice and comment: 'You don't look a bit like my teacher, Miss Roberts.' he remarked. 'Thank you Ronnie', I replied, 'but I don't think I will be filling a vacancy for flower monitor!'

Once incarcerated inside Brent Town Hall, I was shown to a smallish room where three Councillors and an Educational representative, Miss Gupta, were introduced. Perched on a chair and facing this daunting group, I managed to smile and appear in control. I need not have worried (I could hear Ronnie agreeing) for my examiners seemed impressed with my qualifications and track record. My years as an actress did not throw up any probing queries and supposedly, I was not regarded as a fallen woman because of them. One question, however, stunned me. Miss Gupta, a young Indian woman, looking intently at me said: 'Mrs. Herdman, if you were to teach a white child and a black child, would there be any difference in your attitude?' For a moment, I was speechless. 'Certainly not,' I answered vehemently.

Ronnie sat expectantly inside Izzy Swizzy eating bullets. I should point out that sweets, often kept in the glove compartment - 'in case we break down and need sustenance' - were always referred to as 'bullets'. It was many years later that I discovered that this was the name given to a brand of boiled sweet found in the North East. My beloved's cheeks, swollen with confection, still managed a broad smile. 'Have you got it?' he gulped.

Miss Gupta phoned the following morning. She was delighted to offer me the post. It **was** a delight. I must admit I was filled with a feverish hope. I was given some details, including information regarding salary and told that a Head of Section would be outlining the programme for my first assignment.

I was summoned to the Educational Suite where much to my surprise, a Health Visitor met me. I was to help an eight-year-old Turkish boy. This was unexpected but went some way to explaining why Miss Gupta had pumped me about colour and culture. More revelations were to follow, hence the necessity for a Health professional's expertise, for it transpired that young Zeynel Oscan was suffering from a rare muscular dystrophy which only harried the male members of a family. Sadly, his older brother had already died from the condition. Two sisters were unaffected. Language would not be a problem for the family was English speaking.

This was virgin territory for me. I was apprehensive but greatly looking forward to planning my work. Ronnie was happily involved in the adventure and desperate to help in the structuring of this scaled-down curriculum. How valuable Drama would be. I might add that all thoughts of Theatre contracts, TV and Film work were banished from my thoughts. I was pledged and ready to identify with this indigent child.

***

PART 1
THEN

ZEYNEL

I was to be employed every afternoon, Monday to Friday, which fitted in splendidly with the scheme of things as far as Charlie and Phyllis were concerned. When Ronnie was at the BBC I could safely plan my day.

The Oscan family lived near Wembley Park Road. I knocked on the front door of a semi-detached, rather nondescript Council house. Who would answer and meet me? The door opened and I was looking at a dark-haired woman who was smilingly beckoning me inside. 'I am Semsi', she said, 'Zeynel's Mother'. I was ushered into a dark interior. The curtains were half-drawn, but enough sunlight crept into the room to enable me to see its lonely occupant. In a corner, supported by a cumbersome wheelchair, was a boy. He laughed. His dark eyes were unwavering, but his body was jelly-like and out of control. I forgot all except his need. I moved towards his chair and knelt beside him. At once, Semsi intervened and brought a chair. The boy struggled and said: 'I'm Zeynel'. His effort was great but I restrained the urge to help him. I allowed the struggle.

Zeynel said 'Sue'. Semsi hastened to correct him 'Mrs. Herdman!' 'Sue is fine', I said.

Zeynel had a few toys before him on the table and I asked him to talk about them, but the going was hard. Semsi had disappeared and there was a lull. Zeynel studied me searchingly. His trusting eyes darted back and forth. A smile, startling in its intensity, spread over his features and a hand clumsily reached out. I clasped the soft fingers in mine. It was such a fragile, floppy hand and the grip was weak but Zeynel's warmth penetrated through infirmity and illness. We were forever friends. The difference in age was unimportant and in that moment, two souls met.

When Semsi returned, she was carrying a tray laden with fruit: Melon, Strawberries and Grapes. I came to know this Turkish hospitality and teaching did not take place until a guest had eaten.

I looked forward hugely to teaching my new friend. It was uplifting to enter his sitting-room and see his face light up with joy. The room was poky and stuffy, but I did not notice the restriction once our studies had begun. I was learning too, for tasks were different from any I had known. I could hear Semsi pottering in her tiny kitchen and knew that before I left some Turkish delicacy would be produced with the words, 'Some for Ronnie too!' I had spoken of Ronnie, but at that stage he had not been introduced.

Zeynel's abilities were limited, both physically and academically. I decided to jettison any formal teaching and tried to incorporate numbers, letters and words into practical exercises. We played shops, took journeys on imaginary buses, trains and 'planes and sang songs. Videos were very useful for visual learning and all the while Zeynel strained against the confinement of his disease. Walt Disney's animal documentaries were great favourites.

I was becoming familiar with a different culture. I noticed that Zeynel was treated as an exalted member of the family. This was not because of his illness, but because he was male. He was waited on, and when his requests were not attended to immediately, he knew how to attract attention.

One day, the door was opened by one of Zeynel's sisters - he had two, Gulay and Tulay. Both were pretty teenagers and doing well at school. They doted on Zeynel and nothing was too much trouble. Quietly and patiently they nursed and cared for him.

Zeynel's Father, Reza, was a dignified, grave gentleman. Stockily built with dark, wiry, curly hair and a wide smile, he was gracious and interested in Zeynel's tuition. I was respected and honoured within this close family. They trusted me and I was richer for knowing them...

At home, Ronnie was intrigued and impatient to hear all the news. So was Bina and I had much explaining to do. Who was this little boy? Could she see him? Did Charlie and Phyllis know him? The babies, too, were inquisitive when I returned, so off we all went to One-Tree-Hill-Park to work off the thrill of it all.

There was a sudden development. Ronnie was cast in a new BBC television adaptation of Dickens' 'David Copperfield'. He was to play Barkis and needed to grow a substantial beard. The job involved some weeks location filming and the inevitable separation. Nevertheless, I was exhilarant; we were cheering him on!

I did not let on how lonely I might be without him...I had learned when to keep quiet! I thought with gratefulness of the consolations in my life: Margaret, Bina, the Babies, Betty and other dear ones.

Ronnie's beard, in preparation for Barkis, was luxuriant. At first a little ragged, it blossomed into a colourful full-set. I would catch him fiddling and coaxing its growth into a Dickensian masterpiece. 'Ah...' he would mutter. 'You know, my beard is a mixture of colours, some grey and some ginger'. 'Perhaps it's because you're getting on a bit,' I replied. 'Mmn...' said he. This new look suited Ronnie. His hair was allowed to grow and this complemented the effect, especially as Ronnie had been blessed with a natural curl. Barkis was distinguished.

Ronnie had wished to meet Zeynel for some time, but first I needed to seek parental permission and find a suitable occasion. The Oscans were eager to see Ronnie, particularly the beard, for I had told them all about his life as an actor and the coming television series. He was a celebrity and Zeynel's cloistered existence was to be enhanced by this meeting.

Quite by chance, Ronnie remembered a couple of friends whom he believed lived somewhere in North Wembley. He had not seen them for years. Ronnie was a great one for ferreting out whys, wherefors and whereabouts, and, after much detective work, tracked down Wilfred Carter and Alan Barnes. Where did they live? Very close to Zeynel and on the Wembley Park Road. Ronnie decided to pay an unexpected call, but first, a surprise for Zeynel was on the agenda.

Semsi and Reza were expecting us, but Zeynel was waiting for his regular lesson. We arrived and I entered the sitting-room. The little boy was watching television. 'Hi Sue' he said, and then, looking over my shoulder, he glimpsed Ronnie. He shook with excitement, frantically trying to control his palsied body. His eyes shone and for seconds I felt my tears start. Ronnie's face was transfixed. Then Semsi saved the moment. She bustled into the kitchen as Reza offered Ronnie a seat. Ronnie spoke gently to Zeynel. Then the laughter began and Zeynel chuckled until the time came for us to leave. Ronnie paused at the door, looked back, and before he could speak, Zeynel uttered only one word: 'Ronnie'. Some moments are savoured forever. We stepped into the sunlight and made our way to the car. Neither spoke. 'Thank you, Ronnie,' I said, and kissed him.

We found Wilfred and Alan. Their house stood back from the road and in front was a colourful and carefully tended garden. Ronnie approached the door. I saw a curtain snatch. Ronnie waited patiently for quite some time before his knock was answered. What happened next was perplexing, for the tall gentleman in the doorway was gesturing for Ronnie to go away. The door slammed shut and Ronnie turned to look at me. He returned to the car and announced, 'They think I'm a vagrant and told me to bugger off!'

Wilfred Arthur Carter, as he was affectionately known, and his partner Alan Barnes were reunited with their long-absent friend Ronnie. I became very fond of them both over the next few years and gloried in the Theatre reminiscences and leisurely afternoons spent in the garden. There we exchanged plant recipes and listened to naughty anecdotes about celebrated Theatrical personages. All far too risqué to mention here!

Wilfred was most interested in Zeynel's welfare, and, as he lived so close to the family, he paid regular visits. This insular little boy found his circle of friends widening and, through this, I was to be sustained in the weeks to come when Ronnie was away.

***

PART ONE
THEN

THE BABIES AND ME....

Ronnie's day of departure arrived. The bag was packed and his scripts were gripped determinedly in readiness for study on the train. Then - he was gone and the babies and I stared miserably at one another. 'This won't do,' said I and Charlie and Phyllis agreed. Ronnie was to be away for a fortnight. We would go to the Park. Then, we would be busy...

The business of being alone was very new to me. That is, being alone without Ronnie. I had lived alone when working away and hated it. I was self-sufficient, independent, but unused to existing as a separate entity. This time I was intent on planning my life and enjoying the challenge of occupying myself.

Zeynel and his lessons were the mainstay of my afternoons and Charlie and Phyllis were walked twice a day. Ronnie phoned often and the contact was joyful. Friends: Grace and Brian, Margaret, Jasu, Betty and our Church companions were in frequent touch and the days flew by. The babies were repeatedly on the lookout for Ronnie's return. Charlie bagged the best vantage point on the back of the sofa which graced the space in the front bay window.

Reg did not put in many appearances. His girlfriend visited and they seemed to be incarcerated within....

A week had passed when our little household was disturbed, dramatically, in the middle of the night. We were awakened by an alarming noise which seemed to be emanating from the kitchen. Charlie and Phyllis, during Ronnie's absence, had been used to stretching out at the foot of the bed and slept peacefully throughout the nights. This time, however, they were bolt upright, staring wide-eyed at me and expecting an immediate resolution to the dilemma. We gaped at each other, petrified. Not a sound could be heard but a persistent scratching and scrabbling.

There was only one thing for it. I would have to call Michael from the flat upstairs - all at 2.30 a.m. He was very kind and came to our rescue. A cupboard under the kitchen sink was investigated and with it came the declaration, 'You've got mice, or....'. He hesitated before dropping the bombshell, 'It could be a rat!' It took poor Michael some time before he could calm down all three! He closed the kitchen door very firmly and offered words of consolation. We did not sleep a wink that night...

The following morning, on Michael's advice, the Council Pest Control Service was called into action. 'Oh yes,' confirmed the worthy Inspector ominously, 'it's them alright. It's mice and you could be infested'. If only Ronnie was here! Having said that, I firmly believed that he, too, would have been somewhat unnerved. The mice man dealt with the situation, laying menacing and grim powder at the rear of my kitchen utensils.

Ronnie phoned that night. 'Oh fuck!' said he. 'Quite' said I. After mutually sympathetic comment, we came to the conclusion that Mr. Rea would need to be contacted.

Dutifully, the next morning, I reported to our dour landlord. 'Well, you must remember you're in the middle of the country!' Mr. Rea', I squealed, 'we're almost in the middle of Wembley!' 'Ah...the little devils get everywhere. What the hell did you call the Council for? They're worse than vermin. I don't trust hide nor hair of 'em!' With that, he arranged, brusquely, to visit the following day, no doubt with the upright and staunch Ken attending. I was in arrant disarray and confided miserably in Margaret who offered us a bed for the night! Bless her. Inter alia, or, say I confidently, amongst other things, we bravely faced yet another night, hopefully without uninvited guests...

As the sun broke over the yardarm, the limousine drew up at the kerb and a tweedy Mr. Rea disembarked pursued by an overall-clad Ken, who was obviously costumed for the onslaught of vermin extermination. I welcomed them, the babies welcomed them (meeting with a grudging vociferation) and Bina welcomed them with a beaming smile, which disarmed both men. Introductions over, we all trailed into the minute kitchen and dismantled the area under the sink. 'Oh well, nothing you can do about that,' concluded Mr. Rea, 'they'll be disintegrating somewhere in Alperton'. Of course he was right.

Crestfallen, I moved back into the dining-room. Bina summed up the situation with 'Mousey gone.' Mr. Rea glanced around him, taking in the refurbished furniture and decorations. 'Well, I'll be jiggered,' he remarked, 'who's done up my tacky furniture?' looking enquiringly at me. 'My husband really enjoyed the job', said I, 'he says he likes taking care of old things; that's why he chose me.' I knew Ronnie would have volunteered such a piece of useless information had he been present! Mr. Rea was indeed impressed, so much so that he added, 'Might have known it would be a man who'd done it. Women only concentrate on unnecessary cleaning and upright vacuum cleaners. Well, you can take off a week's rent. Anyone who can do that with my bits needs a medal...and I appreciate it. Just don't call in the Council anymore. They're neither use nor ornament.'

Without more ado, Mr. Rea and Ken climbed into the Rolls which made its way slowly along Bowrons.

Ronnie returned at the weekend and listened in awe to the catalogue of events. Bina filled in the details which I had missed. He was very patient and full of praise for the resolute way we had dealt with such catastrophic dramas. He then settled on a plan, 'just in case'. He acquired a harmless trap which was to be placed under the kitchen sink. Any creature inquisitive enough to peer inside it would be enticed by a light snack and, once enclosed, be unable to escape. The plan produced results and... a result we had not bargained for.

One morning, soon after, the words 'Oh, what little bugger have we here?' I dare not enter the kitchen, so Ronnie appeared holding the contraption up for me to see, and what I saw looked very much like a rat! 'Darling, it's a baby one. We'll take it to the Park to set it free!' 'I suppose, Ronnie,' said I, 'its' mother and father will have its breakfast ready'. 'Of course', was the retort, "Wo ist mein Frühstück'? So, after collecting the excited Bina and the babies, our extended family headed for One-Tree-Hill. We did not see another mouse at No. 20. Perhaps the word had got around...

The mouse or rat episode had been a somewhat extreme diversion from thoughts which had occupied me during Ronnie's absence. Playing Barkis had taken him into a different realm. There he was to be placed in situations which might have proved to be disorientating and odd when exploring his new life. After all, how does one deal with sexually stimulating states governing the opposite sex when one is exploring adolescence, let alone when one is fifty? Our faithful Doctor aptly described it as being let loose in a tantalising sweetshop. Also, Ronnie's friends and colleagues must have found the transformation an enigma. Ronnie, however, coped as he coped with everything else in his life - with nonchalance and evenness of mind or temper. He had always been attracted to women and now he was able to enjoy being bewitched. I watched and was glad. He was free.

*

Our wildlife encounters continued with the appearance of Priscilla the pigeon. It coincided with Ronnie's return to the BBC Radio Repertory Company. Late one afternoon, after teaching Zeynel, I returned to find a large cardboard box in the communal hallway. Ronnie burst through the flat door followed by Bina. 'She was in the middle of the road,' explained my husband. 'Who, Ronnie?' I enquired. Bina filled in the gap with the word 'Priscilla!' With that, the box was opened and I peered inside. A rather fat pigeon blinked at me...need I say more? Ronnie went on to say that she had been lolling around in the road, exhausted, and obviously needing a Good Samaritan. Ronnie had happened along.

There, Priscilla resided for a whole week before I insisted that instead of living off the fat of the land, she needed to be re-housed or re-flown. Once more, our little family headed for One-Tree-Hill-Park, Priscilla cooing contentedly inside her cardboard cage. Betty and Marjorie, hoeing in their gardens, wished us luck as we passed by. Priscilla flatly refused to disembark, but it was Bina who came to the rescue and, muttering Indian words of encouragement, shooed the reluctant bird into the air. Priscilla circled once and then flew. There was not a dry eye in the house!

Numerous plates were kept in the air in the weeks that followed. Visits to Margaret were interspersed with Zeynel's lessons and regular contact was kept with Philip and my family.

In the meantime, Bina was growing and starting school was imminent. We did our best to introduce the little girl to books and activities which may stand her in good stead for the future. We saw a great deal of Jasu and spent many hours reassuring her and offering the friendship and consolation she so needed.

A 'For Sale' notice appeared in Reg's garden. We did not press him to share his plans with us, but waited for some contact. This came, as usual, over the garden wall. 'I'm off,' he proclaimed, 'I'm sick of this neighbourhood and we're off'. We presumed he meant that he would be moving in with his girlfriend, who incidentally, had not been introduced. I was miffed about this. Hester would have been upset. Ronnie, true to form, reminded me that it was Reg's business and life changes for everyone.

Removal vans arrived, curtains were pulled and before we could draw breath, Reg had disappeared. We did not meet him again and the curtains remained closed for ever more. Our new neighbour, an Indian gentleman, was a recluse, so the house once a source of Irish laughter and companionship, became a lonely monument to the warmth and kindness of Hester.

***

PART ONE
T H E N

ZEYNEL (continued)

The Oscan family spent a couple of months house-sitting for acquaintances in Stanmore, so lessons continued in a sprawling mansion surrounded by electrically-alarmed boundaries. The house was gigantic, but the family was soon settled. I had been given directions and found myself waiting at the gates. A terrifying barking ensued when the entrance bell was pressed. Slowly, the 'drawbridge' lifted and I was admitted, but once inside Semsi took me to the spacious kitchen at the rear where, through patio windows, I could see a massive Dobermann Pinchner guard roaming the grounds.

Zeynel called shakily from the room beyond, 'That's Lucky'. Unlucky if one happened to be on the receiving end of those teeth, thought I. At a later date, the unfortunate Ronnie nearly had his fate sealed by those very canines. Forever eager to nosey-parker other people's houses, he could not wait for an invitation to Stanmore. Needless to say, when it came, he was straining at the bit.

I had already arrived at the house and was helping Zeynel to write his name. We were disturbed by the ringing bell and furious barking. I heard Semsi shout, 'Don't open the gate Ronnie!' Zeynel and I looked at one another in horror. Where was Ronnie and, more importantly, where was the ferocious dog, Lucky? My heart sank as I moved at breakneck speed to the front of the house. The gate mechanism had failed and Ronnie was pinned against the perimeter fence. Lucky had nosed his way through a hole in the wall and was snarling at my **un**lucky beloved. Fortunately, there was some distance between the two. I could see Ronnie mouthing 'Oh Fuck!' as he turned to stone before my eyes. My thoughts raced back to the day when he was imprisoned by the West Bank goat.

Zeynel saved the day by calling 'Bang his tin!' Semsi struck Lucky's feeding bowl as if her life, or Ronnie's, depended on it - it did - and, miraculously, Lucky streaked through the side passage allowing Ronnie breathing space to get into the house. He sank to the floor, clinging to his stomach and saying, 'Why didn't somebody tell me? I was about to give him a fruit pastille!'

The later months of 1985 settled into a comfortable routine. We were busy: Ronnie at the BBC and me commuting to Zeynel every day, sometimes calling on Margaret on the way home before shopping and walking the babies. Here was a hiatus. I should have known that some time soon new signposts would appear and a new crossroads would present itself. A great shock waited in the wings...

Suddenly and out of the blue, our dear Zeynel died. We had been aware of an approaching gloom. Our little friend had grown more fragile and we sensed his oncoming departure.

Gulay phoned to tell us that Zeynel had been admitted to Northwick Park Hospital and was asking for us. I cannot describe our helplessness when we saw him fighting for breath and life. He passed away two days later and our lives were bereft. The Oscan family was distraught once again. We tried to draw on all our spiritual knowledge to comfort, but their loss was almost too great to bear. We knew it would be presumptuous to impose our beliefs, but so wished to bring Zeynel and his Brother together.

We received word from Zeynel's sister that a funeral was being arranged and we would be contacted. Sadly for us, we did not hear from the Oscan family. Perhaps it was too painful to see us. We were left wondering and grieving. Soon, we resolved to visit and offer friendship. We met with another blow - the house was empty. Years followed and our thoughts were often with Zeynel and his benevolent family. We loved him and his courageous, humble life was a constant reminder of the gift we had received by knowing him...

I was not referred to another Home Student after Zeynel's death. There was a temporary gap before I was to be re-allocated by Brent Education Department. I was reluctant to resume, for Zeynel had been so special, but knew that that was not a realistic attitude. Other children were equally needy. Ronnie suggested the possibility of some private teaching 'just to keep me occupied'. I hastily pointed out that I was already fully occupied and reminded him of mice, Priscilla and all the other unforeseen circumstances which had hindered my progress! All sarcasm was ignored and Ronnie resolved to put an advert in the Wembley newspaper, 'just to see what happens'. What happened was an avalanche of replies! These were, in the main, from Indian parents all wishing for an improvement in their offspring's Spoken English. So, my educational pursuits were furthered and I acquired some interesting pupils: Trishan, Dindi, Prashandth and Gayathiri. All, in time, became proficient. Much to their parents' admiration, examination results for LAMDA were distinctive. I could have gone on, but as so often in our lives, fate or the guiding hand stepped in and turned our complacency upside down...

It was now the beginning of 1986. Ronnie had had a Christmas break and we spent the holiday in the North at West Bank. Our usual practice was to collect my Mother from Beverley and enjoy being with the family, Philip and Jessie. It was never a long break and there was much to do. It was an idyllic interlude, much cherished by us. Our return to Bowrons took place on New Year's Day amidst snow and ice. We valued greatly our two homes; so different and yet these were the sanctuaries where our love of life and each other could be fostered.

Ronnie's work at the BBC was thought-provoking and inspiring. I looked forward to his evening return when I would be feted with tales of his fellow actors and details of how many actresses he had taught to crochet! After, we would sit snug; Charlie and Phyllis dead to the world by the fire. Bina, determined to eke out her stay before bedtime, would pretend she had not heard Jasu calling, 'Bina, it almost late'.

One afternoon, Ronnie appeared much earlier. He came agog with news. 'I say', said he, 'I've met a fascinating lady today'. Now, I was accustomed to Ronnie showing admiration for his feminine colleagues, so this announcement did not surprise me. 'She's the High Mistress of St. Paul's Girls' School', he went on. 'High Mistress', I said, 'sounds like something rude'. 'Don't be facetious, (I thought that was rich, coming from Ronnie) it's the same as Head Mistress and St. Paul's is just about the most significant school for girls in the country', he resumed importantly.

Ronnie had been convened, as an experienced broadcaster, to assist a classicist, Mrs. Heather Brigstocke, in the presentation of a programme for Radio. It appears that Ronnie had been his gregarious self and they had got on like a house on fire. In the course of conversation, between recordings, Ronnie had learned that Mrs. Brigstocke was in charge of a very prestigious school. Unable to resist the temptation of describing my educational background and prowess, Ronnie discovered that he was talking to a very receptive audience, especially when he listed my qualifications, adding that I had acquired a 2i BA Hons. degree in Drama from Hull University.

Ronnie reported this in detail at home and went on to fill me in on further revelations. 'Oh no, Ronnie,' I exclaimed, 'you haven't!' 'Now wait a minute, darling,' he added, 'Mrs. Brigstocke is absolutely charming and very impressed with your Hull degree. She has great admiration for the Drama Department there. I happened', and this is where I tried to interrupt but to no avail, for Ronnie was in full spate, 'to mention that you were out of work and Mrs. Brigstocke then told me that her Speech & Drama specialist was leaving and she did not have another teacher to take her place'. All at once, I saw what was about to transpire! 'She is going to phone about the possibility of you going along to meet her and have a tour of the school'. 'Ronnie you are the limit; I do not wish to go back into teaching!' 'Oh go on,' said my bold agent, 'it'll be fun, and you'll **love** Mrs. Brigstocke!'

The hand of fate took mine. I diffidently dismissed the idea of the impending phone-call. In fact I forgot about it. Not to be disregarded so easily, fortune intervened.

'May I speak to Mrs. Herdman?' a very plummy voice said when I lifted the receiver. It was some weeks later and I was taken aback by the unfamiliar tones. The voice continued, 'I am Secretary to the High Mistress of St. Paul's Girls' School'. I gulped. She continued, 'Mrs. Brigstocke would be delighted to meet you. I wonder if you could bear to come along on Tuesday next at three o'clock?' I was completely taken off guard. I replied, 'Yes, thank you, I will look forward to that.' With those simple words, I set the seal on the next ten years of my professional life...

Ronnie was on cloud nine and promptly began to plan my dress. I was very distracted for I was noting a faint feeling of being rudderless. Someone, somewhere, was engaged in a plan and I was being moved like a chess piece. It was not an unpleasant feeling, more a powerless one. So I acquiesced. Ronnie was at the helm.

The prospect of attending for this meeting was not foremost in my mind. It was something I was going along with, unlike a forthcoming Theatrical audition. It was immaterial what the outcome would be. It was not a job I was desperate to secure. I was, however, interested enough to be at my best and appear to be sophisticated as well as highly qualified. I was confident and, I must admit, curious...

Dearest Ronnie had picked out a very becoming grey Italian coat-dress. Memory fails when I try to recall which nearly-new shop it had come from. It was befitting for the occasion: tailored, sleek and effectual. Matched with high heels and slate-coloured tights, it was a masterpiece of power dressing.

I made the tube journey to Brook Green, halfway between Shepherd's Bush and Hammersmith. Izzy Swizzy was playing up a little and I did not wish to contend with a breakdown on such an auspicious occasion. Ronnie was at work but had not been able to resist being on the end of the phone issuing last-minute instructions about train changes. It was as if I had my own Angel of Magic, wave in hand....and still waving it in spite of the fact that the coach was non-functionae (one of Margaret's quaint expressions).

The day was Spring-like. Such days in London are pleasing, warm and balmy. I made the journey without mishap and strolled along leafy Brook Green. I passed houses which were invitingly expensive. I had always marvelled how London neighbourhoods can vary in the blink of an eye. Here I was surrounded by affluence, where tree-lined avenues were plentiful with flower and the scent of opulence.

***

PART ONE

T H E N

ST. PAUL'S GIRLS' SCHOOL... AS I SAW IT...

The school was set back from the road behind ironwork gates and railings. The building seemed to be a mixture of brick and stonework, certainly dignified and giving an overall impression of interest, character and stability. The main entrance was situated at the centre and approached by concrete steps which led to massive oaken doors. I waited for an answer by the bell-pull.

The door opened and I was ushered inside by a rather stout, middle-aged lady. She introduced herself and I realised that I was meeting the posh Secretary. Before entering the antechamber on the right, I viewed the main long corridor stretching ahead. It was panelled in oak and the floor a plenary of marble. It was affecting.

I was led into a simple room where the Secretary presided over me with a gracious smile and fragmentary remarks about the glorious weather, until her buzzer preceded a command from the inner sanctum, which lay behind a closed corner door. The Secretary shuffled to her feet and, on opening it, revealed the sunlit interior. 'Mrs. Herdman, Mrs. Brigstocke...' I was invited to enter and the Secretary stepped aside allowing me to pass into a most imposing 'office', indeed, my first assumption was 'drawing-room'. Every school office in my livelihood could only be termed plebeian in comparison. High-ceilinged elegance pervaded and furnishings were country-house gentility. My eye managed to assimilate this grandeur before I heard the words, 'Mrs. Herdman, please **do** sit down'.

I was facing the High Mistress in every sense. Mrs. Brigstocke was a sight to behold and one that I had not envisaged. Ronnie was right. She was the epitome of refinement and grace. Her blonde hair, cut expertly into a becoming bob, framed a striking face. One could see at a glance that the accompanying clothing was equally tasteful and very costly. She was weighing me up with the same intensity.

I was momentarily fazed by her 'out' tray upon the substantial oak desk. Recumbent inside it was a cat! A tabby cat, hastily introduced as Orestes. Fortunately, he was comfortable and remained stationary until the interview was over. The next startling disclosure came with the words, 'Now, **what** have you come to see me about?' I could not believe what I was hearing, but she was in earnest. I replied, 'I understand that you have met my husband at the BBC and mentioned that you would like to meet me'. With that, recognition dawned and Mrs. Brigstocke exclaimed, 'Oh **dear** Ronnie - he was **wonderful** and a very good teacher. He tells me that you are possibly between jobs and **I** am between Drama teachers!' She concluded with uproarious laughter. In fact, I was drawn to thinking how well she would fare in the Theatrical profession herself.

Nevertheless, she had a shrewd eye and enormous perception; certainly not fooled by artifice, but, I suspected that possibly she was capable of contrivance in abundance if it suited her.

'Now,' she went on, 'I **know** you are as **well qualified** in Speech & Drama as it is possible to be and, at present, you are **resting** (more uproarious mirth). My Drama teacher is retiring and I **desperately** need someone to replace her. We could do each other a favour. I would be **delighted** if you could come along and teach a few lessons, and, **surely** that would be useful for you also. If a

Theatrical opportunity **presents** itself, then we would have to think again. Now, wouldn't that be **splendid**?' The cut-glass articulation paused....

Mrs. Brigstocke was persuasive and - imposing, as she unfurled herself from behind the desk. Orestes roused himself and, looking balefully at me, stretched. I was right. Mrs. B. was clad from head to all six feet of her in designer ensemble. Her smile was captivating as she drew the interview to a close.

'Now **do** talk the matter over with dear Ronnie and then let me know if you will be able to **rescue** us'. I was then inducted into the care of the benign Secretary.

This had been a unique experience. Still reeling from the idea that I had been very skilfully manoeuvred, I made my way to Shepherd's Bush tube station. Yes, here was the possibility of a very interesting opening.

Ronnie could hardly contain himself when he returned from work that evening.

'Well,' he said, 'what happened? I hope you've accepted, because I am really looking forward to being a kept man!' I then recounted, chapter and verse, the afternoon's events. My dearest sat, expectant, with Phyllis on one knee and Charlie on the other. The Orestes precis brought forth Ronnie's customary risible, open-mouthed, explicit oaths.

I was nagged persistently by Ronnie to follow up Mrs. Brigstocke's invitation to teach. I was convinced that he was already planning an extensive wardrobe, designed exclusively for this exotic place of work. I delighted in his unselfishness and his excitement on my behalf; the unstinting support that he never failed to give. I grew in assurance through Ronnie's love.

So, I made the phone call. Fluent tones expressed great pleasure and I was promised arrangements for a second visit to St. Paul's once Mrs. B's diary had been consulted. The date was soon fixed and another expedition to Brook Green was about to take place, certainly, according to Ronnie, with a follow-up, harmonizing outfit to complete the presentation.

A chocolate linen two-piece was chosen this time. 'Subtle, very subtle,' summed up Ronnie. ' I hope you're not going to say it matches the colour of my eyes,' I rejoined tartly. This comment was met with what I can only describe as an old-fashioned look. My Mother used this saying often and I neglected to ask her about its origin. It seemed appropriate this time.

I was escorted into the High Mistress' 'parlour'. There I discovered that others were present. Mrs. Brigstocke greeted me. 'Oh Mrs. Herdman, **do** take a seat. I would **love** you to meet the Bursar and some of the senior staff'. Orestes slumbered on in his tray while the ubiquitous Secretary hovered over an occasional table where she began to pour tea into minimal china cups. I had not encountered a Bursar before. In State schools, where I had taught previously, they did not seem to exist for the common-or-garden-staff. Perhaps they were shadowy apparitions who remained in the background juggling the figures. This lady, however, was robust and direct. She did not worry me; after all, I had nothing to lose. Briefly, she explained that private pupils' fees were paid on a freelance basis and, although negotiated through the Bursary, I was then paid per lesson by the parents. Mrs. Brigstocke's eyes were glazing over and she had obviously switched off.

Attention was drawn to one of the others. She was introduced as the Surmistress. This, I thought, was gilding the lily somewhat and could only envisage Ronnie's expression when I imparted such a titbit. She was a genteel, mild-mannered lady and although she was scrutinising me, it was in a cautious, sensitive manner. Hers was not an impudent glance. Apparently, she was second in command. My third inquisitor was known as the Director of Studies, and perhaps, the most astonishing of the three. She possessed a low, sonorous voice which was ponderous in delivery. Her appearance could be described as handsome.

'Bursar, **would** you be so kind. I'm sure Mrs. Herdman will be **delighted** with the school when you've given her a short guided tour, perhaps taking in a suitable venue for her teaching?' With a toss of the blonde bobbed hair and an ingratiating smile, Mrs. Brigstocke brought the interview to a close. We were dismissed. The Surmistress and Director of Studies remained, where, no doubt, they would be cross-examined about my suitability for the post. The Bursar's expression betrayed a slight air of irritability. Maybe she had not been apprised of this arrangement. I had a hunch that Mrs. B's spontaneous plans could be a source of exasperation.

My escort walked a few steps ahead and I wondered if I should keep a respectful two steps behind; I allowed myself an inward chortle at the thought. I was led through the main entrance, a glimpse of which I had had on my initial visit. 'This is The Marble and really the hub of the school,' advised my companion, 'visitors meet here and the girls pass through on their way to classrooms. It also leads us to the main Hall'. Here, she paused and I was allowed enough time to observe her more closely. Had I been a young, nervous girl starting out on my teaching career, she would have terrified me. Possibly because I had been a duffer at Maths. Bursars represent numbers, problems and mental arithmetic which had covered me in childhood confusion and panic years ago. Interestingly, this lady had a Northern aura. There was recognition but an unfamiliar barrier prevailed between us. Candour was missing and her practised role of superiority predominated.

The Hall was a magnificent, vast example of splendid, solid oak panelling. An organ was at the far end. Above, I marvelled at the vaulted plaster ceiling. This auditorium was obviously the ceremonial centre of the school. A main staircase and entrance opened on to a gallery which enclosed the chamber on three sides. Classrooms and studios opened or looked on to it. Our feet clattered on parquet flooring as we made our way along the left towards a short flight of steps leading outside.

'I'm sure you'd like to see our Theatre,' the Bursar went on, 'it's very up to date, built recently in memory of a past student who became very famous. I'm sure you've heard of Celia Johnson. This has been a favourite project for the High Mistress and she has spearheaded many schemes to raise money for the building. It was opened by the Queen Mother.'

By this time, we had reached the main vestibule of the Theatre. It appeared to be very modern and the Foyer, somewhat unprepossessing I thought, preceded our entrance into the Theatre itself. Here I was faced with a typical workshop playhouse of its time. 'The seating retracts,' the Treasurer added, 'leaving a very large space for classroom use. It also has to double as an examination facility'. I was drawn to thinking affectionately of the previous school 'theatres' I had known where inadequate platforms were converted into stages and non-existent wing space made for scenery collapse and missed entrances; where intrepid youngsters had made the best of cut-backs and financial strain, developing ingenuity and skill when presenting ambitious choice of play. Perhaps unfair to make comparisons, but what a gulf can exist between State and Independent education.

I went on to learn that this Theatre was complete with Wardrobe store, Scenery docks and, what blessings - Dressing Rooms equipped with Make-up mirrors!

Classrooms occupied the first floor of the complex. I was quite carried away with thoughts of a teaching Studio fitted with stimulating resources where I could practise my craft.

I was then given a rude awakening. On taking our leave of the Theatre space, we paused awhile in the Foyer. I waited for the Bursar to point out where I would be operating. Instead, she announced: 'Now, while this building was being constructed, we erected a couple of Portakabins nearby for contractors to use. These still exist and, of course, you will require your own area for lessons. I am sure this will be satisfactory. You see, your predecessor lived just around the corner - a cottage in Rowan Road - and it was so convenient for her to conduct her lessons there. The girls loved to pop round'. I was astounded, aghast.

Bathed in disappointment and disbelief, I was piloted outside. True enough, there were the Portakabins and compared to what we had just seen, they were 'revolting, repulsive and vulg**aaar**!' to quote an esteemed phrase of Margaret's. As we stepped inside, we were faced with an open lavatory door and beyond could be seen a wash-basin and toilet, complete with the seat in upright position. In one agile, free-flowing movement, the Bursar lunged forward and hastily pulled down the lavatory seat and closed the door on it. I was reminded of Ronnie's Oxfam adversary, Attila. What male occupant had infringed this time?

As if reading my mind, the Bursar explained that I would be sharing the billet with the Theatre Technician. Not to be deterred and having been engaged in Drama in a variety of rendezvous, I summed up the situation as yet one more of life's challenging obstacles to overcome. Another, I suppose, would have asked questions and queried the necessity of being dumped in such surroundings when palatial quarters were on offer across the lawn. What I could not have known at the time was that the Portakabin would become a refuge, a beacon, a place of safety, consolation and most of all, of fun. It is not only surroundings that bring about a holistic development, it is people.

I made several more excursions to St. Paul's in the following weeks. I needed to meet the precursor responsible for Speech & Drama. The Bursar suggested that I would gather all the information I required from my predessor who resided in a minute cottage tucked away behind Rowan Road. I spent a most appealing, agreeable afternoon with this lady and indeed did learn much about the school and its traditions. I began to realise how enthralling the work could become.

This lady's eloquence and the ambiance of her environment lulled me into a world of social ascendancy inhabited by gentlefolk. She was generous in her sharing of advice and description of the work involved. Organisation seemed to be rather hit-and-miss as far as timetabling and the overseeing of curriculum. The process was summed up thus: 'The Music Department is very helpful - I'm afraid Speech & Drama is something of a Cinderella - and a member of the Music Staff will aid with timetabling. It's a bit of a riot really, for of course our subject is very much extra-curricular and the dear girls have to be fitted in during lunchtimes, after school, or, and this is most unsatisfactory, before Assembly in the early morning. Added to that, they are so hard-worked; academia must always prevail'. I began to get the idea. Nevertheless, this was illuminating and I knew I would have to begin, gently, as I meant to go on.

My starting date was in September. I could not avoid reminding myself that I did not know how on earth I had arrived at this juncture. Ronnie, a fine mess you've got me into...

My new occupation seemed remote - months ahead - and we had the whole entrancing Summer spreading before us. I was filled with thanksgiving. Friends pointed out that securing a job at St. Paul's Girls' School was an achievement. It seems that I had landed a big fish. Strangely enough, I did not long for the elusive audition dispatch. That part of my life seemed to be fading into inconsequence. Ronnie was caught up with plans, mostly for my wardrobe, but his pride was patent.

Ronnie requested leave from the Radio Repertory Company and as soon as Izzy Swizzy was laden, we were 'on't roaaad' for Scarborough. Our lives were changing again, but the pull of sand and sea remained as seductive as ever.

Long days were spent sauntering, mooching through the Dales and motoring over to Hartlepool from time to time to visit the querulous Louie, who seemed to be getting used to me. 'Our Violet' - Ronnie's sister - was coming in for some stick, for at that time Kathy was the golden girl and relations were fraught between the sisters. I kept a careful distance and watched from afar as Ronnie trod on eggshells. He, too, was favoured; Mother and Son shared an easy, humorous outlook on life. Poor Violet was on the periphery, but not unduly perturbed when we visited her and her husband Harry, in their scrupulous home. We would make our way back through villages and the awesome Sutton Bank Hill, or take the caravan route which meandered through hamlets and off-the-beaten-track settlements. We savoured these journeys. Izzy Swizzy acquitted herself well and the babies, in seventh heaven, rollicked through grassy meadows and hills whenever we stopped for Ronnie's countless cups of tea.

The Moors, always expansive, rolling and mysterious, threw up minor alarms.

Ronnie had been reading extensively about weather conditions in America and how hurricanes had devastated coastlines. Once, embarking on the last leg of our drive home to Scarborough, the clouds amassed and hung low over heather and gorse. Ronnie seemed rather quiet. One cloud promised to be more threatening than others. His subdued tones 'Oh dear, I hope that's not a twister!' prompted my comforting reply 'Never mind, Ronnie, I'll look after you!' I came to the conclusion that my dearest could be uneasy with the elements.

My Mother joined us for a couple of weeks. By now, Ronnie had won her over and her stays were pleasurable. We even took Mum over to meet the unpredictable Louie and they were extremely compatible, so relief was the order of the day.

Philip was a Godsend as far as my Mother was concerned. He was a keen player of cards: poker, canasta and the like. So, she was his admiring sidekick. Ronnie, also, enjoyed the games and the three of them spent evening hours at the dining-table haggling over winnings; my Mother's cheating drawing howls of indignation. They failed to convert me. I could not grasp the complication of remembering who had what and so became a figure of fun. Not that I minded one bit, but preferred to dole out the gin n' tonics and watch the sheer pleasure, absorption and jollity of my loved ones.

I remember looking and thinking of how these three were so precious to me and that one day, I may be looking at the dining-table and recalling their joy, but sitting there alone after they had gone forever. Such moments in time are transient but indelibly printed upon one's inner solitude. Sometimes, momentary glints occur during our waking hours, but more often in dreams when our dear ones draw near.

We returned to Bowrons Avenue one week before the St. Paul's Autumn Term 1986 began. The flat was busy as we planned for my schedule and Betty's dog-sitting for when Ronnie was working.

I had not received further instructions from the School, so prepared to report for duty some time during the first week of September. I was notified of the official Staff Meeting, so assumed that all would then be revealed. Apparently, the first days of Term were devoted, as with many schools, to meetings of one sort or another. I was nervous but also inquisitive.

Suitably apparelled, I attended in plenty of time and was directed to the Staff Room where teachers were assembled. There, I was greeted by the Head of English, a pleasant young woman - 'I'm so pleased to welcome you under the umbrella of the English Department'. I had slight misgivings for I did not wish to be under anyone's umbrella. My concentration was diverted from this well-meaning lady, for I was focused on the sumptuous surroundings.

The Staff Room, unlike any other in schools known to me, was similar to a vast entrance vestibule of a luxurious hotel. The silver grey décor was complemented by toning carpet and furniture. Comfortable sofas and banquettes were separated by partitions which created seclusion within the open-plan design. The kitchen area, if one could be so bold as to refer to it as such in this wealthy environment, occupied a far corner and there delicate mugs were at the ready together with some very indulgent pastries. These had been placed upon a magnificent oak refectory table.

The lounge, I could not call it a Staff Room, was beginning to fill up. My English Department associate had moved off to hail other assistants, so I found myself casting around in search of a sympathetic face. I was soon rewarded for, as people were starting to take their places, I sought a seat beside a very chic Italian lady who introduced herself as Alessandra. We were confidants from then on and our friendship gave support to us both for many years to come. Linda, Biology and proficient in all things unknown to an actress and humble Drama specialist, made up the triumvirate. We were very close.

All waited with baited breath. Word went round that the High Mistress was about to make her entrance. Did I hear a fanfare? Gradually, silence invaded and the only sounds were those of cups and saucers clicking. The door opened and in swept the First Lady with the Surmistress, Bursar and Director of Studies in hot pursuit. All rose in unison as the top table seats were occupied. I was seized with anticipation. I recall these affairs with some flippancy. There had been a long interval between my Academic career and my Theatrical one. Thespian rehearsal rooms, the liberal attitude of most actors and absence of restraint was vastly different from this formal, obsequious domain. I found difficulty in distancing myself from the irresistible urge to regard the whole ritual as a casket of riches for the stage.

As the summit opened, I found myself much more interested in observing the gathering of men (few, I hasten to add) and women. One thing for sure, there was a marked contrast between Mrs. Brigstocke and her underlings. With the exception of Linda, Alessandra, a very stylish Languages assistant and myself, the dress sense of the assembled flock left much to be desired. As I have discovered with some academics, make-up and an imaginative, groomed appearance seem to them to be a frivolous, unnecessary gratification.

Proceedings centred mostly around changes to the timetable, examination results and forthcoming events. I sensed an air of anxiety when the High Mistress allowed herself to look fixedly at individuals. It was similar to being on the front row of a play when audience participation was expected, or the dreaded moment when a performer would announce, 'Now may I have a volunteer please?'

While this entertainment was in progress, I contemplated those around me. There was the Director of Music, who was given to laughing synthetically at the High Mistress' quips. He appeared to be the only one who possessed the nerve to do so. There was certainly a rapport between them, somewhat sardonically acknowledged, I noticed, by the Director of Studies... I wondered how many times they had confronted each other. What wicked absorptions! How Ronnie would have loved to be a fly on the wall.

I was jolted into taking notice when I heard my name mentioned. I was being introduced and requested to stand so that all could see 'Mrs. Herdman, our **distinguished** new member of staff in charge of Speech & Drama'. I managed to summon as much sang-froid as possible, nodded my thanks and sank, relieved, into my seat. All those who could catch my eye smiled in a most welcoming way and I immediately felt a degenerate traitor! My thoughts had been unfair. I saw humour in the situation, but I also saw generosity and cordiality.

The High Mistress and her entourage took their leave. A hubbub ensued and my new friends drew me into conversation. We exchanged our reactions, which I sensed were very similar and renewed a resolve to stick together. At that moment, the Head of English reappeared and invited me to meet a member of the Music Department. Here was my timetabling saviour. He turned out to be a man of few words. I began to say how grateful I was to receive help with my rather daunting task, only to realise that he had no intention of being a liberator. He initiated his support with 'I've got a list of all girls wishing to take Speech lessons; I'll pass it on to you, then if I were you I'd pour myself a stiff drink and set about sorting them'. I was stricken with sheer panic. He went on to say, 'Just give a notice to whoever is taking Assembly on day one, asking all who have put their names forward for lessons to meet at lunchtime to arrange a slot'. This was proving to be something of a farce. First the Portakabin and now this DIY attitude to organisation. I could not wait to get home to deliver this choice summary of events to Ronnie. I also felt a niggling feeling of doubt and alarm. The Music assistant did come up with the pupil list - about sixty girls expecting to be catered for! I now realised that I would need to take the bull by the horns, ignore previous dogma and do it my way...

Ronnie was open-mouthed when, over supper, I outlined the day's phenomenon. True to form, he tranquillized with the words, 'Darling, I'll help you'. No sooner had he reinstated some mental order within me, when the phone rang. It was the resolute Bursar! She suggested that I contact my forebear yet again to enquire about Drama books belonging to the school, which to the best of her knowledge were being housed in the Rowan Road cottage. 'I suppose you would find them useful', she concluded. At that point, I almost threw in the towel. Instead, I poured another gin 'n' tonic and said, 'Ronnie, did you say that this was a progressive private school?' As usual, my darling and I counted our blessings and found much to laugh about.

The first day of Term dawned and, with some trepidation, I armed myself with a mind-set of determination and goodwill. I had taken advice and looked for whoever was to preside over the first Assembly. Armed with my notice, I approached the High Mistress. 'Of **course** I will tell the girls. They will be **delighted** to meet you - and you look **charming**. I'm afraid I've had to have a word with a number of the academic staff on occasion. They can look **absolutely** dire!' I took my hat off to this most scandalous indiscretion: it was quite delicious.

That first Assembly gave me scope to study the girls. I had been told that they were known as Paulinas...perhaps to some a trifle pretentious. Uniform was not worn and so I saw a motley group of students, their noisy effervescence filling the hallowed auditorium where the organ was being played. A few members of staff were making a vain attempt to stem the chatter but this continued until footfall on the Marble heralded the High Mistress' advent. Silence followed as the congregation rose to its feet. Mrs. Brigstocke's passage to the platform was inviting to watch. She was a commanding figure and in spite of her august height, she was valiant enough to wear high heels. One found pleasure in watching. The High Mistress represented the immaculate role model.

The proceedings were formal and good wishes for the new Term were shared. Announcements made up the final moments of the coming together and mine was included: 'I **know** you will be **delighted** to learn that Mrs. Susan Herdman will be joining us as Speech & Drama specialist. Please meet her at lunchtime today at the...er...Portakabin (did I detect a difficulty in saying this disagreeable word)...to arrange suitable lesson times'. I smiled graciously and one or two of the girls nearby turned and viewed me with such open sincere friendliness, that I was at once pleasantly reassured. Mrs. B. had certainly done her utmost to make me feel revered.

I had been employed as a Part-Time teacher and so presumed that I could choose my hours and times. I hoped to work on Fridays only. Wielding my list, I made way to the inhospitable Portakabin. There I met the friendly Theatre Technician, Alan Owen. He proved to be an obliging colleague and seemed pleased to have an ordinary, un-academic schoolmarm around.

I took in my surroundings which at that point appeared to be utterly devoid of any aesthetic identity. There was a feeling of camping out for the time being. The job in hand was to get the girls' timetable structured. Available windows were limited to lunchtimes, free lessons and after school. I sat at my 'desk', an examination table, an urgent behest from the Caretaker, and waited...

Lunch was non-existent that day, for at 12.00 noon a queue formed at my door and I was a prisoner for the next hour and a half! In nightmare conditions, I marshalled students into group and single lessons; my method could be compared to the duties of a very efficient Theatre Booking Clerk. I soon realised that I was living in a fool's paradise in aiming to purvey for sixty-odd students on one day. So, I judged that my Part-Time duties would, of necessity, have to include Thursday afternoons...

My list consisted of meaningless names. In the quietude of No. 20 I pored over them while Ronnie tried to decipher some of the more perplexing nationalities. 'I say, Alice, isn't it all exciting,' he observed. Mmn...

The days at St. Paul's **were** exciting, for in spite of the frantic search for some sort of Timetable order, I found great pleasure in my meetings with the girls.

They were well-spoken, polite and possessed the essence of London culture. Most came from socially and financially privileged backgrounds. Rarely, if ever, did I encounter arrogance or unruly behaviour. The learning was reciprocal. I was learning about their position in society, its advantage and opportunity for the prosperous. Before, I had not used my skills and knowledge in such an environment. I remember remarking on this to Ronnie and how, in my opinion, I thought I would be superfluous. How could I be needed in this favoured place? Ronnie's wisdom won through: 'Look, petal, wealth and prerogative are not always uppermost. You will be needed for the qualities that sustain one's life'. In the years that followed, I often recalled those words and realised how wise Ronnie had been. Within the ordered, placid atmosphere of the school, I was able to function with expertise and flair.

The students were eager to learn. I had much to impart. They had been accustomed to Speech & Drama in a context of examination work where appreciation of Poetry and Literature had been prominent. Scant attention had been paid to Educational Drama where abstruse qualities such as sensitivity, observation and imagination could be encouraged through communicating ideas and opinions easily, simply via the spoken word - no script, no audience, no stage. I was earnest in my hope to guide these young women to experience being vast numbers of other people in vast numbers of situations. That way, they would value something becoming important not just in academic terms and for school subjects, but for the human being and his sympathy and understanding of other human beings. I had realised that these girls were hand-picked academically and had not won places at St. Paul's through the depth of the parental pocket. They were academically eminent. I envisaged a combination of intellectual proficiency and human empathy. They could leave the school endowed with gifts which would be invaluable to every stratum of society, especially if they acquired influential professions where this could be put into practice.

Routine was established, the Portakabin began to take on a homely countenance and rapport was first-class. Weeks turned into months and although I was hard-working and often very tired, both Ronnie and I found yet another galvanizing, contented period in our lives. We were united in all things and took immense pleasure in our activities. We shared. Our happiness spilled over into the lives of others. Our joy became theirs.

I made many forays into the silver-grey Staff Room where appetizing mid-morning snacks appeared. There, Alessandra, Linda and I exchanged laughter and notes of enlightenment about our surroundings. I was certainly warmly received by other members of staff; only a few eyed me with some inquisitiveness.

Mrs. Brigstocke appeared occasionally, most unexpectedly. I encountered her once as I stooped to retrieve litter from the Hall floor. '**That**, Mrs. Herdman, is the true mark of a future Head Mistress!' Tumultuous laughter followed this declaration. Her laughter was infectious and, as it pealed around the cavernous Hall, I thought of how much I liked her. She was, however, unpredictable and mood changes were not unusual. Although never on the receiving end, I witnessed an icy bearing towards others when she was crossed. Between us, there rested a mutual respect and, I think, admiration, but I fervently hoped I would not face her as an adversary.

Pupils on my list increased and I began to realise that word was going round that the sessions were interesting and different. Undoubtedly, I was busy and between preparation and contact with Staff within my circle, I laboured to make the Portakabin more appealing. The Caretaker was most helpful and managed to acquire a presentable desk for me. My habitat took on the appearance of a Drama Department in miniature.

My private teaching outside school was still ongoing and most Saturdays were taken up with a tour of Wembley, Harrow and Kenton. Dear Ronnie was supportive as always and cooked tasty meals, ironed and made laden excursions to the launderette where he had many Indian lady acquaintances. Charlie and Phyllis were placated around these commitments and all made for a gentle, steady existence.

I should have braced myself for change. Experience had taught me that when all was proceeding with equanimity, a challenge would present itself.

I had begun to realise that the Portakabin was, to put it mildly, a very confined space for group lessons. In spite of numerous efforts and improvised brainwaves, the girls were overcrowded, but I soldiered on in the hopes that it would dawn on someone somewhere that we needed more space. I would gaze longingly at the Celia Johnson Theatre across the path, mystified as to why it remained empty for most of the day.

Word came from Mrs. Brigstocke requesting a meeting and I was ushered once more into the inner sanctum.

'Mrs. Herdman, I am **delighted** to hear about your **impressive** performance'. This was disconcerting. Had she had the Portakabin bugged? She continued, 'As you know, I have left you alone to settle in and **do hope** you are finding everything to your satisfaction'. I drew breath and was about to mention the lack of space, but lost the chance. 'I would be **so** pleased if you would take a

Workshop with the Sixth Year girls. I find their speech **appallingly** sloppy. I am **so** relieved that you are here and I can call upon you for assistance'. What could I say? I was stunned to hear that this meeting was to take place in the Dining Hall! Why was the Celia Johnson Theatre still out-of-bounds?

The 'canteen' was alien territory to me for I was fully occupied at mealtimes with extra-curricular lessons. I resolved to reconnoitre. The Dining Hall was as luxuriously appointed as the rest of the school. Situated towards the rear of the building, it was spacious but rather dark. I wondered if the girls appreciated how very fortunate they were to dine on polished oak tables and be served from gleaming glass-fronted serving hatches. No matter...my visit had served its purpose.

On the appointed day, I made my way along the corridor to approach the Dining Hall and was met with a babbling crescendo. What I had not bargained for was a session with the **whole** Sixth Year group which amounted to approximately fifty plus students. I made my entrance and a hush precipitated. They were throwing down the gauntlet, waiting for me to say something of weighty importance. Not to be deterred, I perched upon a convenient table alongside cutlery and addressed a sea of expectant teenage faces...

These sparky girls were quick to absorb the improbability of the situation and came to the conclusion that the time could be put to better use as an extra 'free'. After all, they had been press-ganged into a Drama Workshop and one could not expect all to be devotees. I decided to release a large proportion of the rally and turn them loose on the Library; the upshot of this was that the remaining students and myself had a very productive lesson. Deborah Chazen and Allegra McEverdy went on to be very successful; one a Restaurateur, the other an Actress so the whole operation that day turned out to be worthwhile!

I did, however, decide to put my foot down and on the following morning I sought the Head of English and put my case. If I was under her umbrella, then I needed shelter. I stated, in firm and professional manner, that I was being asked to teach large numbers of children in inappropriate venues. Added to that, it was beyond endurance to cope with a whole year group single-handed and in my opinion whoever had set up this fiasco needed to be made aware of its short-sightedness.

I wondered if the High Mistress' enthusiasm for Drama's eventual success had filtered through to her minions. I had learned that Mrs. Brigstocke's interest in Theatre had stemmed from her time at Cambridge as a contemporary of Richard Briers and other respected performers. Apparently, they were frequent visitors and the school had benefited from their lectures, appearances on festive occasions and tireless efforts for Theatrical fund-raising. The High Mistress was, I was told, a popular dinner party guest. I could imagine how brilliantly she would unite educational support, while at the same time radiating wit, vivacity and allure. She was a force to be reckoned with and, unknown to me at the time, had been putting plans in motion for further advancement in Drama. There was talk in the Staff Drawing-Room of an advertisement for Director of Drama. No doubt the Celia Johnson Theatre shrine would be at the core of such an attractive post.

Ronnie hopped from one foot to the other in excited preconception. 'Now wait a minute Ronnie, that's a little too far in the opposite direction', I murmured, while secretly I was enticed. I listened and waited...

I was waylaid by the Director of Studies. She drew me to one side at break and asked if I would be interested in teaching an English lesson for eleven-year-olds. This would be Spoken English. I was pleased to agree. It was a timely occasion to meet another group of children, but in different circumstances.

On the appointed day, I entered a formal classroom and was greeted with approximately twenty hopeful faces. I had prepared well as usual and was only into the first ten minutes of the lesson, when there was a knock and there, framed in the doorway was the Director of Studies and the Head of English. 'Please do continue, Mrs. Herdman. If you are in agreement, we will sit at the back and enjoy your lesson'. I was to be observed and by this rather daunting pair. They beamed throughout and, as I concluded, took their leave. The children had certainly enjoyed themselves, so all was well.

'Mrs. Herdman,' the High Mistress began the following day, 'I understand that you acquitted yourself in **exemplary** fashion yesterday, and, I must add in very stringent context. The Director of Studies **absolutely terrifies** me! You, however, came through with **flying** colours. Now' and here followed a very dramatic pause, 'I am thinking of appointing a Director of Drama, a person who will not only be responsible for direction of plays in that **wonderful toy theatre**, but who will begin to build a thriving Drama Department. I am hoping that you will accept the post'. I was discomposed. No preamble, only an uncomplicated offer. Seeing my bemused expression, Mrs. B. went on, '**Do** go home and discuss this with **dear** Ronnie - I'm sure he will be **delighted**!' She added, 'I am also instructing the Bursar that your salary should be no less than ten thousand per year, if you choose to accept the appointment and that your title will be Director of Drama - **and**, may I say, I think you will be **splendid**!' I then realised why she had requested so many extra commitments in recent months. I was being vetted!

As I made my way home with this classic news for Ronnie, I cast my mind back to my Doctor's prediction made so long ago. Like Dick Whittington I seemed to be finding my fortune. His name appears on the roll of the Mercer's Company in 1395. How ironical that the Mercers of London appoint the Governing body of St. Paul's Girls' School...

This was to be decision time. I was relieved as well as exhilarated when I gave Ronnie the tidings. Relieved because this was a settlement on the future for us. It would be a life shift and needed to be deliberated very carefully. Ronnie's opinion was as important as mine. I need not have questioned it.

'Sue, **darling**, Congratulations! This is absolutely wonderful and - have you thought - I suppose you'll get paid in the holidays!' Once more I blessed whoever had guided us and most of all, I blessed the gift of Ronnie.

As he was quick to point out, a salary of this magnitude (in 1986 I hasten to add) was manna from heaven and a luxury we had not conceived of coming our way. It would provide durability and peace of mind. Importantly, this security would allow Ronnie to pick and choose his assignments. He concluded his summing up with, 'For God's sake, get back to Mrs. Brigstocke straight away before she gives it to someone else!'

The Head of English was very generous the following morning and welcomed the Director of Drama Designate under her profuse umbrella. I reminded her, gently of course, that the High Mistress was looking forward to an independent Drama Department, but until then I was only too pleased to receive her support. One learns to walk the tightrope of educational politics very gingerly. There could be a sheer drop on either side...

Mrs. Brigstocke was **'absolutely delighted'** all over again at my acceptance and took the initiative to inform the Bursar without delay. Alessandra and Linda were very impressed with this development and there was much rejoicing all round. I was given to understand that a Formal Announcement would be made at the forthcoming Staff Meeting, so Ronnie, hardly able to contain his pride and jubilance, also announced that stunning new garb would be necessary.

My appointment was very well received and good wishes prevailed from the staff in general. I had a few months to enjoy freedom from overall responsibility and planning, so the time was well spent endeavouring to broaden the horizons of Drama and develop a trusting, caring relationship with the girls. They revelled in liberty to experiment and delve into character and motivation. Those who wished to concentrate on examination work only, did so and results were first-rate. I noticed that Music Department success was regularly mentioned in dispatches, so, cautiously, I began in small measure to raise awareness of an up-and-coming Drama Department. Some eyes did widen in recognition; the point had been made. As Ronnie would have commented, 'We were ont' roaad'.

Towards the end of the Summer Term, we were invited to view two shows in the Celia Johnson Theatre. Ah, at last the edifice was in operation... These occasions provided superb scope for Ronnie to soak up atmosphere and sum up his opinions.

We were shown to our VIP seats for the first performance of 'The Cherry Orchard' which had been directed by a Russian matron of generous physical proportions and a member of the Modern Languages Department. I had noticed that she was a forthright, dominant personality in the work place, but at the same time, an honest, kindly and sensible woman. I respected, liked and admired her. Ronnie's observation on first sight was 'My God, she'd last you a lifetime!'

The production proved to be an interminable exercise and the two Intervals prompted a mini stampede towards the Foyer and refreshments. Ronnie, who had held my hand throughout, as was his wont during Theatrical viewing, made a point of squeezing my fingers meaningfully whenever Feers (the ancient manservant and of course played by an unfortunate feminine Fifth Former) shuffled across the stage, obviously in the final stages of acute osteoarthritis. It was wearisome for all of us.

The Director, riding on the crest of a wave when the final curtain came down, addressed us saying how well Liubov Andryeevna, the leading role, had been played. 'eet is veery useful to cast 'er - ze parents are veery rich, so zey pay for all ze costumes. Eeet is good'. Ronnie nodded, sagely. I realised what a mammoth task awaited me as I met his twinkling eye...

The second programme was a Musical Extravaganza. Certainly pleasing, but sadly lacking in some aspects of professionalism. One overheard archetypal recapitulation: 'So good for a School Production'. It had been undertaken and, I venture to add, with a great deal of hard work by a young Assistant teacher from the English Department.

In the concluding weeks of the Summer Term, I met the High Mistress again and on this occasion, the Director of Music was present. All was very sociable and I was informed that a new Musical Production was in the offing for the Autumn Term. This was to be undertaken by the Music Department and was being specially written for the school. 'In fact,' remarked the Director, who, at that moment in time, was clad in a startling pair of fuschia-pink trousers, 'it is being created as we speak'. I wondered if I should genuflect at that point, but was interrupted by Mrs. B. who gushed, 'This will be the **first showing** - I am **so** looking forward to it. And, of course, as this is to take place, Mrs. Herdman, at the beginning of your office, it will give you **ample** time to settle into your honeymoon period as **Director of Drama**.' Apparently, it was customary for the main Drama production to be presented at the end of the Autumn Term. Admittedly, I was somewhat relieved to be released from such a commitment until I had found my feet.

The Director of Music was lithe and bony, quick of movement and beady of eye. His speech was unfalteringly brisk and while his affinity with the High Mistress was undoubtedly effective, his attitude towards me was dismissive. I was unaffected for I had encountered such transparent antics before. Rehearsal rooms abound with the like and I was not dependent on his approval.

The Summer approached and with it the promise of our trek to the North. The new life which lay ahead stayed ahead and I gloried in thoughts of West Bank, the babies, Philip, Jessie and the simple existence which Ronnie and I loved best of all. We had always believed that the best part of winning a new job was that first flush of excitement when one could tell friends of the success and receive their glowing admiration! After that, there was the winding down and a bizarre niggling sensation of 'Will I be able to do it?' One always does…

The first days of the holiday are often the most memorable because one has the whole holiday to look forward to and so time is wasted faffing or sitting indolently while another glass of wine is poured. Important decisions are placed in the recesses of one's mind to be thought about another day.

We lovingly prepared No. 20 for our going and little Bina, with heavy heart, traced our footsteps. 'We won't be long' I reassured her weakly, 'and we will send lovely postcards of the sea'. It was a tugging farewell for us too.

Ronnie always had a sleepless night before we left early in the morning. When I asked why he replied, 'Oh, I'm very excited!' He adored Scarborough…

Izzy Swizzy was brimming with belongings. No doubt she would be as heavily taxed on the journey back. Six weeks lay before us and I felt quietly satisfied that now I would not be waiting for the phone to ring. Invariably, this happened just as we had settled at West Bank. Now it would be for Ronnie. So many times his agent would insist that he return to London. He would do so at some expense, only to discover later that he had not been successful. This time, he was still contracted to the BBC and so his journeys would be intermittent and the work pleasurable.

West Bank was often in a state of neglect and we discovered that Philip was spending long lunch hours in the pub. We paid no heed and thought instead of the blessing it would be to have sufficient money to spare. We could make some improvements to the house! It was a luxurious thought.

The Secret Garden awaited and Ronnie was in his element. It was a relaxing, quiet time and as the weeks passed, I began to think of the powerful prospect of life at St. Paul's. I was exultant to think that I had been entrusted with such a task and my title of Director of Drama seemed so very grand. In the world of Theatre one is only as good as one's last job. I reasoned that circumstances were not very different elsewhere. St. Paul's would be watching carefully and acceptance of my skills would depend very much on how I carried them out.

Ronnie led me through the sunlit days, joking happily and serenely attending to his roses and clematis. There was no room for nervous tension in his world and he rose in the mornings with the same optimism as he retired at night. Our pleasures and pastimes were leisurely and I lazed, cosseted, on a bounty of love and gladness. 'I say, Alice, do you fancy a bag of chips?' would waken me from vague musing and joyfully I would follow his whistling down the street, purposefully ignoring the neighbours' incredulous countenance when faced with yet another of Ronnie's irregular, rum rig-outs. How blessed is one's mind's eye when it recalls such euphoria.

As our parting drew nigh, I started out on as much devising for departure as I had at No.20 weeks ago. Philip, never slow to comment and always able to draw on irrepressible wit, rejoined 'Little-Miss-Make-A-Job strikes again - did you come home for a holiday?'

Dear Philip, how I loved him. I knew he, in secret of course, appreciated my care and valued even more the well-stocked fridge and cupboards. 'Oh good,' he would remark, 'lots of washing powder!' Now, I wish I could hear his laughter once more. One's memory overflows with image. His glass may have been empty, but his heart was forever full. I hold dear his touching care when I was laid low with 'flu'. As Jessie lay lovingly beside me on the upstairs couch, Philip laboured with coal and logs to stoke up the living-room fire and cooked stimulating meals for his invalid. His only exposition was 'Now, I suppose you want the television on!'

We arrived at No. 20 with a week to spare before I was called to St. Paul's. Late August of 1987 was warm and long tempting evenings in the garden were a delectation of delight. Bina, Charlie and Phyllis were locked in carefree companionship. We were rewarded a thousand fold in sharing their merriment. Margaret, although unable to join us, was included in our lives and constantly refreshed with reports of goings-on. She was particularly intrigued with news of the Director of Drama and I was immensely grateful for valuable administrational advice. She was wise, knowledgeable and adept in the ways of management. In the years to come, I remembered again and again her guidance and intuition. 'Always take a copy, dear and ask for names when on the telephone' she would state. I have not forgotten...

**

PART ONE
T H E N

ST. PAUL'S
AUTUMN 1987

The first days of my prestigious career at St. Paul's were occupied with meetings. All were unhurried, laid-back and without aggravation. Now that I was a full-time Member of Staff, I was able to take on many more students for lessons and soon reached a stage where a waiting list was required.

The Portakabin gradually took on individuality, a peculiarity which the girls came to look upon with affection. I established a friendly relationship with the Theatre Technician and he was able to fill in many blanks as the days progressed. I was becoming a known figure in the Staff Drawing-Room and was received with smiles and good wishes. People-watching, a favourite pastime, was enjoyed even more as one grew acquainted with the cliques and friendships. I became more practised and well-versed in interpreting this newfangled body language and bearing. The hierarchies were implanted and all proved to be grist to the mill.

I should have known: complacency can be an antecedent for momentous events. Sure enough, drama in more ways than one was just around the corner...

Mrs. Brigstocke sent word for an urgent meeting. My heart sank. Where had I infringed upon the sacred traditions?

I was intrigued to find the Director of Music within the inner sanctum. Orestes seemed to have taken on an aura of doom but Mrs. B. was her hearty, intense self. My antennae served me well. There was to be a bolt from the blue. The Maestro fidgeted and trumpeted, 'So sorry, there has been a hiatus and unfortunately the Autumn production will have to be postponed, as, at this moment in time, it is only half completed...'

I strained, charged and on the knife-edge....Why had I been summoned? I was soon to have my fears confirmed.

'Mrs. Herdman, **do** you think you could step into the breach,' enthused Mrs. B., 'I **do** realise that this is **fearfully** short notice, but it would be the answer to a most unexpected and **exasperating** quandary'. Certainly a predicament – for me. I felt panic rise in my throat. How on earth could I agree? Hastily, I attempted to work out a mental time scale. I would have approximately ten weeks to audition, cast and rehearse a show that had not been chosen.

The Music Man was suddenly attentive. Desperate to be released from his chains, he was bright-eyed as he studied my feedback from the depth of the High Mistress' sofa. I was hesitant for a very good reason. This, by chance, if I consented to step in, would be my debut. It was maddening for if I had known what would befall, I could have spent much of the Summer vacation getting ready and laying the groundwork. I played for time...

Now it was my turn to be effusive. 'Mrs. Brigstocke,' said I, quite pointedly ignoring the consummate Conductor, 'I would be **delighted** to help if possible, but I'm sure you understand that this needs considerable thought and I have to have time to decide on a list of possible resolutions. Perhaps we could meet once more in a day or two?' The sofa fidgeting increased. Our exalted musical leader was a fish on the hook. He wished to be thrown back to where he would flounder no longer.

The High Mistress, in her wisdom, concurred that time was '**most important**' and agreed to a further encounter post haste. She, no dilettante in such matters, knew I held all the cards, but, as I left, the discomfort of having to come to a decision on such a vital plight weighed heavily. How quickly I made my way home that evening. Who would find the answer? Why, Ronnie of course! There lay my salvation...

I had not contemplated such a turn of events. Of course I could refuse. So much was at stake. Success would be imperative. I had planned to integrate my professional ideals slowly and did not intend to jump-start any changes I wished to make. Now, all would be accelerated if I took on this huge challenge in so short a time. 'I say,' said Ronnie, 'why don't you do a Pantomime?'

Ronnie's words were another bolt from the blue. A Pantomime! All at once, I began to see what an adventurous suggestion this was. I would be starting out with something quite unprecedented at St. Paul's and yet what a master stroke. 'Ronnie,' I exclaimed, 'you've done it again!'. This, however, would be a mammoth undertaking and to be accomplished in a short space of time with raw amateurs. A sleepless night followed, but, over a nocturnal pot of tea, we came up with the choice of show - 'Dick Whittington'! Triumphant hugs all round!

Before putting our proposal before the High Mistress (I say 'our', for Ronnie was already up-'n'-running with the idea), I decided to make a phone call to Kenneth Alan Taylor in Oldham to find out if he had written a Dick Whittington script. He had and promised to forward a copy that day.

Thus armed, I made an appointment with Mrs. B. Fortunately, the M.D. was otherwise engaged, but a Musical representative would have been useful, for undoubtedly tunes were going to play an important part in this sensational production. Without further ado, I put my case. The High Mistress' eyes became wider as I outlined the plan. She was fascinated and, I suspect, all too ready to champion the idea but requested a short time to ponder and 'could I **bear** to meet again after school'.

The First Lady was beaming as I entered the oval office. 'The academic staff are **enchanted** with the idea', she declared. I explained about the script and with all the benevolence I could marshal, announced in diplomatic fashion, that a copy would be ready for her perusal within twenty-four hours. Kenneth Alan Taylor's ears must have been burning as I described his work as unique in its traditional values. Indeed, I could not have been more confident, for I knew his pantomimes to be legendary.

Weeks later, I realised what a leap in the dark this had been. When the idea was born, Ronnie and I had paid scant attention to the fact that much help via the Art and Music Departments would be vital. We had taken this for granted and also, when the notion was mooted, back-up for costume and scenery construction was put on the back burner of our minds.

The High Mistress was '**delighted**' with the script, Kenneth was very appreciative and from then on, it was all systems go. Whoever had placed us in such a set of astonishing circumstances had done it with good reason. I was constantly aware of guidance, reassurance and certainty that I was realising my destiny. At the same time, I was ceaselessly reminded that anything worth having has to be strived for. We had not been given an easy passage.

The Autumn production of 'Dick Whittington' was announced at the next Staff Meeting. A few 'oohs and aahs' partnered the news, but in general there was a sense of pleasure and animation. Everyone seemed to be of the opinion that it was appropriate for overly academic presentations to be discarded for the time being in favour of 'jolly good fun'. Mmn, thought I. Did they realise how much dedicated expertise went into Pantomime skills?

The Bursar was hovering expectantly. She required a breakdown of show expenses. I was to receive a Budget based on my forecast. Here, I ran into deep waters, for, unused as I was to financial complication, I felt she had me over a barrel and would be ready to say no. Again, Ronnie's canny common sense prompted 'I say, darling, don't despair. Wouldn't it be a good idea to have a quick look at past balance sheets for Dramatic productions and base your prediction on that?' Problem solved and Budget acquired.

***

PART ONE
THEN

DICK WHITTINGTON
AUTUMN 1987

I resolved to hold auditions for the whole school and there was a marked buzz of anticipation when I made my announcement. A synopsis of story and character notes were posted in the Theatre Foyer. Classroom undertaking in the vicinity of the Theatre almost came to a standstill when details were released. Auditionees were asked to prepare a simple song (operatic agility not essential, but rather an ability to 'put over') and tell a joke.

Academia took a back seat for a while. Audition lists were full and extra evenings had to be set aside. Each student had a three-minute slot and Auditions were private. Needless to say, all had to be completed after school so I was not leaving the premises each night before 6.15 p.m. Ronnie called in on his way from the BBC and watched entranced as the girls went through their paces. Many were exceptional, some superb and all were keen to be involved in any capacity. Also, I had advertised for groups to volunteer for Costumes, Front-of-House, Make-up and numerous other backstage posts and it was obvious that competition was rife.

The Chaplain and Head of Lower School made an appearance and offered kind, encouraging observations. He seemed to be impressed that Ronnie too was showing so much interest. Later, we would come to realise how imperative his interest was!

Ronnie and I spent a feverish weekend casting. We were overjoyed with the results and when I reported to the High Mistress on Monday morning, she greeted me with,

'The Chaplain tells me you were quite **brilliant** last week, **and** my dear, you **laughed** at **every** joke! That, was above and beyond the call of duty!'

Audition results were posted and great jubilation took place in the Theatre Foyer. There were some surprises and, much to my satisfaction, a few students who had not been successful on previous occasions, found themselves in leading roles.

I was eager to employ as many hopefuls as possible and, somewhat rashly, invented a chorus consisting of a dozen extras. In total, our Company swelled to twenty-five. Ronnie, with his characteristic foresight remarked, 'Mmn, all to be costumed....' I resolved to think about that later, for my immediate task was to block the show for rehearsal. Also, I was mindful of the girls being unused to my methods, which were dependent on both Theatrical and Educational philosophy.

I called a meeting for cast and crew and outlined the plan of campaign. I was quick to point out that those playing leading parts were on equal footing with Scene Painters, Costume makers and helpers serving Interval coffee. Professional standards were of paramount importance and all needed to be team players. The enthusiasm and goodwill which resulted was heart-warming and, as always, it was brought to mind of how we all thrive on morale boosting and kindness. The Company was allowed one week to rest on its laurels while the novice Director of Drama repaired to the confines of No. 20 and Ronnie's solicitous care, there to work out the intricacies of production.

Rehearsal schedules, all skirting around the demanding academic premise of the school, were computed (no machines in those days) for a week in advance, so allowing students to plan their calls and commitments.

It was an exciting time. The young people worked with a will and gradually became conversant with the skills.

Their only criticism or observation was that the 'corny' script would be an embarrassment to the sophisticated parental audience. 'Oh ye of little faith' was my retort.

Ronnie was gradually introduced, largely through necessity. He was an expert on Pantomime gags, slapstick routine and audience participatory agility. The girls respected Ronnie, grew fond of him and admired his patient cleverness. Most of all, they laughed with him. He was not gifted with an efficient memory for names (often we would attend last night parties or film wraps with the Cast List in our pocket so notorious was he for remembering those he had worked with the day before) and so referred to the girls as Betty, Gladys, Flossie or Doris. They were enraptured, in spite of the fact that their real monickers were probably Philomena, Xanthe or Nyree! To Paulinas he was always Ronnie and never Mr. Herdman. Their affection for him was memorable. He taught them how to sew, to paint, to slapstick and how to organise the Foyer kitchen for Interval refreshments.

The Front-of-House team was split into two groups and each carried its own important title - Refreshments or Foyer Décor and Hospitality. Ronnie drilled Refreshments with regimental precision. On reporting to me later, his eyes widened like saucers when he mentioned that the girls seemed unfamiliar with the words 'dish-cloth' or 'tea towel'. His concern grew when he outlined plans for demonstrating use of the tea urn and after, when the Second Half commenced, how to collect, stack and wash-up the crockery. 'I find that one needs to explain everything in detail,' he wailed, 'don't they help their Mothers at home?' 'Darling', I commiserated, 'let me tell you a story. A previous High Mistress, I am told, when sounded out about the possibility of students learning cookery, replied: 'Paulinas do not cook. They think!' Ronnie's retort was unprintable, but the gist of his acknowledgement was 'For God's sake, what's their old man going to say when he gets home for his supper and his wife says, 'Sorry, darling, I'm thinking!'

Some weeks into rehearsal, I was beginning to be a shade alarmed at the sheer lack of interest and co-operation from the Music and Art Departments. I had submitted designs for scenery and also numerous requests to the Head of Music for an accompanist. These appeals met with veritable silence. On two occasions a very pleasant Sixth Form student attended and was wholly at sea with typical Pantomime music. She did not appear again. Another memo, sent post haste to the Gustav Holst seminary, prompted the arrival of an Assistant Music teacher. Again, quite personable and, seemingly, eager to be of service, but as soon as a requisition for Tiddly-Winkie-Woo, Riding Along on the Crest of a Wave, and (here we did run into trouble) Supercalafragalisticexpialadocious was made, she fled! As a result, Ronnie and I soldiered on and taught the Cast the songs ourselves. Without, I hasten to add, a piano or instrument of any kind. In any case, neither of us could read music, but what fun we had! Eventually, things came to a head and I took advantage of the umbrella belonging to the Head of English. I was given shelter and supported. Even so, the Musical Director did not make his presence felt until two days before the Technical Rehearsal. I fear he went into trenchant shock when witnessing the sheer excellence of performance, galvanised a four-piece band into action and saved the day.

The Art Department came up with one answer to my pleas for Scene Painting - half a back-cloth covered with a large expanse of sea and sky. The abandoned Scene Painting team was sustained by the vision and hands-on adroitness of - yes, Ronnie!

All this was taken on in addition to one's daily teaching. Needless to say, Ronnie was not forever on hand to come to the rescue. He called in whenever BBC commitments allowed and took up the paintbrush. After-school-hours were sometimes not conducive to flashes of inspiration and the girls were often weary. When rehearsal finished at approximately six o'clock on Winter evenings, they would head home condemned to a sentence of three hours homework.

One evening, Ronnie was labouring with the backcloth of a UV scene. I was uninitiated to this effect. Ronnie visualised an underwater scene complete with fish, water-lilies and mermaids! When lighting was directed on to the specialised paintwork, all else was thrown into darkness, thus emphasising shapes and glittering colours. I marvelled. His greeting was, 'Well, we're on't roaad!'

Ronnie found himself in conversation with the school Caretaker from time to time. One evening, this obliging, agreeable chap offered to give my persevering spouse a hand. From then on, they developed a tenacious working partnership and produced wonders of scenic delight. After all, who needed an Art Department?

We had ventured into the precincts of the Wardrobe. There we found a collection of decrepit Elizabethan creations, long-forgotten, dusty and threadbare. I remember with affection, the Bursar, in a moment of expansive explanation, describing these as 'of some value'. Ha! The stockpile was sparse to say the least. It was all very dispiriting for the Budget, the precious Budget, was not given to the profligate excesses of costume hire. 'Panto needs spectacle', added Ronnie. At that point, we decided that a call at the pub on the way home was very necessary.

It was on this auspicious occasion, fortified with booze, that Ronnie undertook, in the absence of a Home Economics Department at St. Paul's - which would have been our Costume salvation - to crack the gargantuan task of Wardrobe Master.

In all, he made fifty-seven costumes and numerous changes for the Chorus. The Dame alone wore seven ostentatious Pearly-Queen robes dripping in bling.

'I hope you're going to include a programme note saying that I stitched on every bloody sequin by hand in my lunch hours' was my darling's piquant elucidation.

At one time, the whole collection hung from every available window-ledge and door at No. 20. Charlie and Phyllis were alarmed all over again. Perhaps it was deja-vu from their infant experiences at Oldham. For all we knew they were awaiting a Slurp-like ghost and a giant on stilts!

Ronnie continued to amaze me. He showed no irritation or a woebegone face. He was a tower of unpaid strength to us all. Never once did he mention remuneration. That would never have occurred to him for his toil was all for me and the girls.

We were well into the rehearsal period when I received a note from the young English teacher who had directed the Summer Musical. I was nonplussed, for I had not had close contact with her except for casual greeting at coffee. She wished to speak privately and suggested that we meet in a classroom off the Great Hall. It was very clandestine.

There, I met with a barrage of dissatisfaction and complaint. It seemed, putting two and two together, that in her opinion, the role of Director of Drama had fallen into the wrong hands. As far as my Associate was concerned, the job should have been hers. This bitterness, however, was not directed at me.

'I've put my heart and soul into the hope that I would be taking over Drama in the school, and now I know she's had an actress in mind all the time!' (Presumably, the 'she' referred to was Mrs. Brigstocke).

I looked on in outright confusion. I was wrong-footed. 'So', my colleague continued, 'I thought at least I could put you straight on a few things you should know'. I shook my head, but there was no stopping her and so determined was she to blacken those who had overlooked her, that all I could do was allow the torrent to wash over me.

'Time and again, I've prepared reports and suggestions for Drama, at the High Mistress' request, handed them over to the Head of English ('umbrella lady', I thought) only to discover later that she had claimed them as her own ideas. You watch her!' she finished, dramatic and drained. It was a tour de force and reminded me of thwarted actresses who had queued for an eternity to audition, only to be sent away because they were the wrong shape.

'And another thing'... I braced myself. 'The Head of Music won't back you. With that, it seemed she had blown herself out and, at last, there was a pause.

'I really am very sorry that you have been so disappointed,' I said lamely.

'Oh, I know you're well qualified besides being an actor. I've looked at the Staff Lists in the office' she fired at me. 'Well, good luck, is all I can say. I just thought that you should know'.

To thank this poor young woman would have appeared asinine and inadequate, but I did so just the same and beat as hasty a retreat as I could. It had been a singular interlude.

Ronnie, when apprised of this catalogue of events, condensed it with the wisdom of Solomon, 'Oh, trouble up at Mill, eh?' This did seem to be an apt summing-up of a most curious incident. I did, however, intend to supervise closely any future delivery of written communication set aside for the High Mistress.

This gambit did not come to fruition before the information I had received was borne out.

The High Mistress made a request for a detailed report outlining my plans for the future Drama Department. Also, I was asked to shape an abstract giving the main features of my Drama Policy, explaining in detail how Educational Drama, Speech Training, Spoken English and school Dramatic productions would operate. I could have done without this taxing task when in the midst of rehearsals. Nonetheless, it was completed on time. I decided to post copies of this document to the leading Academic Staff as a gesture of goodwill. I knew it would be of interest and also invaluable for their understanding of my fledgling Department's aims. On entering the Drawing Room, I found the Head of English poised before the Staff post boxes. She was reading the accompanying notes which I had attached and addressed individually to the Director of Studies, Surmistress and Tutors. Noting my unbelieving expression, the intruder added hastily, 'Oh, I was just looking at your approach for the others. They're all different - I mean, different from mine!'

As time went by, I justified the move as not being an unmannerly one. Insatiable curiosity had gained mastery in an unguarded moment. Although tetchy at times, the 'umbrella lady', in the future, proved to be a supportive and most appreciative force for me, Ronnie and all Drama Department projects.

The Panto was running in tandem with this time-consuming business and now excitement and apprehension were growing side by side. The Art Department had almost relinquished responsibility once having noted the eminence of the Ronnie/Caretaker joint effort. The Company was now united in its dedication to the First Night and four-night run.

The Front-of-House Décor team was particularly stalwart. A beautiful Christmas Tree was the centre piece of the arrangement, but the spokeswoman of the group waylaid me to say that in order to put the finishing touches to the design, more garlands would be needed, so she had asked her Father 'to pop in to Harrods on his way from the Commons' to buy the necessary decorations.

'Will your allowance stretch to this?' I said tentatively, 'Oh, that's alright, Mrs. Herdman, Daddy will pay. Don't worry'. 'If your budget has run out', I avowed, 'then we can do nothing, for when the money has gone, it has gone'.

She was crestfallen, but I like to think a lesson had been learned. Ronnie said, 'Spoilsport!'

Once the Band was in situ, the Dress Rehearsal steamed ahead and every student was fully committed to the Show. On Opening Night and indeed every subsequent night after word got around, the Theatre was packed and queues for tickets swept almost into Brook Green.

Parents exclaimed, parents applauded and parents were ecstatic when invited to sing-along to Maybe It's Because I'm a Londoner led by the diminutive Dame.

Idle Jack converged on Mrs. B. who was Guest of Honour on the front row and said, 'Now, little girl,' (roars of mirth from the audience at the audacity of it all, apart from the allusion to the First Lady's height) 'what's your name?'

'**Heather!**' was the resounding reply as she was led to the front of the Stage. At that point, the audience was unanimous in its glee. The High Mistress was a star.

Ronnie and I, watching from the Lighting Box, were transfixed with delighted pride, our hands clasped as always.

Thrills were interrupted by foot-stamping and chants for 'Director! Director!' I was guided to the Theatre's centre aisle and escorted to the Stage whereby further shouts for 'Ronnie! Ronnie!' promised to create mayhem. It was a moment of great euphoria and emotion swelled. Ronnie beamed on the receipt of a magnum of Champagne. I tried to hide my tears behind a colossal bouquet of flowers. I was also presented with a Filofax - very fashionable in those days and no doubt considered to be an essential part of my future equipment. The expression on the faces of my talented, loyal Company was a heaven-sent reward and a never-to-be-forgotten gift. Those moments graced me with a renewed and unwavering passion for my vocation.

Two more lasting memories pervade my thoughts.

The final night of the Panto presented seating problems. Parents, Grandparents and an entourage from St. Paul's Boys' across the river, not to mention numerous Governors and Guests threatened to overcrowd the Theatre. Requests for chairs in aisles and entrances had to be refused in the interests of Fire Regulations. This caused an uproar and one that Mrs. Brigstocke was not unaware of. She pressed me to allow admittance into the access and escape routes. I, in turn, impressed upon her that if a Fire Officer was to descend upon the production for inspection, he could forbid the performance to take place. 'Oh, I **don't** think he would **do that**..' announced my superior. 'Mrs. Brigstocke,' I stated, 'how would we evacuate if there was a fire? It would be extremely difficult'. 'Oh, **please do not fret**, Sue...**I** will **help** you!' As a result, the Theatre strained at the seams and I **did** fret. The High Mistress reigned supreme.

On the morning after the First Night, a knock was heard on the door of No. 20. A very imposing florist standing on the doorstep was half obscured by the largest and most exquisite Azaelea plant.

The card read: 'Many, **many** thanks - **Heather**'.

The Pantomime, although arduous and an unexpected early start to my career at St. Paul's, rocketed me into a venerated position in the school's system of gradation. I had proved myself.

1988 was coming round and as the memory of the Pantomime's success began to fade, more challenges appeared on the horizon and the New Year brought a search for another choice of play destined for the Summer Term. Ronnie's contract with the BBC was drawing to a close, but my St. Paul's salary gave him the benefit of a well-deserved term of respite. 'For God's sake, choose a piece without a cast of thousands!' was his tart reflection.

Christmas 1987 was interspersed with feasting and chewing over the various possibilities for the next Dramatic production. We envisaged 'Jane Eyre'. I was interested in a new adaptation written by a colleague who later went on to be the Examinations Co-ordinator for the London Academy for Music and Dramatic Art. Very similar to a film script, the arrangement lent itself to an uncomplicated, uncluttered, symbolic setting - much to dear Ronnie's relief!

***

PART ONE
THEN

DOMESTIC BLISS...

It is tempting to dwell on life at St. Paul's, but we did have an existence beyond its revered precincts. Nonetheless, stress shifted from the eagerly-awaited Theatrical phone-call and erratic offers of work, to forward planning around the hectic calendar of Term and vacations.

An unexpected windfall came our way. An elderly Aunt of mine died and left a small legacy. It was a boon. For some time, Izzy Swizzy had been ailing and had shown cause for concern on the motorway. 'Eee, the poor little thing'll have to go', said Ronnie despondently. Auntie Annie's gift made way for us to purchase our first new car! As a munificent gesture, Ronnie bequeathed our little red treasure to my Brother Nick. He was car-less and overjoyed, reassuring us that he would be able 'to fix her'.

We were not imbued with unlimited means, but there was enough money to acquire - a Lada! This was at a time when these motors were the subject of unbridled mockery. That, added to our whimsical persona and two poodles radiant in the back seat, brought gales of laughter from strangers, friends and our nearest and dearest. 'A cat can look at a Queen' remarked Ronnie dryly. The St. Paul's car-park, however, did take some time to recover, so used was it to housing Daimler, BMW and Jaguar. Some things require barefaced cheek...

Ronnie had been hankering after a Conservatory. We were now in a position to take out a small bank loan, and, although loath to borrow, we set a plan in motion. The bank looked kindly upon us, Amdega was contracted and, most important of all, Philip agreed to put up with the considerable inconvenience and mess while construction was underway.

TV's 'Grand Designs' had not been devised at the beginning of that bitterly cold January, but Ronnie mimicked its style and overflowing with careless oblivion, he strutted around the muddy foundation talking about 'being on site'. Philip retired to the mutilated kitchen searching for his empty glass and muttering, 'Remind me to get him a builder's crash helmet; preferably a yellow one. He's **so butch**!'

Dear Philip. He and Jessie were left to hold the fort. Later, we discovered that the end wall of the kitchen had been pulled down in order to lay underpinning for the double Conservatory doors. The East wind had spiralled through the house taking dust, brick and dross with it. Philip retired to the first floor and huddled before the log fire. During the day, Jessie was exalted with new quarters - the Theatre Dressing Room. We were indebted to our friend for he had faced a mountain of provocation. Within weeks, the brick base was in place and our princely, elegant Conservatory added considerable ornament to the neighbourhood! Ronnie was Lord of all he surveyed and Philip and I looked on with loving indulgence...

The early part of 1988 passed with routine and a burgeoning Drama Department. There was, however, time to spend with Bina, now six years old, Margaret and surprisingly, a newcomer to my roll call of pupils. 'I am Ramah,' explained the telephone voice, 'Ramah Samuel and I wish to apply for lessons. You have been very recommended and I am eighty-two. I wish to give a talk at my Club but my elocution is not so good. I will pay'. The elderly Jewish lady was unshrinking in her wish to speak well. 'I will pay,' she repeated, 'how much?'

'Will ten pounds for half an hour be satisfactory?' I replied. 'Make it five and I'll have three lessons'. Ramah went on to deliver a very satisfactory talk about her early life in India, won the coveted trophy for excellence and a place in my memory for unusual qualifications and dear friendship...

It was not always a life of bliss. Consternation followed a visit from Northern friends. A spot above Ronnie's right eye was noticed. He mentioned that he had had trouble healing it. One of our visitors suggested a Doctor's appointment even though Ronnie thought a fuss was unnecessary. He was referred without delay. We did not attach much attention to this and in due course he was seen by an Australian specialist at St.Thomas' Hospital. Imagine my dismay, when he returned covered in a large eye-patch and substantial bandaging. 'G'day, mate, fair dinkum', said Ronnie, no doubt taking a rise out of the Aussie consultant. Noting the expression on my face, he added in more sober tones, 'He said, "Now, Mr. Herdman, we'll take that cancer off straight away".'

I was horrified. 'Oh it's bonza, Alice,' Ronnie went on, 'it's of the rodent ulcer variety, not really dangerous'. I regarded this as disturbing, but kept that to myself. It did heal rapidly and then hospital visits were limited to three and eventually sixth month and yearly check-ups. Panic slowly diminished...but it was my first brush with fear...

Margaret was not well. Ronnie, now able to see her more often, set forth once again on the 83 bus, ushered by Charlie and Phyllis if Betty was otherwise engaged, to visit. Her arthritis was worse, if that was possible and she was frequently 'in a state of deshabille'. Or, as she would add succinctly, 'Drunk again'. Margaret kept her substantial supply of Bell's Whisky in the downstairs cloakroom, hidden partially by the lavatory. Some time ago, she confided to me that visitors were offered sherry - 'I do not volunteer the hard stuff, dear', was the terse explanation. For Margaret, it dulled the pain...

Many a time and oft, Ronnie would find Margaret in disarray and some confusion. Hurriedly, he would begin to put the lounge to rights before Flo, an angelic carer, appeared to attend to the old lady's intimate needs. 'How are the mighty fallen...' Margaret would brood sadly. Circumstances could be very much worse and dear Ronnie would be faced with appalling faecal accidents. On opening the front door, a slurred call from within would greet him: 'Take care dear, cow pats again!' Not to be deterred, he would make his way along the passage and hear the miserable, faltering voice, barely audible and murmuring, 'Revolting, repulsive and vulg**aar**...'

I tried to be there but St. Paul's was demanding. Margaret understood, but I was wretched and so wished to be by Ronnie's side. When Margaret was confined to bed and the situation desolate, it was her beloved Ronnie who took her hand as she passed into a gentler world. Our loss was great and these rich remembrances lived with us throughout our lives. Margaret's humour, her invincible spirit and her refinement in spite of adversity were, for us, a most fitting epitaph.

The Spring Term of 1988 presented me with a monumental waiting list for group and individual Speech & Drama lessons. The subject was not included on the curriculum, so there was an onslaught of students wishing to learn. The successful Pantomime had awakened a colossal appetite for Drama and all that it entailed. I was inundated on Parents' Evenings with Mothers and Fathers determined to enrol their offspring. I was most flattered when a very well-known businessman announced, 'Now, Mrs. Herdman, when are you going to start sessions for parents?'

It was this chance remark that gave birth to the Experimental Evenings of Drama. Parents were invited to an evening of improvisation whereby they could work alongside their children. Sometimes, roles were reversed and much informative discussion took place afterwards, especially when Fathers had found themselves confronted in Role Play by their eleven-year-old daughter saying, 'Well, what time do you call this? Where have you been!'

It soon became clear that the baby had outgrown its bathwater and the load was too heavy for one pair of hands. Mrs. Brigstocke, never backwards in coming forwards, declared '**Sue**, time to call in **Ronnie** once more. **Do** you think he could take on a few of these students? I'm **sure** he would **love** it.' Poor Ronnie, he was momentarily aghast. 'Hell's teeth' was his eloquent reply, 'doesn't she know I'm just a jobbing actor?' The upshot was that three or four groups were allocated to him and he proved to be an excellent teacher with a wealth of Theatrical knack and know-how.

This time, he received financial recompense which made the whole enterprise even more worthwhile. It goes without saying that the girls adored Ronnie.

He had to undergo a medical examination before he could begin. He was given a chest X-Ray and other standard procedures. All a matter of routine they said...yet... that is where it all began. It was not the first time that I had cause to thank St. Paul's Girls' School.

Ronnie was recalled for further tests...just routine they said...He attended and it was weeks before we had word. Ronnie, true to form, was blasé. It was I who followed up, only to be told after a long interval that the Cardiology report had 'gone astray'. Cardiology? Routine X-Ray? Alarm bells began to ring. As the letter went on, relief surged through me: 'I have now got a further letter to the Cardiologist. I should stress that there is no urgency about you being seen as there is no evidence of serious cardiac problems but that the investigations are more in nature of a check-up for some minor abnormalities. I hope that you have not been too worried by being referred'. I have kept that letter from Dr. J.F. Riordan, Consultant Physician at the Willesden Chest Clinic. His words of reassurance were read and re-read in the years to come. The letter became my talisman of hope...

Ronnie attended for consultation at Central Middlesex Hospital, an austere Victorian brick structure reminiscent of a rotting tooth set in a green landscape. At that time, there were many areas of Wembley which were lush with greenery and mature, noble trees. I can recall a particularly dazzling avenue of horse chestnuts, imbued with glorious sugar pink candles, on the Bridgewater Road. I did not keep Ronnie company in those days; he chose to manage alone. When quizzed about the meeting, he was non-committal, save to say that his blood pressure was 'a little high' and his GP would be instructed about prescription. As usual, my husband was entirely positive and dismissed such an episode from his day.

Our GP resided on the Ealing Road. The surgery was placed on the corner of a very pretty, tree-lined avenue and was the one true throwback to the hey-day of an unspoilt Wembley. Partly thatched, the fabric of the building was cottage-like and made for a contradictory sight in the heart of Alperton where streets resembled the heart of Bombay.

We had registered with a female Doctor. Dr. Singh, an Indian lady, was partner to a Jewish gentleman, Dr. Sifman. Ronnie decided on Dr. Singh. He had made her acquaintance once before after he had had the unpleasant spell of enteritis. The complaint had left him with a very sore bottom and so, much to the embarrassment of my dearest, Dr. Singh was the only practitioner on duty.

'Bend over chair, Mr. Herdman,' ordered the sardonic Medic. According to Ronnie, she gave him a **very** thorough anal examination and diagnosed, alarmingly:

'It nothing - fissures!' One can only imagine the visual impact of an Indian woman, in full sari, scrutinising a male posterior which happened to be of princely proportions.

Here, I am reminded of a conversation Ronnie and I had about Chaucer's 'The Miller's Tale'. The vulgarity of the story appealed to us both. We were talking about this shortly after the interlude with Dr. Singh. Ronnie's ordeal was being compared with the moment when the Miller puts his rear end out of the window in full view of passers-by. 'If that was me people would still say, "Oh, goodnight Mr. Herdman"!' observed Ronnie. Mmn...

Once medication was in full swing, regular fixtures were made for Ronnie's blood pressure checks. Other than that, the following months were trouble free and our lives continued in their busy, contented way.

Ronnie enjoyed his teaching. Whenever he had free time, there were costume plans to be made for 'Jane Eyre'; by no means such a massive undertaking as the Pantomime. We had, once again, a talented cast and rehearsals progressed in a fulfilling and professional manner. At the same time, Ronnie fitted in a television job. He played Callaghan in 'A Dog's Life', an episode of 'The Bill'.

'Jane Eyre' was a stylised production. Scenes moved in a series of flashbacks with Jane in the role of storyteller. The main effects were created very simply with pools of light. On this occasion, Latymer School helped us out with the male characters. It would have been inconceivable to cast a female Rochester! Added to that, it was a social exercise for Paulinas as well as an educational one. They were unused to making allowances for the opposite sex in an environment which was, more often than not, a female realm. In turn, the boys had to fight to keep up with the brisk working pace and there was much cracking of the whip.

It was a good production and when the final curtain came down, we looked forward to the end of Term and a Summer holiday which, for once, was not dominated by the pressure of laying foundations for a major Autumn production. The Musical Supremo had at last, belatedly, arranged the finishing touches to an elaborate score and it was to be premiered at the end of 1988 with an orchestral cast which would, in all probability, rival the last night of the Proms...

We headed for West Bank with plans for home improvement and a little more financial wherewithal to carry them out. Central heating was foremost. We had endured freezing Winters in the beloved but draughty house and now it was time to engage in another building project. Philip groaned and filled his empty glass as we filled in all the details of construction. As usual, he was a tower of strength and joined us in the plush and palatial Conservatory at the end of fractious days. The gin 'n' tonics never tasted so good...

Conversation turned to the furnishing of this small but pleasing sun-room. Ronnie, forever a fount of knowledge, described various plants which would thrive in such a milieu. Little did I know, at the time, that a particular floral greenery would be the means of an introduction to Ronnie's Uncle Sandy (of elephant's foot fame) and Auntie Winnie (the formidable Louie's younger sister).

The central heating had to be tried and tested, so the household sweltered for a day or two in extreme temperatures - but oh, the luxury of it. It was regrettable that the Summer of that year turned out to be stiflingly humid. It mattered not for the job was done. Added to this stupendous improvement, we installed gas fires in all three reception rooms and were able from then on to be in clover before life-like flames.

We were gladdened to leave Philip and Jessie in a state of unaccustomed comfort when it was time to leave for London. They would face the Winter months in an avid foretaste of unbroken warmth and repose.

***

PART ONE
THEN

UNCLE SANDY AND AUNTIE WINNIE

We preferred to return to Bowrons a week before Term began. It was a matter of acclimatisation. During this time, we set aside breathing space where we could enjoy day trips. It was on such an occasion that Ronnie suggested an excursion to Hitchin to meet his Aunt and Uncle. It was some years since he had seen them. I associated Hitchin with momentary, irritating train hitches on the line to King's Cross.

The surrounding countryside of Hertfordshire was refreshing and green. The September colours bathed the suburban streets in a golden light which enhanced the red brick estate where Winnie and Sandy lived. The semi-detached house was situated on the edge of pasture and woodland - its front garden awash with colour and foliage. Uncle Sandy was framed in the doorway. 'Where the hell've you been? I'll have you know I've been standing here for over an hour!' This was followed by hearty, infectious laughter.

Sandy possessed a thatch of sandy hair and a moustache that almost matched it. His eyes, of penetrating cornflower blue, complemented charismatic charm. A lady appeared beside him. 'Take no notice of him. He says everything but his prayers!' This must be Auntie Winnie! She was white-haired and tiny; a mass of silver curls framed a pretty, jovial face.

As we were led into the house, Charlie and Phyllis going ahead in inquisitive wonder, our hosts spoke at once so that speech overlapped and it was almost impossible to make out what was being said. Most of the time, Winnie managed to obliterate Sandy's conversation and he was left with an aside, 'You're honoured - she never speaks to me!' One was witnessing a finely-honed double act.

The kitchen, at the back of the house, opened out on to an artistic, immaculately-kept garden complete with lily pond. Beside the waters, a very large black dog sprawled. He rose to his feet and gave one resonant bark. Charlie and Phyllis took fright. Phyllis scuttled back into the house to tell us all about it, while Charlie, in panic-stricken funk, fell headlong into the pond.

'I told you it was dangerous,' shrieked Winnie. 'What the hell did you expect me to do?' returned Sandy, 'Fill it in?' In the melee that followed, Charlie was hauled ashore covered in green weed and algae. Sandy, calmly ignoring the skirmish, towelled the dripping Poodle dry until order was restored.

Winnie could be heard inside, clattering utensils and calling 'I've made a sponge cake. Do you want it now or after?' She was looking through the window at the time and I was enthralled to notice that her teeth seemed to be holding a separate conversation as she spoke. They were magnetic; the effect was hypnotic and totally out of control.

We reclined on a very spacious and comfortable garden swing-seat swigging a rather sickly sherry. Uncle Sandy was most entertaining company. I loved him. Winnie serenaded us with tuneless song from the kitchen. Sandy reminded us that she was hard of hearing and added, 'It's one of life's burdens - the fact that she can't hear it and I can!' Sandy was devoted to the big, black dog Arthur and told us of their long walks by the brook at the side of his house. 'She has her sleep while we're out,' he added, 'then it's television and not another word spoken all night. It's called marital compatibility!

Dear Winnie had most certainly pushed the boat out and lunch was spectacular.

Chat centred around catching up with family news. I was astonished to hear that Winnie and Louie were estranged. 'Well, I always thought that our Louie was jealous of me,' said Winnie, 'you see, I was younger and my hair was red'. Sandy coughed rather pointedly. 'Eh?' said Winnie. 'Nothing...' Sandy hastily replied.

There followed a most noteworthy account of Winnie's early life, some of which Ronnie seemed to identify. Winnie and Louie had been put into service when they were both seventeen. Surprisingly, they were brought South to take household positions in a stately residence. Supervised quite closely by housekeepers, butlers and the like, they found little scope to go astray. In spite of this, it was, however, Louie's misfortune to become pregnant, presumably by the chauffeur!

Ronnie was not taken aback by this resume. He had suspected, but never been told, that he was illegitimate. He was his Mother's first-born. Winnie filled in many details for him on that auspicious day. She went on to explain that their Father had remonstrated with Louie and tried to persuade her to marry the Father of her child who was, to all intents and purposes, an honourable, respectable fellow who had wished to make her his wife. She refused. Her Father transported her back to the North where she eventually married Ronnie's Stepfather, a shipbuilder. Winnie had admired Ronnie's biological Father and blamed Louie for the whole debacle, insisting that she had 'led him on, spending his money without having any real affection for him'. Ironically, it transpired that Ronnie's real Father was a devotee of Amateur Dramatics and spent most of his leisure time taking part. Was this to be Ronnie's inheritance? Sadly, he did not meet his Father, but told me of presents which had arrived on his birthday from an unknown person - heartache for both.

The afternoon was soon drawing to a close and Sandy was hellbent on diverting Winnie from divulging more lurid details from a colourful past. He beckoned me to follow him into the verandah at the side of the house, where I was presented proudly with an exotic houseplant. I admired its waxy tendrils which resembled those of a passion-flower. 'Hoya Carnosa,' Sandy added importantly, 'I got it for Winnie at the market. Very rare I told her, but she said, "Where the hell are we going to put that?", so I thought to myself bugger it then, you can do without!' Sandy's face was wreathed in smiles as I kissed and thanked him. He knew how much I appreciated his sweet, funny nature. By then, Ronnie had joined us and told his Uncle that it was absolutely ideal for our Conservatory. Indeed it was and once planted, it covered most of the brick wall and perfumed the house from floor to ceiling every Summer. Now, so many years later, I look at another Hoya and remember that afternoon and the many subsequent visits to Hitchin. I would so look forward to those outings, Winnie's sponge cake (I have the recipe) and lazy days where we would delight in scintillating repartee while sipping that unpalatable sherry.

We did not take our leave without being laden with presents. The one we held most dear was a pair of antique concrete garden gnomes! Two and a half feet tall, very old, quaint and to quote Winnie, 'a bloody nuisance', they were yet another of Sandy's procurements from his days working on Hampstead's 'dust'. Ronnie almost suffered a hernia in his attempt, aided and abetted by Sandy, to hoist these weighty two into the co-operative, obliging Lada. The little men now stand guard on either side of my kitchen door; visitors are intrigued and amused when told of their chequered history. They have become a lasting reminder of warm companionship and laughter-filled Summer holidays.

After an Autumn Term which seemed to be almost inert we looked towards the end of another year. The months which led into the beginning of 1989 were uneventful but bustling. My Brother married for the second time and Ronnie, contracted again to the BBC Radio Repertory Company, was doing the job he loved and balancing the workload with part-time teaching when he was available. It was a rewarding, satisfying time. My days were consuming and it was a constant exercise in manoeuvring our domestic commitments alongside professional ones.

It is a blessing when the future is veiled in mystery. It needs to unravel and while so doing, we try to follow its path courageously with an equal measure of joy and sadness. We were about to be tested.

***

PART ONE
T H E N

ST. PAUL'S and...

The Nurse appeared in the Portakabin doorway. This was unusual, for if I needed to be contacted, my phone extension served its purpose. 'So sorry to interrupt, Mrs. Herdman. I thought I should let you know in person that Ronnie is over in my Consulting Room and feeling rather unwell'. This was an unexpected shock. My stomach lurched and mouth-dry I leaped to my feet. 'He's resting and quite settled, but the blood pressure is high. I've advised him to see his Doctor as soon as he can'.

My mind raced. Premonition filled my thoughts. Suddenly, our untroubled life began to take an alarming turn. Dr. Riordan's letter of referral formed before my eyes and, as I hurriedly made my way to the Nurse's refuge, I knew I was afraid. 'Darling, I'm fine,' reassured my beloved, 'just overdone it a bit'. St. Paul's, as I grew to realise, was a well of understanding and consideration which proliferated when the human condition prevailed. I was allowed to take leave that afternoon.

In such circumstances, one's thoughts are filled with reasons, possibilities and conclusions. Nearly all are misguided, but we need to hang labels on illness. We are desperate to make a pattern, to make sense. I remembered a friend had noticed some weeks before that Ronnie had swollen ankles and drew my attention to them. 'Might be a good idea to investigate,' he had said casually, 'that can indicate a problem'. Of course we had not investigated.

As the car moved nearer to home and Ronnie sat beside me, I listened as he recalled feeling a little 'under the weather' once or twice on his way to work.

'I thought a brandy might pull me round', he reasoned, 'I would feel a little faint and sickly. Nothing to worry about, so I popped into a pub and sat quietly for a while with my drink. I was as right as rain in no time!'. 'Why didn't you tell me?' said I. 'Oh, you'd only worry' was the reply.

The upright Dr. Singh restored confidence and upped medication - but, she did not hesitate to make a further appointment with the Cardiologist. I calmed. Ronnie, as ever, was unperturbed by events, chalked it all up to experience and continued with his life.

This chapter brought about a watchfulness within me. I became preoccupied with the search for symptoms and changes in Ronnie's wellbeing. Sometimes, this would prompt comment. 'Why are you looking at me like that? I know you are completely infatuated with my handsome physique and pert bottom!' Ronnie would reflect. Fear would be dissolved in laughter and the exchange closed with 'Oh give us a kiss, petal'.

Ronnie insisted on continuing with his part-time teaching. His Cardiology appointment had proved to be useful in that he was monitored regularly and Dr. Singh kept informed. So, well into the Spring Term of 1989, I felt my mind was more at rest. My worry for Ronnie, carefully disguised, ran in conjunction with concern for the pain in my right hip, the severity of which was causing me to walk very awkwardly. This was noticed by my Mother when we attended the Wedding ceremony for my Brother the previous December. With her customary candour, she observed, 'Susan, you're walking very badly'. I was being accused.

In her view, I could be putting it on. She followed this up with a masterly performance at the Reception when not to be outdone either by my Brother's defection or my painful hip, she staged the Mother-'n'-Father of all 'do's' and had to be squired home where she made a miraculous ten-minute recovery.

A colleague of Ronnie's at the BBC recommended a very reputable Osteopath and in spite of exorbitant cost, I enrolled for treatment. Dr. Singh had requested X-Rays for my ailing hip and results had shown the osteoarthritis to be moderate. At that stage, painkillers were to provide the only let-up. This management was of partial relief leaving only the financial strain of fees. I was, however, left with little option for, as Dr. Singh resolutely stated, 'NHS Orthopaedics do nothing until sixty'.

In the meantime, plans were well underway for the Summer Term production.

Mrs. Brigstocke had approved the choice of play, 'Daisy Pulls it Off' as it was ideal for an all-girl ensemble and Ronnie was standing by to costume another cast of thousands. He seemed well and I realised that overt worrying was useless. We lived our lives as before in harmony, fun and gladness. Also, Ronnie was looking forward to playing the one and only male character in 'Daisy' - a schoolmaster!

Mrs. Brigstocke revelled in the prospect of a real-live professional actor taking part. 'The girls will be **enchanted**,' she enthused, '**so** dramatically **educational** for them to see how it **should** be done!' 'Bless', said Ronnie. We hoped that it would be successful, for it would be the last production under the auspices of the First Lady. Mrs. B. was to retire that Summer.

The production was a resounding triumph and Ronnie conjured yet another spectacular, symbolic set complete with magical effects for the buried treasure! Sadly, he was not well enough to play on four nights and needed to share his role with a dear, inspiriting English teacher, Mr. Nicholas Dakin.

Ronnie had been feeling fatigued as 'Daisy' approached. I noticed how pale he had become and was concerned. Fortunately, there was a lull in his BBC work and concentration could be centred on the play. I was torn as impetus increased but had to allow myself to be propelled along in the vanguard of production. I tackled Ronnie about his four-night performance and I could see that he was immensely relieved to hand over two stints to Nicholas. In spite of this setback, the contingency plans were put into action and we coasted towards the end of Term.

Mrs. Brigstocke's successor had been introduced to the Staff. Mrs. Helen Williams made a tour of the school and naturally Staff and pupils were inquisitive. This lady appeared to be a noticeable contrast to the glamorous Heather. Her clothing was elegant, discreet; her attitude circumspect. On first encounter, I warmed to her. Facial expressions mirror the inner self and I could respond to Mrs. Williams' gentle smile and quiet strength. Here was a worthy heir but what a daunting kingdom she was inheriting.

Celebration dominated as the Summer Term closed. The ultimate festivity was the luncheon party for the High Mistress' leaving. Guests from far and wide were invited and Staff partook of a luscious meal in the company of major league educationalists! Ronnie and I shared a table with Alessandra, Linda and some teaching associates who had a similar outlook on life; in other words, the same sense of humour - essential on such an occasion.

Although we had made acquaintances in our St. Paul's circle, we were not unduly involved socially. Rapport came readily with people who operated on the chalk face. We made friends easily with: an engaging chef Tom Williams, Pat the lady who operated a most annoying duplicating machine in the bowels of the building, the articulate and witty Librarian Jacqui Childs - always magnificently attired - and dear Jenny one of the school secretaries who was a devastatingly amusing companion, and, I should add, wickedly informative about gossip and school secrets. 'Will you miss her?' I enquired of Jenny, when we knew of Mrs. B's forthcoming departure. 'Yes, I will - I'll miss the danger!'

Several speeches were made on this day of days. Betwixt these orations, I took a delight in overhearing the most waspish of snippets. A scholastic onlooker was casting judgement on the whole affair and the culminating tit-bit was 'One would presume that nothing had been achieved here until Heather Brigstocke came along!'

***

PART ONE
THEN

SUMMER 1989

We decided to spend the early weeks of the Summer vacation at No. 20. We invited my Brother Nick and his new wife, Heather, together with my Mother to join us for a few days. The weather was brilliantly hot and so dining outside was our daily pleasure. Ronnie was relaxed, jovial and busy. Little reference was made to his health. Indeed, Ronnie never referred to it. I was the culprit on that score and I had to learn not to enquire, however tempting it was to ask. I did not question, but I watched. It became part of my existence. I was looking for swollen ankles, I was looking for any change in pallor and I was looking for peril. I did not have to wait long.

My family's visit came to an end. Soon, we would make ready for our regular trip to Scarborough. Before then, I needed Osteopathy for I was plagued with discomfort and pain. On the appointed day, I left Ronnie tending his garden. He was singing...

When I returned, I found him nursing a very sore back muscle. 'Bloody sciatica! Blame this on the re-potting of my geraniums,' he said glumly. There was no improvement the following day and I suggested that now **Ronnie** visit my Osteopath! 'I'm needed at the BBC, but I'll call in on the way home'.

All day, Charlie, Phyllis and I pottered, chattered and tidied. Ronnie was very late and when he did arrive at dusk he was flustered, white-faced and exhausted. He had missed his Osteopath-bound train after broadcasting, rushed for a bus and reached his destination with pounding heart. 'She would like you to ring her in the morning,' Ronnie announced.

'Please get Ronnie to the Doctor,' my Osteopath urged, 'he was agitated and breathless when he saw me yesterday; his heartbeat was very irregular. I had to give him Acupuncture to stabilise it'. I felt fear grip. 'Don't lose any time in getting word to his Cardiologist - phone immediately'.

I wasted no time with phones and, on the pretext of going shopping, I made my way to Central Middlesex Hospital where I sought Ronnie's Doctor. His Secretary made contact and an appointment was made for the 2.00 p.m. Clinic.

Ronnie had calmed, was feeling better and berated me with 'Fusspot!' when I asked him to get ready.

The Clinic was heaving and we expected to wait. Instead, Ronnie was called at once for ECG. He cast a glance over his shoulder and blew me a kiss. My fingers were entwined tightly and I noticed a slight shaking. Noise around me, the clink of tea machines, a crying child and instructions from the harassed Receptionist made no impact, except to trigger a wish for silence. Musak drove me to sickness and I longed for Ronnie to come back, to see him, to love him...

'Mrs. Herdman, please come this way. The Doctor would like to speak to you'. A nurse had emerged from the ECG room, but Ronnie was not following her. Panic took hold of me. I was unable to move. I felt the colour drain from my face as I willed myself to follow my guide. She opened an ante-room door and there I was introduced to Dr. Dancy, my husband's Cardiologist. 'I'm afraid we must admit Mr. Herdman,' he said, 'his heart is all over the shop'. I struggled with shock and whispered through lips which seemed to be glued together, 'What is it?' There followed an explanation which I could barely take in. It seemed that the first ECG had not registered an abnormal reading and Ronnie was being released. As he was leaving the room, he experienced the onset of symptoms and another test was done. It revealed severe arrhythmia. He was in a dangerous condition and on his way to Intensive Care. I blurted, 'What can I do? Can I phone someone?' What was I talking about? Gently, the physician added 'No, I will see to all that. Would you like to see him?'

I was marshalled to the Intensive Care Unit. I passed through dingy corridors and wards passing Nurses, patients in dressing-gowns and, while completing this agonising journey, the unfamiliar smell of medication filled my being. I was trembling. The threat, the hazard of my darling's death and the sense of unreality was all-consuming and I was on the brink of devastation.

'There he is, in the far bed. Look, he's waving and smiling for you'. The Sister was greeting me, gently ushering me over to where my dearest Ronnie was imprisoned by wires, monitors and equipment. I was shocked and rallying my essential forces was a mighty undertaking. 'Guess what I've just ordered for supper,' beamed Ronnie. 'Fish fingers! I've arrived so late that that is all they had left - I told them they were one of my favourites!'

I invoked every ounce of strength to murmur, 'Ronnie Herdman, thank God your stomach's in good nick!' Ronnie knew. He knew of my turmoil and emotional upheaval. He knew me as well as I knew him.

I could not stay long. I held Ronnie's hands so frantically that circulation was almost impaired. I was so very afraid, so afraid of leaving him for one precious second. 'I'll be back this evening,' I said, hoping that this flash of normality would bolster his confidence, 'I need to get some pyjamas for you'. 'Oh yes, darling, I've just thought, they might think I'm a pouf if I wear my Lungi in here! Now hurry along, you need to get back to those babies. Drive carefully'. I will never know how I managed to turn, wave, smile and leave him. I was distraught.

I was alone. I was walking dazedly towards the car park to make a journey alone. The faint reminder of Ronnie's Bluebell cologne hung in the air as I fumbled for the car key. Did I know where I was going? I knew I had to do things. I had to function and I had to tell someone. Someone else needed to know. I needed someone to know. It is terrifying to realise that one can drive the car without having any recollection of the journey. It must have found its own way to No. 20.

Charlie and Phyllis were just the same, everything was just the same. I was the only one who had undergone a shattering change. I went through the motions. The babies ran into the garden while I telephoned Philip and my family. My Mother said, 'Would you like me to come, love? I can, you know. I'll come tomorrow'. Philip said, 'Oh Sue, please don't cry. Do anything, but don't cry...he's so good, isn't he?'

All at once, I pulled it together. I drew on every reserve of inner strength and spurred myself into action. I had to be practical. Charlie and Phyllis and then pyjamas. Mrs. Doubtfire rallied immediately and her entrance was heralded with 'Now, you two, tea-time!'

Pyjamas. Ronnie did not possess pyjamas. Slowly, realisation dawned and dreamlike, I prepared for salvation and Marks & Spencer. Michael appeared in the hallway. He was concerned and offered aid. My words were blurred, disorientated and vague. Another person knew...

With some order restored, I was intent on only one thing - my return to the Hospital. In trepidation, I rang the Ward bell. There he was, my darling, looking expectantly towards the door, waiting for me. 'Good God,' he exclaimed, 'where did you find these?' on viewing the pyjamas. 'I needn't have worried - these make me look more like a pouf than the Lungi!' I had to admit that they were a trifle outrageous in their stripy hue.

'They've got me on a loading dose of Amiodarone,' Ronnie told me weightily. 'It's peculiar, I feel fine'. Mmn... When it was time to leave, my faculties were returning, somewhat intermittently, but nevertheless I was mustering an element of control. A fragment of apprehension was dispelled when Dr. Dancy's Registrar informed me that Ronnie's procedure was following a common pattern. He would need to remain in ITU until he had been stabilised. It would take a while to assess and put into practice the appropriate dosage of Amiodarone.

I was helpless, inadequate and lost. At such times, one's very existence hangs in the balance. All I could do was wait and care so very deeply. I could smile, I could still smile at the thought of Ronnie in those dreadful pyjamas. Most of all, I could weep and my tears flowed and flowed...

I needed to express gratitude to Isabelle, my Osteopath. She had proved to be one of many guardian angels. She had warned us. My phone call was followed very soon by one from a friend of hers, a Cardiologist who practised at the Cromwell Hospital. That friend called and comforted me every evening throughout Ronnie's hospitalisation. I had not met her, nor did I meet her after Ronnie was discharged; only once, when delivering a bouquet which was a small token of our thanks for the support she had so unselfishly offered.

My Mother, good as her word, disembarked from the coach the next day and was the backbone of behind-the-scenes help. She, at the age of seventy-six became temporary chatelaine for No. 20. Betty, a constant ally, aided and abetted by Jasu and Bina, filled in the gaps. All for the love of Ronnie....Gudgerati Grandma from next door nodded and mimed her sorrowful concern. My Mother was most affected when her counterpart put a finger to her eye and drew it down her cheek in dumb show of a tear...

St. Paul's, West Bank, even our Alperton life and the Church seemed to be obscured by a mist of uncertainty. I was living in an untried world where all seemed to be part of a trance-like existence. My Hospital visits were the centre of my life and every moment was geared to Ronnie and his needs.

Benefactors appeared through the mist. Ronnie had a remarkable coterie of people who cared, just as he had cared for them. Gertrude was such a person. Some time ago, Ronnie had heard of her needs through his voluntary work at the Wembley Community Hospital. How did he make room in his complex and busy life? Gertie was unpopular with the majority of carers, so it fell to the kindness of Ronnie to visit. She was charmed. My life was enhanced as Ronnie's friends became my friends. Gertie listened every evening when I cried and her phone calls became an enduring lifeline in the absence of Margaret. During the final months of Gertie's life we came to know her nephew Brian and his wife Else. They lived some distance away and visiting Auntie Gertie was difficult. They valued Ronnie's philanthropy, showed their indebtedness and became lasting, firm friends.

After two days, Ronnie was moved to a Ward. There, still wired to incalculable diagnostic equipment, he spread his positive word. The Ward was huge. It was an all-male environment where varying ages and heart disorders pervaded. I was a daily pilgrim and soon adapted to the unfamiliar routine of visiting times and rules.

Before long, Ronnie was on speaking terms with the gentleman beside him and he was often included in conversation. 'How many children have you got?' enquired his companion. I must have looked a little confused, for he added: 'He keeps talking about the babies'. When I explained that these were our dogs, I was looked upon with an air of total incredulity and astonishment.

Ronnie's neighbour had a wife with an unfortunate manner. While sitting beside my darling, his hand pressed tightly in mine, I caught her disapproving glance. 'Perhaps she thinks you're going to touch me up,' Ronnie observed raffishly, 'now just you keep your little hand on top of the bedclothes and remember that I've got a weak heart! Look at that monitor; it's going berserk!' I looked at Ronnie's face. There was no hint of self-pity, of worry or uneasiness. He was living through this obstacle with his customary courage and bringing his own brand of stamina to the business of dealing with it.

I visited one day armed with a punnet of strawberries. I was often given instructions from my dearest not to bring too many gifts, and so, determined not to arrive empty-handed, I had been on the lookout for a treat. When I turned up, the neighbouring, judgemental spouse was already in position, partnered by an equally critical female comrade. 'It's Rosa Klebb,' quipped Ronnie. In order to stem my chortles, I grabbed a strawberry. We shared Ronnie's treat and admittedly I did seem to consume the lion's wack. Unable to resist a glance at Rosa, I was in time to see her mouth 'She's eaten all them stawberries'. Is it possible to enjoy Hospital visits? Yes, for such fleeting comic moments obscure the real reason for us being there and once more, our spirits rise...

Ronnie took great delight in drawing my attention to a Japanese Nurse. I caught sight of her at the far end of the Ward. Ostensibly, she wore white surgical clogs and even at night could be heard from afar making her noisy way to the bedside. Pausing to read notes, she would say to Ronnie, 'Mus Haardman. You comfubble?' 'Yes, thank you, very comfubble' would be Ronnie's saucy reply, before she added, 'I fink you 'umerous, Mus Haardman. Ha! Ha! 'ery 'umerous.'

Being 'umerous got us through. Ha! Ha!

Soon, Ronnie was disengaged from his wires, and, irrepressible as always, was up and about, ministering to less fortunate patients and being his selfless self. His drugs were the crutch and Amiodarone, Frusemide and Enalapril became common parlance in the Herdman glossary.

Gradually, Ronnie recovered and grew in strength. His heart was in its early stages of being nursed and we would have to adopt a new way of life; a way that could reinforce and not interfere.

I wrote to Dr. Dancy towards the end of Ronnie's stay in Hospital. I needed information. It was important to know more and I knew that Ronnie would not ask. There was to be a revelation. We were on the brink of learning to live with a condition that was not going to go away.

I received a prompt reply from Dr. Dancy. It referred to my 'cry for help'. Indeed it was. I did not tell Ronnie of my plan. I would have been urged not to fuss.

Dr. Dancy was a man of few words and came straight to the point. Mr. Herdman has Cardiomyopathy. His heart is enlarged. We do not know the exact cause of this illness, but it can be brought about by a virus or, in some cases, alchoholism'. 'Certainly not that,' I replied, 'Ronnie is not a drinker'. 'We now have pictures of his heart', the Doctor went on, 'and, interestingly, Mr. Herdman has not shown many symptoms until now. This, however, is a progressive heart disease...'

My own heart pitched in my chest and once more my tongue was sticking in my mouth. He spoke again and I watched his lips moving as the news began to penetrate. One needs to know, yet one does not want to know. One must ask questions, but does not want to hear the answers. One wants to run away from the inevitable, but one cannot. The blows of truth rain down on one's head and they have to be endured. They cannot be returned.

'It is difficult to give a prognosis,' the voice carried on as I struggled, wrestling with the word 'prognosis'. What did it mean? I knew what it meant, but it was as if I had not heard it before. 'You do need, however, to have some light at the end of the tunnel'. What? 'In time, there is always the possibility of a transplant'. What? 'There are patients now at Harefield who have hearts in a very much better state than your husband's'. My mouth seemed to be working independently and co-ordination was in the charge of an alien power. 'At present, Mr. Herdman's illness can be controlled with drugs and I propose to take one step at a time'. I hung on to this scrap of hope and rallied. Dr. Dancy had thrown life-belts and I, because there was no choice, had snatched at them.

'Does he know?' I asked. 'I have been direct in answering and Mr. Herdman being Mr. Herdman has absorbed the news with his typical optimism'. 'I can imagine,' I agreed. The kindly man resumed, 'Patients respond in different ways; some will sit in an armchair and sink into depression, others will be determined. We both know which preference Mr. Herdman will plump for.

Will you be in the driving seat, Mrs. Herdman?' Dr. Dancy added wryly. He must have known.

Ronnie was in exuberant mood when I appeared for visiting. 'They think I can come home in a day or two,' he laughed, hugging me, 'now what have you been doing?' 'I've been to see Dr. Dancy,' said I. 'Oh yes, did he tell you that I've got Cardiomyopathy? Fascinating, isn't it? Oh well, I'll just have to keep on taking the tablets!'

A new phase of our life had begun. The odyssey was taking a different direction.

Ronnie was out of Hospital and while we strove to arrange what was left of the Summer holiday, we received another shot across our bows. Mr. Rea, our landlord, died. We were shocked. The steadfast Ken informed us of the news.

Mr. Rea had every intention of leaving the whole house to you. He was very struck with the way you had looked after his property. He just did not get round to it'. We were astonished at the news and grateful for Mr. Rea's intended goodwill. That being said, the future was uncertain but, at least, we rested comfortably in the knowledge that our tenancy was secure.

Ronnie was soon feeling much stronger and, inevitably, ready to carry on with an active, well-adjusted everyday programme. I hovered on the fringe, equally undeterred in keeping a watchful eye on proper recuperation. My Mother needed to return home and so, perhaps with some apprehension on my part, we agreed to motor North. 'It'll be a lovely break', said the vehement Ronnie, 'and so good after my enforced indisposition! Pompous twat, aren't I?' In future, nicknamed Mr. Pomp', he rued with indignation the hole he had dropped himself into.

This was no ordinary holiday making ready. Unbeknown to my husband, I toiled in secret, swotting up on road numbers, the nearest hospitals and emergency telephones. From this time onwards, my thoughts were preoccupied with the likelihood of crisis developing. I did my best to disguise tension and to a large extent, succeeded, but the heaviness in my gut never disappeared. It was an invisible burden.

Ronnie was eager to visit West Bank and it would have been a bitter disappointment if I had refused. I did, however, suggest that our stay was leisurely, short and the subsequent return to London sooner rather than later.

Ronnie had been right. The change did do us good. We were refreshed and with minds diverted from the ordeal we had lived through, we contemplated a future which, although unpredictable and strange, held promise. We never relinquished our loving contentment.

***

Ronnie & Philp

Above: Ronnie with his Mum Louie
Below: Ronnie (with the beard he grew for Barkis), Zeynel and Sue

Sue, as Madge in Time and the Conways

And, Sue in her 'young costume in Time and the Conways'.

Above: Charlie, Sue with Phyllis and Jessie
Below: Sue's Mum, Jessica

Nick, Sue's brother, and sister-in-law Heather
Below: Lucy

Above: The Babies
Below: Margaret Rankin

Above: Winnie and Sandy (With Sue in the middle)
Below: Bina

Above: Ronnie in our garden
Below: Bina, Ronnie and the 'Babies' in our 20 Bowrons garden

Ronnie in our Secret Garden at West Bank, Scarborough
Below: And the same garden in winter

*Ronnie as the Schoolmaster in St Paul's Girls' School
production of 'Daisy Pulls It Off' 1988*

Ronnie, above and below, in 'Will Shakespeare'

Left:
Ronnie as 'Moley' in the
TV production of
'Wind in the Willows'
and below,
as Barkis in
'David Copperfield'
1987

And, last but by no means least, and very important in our lives was Betty, our very own 'Mrs Doubtfire'.

PART ONE
THEN

DOMESTIC STRIFE...

A solicitor's letter awaited us. No. 20 was to be put up for sale. We were requested to make an offer on the flat. Michael and Carol also awaited us with an invitation for drinks. They planned to volunteer a proposal to buy the upper apartment. We postponed any social gathering for the time being.

This development was happening very rapidly. We were unsettled, uncertain and reluctant to be jockeyed into position. We needed time to think and consider. The dilemma did have some attraction. It could be advantageous to buy. A property investment is always useful, but we did not possess the funds. West Bank would need to be sold, half the proceeds given to Philip, and even then, would there be enough to purchase a London home? We did put forward a very low offer, which was rejected. We declined to up the price. Without more ado and post haste, our neighbours had bought No. 20 lock-stock-and-barrel. We were under the aegis of a very different landlord.

The dust began to settle. Soon, we were in the throes of making provision for St.Paul's Autumn Term and Ronnie was looking forward to returning to the BBC. I was anxious about him travelling back and forth by Tube. We take these mundane tasks for granted when health is robust. Fortunately, Ronnie looked upon his stretch in Hospital as merely a hiccup, a temporary hold-up and nothing would be permitted to stand in the way of our nonchalant existence. I needed to deal with my fear and because I needed to, I confronted it. Ronnie fought on, fortified with his armoury of medication. His courage strengthened me and it became a priority to live for the present day and allow tomorrow to take care of itself. Mmn....

We received yet another invitation from the upper flat. This time we felt able to accept. Ambiance and atmosphere was pleasant amid conversational ease of manner. Michael, however, wasted no time in broaching his purpose. All at once, we realised why their request for a meeting had seemed so urgent.

'Of course, our buying the property has somewhat altered the relationship with you', declared the haughty Michael. 'We wanted to explain that we are hoping to convert into a family home. How soon can you move out?'

We were confused, embarrassed and very disturbed. Hastily, I replied, 'We cannot leave for some years. I am nowhere near retirement at St. Paul's and therefore, we intend to remain here.' Ronnie did not utter, but instead, rose angrily to his feet and - left. Distracted, I muttered concern for Ronnie's health and made my getaway. We had had another monstrous jolt.

Ronnie was trembling with anger rather than shock. We faced each other in disbelief. Silence reigned between us for several minutes. I was more anxious to bring about calm and in so doing, made a few inane comments to Charlie and Phyllis, who were overcome with delight that we had reappeared earlier than expected. 'What a shit!' said Ronnie venomously. 'Darling, we are in a secure tenancy and legally protected' I replied, trying to appear assertive, knowledgeable and supremely in charge. We both, however, sank into a mire of vulnerability. This was a cruel thrust especially in view of Ronnie's frail state. 'Come on, love, cheer up. We'll find a way. We always do'. I said, lamely. 'What an arsehole!' was my dear one's urbane riposte. Ronnie's language was wondrously specific in times of rigorous conflict. If he could curse, I knew he was well enough to do so! Mmn...

From then on, the atmosphere at No. 20 was tense. Our upper neighbours made a vain attempt to cover their lack of ingenious tact in dealing with the situation, but Ronnie was having none of it. We were alarmed. Much time, effort and money had been invested in our London home and now, faced with the prospect of possible eviction, we were on the verge of being excessively hasty. More importantly, Ronnie needed to be protected from unnecessary stress. I did engage in conversation with Michael and Carol while Ronnie was at work, but soon realised that rationalisation was not on the agenda. They wanted us out.

I decided that it was essential to foster calm. This presented some difficulties. School began in a matter of days. I persuaded Ronnie to view these unstable circumstances with his innately hopeful disposition. To reinstate equilibrium, we needed to ascertain our legal state. A visit to Wembley Council Offices consoled us. We were advised to take no action, were secure and could not be moved unless, as tenants, we erred or infringed upon the law.

Heartened, we became more settled and, although sensitive to reaction from above, we pursued our busy, productive life. The Autumn Term was about to commence, a new High Mistress would be in office, and, most crucial of all, Ronnie was well. He was responsive to treatment and thankfully, the Hospital began to fade from memory. More Television and Radio work was in the offing, and his agent seemed to be very obliging in her ambition to further his career.

All was brighter and we began to look beyond the officious bullying of our landlord. Still, we had not predicted harassment. Much to our horror, this began piecemeal, but increased in intensity until our position became untenable.

***

PART ONE
T H E N

BACK TO WORK...

Mrs. Helen Williams came to St. Paul's having spent fifteen years as an academic who taught English Literature at Edinburgh University. She then went on to be Headmistress of Blackheath School. 'I think my best approach is to be different. I am more interested in substance than image' was her opening statement.

In contrast, Heather Brigstocke had been very popular with parents. They identified with her and her cosmopolitan prestige. They wanted their daughters to be like her. As a public face of the school, she was inseparable from the institution she had created; a hothouse of sophisticated beauty and brains. It was a hard act to follow.

My professional life was ongoing. I made up my mind to adopt a laissez faire attitude towards Ronnie's illness. I could do nothing to change the scenario. It was now a reality and lived with me on a daily basis. It was impossible to know how far his state affected Ronnie. We did not pander to searching talk, but distracted ourselves with the joy of living, come what may.

St. Paul's, settling into a new premiership, progressed like a well-oiled machine. I marvelled at its complacency. Those in greater command than I thought it a sensible idea to opt for a less ambitious End-of-Term production and, one geared specifically to senior girls. I welcomed this proposal for it would give me a window to concentrate on our domestic fix, which was unchanged.

The conventional meeting was held and a rendition of Enid Bagnold's 'The Chalk Garden' was agreed upon. I did mention the likelihood of a full-scale portrayal of 'A Midsummer Night's Dream' the following year. 'You're a glutton for punishment!' Ronnie mused. This was vigorously endorsed and Mrs. Williams beamed appreciatively.

I did not encounter the High Mistress often in those early days, but when we did connect, she appeared to be very interested and supportive of my Educational aims. I did need to consult her about engaging another Assistant, for it was obvious that Ronnie could no longer step in. The Drama Department was not insignificant in size and help was essential. 'Sue, you're a victim of your own success', Mrs. Williams declared, smiling. I was given permission to advertise.

The High Mistress' study had taken on a new distinction. It became a tasteful restoration of Arts & Crafts elan, so in keeping with the building's period character. Polished wood floors replaced pile carpets so revered by Mrs. B. and furniture had been chosen with knowledgeable panache. The high-ceilinged, spacious room was not dominated by this Superior's desk, but tables and chairs were arranged in groups. A Head of Department was heard to remark unkindly that the Office resembled Fortnum & Mason's teashop. I nursed a desire to retaliate. The offender was totally lacking in artistic flair if her choice of clobber was anything to go by.

I wasted no time in placing my advertisement and was inundated with replies. The business of Interview was left to me, but my shortlist was to be appraised by the High Mistress. Mrs. Moragh Gee joined my Department and I was delighted to welcome her wit, humility and sophisticated competence. She became a trusted friend. The girls, with whom she identified instantly, warmed to her gentle, forthright demeanour.

***

PART ONE
THEN

HOME IS A HAVEN.....?

A sinister aura hung over No. 20. We became sensitive to a lull before the storm. This despondency was detrimental to Ronnie's health and I became increasingly concerned for his security and welfare.

Michael requested a viewing of the flat. We agreed. I arranged a mutually convenient time, but making sure that Ronnie was at the BBC. I found the whole scene perplexing, especially when a tape measure was produced and measurements taken. I have no doubt that the intention was to intimidate. Few words were spoken. I refused to ask questions or to appear browbeaten. Three days later, we received a letter outlining our landlord's intention to increase the rent. We took advice and were assured that this would have to remain within the bounds of comparable lets. We were playing for time. None of this could be finalised overnight. We remained silent.

Much to my relief, dear Ronnie seemed to be taking all in his stride. 'Arsehole,' he muttered. While he could still use foul language, we were home and dry....

Some weeks later, a Saturday afternoon, I was giving a couple of private lessons in Hendon. Persuasive Indian parents had implored me to see their children through exams. Imagine my shock when a distressed phone call from Ronnie hurried me home.

I drove blindly in a haze of anxiety. To my horror, I found that a Police Patrol Car was stationed outside No. 20. I forced my key into the lock and blundered into the living-room. There, I found a Policewoman comforting my white-faced and shaking husband. He pointed to the garden and there, saw in hand, was Michael in the company of his Father-in-Law. Smirking, they were hacking down Ronnie's beloved cherry tree. 'She can't do anything...' said my frantic darling.

'I'm so sorry, Mrs. Herdman', said the Officer, 'it's his property and he is entitled to do whatever he wishes. I have cautioned him, but he is adamant that garden improvements need to be made'. We were defenceless. I felt choking anger, but I became frightened for Ronnie's sake. I was open-mouthed when he said, 'Well, the bastard's not going to get the better of us. It's a terrible shock, but we'll cope, my sweet'.

We did cope, but the terror of the crisis left us in a state of fearful premonition. We came to dread future developments, which led to unease when at work and uncertainty whenever the flat and the babies were left unattended.

A portentous silence oozed into the anatomy of No. 20. We were suspended, waiting fearfully for the next onslaught of menace. We attempted to ignore this tenuous tone, while at the same time being on the lookout for the hit man upstairs. Nervously, we outlined what was happening to Jasu and then to Betty. Mrs. Doubtfire was shaken. 'How I wish Jo was about to leave,' she said, 'I know she wants to return to New Zealand'. Jo was a student who occupied the first floor rooms in Betty's house and seemed very settled. So had we been. The thought of leaving our dearly loved roots was sickening.

An insufferable event, brought about by our odious lessor, changed our minds and precipitated a plan of campaign.

We received a polite request from Michael. He wished to replace window frames in the front bay and needed access to the flat. This was fair enough and not wishing to be petty or unobliging, we agreed for this to be done. Michael was already in possession of keys. In previous, happier days these had been entrusted as part of a cordial link.

We thought it opportune to disappear for the day and chose a Saturday for a spin to Hove, where a devoted BBC friend of Ronnie's resided. The weather was glorious and it was invigorating to drive through the Autumn countryside, free from baleful acrimony. Kathleen, a wonderful Geordie lady, was disgusted with the lamentable tale and spent the day cheering us with saucy BBC stories, Theatrical experiences and colourful language which rivalled Ronnie's barrack-room expletives. 'What a prick,' was Kathleen's overview. This was doubly effective coming from a little lady of advancing years who resembled the fragile, unsteady, frail, elderly gentlewoman in 'The Ladykillers'.

'So long, kidda,'...said Ronnie as we took our leave. 'I love you both,' replied Kathleen. She had rejuvenated mental order in us with simple fun and the inestimable gift of friendship.

All seemed quiet on our return to No. 20. The only visible evidence of the artisan's toil was the discarded panes of glass from the window. These had been reared up underneath and were resting against the snowcemmed brick. Our home was tidy. Sadly, I thought of how it had changed. It was no longer a place of safety and peace. It had been breached.

Awakened in the middle of the following night and clinging together in terror, we listened to the sound of glass being smashed. The noise was coming from the front garden. There was shouting and laughter as yet another pane was splintered. Drunken voices could be heard gurgling and spluttering. We sat on the edge of our bed, Charlie and Phyllis clutched in our grasp, sweating with fear. Footsteps hurried down the stairs. We began to tremble. My immediate, desperate thought was to dial 999. Ronnie's heart was uppermost in my tangled mess of panic. Before I could move, Carol's urgent words were heard. Men's voices, hoarse and threatening, were answering. Suddenly, a hush descended. Our tormentors, having been intercepted, had repaired to above. 'Do you think this is how the Babes in the Wood must have felt?' concluded Ronnie. 'Any chance of a cup of tea, Alice?'

We calmed, we recovered and we planned. This act of selfish cruelty in light of Ronnie's recent illness, was inexcusable and we made the painful decision to leave No. 20. In my innermost thoughts, I knew that there could not be more risks to Ronnie's health and peace of mind.

We began by making enquiries. Visits were made to Estate Agents, Council Offices and Housing Associations, all of which proved to be fruitless. It was an exhausting and unsettling time. On each occasion, we were told to hold fast. We could not be evicted and if harassment continued, then legal proceedings against the offender could be initiated. It was alarming. I knew the only solution was to rid ourselves of this oppression and bring harmony back into our lives.

Perhaps Michael's drunken night had warned him to apply the brakes. Certainly, there had been some admonishment from Carol. Had realisation dawned that they had gone too far? Whatever the outcome, we were left alone...for a while.

Term progressed and before long the end was in sight. Fortunately, work on the play was not an arduous exercise and Moragh was proving to be a strong accessory in the Department. Mrs. Williams continued to feel her way and all loped along in an uninterrupted fashion. Worry, however, played an important role in my life and the sources of anxiety could not be rectified. Alternative accommodation was unforeseeable and while we were in a state of flux, Ronnie's health was in jeopardy.

We were going home to West Bank for Christmas 1989. Family knew something of our fix and it was comforting to know that they would be there to bring faith back into our lives.

Ronnie was being devious. Minutes before our departure, I found him placing two smallish tomatoes beneath the carpet on the inside of the flat entrance. 'That'll nail the bugger,' he proclaimed with satisfaction, 'I'm pretty sure he'll come in while we're away and if he does he'll fuck my tomatoes and that'll be trespassing!' I was astounded. Most of all, I was flabbergasted at Ronnie's ingenuity. Dr. Dancy had been right. Sitting in an armchair was not my darling's province. We boarded our Lada with an element of smug satisfaction and for the time being, tension loosened its grip. We were on't roaaad....

New Year's Day 1990 brought a chill to mind. Our spirits on the journey South were shrouded by an unfamiliar feeling of malevolence. What mischief awaited us?

Jasu and Bina were there to greet. All was quiet and the house was in darkness. Mysteriously, Ronnie asked our friends to usher the babies round to the back door, while he, on the pretext of helping me to unload presents and the customary baggage from West Bank, stealthily unlocked the front door of the flat. As it opened, he groped beneath the carpet. 'I knew it! He's been in!' There, flattened in the palm of my Sherlock's hand, were the tomatoes. The most serious things in life can appear to be utterly ludicrous. I was violently seized with laughter as I saw Ronnie's face. It was a manifestation of triumph.

Our persecutors appeared to be away and we spent the next hours in after-Christmas fun 'n' games with little Bina. Later, earnest discussion took place. Michael had definitely entered without permission. Our belongings seemed to be in order, but privacy had been invaded and enough was enough.

A warning letter was delivered to Michael. It accused him of trespass and in turn, threatened proceedings via a solicitor if he continued to hound us. The master and mistress returned from holiday. The following day brought complete and utter silence from above.

In the few days before the onset of the Spring Term, we sought the advice of a solicitor who had been recommended by Brian and Grace. Protection was essential while a sound plan was being put into action. He provided beneficial information and we were soothed by the security it fostered. We continued to search for another home, but without success. Michael, however, did not reply to our letter, nor did he make any attempt to contradict its contents. Ronnie's tomatoes had granted us breathing space...

As the St. Paul's apparatus revved into life, Mrs. Doubtfire saved the day. 'My dears, some wonderful news! Jo is returning to New Zealand sooner than expected, possibly at Easter, and the top floor of my house is yours if you would care to share with an old, arthritic lady!' Ronnie and I were in a state of euphoria. We were able to escape from trickery, danger and stress. I was in awe. Once more, a guide had materialised. We were not alone. At the eleventh hour, help came....

***

PART 1

T H E N

HOPE SPRINGS ETERNAL...

Many years ago, a friend had observed that certain people could swear charmingly. It occurred to me that Ronnie was such a person. His voice was rich and his accent impeccable. Profanities issuing from the mouths of some are indeed coarse and offensive and while Ronnie had an extensive vocabulary of curses, none seemed to shock; his enunciation, accompanied by precise diction and the occasional lapse into Geordie dialect, succeeded in reducing one to stitches. It goes without saying that he knew exactly when to put a curb on this natural inclination to eff and blind. Perfection of speech and sensitivity to the delicate perception of others, were to him, of prime importance. I was not so fortunate and referred to on more than one occasion as 'the old trollop', or worse. If I was foolish enough to murmur 'Oh, I'm a silly old bugger', the echo would be 'Oh...you're not **old**!'

I trusted his sensibility and was secure in the knowledge that he would temper his repertoire to any circumstances. The High Mistress, Staff and pupils of St. Paul's looked upon my husband as the perfect gentleman. I wholeheartedly agreed, but how rapturous it was to behold the flip side.

All knew of Ronnie's illness. I did not labour the point, but at the same time was aware of genuine concern when colleagues were enlightened. How lucky we were...

We were now making plans for casting 'The Dream'. Groundwork needed to be done long before the Autumn Term. Again, we hoped for a chorus, this time fairies, goblins and the like. Ronnie was as involved as ever and there were many visitations to the Brook Green Red Cross second-hand headquarters for lengths of material. The most delicious acquisitions came from the Ealing Road sari shops, or rather the Darjeeling Road, as Ronnie affectionately referred to it.

Nothing deterred my husband and Cardiomyopathy was relegated to the distant recesses of our memory. I should say, Ronnie's memory for I was permanently on the lookout.

Moragh was a rock of dependability, but I came to realise that she too did not enjoy good health, but...we all forged ahead, our minds focused on the job in hand.

In the background, our passage at No. 20 still teetered on a knife edge. We lived with the risk of tyranny, but the promise of Betty's asylum shone like a beacon before us. We plotted and planned for our departure. We knew that as soon as Jo had left, we could begin the move...

Our saviour had already given a guided tour of our new home and permission to refurbish and arrange to our taste. Betty's garden, much to Ronnie's delectation, was also at our disposal. We had been delivered from hurt, inconvenience and arrogance.

I had invested much time in the initial preliminaries for 'The Dream' and was hurrying to finish all the scene blocking plus rehearsal schedules by the end of the Spring Term. I made the acquaintance of a gifted Dance specialist, Frances Clarke; with the High Mistress' co-operation, she was employed as an Assistant for all the Movement sequences to be choreographed during the Summer Term. Ronnie was already creating magical designs to complement my woodland set. We, much to Alan Owen's consternation, conceived of a grassy bank dipping down to a forest pool. There was to be a swing device concealed by greenery and foliage. 'The Fairies will **love** it,' beamed Ronnie. 'Mmn,' said Alan with sighing acceptance. He proved to be one of the most accommodating team-mates. His patience, friendship and unflappable conduct in trying Technical Rehearsal resources, where he was often surrounded by demanding, giggling schoolgirls, was nothing short of laudable.

The atmosphere within the Drama Department and school was smooth and productive. Ronnie was fully immersed in exciting work for the BBC where he was happiest. He was in daily touch with close and amusing companions there and the assignments gave every favourable situation for his clever performance. He still found time for his costumes - more important, he was well.

Meanwhile, back at the den of iniquity, No. 20, all was quiet. Harassment, much to our relief, seemed to have taken a temporary backseat. We conceded that as this may continue to rankle beneath the surface, we could not let-up on vigilance but, a little more secure in the knowledge that our bane was powerless to act further, we established moderate calm...

Bina and the babies took up our hours at home and the Spring weather lifted our frame of mind. We told no one of our coming move. Betty's student guest was leaving after Easter. We were then free to lambast Betty's somewhat post-war decorations. 'You know,' thought Ronnie, 'the Frank family must have been as secretive as us when planning their hideaway'. 'Yes darling,' I agreed, 'but at least our lives don't depend on it - at least, I hope not!'

Before departing for Scarborough and the Easter break, we arranged for our flat locks to be changed. This was safely carried out while our landlords were away for the weekend and, as we loaded up for an early getaway, we whistled while we worked. With some ease of mind, we could look forward to a trouble free stay. 'He'll be apoplectic!' said Ronnie.

The day of our return would be hectic. It would be time to put our covert plan into action. Once more, at last, we were in control...

'Jo's on her way to New Zealand,' said Betty excitedly, 'upstairs is now clear and ready for you to begin.' Dear Betty, she was chattering, clucking and hardly able to contain her happiness. 'Come and go as you please. I know there will be much to do, so plan your moving when it's convenient and I will mind the babies if you find yourselves in dire straits.'

Our activities were veiled in mystery. We had no intention of providing Michael with ammunition. We arranged for paint, brushes, ladders and the like to be transported directly to Betty's. Fortuitously, her house was situated at the top of Bowrons Avenue and well away from scrutiny. Ronnie booked a couple of weeks leave from the BBC and intended to decorate. Brian, always ready to lend a hand, agreed to hold ladders, on one condition - Ronnie was not to wear his Union Jack shorts!

We could foresee a grand removal day towards the end of St. Paul's Summer Term. There would be a couple of months to plan our new home and surreptitiously transfer hand luggage, ornaments and clothing when the opportunity arose. Once committed to a definite date, we booked a small van to carry the remainder of our goods and chattels.

I was immensely relieved that Michael had not requested access to our flat. He had, it seems, made no further attempt to encroach. He was lying doggo, but for how long? Our furtive comings and goings, carried out in his absence, provided ample leeway for us to operate without hindrance. Ronnie, flushed with success, repeated 'Well, we're on't roaaad' with boring frequency. He was working hard, which troubled me slightly, but, he was not overtaxed with strain or fear. He was creating a stronghold for us - it was to be Betty's bastion against the foe. He was content.

Our lovely Landlady-to-be was in her element and appointed herself as resident tea-maker when there was a pause for juicy gossip. Ronnie could certainly come in handy there...

My Term was very busy. My mind was put at rest, knowing that Ronnie was being kept under surveillance by our friends. I could draw breath and apply myself to 'The Dream'. Frances, my Dancing lady, was working wonders with the Fairy chorus. I was faced with massive lists for the main auditions. Many girls wished to be considered for leading parts. It was hugely time-consuming. Ronnie sat with me at times, a little paint-spattered I noticed, and supplied invaluable fragments of cheer. Soon, as the weeks melted away, it was done and we were looking ahead towards the inviolability of Betty's and the end of the school year.

Mrs. Williams had settled in amicably. Some would say that time would tell. Bombast was not her strong suit and she established her presence with taste and composure. The Surmistress, now retired, had been succeeded by the Director of Studies. She, no doubt, was an invaluable support and in view of the years she had spent at the school, was qualified to reinforce the High Mistress' responsibilities. I was given to understand that she was well versed in the running of such a traditional machine as St. Paul's. So, all boded well. My arrangements and duties were not subjected to interference, and, after furnishing senior Staff with progress and detail, I could work in peace. I was trusted.

As the days drew near for our exodus, I had one more objectionable meeting with Michael. Ronnie was finishing off his bedroom painting at Betty's while I shopped. I closed the front door of No. 20 before making my way to the car. Michael was trimming the front hedge with electric clippers. I ignored him. He called, 'You'll be receiving a solicitor's letter about the rent. It's going up'. I replied, 'Well we'll have to cross that bridge when we come to it'. In a trice, Michael moved and was facing me, clippers snatched menacingly in hand. He was close enough for me to feel in danger. Luckily, Carol appeared and intervened. I did not tell Ronnie. He did not need to know...

During the forthcoming week, a letter was delivered to Michael, giving the required notice and stating that the flat keys could be collected from our solicitor on the final day of occupancy. It was not acknowledged.

We were ready by the appointed day and the final personal effect which had to be dismantled was a brass Art Deco fire-hood given to us by Margaret some time before she died. It had been an attractive addition to the sitting-room fireplace. We had no intention of leaving it in situ.

With nearly a week's grace we vacated and lodged the keys with the solicitor. By the time Michael was able to take possession of the flat, we were journeying North to Scarborough for the Summer. All our worldly goods were safely gathered in under Betty's bolstering roof.

It came to pass that Michael had indeed been stricken with apoplexy as Ronnie had predicted. On discovery of the missing fire-hood, he had called the neighbourhood Policeman to accompany him to Betty's, whereby he accused us of theft! Dear Betty pleaded ignorance and in due course, phoned to tell us of the calamity. Michael's thoughtless, intrusive behaviour towards Betty enraged us.

We prompted our solicitor to forward a caveat which rendered him mute, leaving us at liberty to spend several happy years in our new home.

***

PART 1

THEN

SCARBOROUGH

The Summer of 1990 was sublime; the skies shining and brilliant. Our other life in Scarborough was a simple one. We did not have any inclination to go abroad. Beach walks, paddling with Charlie and Phyllis and tending our precious home and garden was all-embracing. Occasionally, a Hartlepool day was on the horizon, so, armed with a picnic basket and a generous supply of treacle toffee and Mills & Boon for Louie, we made off across the Moors, or tarried awhile in Whitby. Sometimes, we would take the route over Sutton Bank, via Helmsley. We had accumulated a collection of lavatory stops, so essential in answer to Ronnie's unrelenting diuretic tablets. My considerate, humorous Brother had presented him with a portable plastic bottle, similar to those used in hospital, as a Christmas gift. It was, however, a rather conspicuous red in tone. Part of the journey took in a busy stretch of the A19. Needless to say, my darling's calls of nature became apparent when it was impossible to pull in to a Service station.

'Well, when you have to go, you have to go', declared my beloved as we motored along in the middle lane. Ronnie produced the red receptacle from beneath his seat while the babies looked on, fascinated. I could not look, which was probably just as well. 'Hell's teeth,' said Ronnie, 'pity I'm not more generously endowed, can I hell as like find the aperture'. 'Would you say that that was the story of your life, my love?' I replied testily. By then, Ronnie was piloting apparatus of various kinds and protecting his modesty with a large travelling rug. All at once, while poor Ronnie was thus occupied, a particularly antagonistic articulated wagon was bearing down upon us and flashing a multitudinous number of headlights. 'He can fuck off for a start,' was my husband's summing up of the situation. To my relief, a traffic gap appeared on the left and, as I was in the throes of pulling over to allow our aggressor to overtake, Ronnie began to urinate into his trusty vessel. The lorry plunged ahead as its spiteful driver blasted us with his horn. Ronnie jumped in shock and his invalidity aid emptied its substantial contents into his lap. 'Fuck me! Somebody - please!' was Ronnie's erudite reaction. He was soaked.

Our arrival at Louie's necessitated immediate action. 'You'll 'ave to borrow a pair of my bloomers, our Ron', Louie decreed helpfully. Indeed, those voluminous knickers amply covered Ronnie's vulnerabilities and a lot more besides. 'I say,' said Ronnie, 'when these are hanging on the washing-line at home, people will think they're yours! Oh, and I say, imagine the Doctor's face if I'd had a do and needed to strip off in A & E!!'

As the day drew nearer for our return to Betty's and 'The Dream', we looked back on a merry, sunny and smiling holiday. Ronnie had been wet but well and I was content. Our life was full of pleasure and we rejoiced.

We were shored up through steadfast friendship. I have not yet mentioned how the fellowship of those dear attachments made our lives whole. Philip was greatly loved and regarded as family; my Mother and Brother likewise. They were constant. Furthermore, our fortune was graced by loyal friends who were caring; they expressed a kinship which formed a supreme bond. Within this companionable, outgoing atmosphere we thrived and lazed away from threat and danger. Laughter was predominant and there were long, warm and affectionate dinner parties, lunches and conversations. Our friends came from many walks of life: Theatre, the Church and the School. Neighbours and helpmeets joined the bunch. At every juncture of our lives we gave thanks for them - they have remained, faithful and true.

***

PART 1

THEN

BACK AGAIN....

We returned to Betty's at the end of August. We needed time to be accustomed to inhabiting a first floor. While I concentrated on all my Little-Miss-Make-a-Job activities, Ronnie, enthusiastically pursued by the babies, took in the garden's potential. Mrs. Doubtfire bustled, her cheerful fervour touching to behold. Betty's ground floor proved to be basic and functional. Her sitting-room was situated at the front of the house and her bedroom overlooked the back garden. On waking, she was able to take in Ronnie's improvements to her existing cultivation - at least, I hoped so...I thought of how our presence would ease her loneliness and relieve the tasks which exacerbated her painful arthritis. It was an effortless, edifying sentiment. Betty had acquired a family...

Term began with the usual round of meetings and greetings. Once the mechanism was in place, the pedagogic engine took over and woebetide any unwarranted infiltrator who bunged up the works. I welcomed its smooth flow. Once that was installed, I could get on.

The Art Department, under new management, had now rallied and Ronnie was exempt from the exacting job of scene painting. All other areas of production were in full swing and I was satisfied that 'The Dream' would captivate. It did, and suffice it to say, the Autumn Term and its accomplishments were rewarding.

Dearest Ronnie remained well throughout and his lavish costumes once more drew a sharp intake of breath.

Work on 'The Dream' had been merciless and rehearsals had leaked into Half Term and Saturday mornings, where, single-handed, I managed over a hundred students without additional support from Staff. Ronnie and my staunch Theatre Technician, Alan Owen, were my only helpers. The dedicated girls' conduct was assiduous. The play, teaching commitments, Drama groups and School responsibilities in general had left me exhausted.

On the third night of the play's run, a puzzling invitation arrived from the High Mistress. I was asked to join her and the Director of Studies for a quiet moment before the curtain went up.

Dutifully, I found myself knocking on the High Mistress' portal. 'Do come in, Sue, it's only us'. Extraordinary. I was treated to a show of generosity and manifest praise for the production. In fact, the appreciation I received was exceptional. Before leaving, it was made known to me that their interest in my academic performance was exceeding the boundaries of the Drama Department.

Ronnie was filled in with the details. 'Mmn', he titillated (would be his choice of word - typical!) 'Where's the catch?'

Moragh, my dear friend and colleague, was leaving. Shortly after 'The Dream', she confided that serious illness was interfering with her life. I felt the loss deeply. One does not encounter such concord many times in life. I knew that it would endure, but Moragh's wisdom, unselfishness and invigorating attachment to teaching and the girls, would be greatly missed.

Once again, the volume of work and growing Department required assistance. I had instituted various departments within a Department: Private Speech Training lessons, Dramatics Clubs, Student-led Productions, Spoken English, Educational Drama for the junior school and at least two major Theatre Productions a year.

Much to my delight, Drama was introducing itself as a Cross-Curricular asset and as a teaching aid, was merged by other academic areas.

Helen Doust joined the Department in the Spring of 1990. She proved to be a gifted and natural teacher. The girls responded readily to her humorous, resolute attitude and I was left in no doubt that her unwavering sponsorship would enhance all that I had worked so hard to found.

Ronnie's progress was steady. He was the bulwark. Without him, my work would not have been possible. He would listen, enthralled, while I gave a root and branch depiction of each development. In turn, Betty became a mainstay in our domestic life. Her devotion to Charlie and Phyllis was boundless and when we were diligent or preoccupied, she was there to boost and prop up.

I was happy that most of Ronnie's work centred around Radio. He was fond of broadcasting and he was good at it. Line learning and adrenalin-boosting Theatre performance could have proved to be stressful and dangerous. Members of the Radio Repertory Company were booked for specific roles and working blocks. This was an added advantage, for it permitted Ronnie to have the benefit of time off to spend in the garden, or skulk around his favourite stamping grounds in search of an outlandish oddity - oddity being the operative word.

My dearest wasted no time in re-designing Betty's plot. Fortunately, she was very compliant. It was Ronnie's intention to dream up a patio area where one could 'Sit and ruminate', he explained. 'I know I like to sit among flowers and chew over a few things', he added in courtly mode. Betty was bewitched.

I did, at the same time, ask Ronnie to heed his language. 'When you're grappling with undergrowth,

darling, do think before you vilify the air with "Oh Fuck!".
Betty may be very sensitive, not to mention Marjorie next
door, or the Indian neighbours'. Ronnie answered
impudently 'When have you known me to be foul-mouthed
in the presence of a lady?' 'Well, you are frequently so in
my presence,' I acknowledged and could have bitten my
tongue out. 'Hmn...' was the reply, 'If the cap fits...!'

In spite of all, Ronnie behaved impeccably when within
earshot of discerning old ladies and those of another
culture. His seating plan was taking shape, complete with
trellis and Handel, a gorgeous climbing rose. The
perfumed blooms were shell pink, their petals fringed with
a deeper tint. When all was finished and Betty sat,
ruminating, beneath this display, she launched the vista
with 'God Bless this Royal Enclosure!'

Years later, when I became a gardener, Handel was one
of the first roses I planted, in memory of Betty and the
rapture of rumination....

***

PART 1

THEN

ST PAUL'S GIRLS' SCHOOL....AS I SAW IT... (continued)

My meeting, before Christmas, with the High Mistress and the Director of Studies had been almost forgotten. In truth, I had paid scant attention to it. Our lives were filled with enough incident for it to be delegated to the recesses of one's mind. As far as I was aware, my following in the path of Dick Whittington was at an end. 'Are you free tomorrow afternoon, Mrs. Herdman?' enquired the school Secretary. 'The High Mistress would **so** like to meet you'. Dear Heather flashed across my consciousness....

When I entered Mrs. Williams' study, I was a little surprised to find the Director of Studies there. She seemed rather flushed. Mrs. Williams was quietly effusive as I was invited to take a seat. 'Thank you so much for coming along, Sue. We have looked forward to speaking to you about a matter which is of much interest to us and - we hope, to you'. I did not reply, but waited.

The Director of Studies watched silently. 'For some time, we have been aware of your continued success in the Drama Department; most of all, we have noticed the understanding you have with both junior and senior girls. We agree that this could also be invaluable beyond the reaches of your own Department.' Still I did not speak. She proceeded: 'The Head of Middle School will be taking a Headship from September of this year and her position will be vacant. The Director of Studies and I feel sure that you would be an admirable successor'. This was the drift of the dialogue. The situation was indelibly printed upon my memory. It would be fair to say that, at the time, I was thunderstruck and I remember expressing shock. My assumption was that the Head of Middle School, responsible for the welfare of two Middle Year groups and six Form Teachers, was an academic post and by no stretch of the imagination was I scholarly. I reminded them of this very forcibly.

I had never overestimated my qualifications. An eminent Theatre specialist once advised, 'Do not, when called to Audition, say you can ride a horse if you cannot. You will be easily found out!' How true...

'We envisage a different role,' my Chief unfolded, 'that is, one of a pastoral nature. You are particularly gifted in this respect and we know that those difficult intermediary teenage years need very careful treatment.

I was on the receiving end of a very persuasive argument. This suggested promotion was in a different league and undoubtedly out of my comfort zone. Before I could say more, the Director of Studies interceded, 'Look upon this, Sue, as a transference of skills'.

I had been assured most precisely that the post would be well within my capabilities. The expectations would be different. 'We realise that you will need to think about this most carefully, Sue. We would be delighted to consider you for the post. Perhaps you will come back to me within the next few days'.

I think it would be fair to say that I nearly staggered from the High Mistress' quarters. I could not conceal my satisfaction. As usual, my first thought was - Ronnie, Ronnie and his reaction, Ronnie and his perceptive comment after that initial meeting a while ago - his, 'Where's the catch?'

There was much to talk about. I needed Ronnie. I needed his comfort, his logic, analysis and advice. We would ruminate beneath the arbour's Handel retreat and be rooted in common sense.

'Sue, this is very important,' Ronnie said, 'and, while we do need to think it over very carefully, it is an immense breakthrough. Think of what you have achieved so far. You have given those girls insight into human nature and all it entails. You have set out to make them think, to empathise with others and understand them. In that safe environment, you have shown them how to develop sensitivity and imagination. Darling, you have introduced them to those qualities through some wonderful Drama. You know as well as I do, that to have neglected them could have resulted in an unbalanced development'.

'Oh, Mr Pomp!' I giggled.

'Yes', - Ronnie was well into it all now - 'these girls are academically smart, but important as they are, there is more to life than exams. Now, they can respond to other people. They're going to need that wherever they go. And - not all Paulinas are brimming with sophistication and confidence. What about those poor little souls?'

'Are you done?' I nodded. 'Most important of all,' Ronnie continued, 'this position in the school is central. You can help them even more through a very tricky period of their lives. Somebody is putting you there for a very good reason and I don't mean the High Mistress. All you have to consider is the Drama Department and will you be able to do both. Who is going to carry that? You can't allow all you've worked for to go under. Go for it, my darling. I'll be here - always. You know that.'

Tears welled. Where had he come from, this guardian? Strange...one can wait for half a lifetime before finding such cornucopia...riches come in many guises.

'Come on, petal, get the kettle on,' said Ronnie, plucking a Handel rosette from the awning, 'put that in a vase, Alice. It's for a star!'

Days elapsed before I gave my decision. Mrs. Williams was delighted. I was still given to thought. My mulling over took place on car journeys. I recollected that not long after joining St. Paul's, Mrs. Brigstocke had alluded to a request being made for me to become a Sixth Form Tutor. Apparently, the Director of Studies and another Staff Tutor had appealed for this,

'I refused, **of course** and not because you would be incapable, **certainly not**, you would make a **sterling** job of it' stated Mrs. B., **'but**...you could **not** run that growing Department **and** take on **such** responsibility. It would be **much** too **much**...'

I was interested to note that, again, the same person, together with a different ruler, had put me forward for this added leadership. Now, the workload would be a colossal accountability. My thoughts probed no further...

Helen Doust carried all before her. Her excellent teaching mirrored my own methods and our like-mindedness made for an unruffled, effortlessly-run Department. At the same time, we fostered good relations with the English Department and it was always included in discussions of our aims and policy.

The Head of English was leaving. Young and hoping to increase her family, she was also ambitious and not keen to remain under another's umbrella. I could identify. Her successor was unreservedly different, largely recognised for her mondaine fashion sense and open, unconventional attitude. She was not anyone's 'creature'. Her predecessor was heard to use this curious allusion, presumably fearful of what she could become. With reference to whom? It was an engrossing riddle. It seemed there were reasons for her wish to escape.

The Staff Room was buzzing with raised, excited voices. There was an air of expectancy and commotion. Attention was focused upon a large, imposing and formal notice. I bided my time, then approached. By then, Staff had dispersed to attend to various duties and I could peruse the statement more closely. I was stunned.

Here was an advertisement for Head of Middle School! Surely, there must be some mistake, thought I. No, the post for which I had been propositioned was being plugged internally. There followed details for application and a précis of procedure. I retreated to the Portakabin, trying to rationalise the event. I rang Ronnie. He, too, was confounded. I tried to skim the surface, but Ronnie as ever was quick to grasp the nettle. 'See her, Sue. Find out what's going on.'

The High Mistress was unavailable and I sought advice from her Deputy alias Director of Studies. 'We were obliged to advertise internally before we could officially appoint. I do hope this will not deter you from applying, Sue'.

'I do find this somewhat disconcerting,' I replied, 'I will, however, give the matter immediate consideration'.

That, of course, is where the concern should have been laid to rest. I should have closed the episode forever by declining to apply. I had allowed myself to be flattered - always unwise. Ronnie, equally unsettled, assured me that in view of what had taken place, this was possibly a formality and they would not renege on previous obligation.

Together, Ronnie and I reflected upon the inconclusiveness of the affair. There would be many highly- motivated individuals, scratching out their applications, little knowing that someone else had been earmarked for the job. I should have backed out and I did not. In not doing so, I condoned what was happening. I reasoned that by making an application myself, I could still be the winner of a trophy I dearly coveted. We reap what we sow....

I allowed time before submitting my petition. It was a sound, powerful tender of personal, Educational beliefs based on extensive experience both Theatrical and Educative. It was a passionate expose of my vocation.

It must have been a measure of subconscious reluctance to take part in this affair that prompted me to delay proffering my bid. It was a jogging memo from the

High Mistress that eventually sealed my fate. The next and final stage of what seemed to be a bungling formula was the holding of Interviews. Called to attend, I was unfazed by question and answer. They were well acquainted with my views and aspirations; repetition was boring and unnecessary in the circumstances. Yet I had allowed myself to be party to this exercise and now the consequences lay before me...

The weeks went by. I make no secret of the fact that I was half hoping to be unsuccessful. I would then return to the peace of my Portakabin without further heartache. Ronnie was his loving self and we spent happy hours together, savouring the garden, Betty residing in the Royal Enclosure and excited visits from Bina and Jasu who filled in the gaps about the pervasive Monsters of No. 20. 'We miss...very much..', concluded Jasu.

In the intervening time, I found myself being alert, watching other members of Staff much more intently than before, particularly those who had applied for 'my' job...various Heads of Departments were in the running. Nearly all were formidable. There was only one candidate whom I thought qualified. She was a member of the English Department and an intelligent, capable young woman who possessed joie de vivre, femininity and style. I sincerely wished her every success.

It came to pass that she did not succeed; nor did anyone else. The post was awarded to me after all. A notice was posted and it met with undisguised dismay. I read their faces like a book - an ex-Actress to be Head of Middle School! Had they taken complete leave of their senses?

My Appointment was announced at the following Staff Meeting and met with total, belligerent silence. The Deputy Head attempted to gloss over the reaction with her congratulations, but all in vain. I was to be skewered....

From then on, life in the Drawing Room became a trifle uncomfortable. My closest friends were very complimentary and glad for me, but the remainder distanced themselves. I discovered that promotion of this nature brought about a climate of change, not to mention unrest. One became one of them rather than one of us...there was a tinge of distrust and a chariness seeped into the mien of those with whom I had been on friendly terms. I had not changed, but others thought I had. Perhaps I would be looked upon as a stoolie...

The forerunner of my Appointment was popular. That did not surprise me, for I had found her to be upright, high-powered and assertive. At the same time, she was approachable, jolly, extremely co-operative and kind towards me. She sacrificed much time to familiarise me with her duties. Obviously, she had not been advised that, in future, the office was to operate on a very different footing.

As a result, I was apprised of administration and managerial strategy. Most of this dreary business involved organisation of numbers for exams, room allocation and copping recalcitrant pupils and Staff. Where was the creativity? Would I ever get around to implement the job I had been elevated to do? The magnitude of the whole weighed heavily and getting a grip of this pedestrian detachment was going to be unnerving. Most importantly, this was not what I had negotiated and acceded to. Only time would tell, and I had to start somewhere. Ronnie said, 'Darling do it your way!'

Helen Doust had been briefed about the coming changes. I had been contracted for an initial period of two years as Head of Middle School. This came with an increase in salary which went down very well with Ronnie who predicted more trips to the Portobello Road. I was to remain as Director of Drama, but Helen would deputise. Secretly, I determined not to release the reins entirely of my precious province. We would liaise, plan and govern together.

In my new capacity, I was to be berthed on The Marble. The office was small and I endeavoured to create an inviting aura within its limits. My worthy antecedent had carried out assignments in the glare of searchlight illumination. I did not intend to put the screws on my charges. So, mid filing cabinets, a desk and word processor, I installed lamplight, a kettle and teacups. Pastoral care would take on a measure of Portakabin intimacy. I would not be inveigled into becoming a commandant.

The Drama Department arrangements were finalised. Helen was to direct the Autumn production. She chose to present a musical, 'Salad Days' which was certainly ambitious. I had no doubt that she could pull it off and was thankful to be able to delegate this sensational project.

The Summer Term was ending and my forbear was about to disappear forever, taking with her the safety net on which I had come to rely. In all probability, I was to be cast adrift in hostile waters. Determined to think about that tomorrow, I returned to the sanctity of home. I could hear a sparkling rendition of 'Hey, Mr. Watchercaller, what ye doin' tonight...' radiating from the Royal Enclosure.

'Now close your eyes'. 'Ronnie, what have you done?' I exclaimed as I opened a tiny leather box. It contained an Art Deco diamond ring. 'Well, I thought that if you were going to hobnob with wealthy parents in your new job, you should have diamonds. A girl should always have diamonds'....

I was beginning to feel physically sick at the prospect of being Head of Middle School. Our holiday in Scarborough had uplifted me and now I was facing the unknown. I had not been issued with anything resembling a Job Description. I feared the blitz of sleepless nights as I attempted to make sense of Form Lists, Agendas, information for Form Teachers and a jungle of documents and data. I felt that I had been deserted.

All too soon I was to realise that the High Mistress had enough misgivings of her own. Life-belts were needed elsewhere...

I longed to renounce all. Abdication shone like a pharos before me. No, I would not run from this fear. What? Give in to those who were certain an actress would succumb to failure? Never!

From day one, I created my own lists. I took paths which were familiar to me; those within my charge came under my jurisdiction. These were my methods and I insisted on adherence. This brought its own brand of unpopularity. The worm as they knew it, had turned...

I was hoping to lead a Team. I knew there would be a differing of opinion but vigorous discussion could be worthwhile, provocative and forward-thinking. I collected the Form Teachers together and outlined ideas for future schemes. Some women, with the exception of one, were control freaks; there was only one way, one process - theirs. I was a novice and to be humoured. Patience, tolerance and flexibility were required - from me. As an actor, I was aware of body language, facial expression and physical bearing. I encountered the lot during those meetings and there were few signs of generosity; instead, I met with personality clashes and impediment.

A few weeks into the Term, I was faced with my first altercation. The weekly meeting had been particularly tiresome. Valuable minutes had been squandered and given to discussion about orange peel jettisoned on the main stairway. The youngest Form Teacher labelled the meeting a waste of time and walked out.

After, while agreeing with her sentiment, I explained that I would not permit rudeness and however facile items of Agenda were, they would be dealt with consecutively. In future, a formal schedule would be submitted and she and her colleagues expected to maintain it. I was fair but adamant.

The following morning, I received a letter of apology. It outlined her regret, mentioned a sleepless night and the hope that our pleasant understanding would not be spoiled. I had anticipated that pastoral care encompassed my custody of the girls; I had not portended that it would embrace adults.

I never failed to marvel at the reactions and observations of these grown women. Ronnie was very amused when told of a visit by the Nurse. She came to my office groaning under an imposing armful of medical examination lists. Presumably, she was taking a breather, or some respite between doses of Paracetamol. 'Oh, it's just like a boudoir!' she exclaimed, gawking about her. 'All psychological Nurse,' I returned. She was caught in the headlights and so made a quick getaway. 'Perhaps she thought you were, in your new capacity, going to put the 'fluence on her', noted Ronnie.

I coped. I coped with lists. I coped with attitude, hurtful comment and emotional immaturity - that is, I coped with the female Staff. The girls were fine. I was left alone to sink or swim. Some guidance was given when there were Parental Meetings, but on those occasions, I left it to the expertise of the Director of Studies/Deputy to outline the knottiness of curriculum. I made my own headway, maintained a good relationship with the girls and formulated the contents of an impressive filing cabinet! Yes, there were some frantic spells, but I survived - alone.

I was alone. As Director of Drama, I had been alone, but this novel, untried and unexplored territory presented loneliness of a different calibre. Ronnie delivered me from the realms of desperation on several occasions. He was there at home ready to listen and advise. He was able to ground me, to love me and to understand. I could laugh hysterically at his mischievous impersonations of the more outlandish members of Staff. Ronnie was my anchor and my home, a bolt hole for sense and stability.

I did find instances of amusement as I grew more accustomed to my role.

I noticed a couple of Staff patrolling in unison; they could be seen on sentry duty at Break times, Lunch times and before morning Assembly, on the watch for those intent on flouting their petty rules. The heedless girls wielded their own brand of savoir faire and flummoxed them. As a result, peccadillos were reported to me and oblique references to lack of discipline were implied. I suppose these were made in a vain attempt to have a go. Admittedly, on one occasion my reaction and retort was a trifle acerbic. 'As to lack of discipline, I wonder how you think I manage one hundred and fifty girls on Saturday mornings, without Staff support I hasten to add, for play rehearsals'.

I had invited this meritorious teacher to take a seat at the beginning of the aforementioned exchange. I happened to be leaning by my office filing cabinet. Her audacity knew no bounds for she went on to accuse me of adopting a superior position if I continued to stand. 'Very well, I will sit at my desk if it will make you feel more comfortable. Please do not infer that I am incompetent. Perhaps you need to put your own house in order'. Her face reddened as she tried to reassert herself. Having failed to do so, she excused herself and beat a hasty retreat. Later, it came to my notice, or rather hearing, that she was reclining in the Drawing Room and near to expiration with the injustice of it all.

Ronnie was entertained with a blow by blow account. When I mentioned to Mrs. Williams, in passing, news of how I was grappling with the tiresome, immature conduct of some Staff, she in turn mentioned it to her Deputy who was most reassuring and knew the identity of the culprits without having to be informed!

The administrative side of the post was more of a nuisance than an occupation. I did, however, make time to keep a watchful eye on the Drama Department. Helen was making excellent progress with the Musical and I was pleased to entrust my realm to her care.

This new position was all the more difficult because I was bending over backwards to lay the foundations for it without assistance. I was expected to fill the shoes of my forebear. To be fair, the Staff it seemed had not been advised of change. My passage might have been smoother if adequate explanation had been given in the first place.

Ronnie was well. He was never far from my thoughts. He managed our domestic life and set me free to concentrate on the excessive demands of the school.

Weekends and brief Half Term holidays brought favourable situations to rectify my feeling of neglect. Ronnie did not even consider the possibility of disregard. 'A trip to Portobello is what you need. We can spend some of that extra dosh you're earning!'

Furthermore, I was experiencing agonising hip pain. In fact, I was lame. I could not control the limp which was becoming more and more pronounced. It was very noticeable to everyone. The hassle was debilitating and not calculated to produce an image of crème de la crème. Added to this annoyance were some niggling menopausal symptoms. Heaving off the duvet in the middle of the night to reveal a shivering Ronnie, became a regular vexation.

I was making headway. I disliked meetings, largely because I did not feel au fait with those attending, but management of affairs was becoming less exasperating and I felt some sense of achievement in having fought my way through. One advantage in working a blank canvas is that one invents a scheme peculiar and acceptable to oneself. My practice was honest and true. I had no time for the devious and power-hungry. The word soon got around...

My meetings with the High Mistress and her Deputy were friendly and encouraging, but in the main vague. I was far too busy keeping the plates spinning to allow my attention to wander too far in that direction. Fortunately, the two of them seemed to be enjoying a useful alliance, which augured well for the rest of us toiling in the engine room.

I suspected that Helen Doust was incredibly tense about the Musical. Her minute consideration for detail was bringing about petulance in rehearsal. I called in and engendered some revitalization into the session. After that, although Helen remained in a state of suspended anxiety, the show ran its successful course and many, including the Deputy Head, termed it a 'triumph'. Poor Helen, although stricken with bouts of nausea and vomiting on the First Night, came through victorious.

The last day of Term brought me almost to the brink of delirium. Relief surged through every fibre of my being. The High Mistress gave munificent congratulations on a rewarding first Term, but I was, inwardly, on my way to our other life. Scarborough awaited us and there I would find repose. I was tempted to say 'a cessation of hostilities'!

Little did I know that in the fullness of time a series of events would trigger a precarious and miserable state of affairs. They would be beyond my control...

In January of 1992, I made a very important decision. I refused to allow administration and the preoccupation of office minutiae to obliterate my chief quest. I wished to care for the girls' wellbeing, happiness and development. Drama was my device. First, I made sure that Head of Middle School had dotted all the I's and crossed the T's of governmental regime. This was vital for those who were slavish to routine and form-filling; for those who were part of a mechanism and directly dependent upon another bureaucrat.

I had given Ronnie a thumbnail sketch of my plan. Now was the time to put it before the High Mistress. Mrs. Williams and I shared the same views about what constituted Education. We believed fervently that learning should be for life, holistic and in the pursuit of breadth. So, in my meetings with her, I was preaching to the converted. We were vehement in our concern for the children, each and every one of them. Not all at St. Pauls' were able to succeed, excel and conquer. Many Paulinas were lacking in confidence and, although academically clever, were ill-at-ease. I came across disparate students who were afraid of their multifaceted and often beautiful peers.

Ronnie had espoused my proposal and so did the High Mistress. My scheme would involve the whole of the Vth Year. It was to be a Drama/Documentary programme entitled 'The Fragile Asset'. Its central theme - Confidence. All students would be performing in role play, improvisation, movement and music. Encouragement to develop self-assurance by experimenting and concentrating on areas where they were least confident, was the object of the exercise. The Study was to be presented before an invited Vth Year Parental audience.

Rehearsal was intensive. Many students had not taken part in such a gamble before and it required courage and perseverance to master skills for which they were unaccustomed. This project was in addition to my daily school duties and it was a gruelling assignment. The result was rewarding beyond measure, both for the girls and me. Vth Year Form Teachers, the High Mistress, her Deputy and all parents backed the performance and were astounded at the girls' professional achievement. It had been a revelation and an accomplishment.

As Ronnie, ever faithful, and I made our way to the car at the end of the evening, we were followed by Form

Teachers and some colleagues. None offered words of praise of the girls or recognition of their huge attainment. All were silent.

The following morning, the youngest Vth Year Form Teacher in my charge whispered conspiratorially 'Sue, I don't know how you managed to do it, in view of all your other obligations'. In addition, I received warm congratulations from the High Mistress. Her card read, 'That was a real Head of Middle School production. Thank you'. Likewise, her Deputy was equally ebullient: 'Do it your way, Sue!'

Ronnie's glimmering message of goodwill meant more to me than any: 'You were beautiful, Alice!' At last, I had found my purpose. My efforts were rewarded ten thousand fold when a Vth Year student tapped on my office door. 'Mrs. Herdman, I just wanted to thank you. I am thrilled. I managed to do it. You said I could and - I believed you!'

The High Mistress called a meeting for the entire Staff. Usually, these followed a standard pattern and the same people were tediously vocal. The careless scattering of orange peel was, mercifully, avoided.

A provoking, but very interesting motion was aired. The High Mistress put forward a radical plan. Her theory was that to students almost certainly bound for higher education, GCSEs, easily acquired, were largely irrelevant. She suggested that it may be possible to devise original study schedules and restrict the number of GCSEs to seven. That way, more demanding courses could be supplemented and assessed by the school.

Her inclination was that broader education of bright girls at St. Paul's should take precedence over monotonous, automatic examination work. I thought it seemed to be an admirable idea and, as far as I could speculate, so did my colleagues. The theory was met with animation and agreement. I recalled that this had been a view shared by Winchester and Manchester Grammar schools. I found the meeting very interesting. I observed and listened. Much of this would reflect on me and my work, for I was directly in charge of the girls whom this would affect. After that I removed myself from its implications for the time being...this was within the sphere of pure academia. I preferred to keep all that it entailed at arm's length. My responsibility had a boundary and I was not disposed to cross it. At the same time, I could see, very clearly, what Mrs. Williams was trying to do and it was an aspiration I would uphold.

There followed a peaceful hiatus. The Staff despots had other rousing fish to fry and were intent on ardent discussion, so I was left in peace. Criticism of my tactics occupied unimportant status and I rejoiced in a ceasefire. I caught fragments of frenzied dialogue and noted pow-wowing groups in isolated corners. I had no doubt that the topic of discourse was the High Mistress' objective. I was not given to hanging around in the Drawing Room, except to have words with close friends. Much occupied me and I was concerned with minding my own business.

Helen had had enough of responsibility, was tired, stressed and ready to go. I was disappointed for she had been such an asset to the Department, but, consideration for a young husband and family was her prime concern at that time. Fortunately, she agreed to stay until the end of the School Year and I was able to arrange interviews for her replacement. Eleanor Zeal joined the Staff of the Drama Department in the Autumn of 1992. A great deal of water was to pass under the bridge before then...

Parents of Middle School girls were encouraged to attend a meeting. Ronnie encouraged **me** to make sure my diamonds were in evidence on that occasion! I did need to invigorate my nerve-wracked energy. I found that, in this context, encounters with powerful, influential Mothers and Fathers could overawe me. I was feeling my way. The High Mistress, ever sensitive to my probationary state, said, 'Leave it to us, Sue'. In my role as Director of Drama, my natural province, I was a superior master of my craft. Here, I was placed upon shifting sands.

Mrs. Williams unveiled her theory. Her audience listened, eyes fixed in glassy stare. Pins dropped but no one could hear. The High Mistress reached the closing words of her address and questions were invited. The tone was contentious. The tense atmosphere and cavilling exchanges brought about unease. These guardians, exam-fevered and dogmatic about their offspring securing at least ten GCSEs, were obdurate. What now?

In all probability, the High Mistress was reinforced by the advice of her contiguous academic circle and steamed ahead. It came to pass that Parents did not want Education in its broadest sense. They wanted results. What a pity. I could appreciate that Mrs. Williams' brave foray had been destined to enhance, not lower academic standards. I can only assume that those who advised and agreed were nowhere to be seen when the axe fell...

I was aware of disturbance within the School. Uncertainty filters through and cracks appear. By the end of the Spring Term, I was saddled with administration and once more taken up with lists, numbers and examination arrangements.

Ronnie and I relaxed into the Easter break. The turbulence of St. Paul's was placed at a distance and I could step into the tranquillity of West Bank and its solitude. Philip tempted us with delectable banquets and time spent in the Spring garden was ameliorating. It was good to be free from discord.

'What do you think she'll do?' enquired Ronnie as he fed his roses. 'Do you think Mrs. Williams has been adequately supported? After all, she came into a horrendously difficult regime and as far as I can see, it would be almost impossible to survive without the help of someone who knew the ropes'. Ronnie was making a very concise observation. 'What are you driving at, Ronnie?'

'Well, what's her Deputy doing? How long has she been at the School? She must know it backwards. From what you tell me, she did much of the spadework for Mrs. Brigstocke. I wonder if Mrs. Williams has been encouraged to break eggs with a big stick too soon? I mean, couldn't she have been steadied? Interestingly, and this is something I've been thinking about recently, her Deputy must have known what a furore **your** appointment would create. So why did she encourage it? She had known all those women for years! You'd need half the Household Cavalry to deal with that lot!' Ronnie's imagery - priceless, as usual! 'As I ruminate,' he continued with significant pomposity, 'I wonder, did **she** apply for the job? Mmn...'

Ronnie's street-wise summation of the circumstances made me think. Whatever the mise en scene, I could do nothing but see my part through.

The commencement of the Summer Term brought a lighter mood within the School. Examinations hovered, but girls could be seen taking advantage of the sunshine on terraces and tennis courts. My energy was renewed and I tackled burdensome tasks with something akin to resourcefulness. I doubted that these chores would ever fill me with a pinnacle of anticipation. The High Mistress appeared on the threshold of my office several times. I sensed her nervousness and a quavering uncertainty. What had transpired? I had noticed that her link or congruity with the Deputy seemed strained, whereas before there had been a noticeable bond.

'Sue, things are not going well with my plan. Parents, Staff and now the Governors are undecided. I fear there has been some obstruction and, in turn, dissatisfaction with the way I'm handling things'. I was in a very awkward position; all I could do was listen and try to reassure. I was incredibly sorry, but remained in a cleft stick. I did not feel qualified to venture further.

As the Term progressed, I became aware of rebellious Staff groups; many individuals bold enough to voice criticism of the High Mistress and her managerial skills in weekly meetings. I quashed the offenders, but gossip suggested mutiny. 'The School may well implode', was a phrase dropped in my hearing. This discontent, as far as I could see, stemmed from the High Mistress' supposed inability to call the shots. I was detached and oblivious of detail or fact. I confess, I found that this was a comfortable bearing. I gave consolation to Mrs. Williams when I felt able to do so. I liked and respected her. She was a dignified Director who placed emphasis on academic excellence, respect for authority and a sensitivity towards the less privileged.

I had had great regard for Heather Brigstocke, but all incumbents are different. As time went on, I began to see that this quiet, gentle lady was being trampled underfoot by those who knew how to make enough noise. The fact that she was discriminating and aesthetically pleasing rather than glitzy or imperious, led some to question her authority. For me, a picture was forming...

With each visit from the High Mistress, I became more conversant with her standpoint. The inordinately demanding Parents I had surveyed during the meeting for the GCSE debacle, had, it seemed, misunderstood the recommended course of action and complained to Governors. In the meantime, the feeling in the Staff Room among the cabal who had also tried to victimise me, was escalating. Our ruler's lack of authority, as seen there and with the fast set, seemed to be the problem.

As I suspected, a large proportion of the Staff were decent, industrious individuals who were ignorant of the power game that was being played out. This unfortunate consensus had rubbed off on the girls and authorization seemed to have become linked with the High Mistress' conduct and personality. She had not set out to be intimidating and so was branded weak or ineffectual.

I, too, had been hounded but unlike Mrs. Williams, I retaliated. Like her, I preferred to work with co-operation and fellowship, but some will propel, shove and, as a result, force animosity. It might be argued that moralistic and scholarly virtues are not necessarily negative, but appropriate to a Head teacher. Presumably, Mrs. Williams had not presented herself to the Governors as a starry, in vogue, modish figure. She must have thought that they were quite happy for her to take a different trend. One does not change one's public face for purposes of the job. If a media luminary familiar with the ways of the beau monde and of charismatic clout had been required, they could have offered the post to a megastar. I carried all this reasoning home; Ronnie and I ruminated far into the night about a very worrying state of affairs...

I had a casual, friendly and interesting brush with the Deputy Head. We were moving towards the middle of Term. As always, she was personable, softly spoken and - manipulative. Again, I listened and watched. I realised how easy it would be for the naïve to be beguiled. I was amused. Yet the following colloquy was unnerving. 'I am here to let you know that I propose to begin a Sabbatical year and (pause) the plan is not to come back'. Ah...

What followed, in the course of our strange conversation, put a possible stamp on Ronnie's wily theory. 'When I was unsuccessful in my application for the post, I said that I would not bear any resentment toward the new High Mistress'. My thoughts raced. If one does not feel resentful, it does not occur to one to mention it. I wondered... Only time would tell and the political rollercoaster would have to run its orbit.

I carried out my duties efficiently. At the same time, I noted all tasks and listed them into a comprehensive Job Description. Whenever I could foresee a break, I walked about the School, intent on observation and deliberately making time to talk to students and answer questions.

There was a need to absorb tone. How far had the canker spread? All seemed well...

I adopted professional detachment. It was imperative to remain objective when the High Mistress' urgency to unload her sorrowful grievances brought her again and again to my door. I sympathised, but I had to remain neutral.

I remained reserved and kept my own counsel. I did not know the whole story...

Towards the end of Term, the disagreeable, appalling matter came to a head. Mrs. Williams confided to me that she had been asked to resign. She had the will to resist and continued to make a stand. Her address on Governor's Day was a tour de force. Throughout, Ronnie and I made no secret of the fact that we were advocates. At home, Ronnie was vociferous, and, needless to say, colourful in his compendium of insults fired at the enemy. True, it seemed to have been a vindictive campaign.

Granted, the High Mistress may have fallen short in areas where she was not gifted. None of us have unlimited talents or, maybe, predilection for the dispensation of management. Perhaps she had been let down by the lack of administrational backing, some of which could have been infused by her Deputy. Perhaps a bitter rivalry had existed. The business, however, was still ongoing and when the chips are down, the fight for self-preservation predominates.

I had always been on good terms with some of the Governors. Many expressed great interest in the progress of the Drama Department and I had had some dynamic discussion with members of the Board. There was, I am sure, a mutual respect. The Governing body was out and about on Governor's Day.

On this occasion, I was in for a further shock when an acquaintance took my attention. 'Mrs. Herdman, I feel I should make you aware of a very perplexing and ungracious letter which was forwarded to the Governors by a senior member of Staff. It objected to your appointment as Head of Middle School, saying that you were totally unsuitable for such an academic post. I will leave that with you.' The Letter Writer was then identified.

I was transfixed with astonishment, shock and a great deal of anger. I retired to a bench on The Marble. I was trembling. A caring Upper Fourth student came across. 'Mrs. Herdman, are you OK? May I get you a glass of water?' How I loved Paulinas! 'You make everything worthwhile' were the only words I could manage to utter.

Bewildered, I made my way to the silent, empty 'boudoir' and wept. I thought of how the world of Theatre, so often maligned and criticised for its malice, could not hold a candle to this kind of vicious cruelty. This I knew would have to be dealt with. When? I recovered and made my way to the Hall for the commencement of the Governor's Day address. I pinpointed the Letter Writer. She was seated in the upper Gallery. I watched her with undisguised dislike. As one of the Form Teachers in my care, she had gone out of her way to be a thorn in my side. I had excused her, tried to understand her reasoning and made allowances. Had she applied for my job? I thought I had found in her a grain of geniality. I waited for the High Mistress to lead the Governing party from the platform and then walked to the foot of the Gallery stairs.

'I wonder if I could have a few words. I know you'll want to be off, but this won't take long'. I led the antagonist into my office. 'Do sit down'. I made plain my reason for the consultation. Her face blanched and she shifted uncomfortably in the upright chair. 'I feel so much resentment for you,' I continued, 'that it will be quite impossible for me to accept you as a colleague. You have behaved in a despicable manner and I can only presume that you would have gone on to discredit me even further'. I can hardly bring myself to write her reply!

'I was undecided when I was putting the letter into the post-box. I did not know whether I would be doing the right thing...' 'Well,' I said, 'it seems your unkind action has not gone without note'. By this time, I was aware of her tears not far from the surface. 'I hadn't thought you could be steely,' she blithely admitted.'I always felt that you were too soft for the job'. 'Life is full of surprises, isn't it?' I replied. 'Tell me, is that the underhand method you always use, for it's just as well that we know where we stand'. Then the tears ran. 'I'm sorry'.

'Perhaps we should wipe the slate clean now that you know I can be, as you put it - steely. Thank you for coming to see me'. I ushered her to the door. I was not sorry to see her go. I would wipe the slate clean, but would the softness she spoke of return, or would I remain forever - steely!

'Oh, I always knew you could be steely,' remarked Ronnie raffishly, 'come 'ere Miss Jackboots!' We then went on to agree that it was pathetic to have to resort to unpleasantness in order to function. 'Jealousy is a destructive and contemptible trait,' said Ronnie, 'now some of the other deadly sins are much more interesting - now what about lust!' Things at home were back to basics...and I was comforted...

A few days remained before the Summer holiday. When all was done, I had time to dwell on an unmitigating contingency. It was not only substantial Parental opinion which had found its way across the Governors' table. Staff had put in their two pennyworth. Parents worries could not be discounted, nor could managerial slip-ups, but in my opinion, the most virulent attribute in the whole episode was the conduct of a Staff coterie. Without that, much dissatisfaction could have been appeased and, the pace checked. Mrs. Williams did not stand a chance and I feared that for her, all was lost. I will never be able to erase the memory of her sadness, nor her distress.

I could do nothing for all was in abeyance. I knew which scholarly individuals made up the repellent faction;

being compelled to witness their self-satisfied smirks, was a test of my forbearance. All I could do was wait.

We had revelled in the initial three weeks of our Summer recess. The cares of the School were far away.

A phone call from Mrs. Williams interrupted our Scarborough stay. Apparently, a further meeting with the Governors had given her renewed hope. Relieved, we continued with languid days by the seaside. Was this beleaguered blue-stocking to rise as the phoenix from the ashes of dissidence? We tempted providence and dared to mellow.

Within a week, Betty had forwarded post which included a letter from the Chairman of the Governors informing all Staff that on 14 August, Mrs. Williams had resigned. Ronnie and I, dismayed and uncertain, made up our minds to return to London at once. I was aware that arrangements would be imminent for running of the School and I needed to be available for news. Soon after our return, I visited Mrs. Williams. Naturally, she was desolate and her heartache was unmistakeable. Her dilemma had been indefensible. Immediate advice for me was to make sure the Chairman knew of my duties with details of what I had accomplished. I was to leave no stone unturned.

Within days, I completed the full Job Description for Head of Middle School and an abstract of the year's achievements, difficulties and expectancy. It was forwarded to the Mercers' Hall towards the end of August. It coincided with a communication to Staff stating that the Deputy Head had agreed to postpone her Sabbatical. Ah... She was to be Acting High Mistress for a maximum of two years and would be announcing administrative, academic and tutorial planning before the beginning of Term.

All was sobering. Ronnie and I were gloomy and could foresee massive turmoil. I did not have time to draw breath before I received a summons for interview. At that time, the Acting High Mistress had not taken over her 'Acting Drawing Room' and was still holed up in her usual quarters.

The meeting was, I recollect, civilised but deeply shocking. 'I have decided to do away with Head of Middle School'. I think it was the phrase 'do away with' which I found most implacable. I was told that I would return, or 'be returned', to the Portakabin. There, I would retain the title of Director of Drama.

Co-ordinators for each Year Group were to be put in place, but as I was not invited to perform such a duty, I was condemned to face the humiliation of absolute demotion. Would my epithet be 'failure'? It was an abysmal outcome and, seemingly, a blow dealt by a hitherto friend.

I was crushed. I had worked very hard to make the job a success, so I experienced great difficulty in coming to terms with the sense of betrayal. Throughout, I tried to dilute the anguish. Ronnie was very, very angry and I was fully aware that this destructive emotion could harm him. I was not able to hide my entire feeling and on one occasion, when I could not restrain my hurt, he was there to hold and strengthen. Without his heart-warming, pragmatic slant on the matter, I would have been reduced to bleak dejection and despair. 'Come on, Alice, this has happened for a reason. So, we pick up the pieces and start again. We have our treasured life together, Bina, the babies and everything else that makes us so happy. Do they have that?

At the end of August, the School was deserted. Its emptiness reminded me of Theatres, dark before the public are allowed to invade the silence. St. Paul's, inhabited by Caretakers and the academic zealots in search of examination results, reeked of floor polish. All was in place, ready for the adolescent squeals which would soon rock the quiescent corridors.

My 'boudoir' was as I had left it. My kettle was missing. Astonishing how one notices extraneous detail.

Purposefully, I emptied the contents of the filing cabinet into black bags and steadily dismantled the whole office. It went through the process of liquidation, as I had done a few days before. All at once, a figure was framed in the doorway. 'Sue, I am most terribly sorry'. It was The Letter Writer, surprisingly contrite, who seemed to have grown a heart. She disappeared. Across The Marble and issuing from the Acting Principal's office-to-be was the voice of another member of Staff. Ah... was she destined for High Office? She was supervising the fitting of a new carpet. Mrs. Williams' impeccable taste was also being exterminated. In spite of this dismal take-over, I could see the buffoonery. I recognised the grating voice as it took on human form. In the doorway appeared the presumed appointee, clad in a strawberry pink linen jacket. Who had advised her of its a la mode finesse? 'They should be locked up' would have been Ronnie's pithy exposition. I completed my evacuation and left. My kettle was not recovered.

I received a most encouraging, courteous letter from the Chairman of Governors, Mr Henry Palmer. He acknowledged my communication and Job Description and took great pains to reassure me that the new structures being put in place were no personal reflection on me. He went on to mention that I was valued as Director of Drama and recognised the tremendous amount I had done for the School in that capacity. He appreciated my worry over the proposed alterations, but pointed out that I was well respected both inside and outside the School. I appreciated his kindness. I have kept that letter, and, over the years, it has become a token of remembrance and appreciation. At the time, however, it was, as Ronnie and I were aware, only half the story...

The entire Staff attended the first Meeting of a new School Year in September 1992. In order to accommodate everyone, this was held in the Singing Hall. The Chairman of Governors, adopting the role of protection officer just-in-case, escorted the Acting High Mistress. A significant number of Staff members were baffled by Helen Williams' departure. Many had not been aware of the strife within and were gravely shocked.

I look back now with deep regret. That day, I should have thrust my head above the parapet and, in speaking out, aired my concern and misgivings. As my eye roved over the diverse body of tutors, I looked for loyalty. I knew it was likely I would not find it; I may be a lone voice. I adopted the coward's way out and stood back for several reasons. I needed my job; mine was the major salary and I could not afford to jeopardise it. I was deeply concerned with Ronnie's illness and his need for permanence. I dare not gamble. I was afraid. There was a marked silence. The meeting closed.

As I reached The Marble, a member of Staff, for whom I held great regard, drew me to one side. 'Sue, are you aware that members of a junta, partially responsible for bringing about Mrs. Williams' downfall, circulated a letter during the holiday. It urged all members of Staff who supported their detestable insurrection to sign the enclosed petition. I, of course, refused as did many others who were got at. I could not speak. It seemed that letters had been in full flow and the milk of human kindness in very short supply.

After that, nothing could be done. Ronnie and I were in conference for many troubled hours. Drama, the warmth of the Portakabin and the refreshing gaiety of the girls made up for my unhappy state. This lovely School and its exceptional, invigorating young people did not deserve to be associated with such unhappiness.

I returned to work and filled my days with an unerring, unflinching desire to carry out my calling. Freed from crippling administration and pettiness, I burgeoned once again and did my best to offer support to the Acting High Mistress. All could see, however, that a controlled game of power had been played and won by a clique that many Staff disliked and mistrusted. The School, as time went by, worked reasonably well on the surface, but Staff reverted to groups of intense personal loyalties or intimidated, suspicious gatherings and individuals. For me, the life of the School was changing...

Helen Williams left me with an invaluable parting gift. She was closely acquainted with the Mother of a Paulina. The lady's Son-in-Law was an eminent Orthopaedic Surgeon and highly recommended. Helen urged me to make contact if a hip operation became necessary.

I continued to be in considerable pain, but at that stage was so caught up with School duties, the instigation of an unfamiliar, dreary regimen and the threat of further disruption, that I chose to grin and bear it. I spent time based in my Portakabin office, only visiting the main School for administration and meetings. It was a means of escape and lunchtime teaching provided me with a convenient excuse for staying put. I was feeling very vulnerable.

For me the joy had gone out of St. Paul's. It seemed that its sophistication, panache and ardent, exuberant enjoyment of life had vanished, largely because those at the prow seemed lacking in such elements - bete noire, comes to mind. But.... unbecoming thoughts and outlook needed to be submerged. As Director of Drama, I worked with renewed vigour.

The Autumn Term of 1992 presented me with the accustomed slot for a Dramatic production. I was constrained to request authorization for any suggestion I wished to make. I discovered that a presentation for the Junior Year Groups was required. I advocated two

Workshop productions: the themes for these to be 'Humour' and 'Bullying'. How very pertinent, I thought.

No eyebrows were raised, and so, permission granted, I put the wheels in motion.

The Junior presentations were given a hearty reception. The Acting High and Chairman patronized 'Only a Joke...', and were generous in congratulatory comment. I was polite and courteous. Their absence, together with the School's coalition, was conspicuous for 'Only a Game...'.

Shortly after, I was called to a meeting to discuss future plans for the Summer Term. It transpired that the Initiate had her sights set on a selection of Shakespearian offerings. This suited me. I was to be allowed a free hand for choice. 'I do hope that this will be an elitist presentation', was her strange command.

Ronnie remained under medical supervision. He worked successfully in Television and Radio as well as continuing to be confidence booster in all our domestic activities. I am sure he did not find my preoccupation with School an easy cross to bear. He was patient and forever engaged in all developments, but the strain weighed heavily. Added to that, my hip pain was proving more and more to be a serious disability. Osteopathy and pain-killers were becoming ineffective. In turn, this was bringing about increasing irritability and fatigue. At night, it was a battle with hot sweats and excruciating spasms. We were fighting to recapture the beatitude of our early marriage. It was slipping away and becoming lost in the melee of day-to-day living.

The next chapter in our lives is painful to recall. As my thoughts meander through events, it is so very simple to understand how such a distressing change could come about. Undoubtedly, the menopause affected my mood swings. It is only with hindsight and increased knowledge, that one can sift the mysteries of hormonal chaos. At the time, denial becomes an avoidance route. Absorbed with worry, School duty and pain, I lost sight of the fact that my dearest Ronnie had travelled only a decade into his new life. How disorientated he must have felt.

I remember so clearly the telephone ringing. It was Half Term. About to leave for Osteopathy, I paused to say 'Cheerio', as Ronnie picked up the receiver.

'I can't talk now. We're going to Scarborough at the end of the week'. Ronnie turned and I was gripped with fear, for his face had turned a deathly pale.

'Whatever's the matter?' I whispered. 'Nothing,' Ronnie stuttered, 'I'm fine'.

'Who was that? Ronnie, who was that on the phone?' Ronnie seemed to be rooted to the spot and unable to answer. I sank into the armchair. 'I cannot go out until you tell me'. Ronnie refused and urged me to leave for my appointment.

In blunt silence, I left. I drove blindly. I remember sitting in the car outside my destination trying to make sense of my feelings. What could it mean?

When I returned, Ronnie was stressed. Striving to remain calm, I asked why he would not tell me who the caller had been. 'Just a friend,' he stated. 'Why be so secretive then, and obviously very disturbed?' I insisted. Ronnie remained uncommunicative and fixed.

I was shaken and apprehensive. The evening was spent in eerie silence and, earlier than usual, I prepared for bed. 'Ronnie, I refuse to go to Scarborough unless you tell me what is happening. We have never had secrets and I cannot understand why you are behaving like this' I said. I left the room.

I lay in bed, unable to stem the weeping. In a while, Ronnie came to lay beside me. 'Sue, I have been so miserable. I have been seeing someone, for I did not know what to do when you were away at School. That was the person on the phone. I was so unhappy and lonely. 'Who is this?' I replied, 'Why have you given our phone number to someone unknown to me? Presumably, they have our home address as well. Has anything happened between you?' I blurted through my tears. 'Have you been having an affair? For if you have, Ronnie, I'm afraid that will be the end. I cannot endure that'. 'No, I just needed someone,' said my dearest, 'Sue, I love you so very deeply. Nothing will ever change that. I finished it, for I knew our lovely life would be spoiled. You are my dearest love, and nothing could ever change that'. In that dreadful moment, I knew Ronnie's words were true. In my innermost being, I knew how very much he loved me and that is why in that instant, we did recapture all the bliss of our early marriage. It returned that night, and never went away, ever again...

The following days were not without sorrow. We did go to Scarborough, and there we found peace once more. I did not ask any more questions. I did not need to. As the hours and days went by, we strengthened and consoled. We had been wounded. The pangs would heal. We were together for always....

There was an ache in my heart. In quiet moments I dwelt on innermost feelings. I had time to realise that Ronnie had needed me to talk and listen. Talking and listening, so much a part of our lives, are the crucial elements of closeness. I had been a slave to tedium and obligation. Talk had revolved around routine and professional duty. Surplus consideration had been devoted to pain and indisposition. I was now at an emotional crossroads, for I realised that our intimacy and affection had been taken for granted. I had been distracted. I had not supported, cared for and loved Ronnie in my usual way. I had not been attuned to giving the emotional warmth for which he craved. Instead, prepossession with Educational demand had been allowed to take precedence. Healing had begun, but I was miserable...

Christmas 1992 came and went and the Spring Term of 1993 was soon upon us. Eleanor Zeal took up part-time teaching in the Drama Department and proved to be an inspiring, dependable colleague. Zeal by name and Zeal by nature, she introduced ideas and projects which promised to be exciting and progressive.

I continued in my struggle to live through a strange interlude in our domestic life; this intrusion into the trustful continuation Ronnie and I had shared. Eleanor's arrival, the planning of the 'elitist' Shakespearian Evening, together with possible ideas for an Autumn major production was my purpose and kept feverish thoughts at bay....the practised, professional machine ground on...

Further diversion came about. My Mother's application for sheltered housing received a favourable answer. Instead of welcoming the news with good grace, she was thrown into panic and almost declined the delightful offer of a brand new apartment in a complex which overlooked the magnificent Beverley Minster.

'Those bells will drive me crazy' she announced.

Ronnie sequestered events, requested leave from the BBC and made plans to travel North. He masterminded the whole operation and by the time I arrived at the weekend to shore up the ranks, he had successfully mopped up my Mother's tears and arranged, with the help of my Brother and his wife, furniture, ornaments and (very important) a new television! My Mother, insisting that she would never become used to this fresh environment, was, nevertheless, very grateful to Ronnie. It was another demonstration of his love for me and the sadness faded from my consciousness, never to return.

'Won't it be lovely, Jessica, to look out on that view of the Church,' Ronnie encouraged. 'Mmn, well...when you've seen it, you've seen it' was my dear Mother's dour reply. It reminded me of her first visit to Kew. We had been looking forward to introducing my Mother to the grandeur of a sumptuous garden. 'Isn't it wonderful, Jessica,' enthused Ronnie. 'Mmn, we've got all this at home' was the shattering reply.

The journey home instilled all the peace of silent companionship and love. The countryside in its Spring stirring, cheered and calmed. We were 'on't roaaad' once again...

I knew that a Shakespearian programme would be popular for the Autumn Term of 1993. At the onset of the Summer Term I met the Acting High to discuss details. I had deliberately kept clear of her for some time, but this meeting could not be avoided. I did have influence when it came to choice of Dramatic presentations. All I needed was her dispensation. 'Taming of the Shrew' was a favourite of mine and within the realms of possibility for the girls. There was no hesitation and consent was given. My Superior seemed happy to fall in. At this time, she was amiable but condescending. Her room had become an office, functional and sparse. Notes of femininity and finesse so characteristic of Mrs. Brigstocke and Mrs. Williams were replaced by bold utility. The space, was spare. In a moment of mental abandon, I thought wickedly of Orestes.

I planned to run play Auditions and work out Rehearsal schedules alongside Shakespeare Evening practices. The going was hard, for my hip agony was becoming intrusive. As circumstances became increasingly difficult, a pathway opened before us...

A Church acquaintance vouched for a possible solution. She knew of an excellent Chinese Acupuncturist and suggested that we contact her. Ronnie, always quick to act on such advice, secured an appointment and our lives were steered towards deliverance. Once again, destiny interceded....

Lily Clark attempted to treat my condition, but it soon became apparent that Acupuncture was not going to solve the problem. To digress, it turned out that Lily's partner was Nigel Lambert, an actor and professional associate of Ronnie's - such a small world.

In the space of a very short time, I was advised to see the redoubtable Dr. Singh to request further X-Rays. 'NHS Orthopaedics do nothing', was her damning conclusion. 'Not till sixty'. At the ripe old age of fifty-three, I had no alternative but to inform her that private medicine would be my only salvation. 'Ah'...ah,ha', she stated, 'very expensive road down which to go'. And that was that. Not to be deterred, Ronnie and I forked out for private X-Rays. Lily studied them in dismay and broke the news, 'Well, I do not prefer to advocate surgery, but you have no choice. Both hips will need to be replaced'. That evening, shock consumed us.

All was not lost. Fate intervened once more. While struggling along the pavement of Brook Green the following morning, occasionally propping myself up on convenient garden walls for respite, I was noticed by the Bursar. Unknown to me, she had followed in my footsteps. 'Sue, you're in a bad way. You need to go somewhere nice and have that seen to. Come to my office at Break today.'

Taken aback, I reported to the centre of financial affairs as instructed. 'Now Sue,' the Bursar said kindly, 'you are entitled to our Private Health Scheme for you have been at St. Paul's for over five years. Please fill in these forms and we'll take it from there. We need to get you well again. Do you know of an appropriate Surgeon?' Instantly, I remembered Mrs. William's testimonial. I would follow it up. I was very touched by the Bursar's thoughtfulness.

We had been rescued yet again and were to be provided with a hiatus. Ronnie and I were about to embark upon an enforced interval from the stress of academic active service.

***

PART 1

THEN

THE LONDON CLINIC....
SUMMER 1993

Mr. Cobb's rooms...' an elegant voice answered. Startled, I almost rang off.

The Surgeon resided in Harley Street, an address Ronnie and I had not had cause to frequent except on expeditions of exploration. I made a request for an appointment. Within days, I was to present myself. Ronnie and I had been catapulted into a different sphere. Little did we know that this change in our lives would offer yet another shared involvement and provide a breathing space, where we could concentrate on our precious life which had been so neglected.

We were steered into palatial consulting rooms. Justin Cobb was a young man. It was easy to warm to him, for he was uncomplicated, efficient and quite charming. I was examined, X-Rays were studied and then came the final diagnosis. 'Mrs. Herdman, your right hip is in parlous state. The muscles in that leg are wasted, so I can see that you have been almost unable to use it. You must have been in extreme pain. The left hip is nearly as bad, but will probably last a further two years after I've replaced the right one. I would like to admit you within three weeks'. I was thrown into confusion. I had not realised that the outcome would be so serious, so soon. 'Where would you do it?' I asked, rather stupidly. 'Why here, round the corner, in the London Clinic. Now, don't you worry, all will be taken care of by my Secretary. I will introduce you to her now - you can liaise with your

Husband and make arrangements. She will see to everything'.

Dazed, I repaired to the waiting room where Ronnie was in suspense but at the same time, thumbing through the latest edition of Country Life. The Secretary presented us with a very large, distinguished brochure and explained that all I needed to know could be found within it. She closed with, 'Please don't be concerned, Mrs. Herdman, I will be in touch about your pre-assessment date in due course'.

We boarded the Lada, having had the sauce to park it in the revered Harley Street quarter. Ronnie's head was buried in the pages of the London Clinic pamphlet. 'My God, Sue, are you sure that the School is going to foot the bill? A private en-suite medium-sized room which corresponds with a Scale B cover is **only** £375 per night and that doesn't include treatment'. Dr. Singh's words rang in my ears. Yes, it was a very expensive road down which to go. The remainder of the journey home echoed with 'I say! Darling, listen to this...! It's a five star hotel!

My beloved was in his element. Yes, we were on the brink of another world and my first thought was 'someone has made a mistake'.

I started to panic and it was not until I had spoken to the Bursar the following morning, that I began to relax and realise that, yes, it was really true...I was to be treated in a lap of luxury which was beyond our wildest dreams.

My visit to Mr. Cobb had taken place two weeks before the end of Term. Before planning for my operation, I had to launch the Shakespeare Evening, which went off remarkably well. Earlier in the Term, I had cast 'The Shrew' so all was secure for the Autumn. Ronnie decided that an errand to the Portobello Road was of supreme importance. He had already made sure that I was purveyed with suitable nightwear, negligees and the like for such an imperialistic Hospital stay.

All at once, I became anxious; not for myself, although I was apprehensive, but for Ronnie. I was to be immobilized for some time. He had a film, 'Century Falls', to complete and a week or two later, was needed for location at Betchworth.

He had been cast as the first Vicar in a low-budget film 'Four Weddings & A Funeral'. It required one day's filming. Fortunately, he was scheduled to finish before returning to the BBC for more Radio work. Would he be alright?

Our visit to the Portobello took place on the Saturday morning before the last week of Term and my pre-assessment at the London Clinic. I remember the occasion so vividly. The day was warm and we began with breakfast at our favourite Italian patisserie. In a very few days we were to face an unnerving trial and I made every effort to hide consternation and dread. We sauntered along, stopping now and again to sit on seats or grassy banks. 'Won't be a minute,' smiled Ronnie and hurried to a corner stall which was festooned with every flower imaginable. When he returned, he was carrying a vast armful of Stargazer lilies. 'For my darling,' he said, 'these will always be a reminder of how much I love you'. That was to be the first of many such bouquets over the years. Those lilies became a lasting amulet of Ronnie's love.

Dear Betty was ready as domestic bastion. I knew the babies would be spoiled in epoch-making fashion and Ronnie would have no cause for concern. The day of reckoning drew near...

***

PART 1

T H E N

AN EVENT TO REMEMBER......!

It was the custom of 8th Year students to offer a Revue before leaving. This end-of-Term entertainment was written, directed and performed by the girls. The content was topical and good-natured - as a rule...

The School was staggered and the pupil audience was seated for either the first or second house. This year, Ronnie and I, together with close colleagues, took our seats and awaited a run-of-the-mill gig. Imagine our glee, satisfaction and wonder when we beheld the daring impudence and effrontery of this rendition. We witnessed glorious, accurate and reckless take-offs. These brave girls had nothing to lose; they were leaving. They had nerve, and gall to use their wit, perception and sense of justice. They would never know how close they had come to passing rightful judgement. They did, however, use a time-honoured weapon known to uncover bullying, ignobility and narrow-mindedness. They used Drama. In their parody, they settled scores with those who had made life uncomfortable. Of course, all hell broke loose, but the 8th were victorious when they received their standing ovation. Needless to say, subsequent 8th Skits were closely vetted and re-writing became the order of the day. Never again could truth rise to the surface. The iron fist of censorship and control was omnipotent. It was, nevertheless, an unexpected victory. Beware all those who dare to lean on complacency when dealing with Paulinas; they do so at their peril. The joy of retribution on that occasion lived with us all for some time. Often, life takes a most unusual turn and blows are dealt in an unforeseen manner, always more potent when struck innocuously by children.

We left Brook Green basking in the warm glow of circuitous conquest. At the close of the Academic Year the School was informed of the Acting High's promotion. She was to become High Mistress.

On Thursday, 15th July 1993, I was admitted to the London Clinic. We took an emotional journey by taxi having said farewell to Charlie, Phyllis and Betty. Tension mounted and, as Ronnie held my hand in a coaxing grip, I was close to tears. My anxiety was not for the forthcoming operation but for Ronnie's vulnerability while I languished in a Hospital bed. None of these fears were voiced. To speak of fear would have undermined Ronnie's exceptional management of the situation.

We found ourselves being led into the opulent vestibule of the Clinic. Stylish attendants were bustling and escorting. We were greeted and guided through entrée procedures, before being dispatched by lift to the relevant floor. My room was an indolent retreat; an indulgent hideaway equipped for comfort and privacy. Within the space of an hour and a half, orders for meals - 'Can't see fish 'n' chips anywhere' teased Ronnie as he perused the plush menus - and visits from Nurses and Filipino assistants teemed. All was awesome and unknown. Dejected, I began to remember a youthful unsettlement. I had stayed for a weekend in the glitzy Guildford home of a Drama student friend. In the comfort of my spacious guest-room, I pulled on the light to see into the wardrobe. Much to my embarrassment, a housemaid in full uniform appeared in the doorway. 'Yes, miss?' she enquired, 'you rang?' Covered in confusion, I tried to explain my mistake. 'Thank you, miss...' she replied, and soundlessly vanished. I was yanked from wayward musing. 'Come on, Alice,' said Ronnie, prodding my arm, 'what have you ordered for supper?'

Then....Ronnie was standing in the doorway smiling and blowing kisses. 'I'll ring as soon as I'm home...must get back to the babies, before Betty entertains any gentleman callers!' All at once, the opening was empty and so was my heart. He was gone.

It would be monotonous and boring to recall all developments, but, as with many life experiences, some happenings are worthy of remembrance.

The aftermath of my operation was painful. According to my sympathetic, gentle anaesthetist, Mr. Armstrong, my hip had been 'an awful one'. Certainly, I found myself in extreme torment and was wired up to large dollops of morphine. I had superlative treatment and care. Ronnie visited and noticed that I was on an impressive medicated high. The story goes that after falling asleep for ten minutes, I would wake and say, 'Oh Fuck! Is it morning already!' At least, that was Ronnie's account of my malaise. It seemed I had acquired a propensity for foul language.

The first days were spent in soporific haze. While I was thus cast down, I dreamed many a time and oft. In my delusion, a vision took shape and an unmistakeable voice uttered 'Oleander, Jacaranda...' over and over again. In actuality, these words were repeated at Assembly with interminable, reverent regularity on every distinguished or scholarly occasion. On my waking, it was almost worth dropping off once more for the likelihood of hearing the fidgeting, twitching and sighing reaction of the snared teenage congregation. I blamed the opiates for this vexatious flight of fancy.

My room resembled a florist's shop. Flowers arrived from friends, family and the St. Paul's Staff. These tokens of love and good wishes lifted me from the threat of doldrums. My initial recovery was slow and beset with some difficulty for I found myself passing out with frightening persistence. As a result, anaemia was diagnosed and a transfusion became necessary. That aside, Mr. Cobb and his committed team were peerless in their professionalism and skill.

Ronnie was coping in his loving, good-natured way and called in, always under the weight of presents for the invalid, when Broadcasting was finished for the day. At times, he would bring friends to laugh with us and Douglas, in particular, relished his couple of hours at the bedside.

Ronnie's most favourite stunt was the ordering of Room Service. We were disported, forever grateful to St. Paul's for this unprecedented, pampered territory of the well-heeled, and having a field day in being able to afford the financing of extra refinements. 'I've ordered some Smoked Salmon sandwiches, Doug,' divulged Ronnie. 'Christ,' replied our dear friend with undisguised alacrity,' and all for an impoverished Australian pouf!'

Hospital nights were long. Nurses, immaculately uniformed, in the small hours, would appear without being summoned. 'Like a pot of tea?' were the most heartening words to hear. A tray then materialised, tastefully set and loaded with biscuits. 'Night starvation!' would be the cheerful accompaniment. My thoughts were of Ronnie, sleeping serenely beside his devoted Charlie and Phyllis. I dwelt too on gratitude. St. Paul's Girls' School had been good to us...at that time, I did not know how greatly I would go on to be indebted to it...

I waited again near the doorway of the London Clinic. A fortnight had passed and I was going home. Ronnie supported a faltering me and my robust crutches into Jenny's waiting car. 'I say,' she chuckled, 'you look rudely healthy! Get in, I've been waiting ages with all the gossip!

The first weeks of my convalescence were spent without the luxury of driving. My Mother visited and was a great help to Ronnie. Between them, they managed many of the household chores with efficiency and equanimity. I gave thanks for my capable, loving husband and the affection of my Mother who was very adept at overseeing the ironing, vacuuming and scouring of bathrooms. Relief filled my being, for it took all the strength and determination that I could call up to wash, dress and tussle with crutches. Driving the car would have been an impossibility.

In spite of painkillers, I was still in considerable discomfort and on less positive days, filled with despair. Would I ever recover? It was fun, in the meantime, to listen to Ronnie and Mum's gripping kitchen confabulation. They were hysterically reminiscent of those one might overhear when tapping in to dinner ladies or heroic Yorkshire nannies.

The time came for Mum's departure. I thought of her courage, for I knew that a five-hour coach mission was off-putting for one who had not gone far beyond the boundaries of the North East. Ronnie squired her to the Golders Green terminal where she was waved off, besieged by the weight of a generous tuck box. Dear Ronnie... dear Mum...

I was on edge. I knew that work needed to be done if 'The Shrew' was to get off to a flying start in September. Perhaps against my better judgement, I waded into Scene plotting and Rehearsal schedules. Before long, I was bedevilled with tension headaches and compelled to rest. It was frustrating and not a little worrying.

As I wrestled one afternoon, Ronnie's attention was zeroing in on the road outside. 'Sue, look at this'. 'Ronnie, must I, it takes me ages to get out of this chair'. 'Oh, give over Alice,' said he, 'it'll do you good...' How annoying!

Ronnie was looking at a white estate car parked on the opposite side. 'That's a wonderful car, look at the shape of it. I wonder...' 'No Ronnie!' I said with some emphasis. 'I'm going to see what it is...you know, just for interest...' I sighed. How many times had I heard those words. I knew that a fait accompli may be on the horizon.

There was an air of inevitability as I watched Ronnie making a meticulous inspection of what I had to admit was a very seductive vehicle. He returned my gaze, his face wreathed in a bewitching smile and I knew all was lost.

'Now darling,' reasoned my beloved, 'has it occurred to you that the Lada does not have power-steering? You cannot have added pressure on that new hip'. Ah, so that was the way the wind was blowing...I reminded Ronnie that funds were limited, but could have saved my breath. 'Oh, it's only money!' was the blithe response.

The following morning, I received a phone-call from the new High Mistress. 'Sue, I have given 'Taming of the Shrew' a great deal of thought and I do think it would be very taxing for you so soon after the operation. I know you would wish to fulfil this assignment, but in this instance, I must over-ride your sense of obligation and decide on a postponement. I realise that this will be disappointing for you and certainly the girls, but you will need time to recover fully. I will meet the Cast with you at the beginning of Term and explain what is to be done and why'. **This** was a fait accompli that I had not contemplated.

I sank into the chair. An overpowering sense of relief consumed me. I had not realised how debilitated I had become and the load, carried for some days, had been taken away. I was appreciative of the High Mistress' sympathy.

'Not before time,' was Ronnie's terse summary.

We were left to prize the remainder of the Summer holiday. Mr. Cobb gave permission for me to drive within the next week, Brian revved up the battery of the hardy, sturdy Lada and we made plans for a day trip to Brighton. The sun shone once more....

***

PART 1

T H E N

MAZDA.....AND.....!

Our return drive from Brighton could take us through Twickenham and then on via Hampton and prettier scenery to Wembley. Ronnie seemed rather set on a ride to Twickenham and soon I was to know why. He had researched the whereabouts of the Mazda showrooms and main dealer location and of course this just happened to be in Twickenham and on our way home. 'I say,' began my devious beloved, 'look at that. There's a car just like the one we noticed in Bowrons. Oh Sue, isn't she lovely!' A closer look gave me a closer price shock.

'Ronnie, I know that this is a second-hand car, and it is absolutely wonderful, but it would wipe us out'. 'Oh, we'll soon put that back,' Ronnie declared airily. 'A few repeat fees and we'll be home and dry. Darling, just think of your 'ips!'

I knew that Ronnie was right. I had discovered that the Lada's hefty, sluggish steering was putting unnecessary stress on my limbs. I admitted defeat, Ronnie beamed and a decision had been made. We would take the plunge.

Sad news awaited us at home. Dear Sandy had had a heart attack, was in Hospital and Winnie, although worried and upset, flatly refused to let us visit. We were to be kept informed.

The start of the Autumn Term was upon us and Ronnie hurriedly set the wheels in motion, as it were, for the purchase of our new car. 'You **must** have it for the first day, darling'. With negotiations underway, a delivery date was agreed upon.

Just prior to the commencement of the new Term, we acquired the white Mazda Estate car. We collected our trophy after being given an illustrious send-off by the dealer. Resplendent, I drove effortlessly through Alperton. Ronnie, nodding indulgently to passers-by whether he knew them or not, was ecstatic. The majestic motor was stationed amid great ceremony outside Betty's. All came to admire. After the modest Lada, this awe-inspiring conveyance measured up admirably to Ronnie's royal patois - **she** was deserving of her title.

The excitement did not mask the need to contact Winnie. Sandy was improving. Winnie chattered to us as only Winnie could and peace of mind was restored to all - for the moment.

Car or no car, I had to concentrate my thoughts on the coming School Term. I contacted Frances Clarke, my talented Dancing associate, to break news of 'The Shrew's postponement. It was disappointing to learn that Frances had a long-standing commitment the following year and so was unable to offer her skill and professionalism.

The Term began, the High Mistress spoke to all concerned with 'The Shrew' and, as expected, the girls were crestfallen but very understanding of my condition.

I was free from pain and each day became a smooth, pleasurable entity instead of a wracking, searing toil. The Department was busier than ever and eighty per cent of the School was involved in a Drama activity of one kind or another. On many occasions I mentioned this to the High Mistress for it was becoming clear that another Assistant was needed to cope with the volume of work. It was splendid to know that all the exertion had been worthwhile; the Department was flourishing in its own right and my ambition for it was steadily moving to maturation.

***

PART 1

THEN

MAZDA MAYHEM!

The Mazda behaved **herself** for a week or two. Then, with astounding recurrence, she developed annoying faults. First, the radio refused to operate and **she** (perhaps no longer worthy of the royal appendage) ended up in dock for at least a week. A catalogue of disaster then ensued. I was on the receiving end of a series of major breakdowns. These took place in the most inconvenient locales: Marylebone Road, Hanger Lane gyratory system and Shepherd's Bush roundabout. At least, **she** managed to keep going while getting the better of Hammersmith one-way tracks and the North Circular Road. I cannot overestimate the sheer terror of being marooned in a stationery car while a ruthless and unyielding volume of traffic promised to obliterate me. On each occasion I was doomed. Eventually, rescue came by way of a coasting Patrol car; Policemen smiling benevolently at the nerve-wracked woman behind the wheel and who, miraculously, persuaded the truculent Mazda to resuscitate. As a rule, after each bout of malfunction, **she** was hoyed back to base for repair and, in atonement, we were given a range of speedy sports models to assuage our exasperation and regret. Ronnie, and indeed, Phyllis and Charlie whooped it up in a Brands Hatch spree while sitting in a GLX 326 Mazda Sports along the Kenton High Street. We were home in twenty minutes!

There was, however, a final straw. The dealer assured me that all was now well and I should relax knowing that such disasters were a thing of the past. I was enticed into believing that the car was in immaculate condition and had been put through the mill in a programme of healing; I could put my mind at rest for **she** was deep-dyed reliable. Defiant as ever, **she** stopped once more in Shepherd's Bush and refused to budge. Paralysed by a seizure of rage, I flung open the car door and burst into a nearby phone box. The Mazda dealer, about to leave his office, spluttered, 'Stay in the car, Mrs. Herdman - whatever you do, stay in the car!' 'How the blazes do you think I'm speaking to you? By sitting in the car?' (I hasten to add - no mobiles in those days!) To add insult to injury, I was, in due course, loaded on to a huge, conspicuous breakdown truck together with the neurotic Mazda and carted home. Ronnie, Betty, Charlie, Phyllis and most of the Asian community living in Bowrons Avenue, turned out to welcome us. Ronnie opened his mouth to offer greeting, whereupon I hissed, 'That's it, don't say a word about **her**. **She**'s a **cow**!'

I reconciled myself to the fact that a strong letter of complaint was forthcoming. I wrote to the Mazda Head Office, giving a full history and demanding a replacement. I received a craven apology, a LARGE bouquet of roses and a new car. Ronnie cooed: 'I say, this one's Mint Green, darling. How lovely! One of my favourite colours!' 'Ronnie, sweetheart, I'm so glad that **she** meets with your approval'. His reply was true to form, 'I say, Alice, you looked so regal in the passenger seat of that breakdown wagon!'

In many ways it was fortunate that I had been relieved of an Autumn production. It came to pass that domestic events far outweighed professional duties in order of priority. Work was completed proficiently and I did not encounter aggravation from those on high, so I was able to apply myself to other developments.

At Half Term, we visited Winnie and Sandy. It was a jolly day, but we were downhearted when we saw how Sandy had failed. He was fragile and his natural exuberance was much diminished. We left not knowing if we would see him again and, as we turned to wave goodbye, we knew it could be his last farewell.

The Department's workload continued to increase and I was snowed under with Administrational duties, one hundred and fifty Reports, Timetabled Drama for MIV and UIV, Workshops, not to mention the numerous optional private Small Group and Individual lessons. I had no choice but to inform the High Mistress yet again that the Portakabin could no longer accommodate the volume of students, let alone a waiting list which was considerable.

Towards the end of Term, I received a memo from the High Mistress requesting a detailed Timetable of pupil numbers, year groups and Staff teaching them. This was to be forwarded to the Deputy. A week before School closed for the Christmas break, I was asked to make an appointment with the High Mistress - not immediately, but at the beginning of the Spring Term 1994. The Staff came to know that this was a favoured line of enquiry. In the time that elapsed before interrogation, one was supposed to sweat with fear; this was often the case with nervous, timid colleagues. I was, however, conversant with such tactics and they left me amused. Nevertheless, were things changing?

*

Betty, our dearest Betty, was taken ill at the onset of December. She lay, stricken with diverticulitis, in Northwick Park Hospital. We were adrift without her, but most of all, Charlie and Phyllis were distracted and miserable.

Mrs. Doubtfire's absence was a mystery to them and Charlie, precariously balanced on the back of the sofa, looked longingly from the front window. Phyllis, much more sensible, was prepared to sit out the separation on Ronnie's lap. To our relief, Betty recovered and convalesced at her cousin's home in Stanmore until long after Christmas.

Doom and gloom travelled with us to Scarborough. The warning of illness and discomfiture sat on our shoulders and bothered us at every turn. The Mazda, however, was a source of much satisfaction, and, groaning with kit and clobber of every description, **she** bowled along the A1 to the manner born. With ill-concealed excitement, we drew into West Bank, intent on showing off our polished, state-of-the-art carriage. I refer to 'polish' in wry mode, for Ronnie was still enthralled enough to enjoy a penchant for washing the car. 'Such refined lines,' he purred, 'such a pleasure to shampoo and shine...' This inclination soon wore thin and the local car-wash, according to Ronnie's surveillance, was more than capable of ousting 'all that elbow grease'. Mmn....

We were not prepared for the change in Philip. We were profoundly shocked to see how haggard, thin and weary he appeared to be. With obvious effort, he tried to rally some enthusiasm for our arrival. Ronnie and I, with telepathic insight, realised that admiration of the Mazda was way down the pecking order for consideration and made an urgent request for a pot of tea. Our dear friend seemed loath to offer any explanation. Our whispered bedroom conversation on our first night of the Christmas holiday was fearful, jarred and perplexed. How were we to deal with this impasse? We concluded that Ronnie should find some golden opportunity to talk to his dear friend. It seemed important to respect Philip's privacy, unless he wished to confide or explain to us how he felt.

Fate intervened once again and our way became clear. We planned a ride to Hartlepool before harsher weather set in and invited Philip to join us. We promised a pint in his favourite Moorland pub. The offer was too good to miss...

Armed once again with a liberal supply of Christmas Mills & Boon and treacle toffee for Louie, we made Philip comfortable in the front seat (Phyllis doggedly determined to sit on his lap). Ronnie rode shotgun and with his irritating habit of backseat driving, skippered the whole junket. Diversion paid off and Philip's energy revived enough to admonish Ronnie at every verse end with bantering, waggish put-downs.

We noticed that his renewed stamina took a dip while at Louie's. It's true to say, that everyone took something of a dip when sidestepping Louie. Our departure met with some ease and soon we were homeward bound, or rather, en route for the aforementioned pub.

It was noticeable that Philip was not smoking. Cigarettes and beer were partners in crime - what had happened? 'I can't face a fag anymore, Ron...the cough is the worst...it's ridiculous, the smoke kills me...' We did not need to open a halting conversation about Philip's malady. He knew and we knew... In the following uncertain days before Christmas, Philip was tested, X-Rayed and left to wait and hope...

Philip had lung cancer and we were devastated.

My Mother came to stay. She was her sweet self, kindly and easy to please. Ronnie, over time, had reached the real Jessica and she was at home. Christmas, that year, was a distant affair, but Philip seemed to welcome the activity and hurried preparations. Our distraction was hidden and spoken of in hushed tones when all was quiet.

After my Mother's departure, the time came for plans. Philip's Doctors devised treatment and this was put into operation before our return to London. The prospect of leaving our beloved friend alone with only Jessie, presented us with hollow, defenceless emotions. How intolerable it would be to abandon Philip...

Schemes and arrangements fought for supremacy in our minds. We were faced with the insoluble predicament of trying to be in two places at once - our place of need and our place of work. 'Penny will come in, Sue; don't worry. I'll still be able to cook a spud or two'. I was reminded of Philip's self -sufficiency. He hated fuss and his desire to be the independent, positive joker remained intact. His tacit encounter with this scourge would be reduced to a nonentity, a nuisance which would not be permitted to intervene.

Penny was a staunch, enduring friend. Her relationship with Philip had been ongoing for many years and their memories and affiliations were legion. After-show drinks and Scarborough scandal or tittle-tattle sustained them. Penny was confidant, crony and companion; her cosy bungalow became a Sunday lunchtime den where Philip was denizen. She would never permit his glass to be empty.

With these thoughts of comfort, we left our dearest friend in the care of Jessie's unwavering trust and unconditional love.

Ronnie knew that he would return to West Bank soon. He was needed there. It only remained for him to secure leave. My thoughts were tumbling, shifting and dishevelled. I was wrestling to dispel anxiety. We were in a maelstrom of uncertainty and dread. I turned the inescapable key to this puzzle. I resolved to place my faith in foresight. After that, I could do nothing. Ronnie would journey back and forth to nurse his loving friend and I would sanction all his heartfelt inclinations. He would be protected.

The High Mistress' gambit was surprising. She opened the Spring Term 1994 meeting with enquiries about my health. Of course, this probing could be interpreted as a genuine desire to offer sympathy and understanding. Her abstruse expression, however, roused misgiving within me. She warmed to her questioning. Had I looked to the future? What was I planning to do? Finally, she fired an impertinent query. How old was I? I smiled. 'A couple of years older than you, I believe', I parried.

'I have decided to **do away with** all the optional private Drama lessons and instead, make plans to include Drama on the Timetable. Many children wish to take part in Drama and this will solve the problem of numbers. I now propose to place the Subject under the auspices of the English Department. You will, of course, retain your title as Director of Drama. Members of the English Department will assist with teaching and so lessen the need for another assistant'. The impact of this left me sickened, undermined and severely shaken.

This pejorative address left me in no doubt. But...why was I to be eroded? The Department, lovingly built over seven years, initiated and spurred on by Mrs. Brigstocke and Mrs. Williams, was to be taken away. It seemed that I must be **done away with** yet again.

My mouth curved to a smile, but my eyes delivered an intransigent message. I fired a broadside: 'I am aware that you wish to bring about a closer link with the English Department. I must point out, however, that its members are not Drama specialists. It is not my function in the School to teach English teachers how to teach Drama'. I took my leave. I remember having some concern for H.M.'s blood pressure. Her face had taken on an alarming reddish-blue tinge.

The elegant Mazda bore the brunt of my anguish and sorrow on the way home. At traffic lights, I was oblivious to what must have been doubtful stares from motorists coming to a halt beside me. I backed the idea of Timetabled Drama. It was a praiseworthy strategy. Every child should be given the chance to take part, but not at the expense of other Specialist areas such as Spoken English, Remedial lessons for speech impediment and defect, one-to-one aid for those lacking in self-esteem and confidence. The prospect of Examination work being demolished after my striving to build up excellent results with Lamda and The Guildhall School of Music & Drama, was mind boggling. All was to be laid waste with one heartbreaking swipe. Why? Oh why....

At this juncture, I am reminded of a fitting quote from Cicero - 'A nation can survive its fools and even the ambitious, but it cannot survive treason from within'. What an apt précis of current events...

All too soon, I discovered that my Administrative workload was being increased. Bearing in mind that at that time an inordinate proportion of the School was engaged in one form of Drama or another, each activity demanding its own governance, the High Mistress insisted on my fulfilling the role of Form Attachment. This added task, with its accompanying duties of supervision, registration and lunchtime monitoring, seemed to be a further demonstration of constraint and duress. What was happening?

Another worrying ingredient added itself to the mix. My left hip was starting to make its presence felt in contrary fashion. I was in very noticeable discomfort. A quick call to Mr. Cobb confirmed my fears. The offending hip had compensated for the other and new X-Rays were required. Culmination resulted in a decision being made not to operate in the hopes that the pain would settle. It did. Relief from adversity resulted in more ways than one.

I decided on an unusual course of action. Something had to be done to ease the flow of uncertainty I felt I was experiencing.

I requested an interview with one of the School Governors. In due course, a pleasant, thoughtful gentleman called at my Portakabin. Within this salubrious interior we put cards on the table. I made no secret of my fears. He knew of the Department's progress, had often praised it unreservedly and was clearly shocked by my disclosures. Thereafter, he brought about a lull. The dust settled and for a while I was left alone.

Ronnie remained well. In the weeks that followed, he made brief trips to Scarborough to tend Philip. Further heartbreak descended upon us when Jessie died. Our beloved Jessie...Philip was inconsolable, but within a solitary, quiet sorrow which enveloped the house. The news was not good and Ronnie's frequent phone-calls were forlorn and sad. I sensed his loneliness. When we were three, I became the catalyst. Ronnie, in spite of his love for Philip, was always ready to come home.

March 1994 brought another request for a meeting with the High Mistress. There was to be discussion about a Summer production for the Junior girls. I researched some ideas. I discovered a new adaptation of 'The Railway Children'. I thought how pertinent this would be; how Educationally valuable in content - a single parent, three children and a Father wrongfully imprisoned, good triumphing over evil once more. Much to my astonishment, the High Mistress seemed unfamiliar with the Nesbitt story! She would have 'to think about it, perhaps discuss it with the Head of English'.

When she eventually 'came back to me' she remarked that in her opinion it was too sentimental, but, that there was a very good part for a train!

I suppose I lost all sense of reality at that moment! 'Perhaps **you** would prefer to choose a piece, High Mistress' I replied. 'Yes,' she went on, 'I think 'School for Scandal' would be an admirable choice'. I found difficulty in accepting that such adult themes of adultery, malicious gossip, wrongdoing and dishonourable behaviour could be preferable to a wholesome family entertainment. My heart swells with joy when I think of 'The Railway Children's location so many years later in 2011 - Waterloo Station, where families flocked to see such an excellent part for a train!

I was subjected to the odious mission of putting old heads on eleven and twelve-year-old shoulders. Ronnie, true to form, came to this new obstacle with his usual verve and set about designing a collection of delectable Restoration costumes. The young Cast worked with a will, much laughter ensued and many questions poked into the wayward lives of the characters. I was engaged in searching analysis of their motivation. The theme of infidelity reared its ugly head and was a target for adolescent relish. The production was, in the end, a piece de resistance, a jewel in the crown of Educational and Theatrical expertise. All was well again and our determination to succeed in spite of hardship, was rewarded with accolades and parental recognition.

An invitation to attend the preview of 'Four Weddings & A Funeral' arrived. The Cast, Film Crew, Producers, Writers gathered one Sunday morning in a Curzon Street studio. From first moments, we knew...we knew that an enormous success was possible. We did not know, however, that the film was on the brink of worldwide celebrity and stature. After the premiere in May 1994, Ronnie, my darling Ronnie, was famous! We were robustly fortified for any impediment, barrier and block! It was a happy and welcome entr'acte for me before facing trying and taxing academic pressure.

I was reminded by the High Mistress that my title and salary would remain unchanged when her 'Plan' went into operation. At the closure of the Summer Term 1994, I had come to notice other disturbing elements which led me to believe that I was being disabled and worn down. Why?

I was instructed to discuss all proposed plans and projects for Drama with the Head of English. This had not occurred before; my judgement had never been investigated by another Department. Undoubtedly, I felt insecure and threatened. Via the grapevine, I heard about Appraisal Schemes and Head of Department meetings. I was not invited to take part or attend. I requested the Deputy Head to view a lesson for my Appraisal. She failed to turn up. I learned that Heads of Department had received a booklet outlining plans for the amendment of Middle School Courses. I did not. Was I becoming peripheral, marginalised? Was I being made redundant? Was I, yet again, to undergo the humiliation of being reduced in status? Why? What had happened? Why did I deserve to be so degraded and brought low? In my crestfallen moments I looked upon this time as a fleeting time.... A helpless, ambivalent, shifting...

***

PART 1

THEN

PHILIP

When we returned to West Bank for the six weeks of Summer, we found Philip in a precarious state. The disease was wreaking havoc upon his sparse frame and we were frantic at the thought of losing him. We devised schemes for making his days luxurious, comfortable and as pain-free as possible. The Doctor suggested a period of respite care in the Hospice. We were immensely relieved when Philip agreed. St.Catherine's Hospice in Scarborough was an idyllic retreat, a peaceful sanctuary where Philip could be cushioned. There, his medication was assessed and monitored. We called daily and were overjoyed to see our dear friend's gathering composure.

Ronnie was enveloped in practical goings-on. He would re-decorate Philip's bedroom. Together we worked unstintingly to have all in place for his homecoming. How thankful we were to be free from duty and ties. Nothing would be allowed to intrude upon this dedication. The Summer was fair and we could come and go without liability. Philip was dying and we were devotedly helping him along his pathway...

'Ron, this is five-star', Philip murmured, on his return. His face, although gaunt and hollow-eyed with sickness, broke into an air of radiant appreciation. I will remember forever his thankfulness, his love for us both. It was a fleeting moment filled with yearning. His eye took in the pristine bed-linen, the polished furniture and the new television. 'Before you get in, Philip, I'll just fetch our eiderdown from upstairs in case you're cold' said Ronnie.

'Oh, don't worry Ronnie, she's been down three times already!' All at once, the old Music-Hall joke reduced us to euphoria and daftness. In an instant, I realised that frightful illness can never get the better of a gallant spirit. Our time was Philip's. Our life together became a cherished passage of time...

Early one morning, I was passing Philip's door when I heard him calling. 'Philip, I thought you were asleep...' 'Come in, Sue, and sit down. I don't want you to say anything, so listen carefully'. Philip produced a wallet from under the pillow and said, 'Now, I have quite a bit in here. As you know, I have not been able to down a pint or smoke a fag for some time and I've managed to accumulate some cash - no, don't say a word - I want you to have it. I would like you to go to Tesco's or whatever and have some fun with it. I have never forgotten how you have always made sure I have had all I needed and you have saved me many times when I've been in the shit. This is my way of giving something back. Now off you go and tell Ronnie that I would like a salad for lunch, but only if **you** make it, and with that tasty dressing I've grown to like'. The tears did not flow until I had left the room...

It was Phyllis who knew that Philip had died. She came to the bedroom to tell us. It was early. The night before, Ronnie had been asked to retire to bed. Philip had wished to be alone. Perhaps he knew...

Only a week or two sooner, I had asked Philip's Macmillan Nurse how long he would have to wait. 'He will do it his way, in his own time', she replied. We were facing time once more. We had two weeks left of the Summer vacation. Philip knew that. I have often thought that the fearless are merely fearless. Those who act in spite of their fear are truly brave.

Philip's passing was very hard to bear. The simplest remembrances are the most plaintive. 'Oh dear, my glass seems to be empty' is such an anamnesis.

***

PART 1

THEN

'THE SHREW' - AND OTHER THINGS...

My busy preparation for 'The Shrew' was a partial antidote. The desolation of life without Philip was not lessened, but the frenzied introduction of Rehearsal, lesson-planning and Costume fitting filled the empty hours for us both. Out of necessity, the loss had to be relegated to West Bank. There we would grieve.

The Production was a stellar undertaking. Ronnie was making repeated excursions to the Ealing Road sari shops where he found very beautiful fabrics destined for Katharina, Bianca and the like. The inexorable wheels were turning again.

Yet - the hand of fate touched us. Ronnie was stricken with ghastly pain at ten o'clock one Autumn evening. He was rushed to Central Middlesex Hospital where, after tests, the Medics decided his heart was safe. An inflamed gall-bladder was the suspected culprit. At one in the morning and exhausted with relief, I made my way across deserted wasteland which was the car-park. My mouth dry with fear, I hoisted myself into the driving-seat. How agonised Ronnie would have been if he had known I was alone in such a district. He, who was unfailingly protective.

It was elected that the offending gall-bladder should be left alone for the time being. Suitable medication calmed symptoms down and it became one more thing to live with; one more shock to overthrow.

Hour after hour the machinery of Rehearsal ground on and as ever, the fruits of such intensity began to appear.

Angela Hardcastle, a gifted dance instructor stepped in to Frances Clarke's shoes and Sumptuous Costumes amid Elizabethan settings   put the finishing touches to a grandiose pageant. The Production neared its spectacular end and as the Technical and Dress Rehearsals were in view, my left hip began to go into repeated spasm and I knew I would have to recognise the severity of such a token. I was in for another run of infirmity.

Pain persisted during 'The Shrew' performances. X-Rays were taken and Mr. Cobb broke the depressing news once more. My left hip would need to be replaced and without delay. The High Mistress was duly informed. This time I could not recline on a Hospital bed during a convenient vacation. My condition demanded immediate attention.

The High Mistress was sympathetic. I was led to ponder, de facto, that there appeared to be a dash of the old friendship hovering. 'You have no choice, Sue, but to take leave for the whole of the Spring Term and I will arrange cover for you'. I was immensely grateful, but reminded by shrewd friends that the School was eager for me to be well enough to continue giving good service. Ergo, makeshift provision was vital. My absence would also provide timely scope for the Head of English to act as commander. So, in all, I was not hoodwinked into believing that I would be missed. I was not indispensable and there were more pressing worries to fill my thoughts.

The Head of English did not seek assistance. She was in full sail and I saw no reason to enlighten her about the Department's conundrums. These riddles were sacrosanct: I had no intention of edifying the arrogant. Ronnie, informed of the sequence of contingency, said, 'Who's the poor sod they've got to stand in? I don't envy whoever it is!'

***

PART 1

THEN

THE LONDON CLINIC....AGAIN!

So, it transpired that 1995 was to be a year to remember. Before my arrival at The Clinic on 12 January, Ronnie had an appointment with his Cardiologist, Mr. Dancy. We attended the evening before my operation to hear results of tests he had had several weeks earlier. Angina attacks had become more prevalent. It was perturbing.

'Mr. Herdman, it seems that the lower muscle of the heart is not functioning and you have a blocked artery. Of course the rest of your heart is sluggish because of the Cardiomyopathy. We are going to increase your Enalapril doseage and I recommend half an Asprin daily. In the near future, we may be looking towards by-pass surgery.' I was reeling with inner shock. As Ronnie rose to depart and made his way to the door, I turned to whisper before leaving. 'I am concerned about my husband. I'm to be out of action for a couple of months. Is he going to be safe?' 'At the moment,' replied Dr. Dancy, 'Mr. Herdman is on ice. It could clot'.

The intricacies of St. Paul's seemed very distant. I was frozen with fear. Ronnie yielded to his trust and reliance on Doctors. I think 'kismet' was the word he used. I was jostled into an auspicious frame of mind once more. As far as my darling was concerned, it was onwards and upwards towards a pain-free hip...nothing else was permitted to impinge.

January's weather was, to put it mildly, inclement. In spite of the bitter cold, Ronnie travelled to and fro to visit the Clinic where I wilted under post-operative haze and fug. We were cheered by messages of goodwill from School and delightfully, numerous visits from the most unexpected people. This diluted, to some extent, my constant worry for Ronnie. He did, however, seem to be impervious to defeat. Fingers remained crossed for most of my detention.

A well-qualified young Theatre Director had been appointed to take over my duties. I would have assumed that he was holding a winning ticket when thrown headlong into the midst of so many Paulinas, but it seemed that he had found himself at a disadvantage. According to arch and rascally student reports, girls were comparing him, unfavourably, with me. I felt very sorry for him. Where was the staunch defender, The Head of English?

This information came my way, unsolicited, from Senior students. These, when visiting my sick bed, seemed compelled to set the record straight. Their loyal affection touched me; such allegiance is a wonderful gift.

Shortly before I decamped from Hospital, my door opened to reveal - The Letter Writer! I could hardly conceal my amazement! She, clinging to a flower arrangement of princely proportions, sheepishly took a seat by my bed. Once constrained pleasantries had been exchanged, she embarked upon an offensive of derision, complaint and concern over the future of St. Paul's Girls' School. 'I have come to the conclusion that the Deputy Head is no more than a poisoned chalice. (Surprise! Surprise!) We are in the throes of a most unsatisfactory regime and I fear the School will soon find itself in an unholy mess,' she announced bitterly. I found myself on the receiving end of an astounding, dissatisfied monologue which finally came to an end two and a half hours later. I was, nevertheless, left mustering enough reserves of strength to laugh uproariously at the absurdity of it all! Truth will out....

In the days that followed, I was indulged with many visits from Staff and girls. A dazzling flower arrangement from colleagues was delivered by a most caring, gentle young Maths teacher. Ned Sherrin's collection of anecdotes was delivered; the Sixth Year had been cajoled into making a memorable contribution towards my recovery! I was touched and comforted by the strength of my ongoing closeness with the girls. That very thing, the most fundamental facet of my work, could not be crippled by anodyne meddling and interference.

Ronnie, as was his wont, almost brought the entire London Clinic medical team to a standstill when, on route for a farming commercial interview, he appeared for visiting clad in corduroy plus-fours, horticultural apron and cloth cap. It was phenomenal that he, suited thus, had circumvented the Hospital Commissionaire. Mr. Cobb was very amused. Ronnie's formula for fun was irresistible; his truth shone through sham and pretentious posturing. I am sure he was not unaware of effect: his sparkling eyes betrayed him. Throughout, his illness remained a closely-guarded secret. If it was mentioned at all, then I was the transgressor who imparted intelligence.

My convalescence at home was hampered by repeated fatigue and intermittent pain. Ronnie was assailed with chores, expeditions to the launderette, supervising an increasingly weak Betty, coping with Charlie and Phyllis and, as if that was not enough to floor him, he made time to visit School thereby to assist with Costume for the VII Year John Colet production of 'The Women'.

He encountered my 'replacement', the young Theatre Director, on his travels and learned that the unfortunate fellow was expected to teach twenty or more students in the confined space of a basement tomb adjoining the Dining Hall; the High Mistress had designated this venue as an appropriate and supposedly imaginative Drama Studio. In her opinion, this became an admirable facility for Dramatic purpose. Again, the vacant Theatre had not gone unnoticed...ah well, all comes to pass in time. My discreet spouse was non-committal; his cautious, wary self-overruled! Later, he had not been able to resist the temptation of dropping in to the Staff Drawing Room. There he was met with congratulations for his Vicar in 'Four Weddings', for by then many had seen the film and were thrilled to know an Actor who had found fame at last - certainly not fortune, I hasten to add. Providence, nevertheless, bestows its own rewards... and, in the fullness of time, makes itself clear.

Early in February 1995, Ronnie had yet another medical appointment. This time his gall-bladder needed attention. A Mr. Menzies-Gow, a specialist at that time in key-hole surgery, explained that the gall-bladder wall had thickened which would suggest infection and therefore it would be advisable to remove it. Ronnie waited until he got home before cursing 'Oh Fuck!' which was his precise oath when he was hard put to think of anything else to say. The upshot of the matter was that he could be admitted to the nearby independent Clementine Churchill Hospital for the operation. Recovery was estimated in a couple of days.

Ronnie qualified for private medicine under my health insurance with St. Paul's. We were eternally grateful for this invaluable assistance. I came to realise over the years how immensely fortunate we were to be so protected. This financial subsidy was repaid, I hope, with our unwavering, dependable and conscientious hard work. The School was a fine establishment which was evolving and being enhanced, in the main, by like teaching. I was saddened to realise that, at present, it seemed to be in the sway of fervent personal ambition. It was comforting to know that perpetrators of such an obnoxious trait cannot prosper. Often, they turn on each other. It was happening already.

Within a few weeks, Mr. Cobb gave me a clean bill of health and I was sent forth to 'get on with my life'. He added a footnote; he could vouch for Ronnie's gall-bladder care under the protection of Mr. Menzies-Gow. It put my mind at rest. Before parting, Mr. Cobb gave me a farewell shot - 'I do hope you will find the High Mistress in good form!'

Ronnie was to be admitted into Hospital on March 20, so we decided on a short break in Scarborough, but before leaving, called on Winnie and Sandy. We were so relieved to see our dear Uncle looking much better. 'Winnie's looking after me - as only Winnie can!' said he, and winked meaningfully.

We collected my Mother in Beverley and she spent the holiday with us...enough said about that! West Bank, our home, our sea and sand - we were content.

Philip and Jessie were sorely missed. We could not fill the emptiness. The ether filled the atmosphere with intangible laughter and barks which were a constant evocation of emotion and wistfulness.

Christmas, after Philip's death, had been a remote festivity; a reclusive, thought-filled, pining space. Now, the year had moved on to sunlit days and stirring gardens. As a part of this new beginning, Philip and his faithful Jessie were an indelible presence remaining with us for evermore...

The middle of March brought a shaky afternoon return to School. I was still operating on a stick, but driving was a boon and, filled with optimistic anticipation, I made my way through the Great Hall. My stopover was to receive an audience with the High Mistress, agenda unknown. On my way, I met various members of Staff who were all very pleased to see me. Girls were leaning out of windows or classroom doors in happy greeting.

The High Mistress was cordial. After polite enquiries about my health, she launched into her purpose. The choice of Autumn production was foremost and much to my surprise, she regurgitated the idea of another Pantomime. This had been light-heartedly mentioned earlier in the year, but I remembered the workload from before and was hesitant to repeat the labour involved. I attempted to remind her of the difficulties, but she had obviously invested some thought into the possibility and elaborated further on her suggestion. She predicted the English Department (I squashed my irritation) making a written contribution of topical ideas and cross-Departmental influences, not to mention the Music Department's exhilarating input. I groaned inwardly. I recalled my efforts to fire it into action on the previous occasion. Also, I abhorred the idea of not being solely in control. I could see that I would be expected to bow to the Head of English on a regular basis.

I did, under duress, make a concerted bid to be accommodating, and, in so doing, volunteered to contact my worthy friend in Oldham for one of his home-grown Pantos. Ronnie was incandescent. 'If you think that I am going to burn the midnight oil again, this time coming up with a costume for Mother Goose, or worse, you can think again! (Pause) Now, when do you want it for?' Kisses and cuddles followed....

Ronnie's gall-bladder came out mid-afternoon on March 20. All had gone very well - just. When he was admitted, I made sure that he had a list of medication and full information about his condition. 'Why do I need that? You're fussing', said he. Mr. Menzies-what's-his-name knows all about me. He's a Doctor'. Imagine my annoyance, when visiting in the evening, to discover that the Staff Nurse had come across this written message quite by chance, cast adrift on the bedside locker. 'I was alarmed, Mrs. Herdman, for your husband was already in Theatre. Often, Consultants do not pass on such details. I had to run all the way'. I could not wait for my darling to come to, so that I could read the riot act. Of course I didn't. Ronnie said, eyes twinkling, 'Well, I was planning the Panto costumes at the time - got to get my priorities right! I say, Alice, look at these little holes, that's where the key-hole comes in...two more orifices to add to my collection!' Overwhelming logic!

*

Kenneth Alan Taylor forwarded enticing scripts and Ronnie and I did burn the midnight oil reading. The time-honoured gags and jokes, tried out with gusto, brought about hysterical mirth at one in the morning...

It only remained for me to furnish our High Mistress with details. The scripts were delivered and before departing for the Easter break, I met the new Head of English and the Theatre Director. This get-together was contrived to be a hand-over before I recommenced work. He was an amiable young man who seemed to have done his best. In the course of conversation and planning for the next Term, the Head of English, in a bid to be jovial, said she experienced a feeling of being caught between two forces when meeting the High Mistress and myself! Wonders never cease, I thought. I did, for different reasons, feel a trace of compassion for them both.

As I adjusted my sticks and made my way through the Great Hall, my double-dealing peer, the Letter Writer, swept towards me. Her baleful expression led me to believe I was in for another basinful of dissatisfied disparagement.

'She's dismantling the Design Technology Department. It's all falling apart!' she screeched, without losing step. I was fearful of being engulfed in a puff of smoke.

St. Paul's Girls' School inhabited most of our waking hours one way or another.

Soon, Scarborough brought about change and the wherewithal to spend leisure time with friends and family. Not all was plain sailing and co-operating with my Mother's needs, Louie's unpredictable moods and the advancing years of Charlie and Phyllis were ongoing issues which presented us with some aggravation and a certain lack of peaceful recreation. Spasmodic pain in my hips did not help when dealing with the domestic pressure and transitory thoughts removed me to Bowrons Avenue, Betty and the cool sanctity of the Spiritualist Church!

Such escapism was short-lived, for I was deeply happy. Ronnie and I squabbled, laughed, cried (me only, when, as Ronnie said, I was 'overwrought'!), walked, rescued Charlie from crabs in rock-pools, drove over the Moors and whispered sweet-nothings as the sun went down over the sea. Our visits to car-boots, table-tops and jumble sales were legion. Such trips yielded a flood of ornaments, garden tools, plants and strange handiwork. To Ronnie, all were of use, or a feast for the eye...we were bathed in simple pleasures which rejuvenated and warmed the soul. During this blessed interval, Ronnie was well; he thrived on transient relief from the curse of breathless angina. We were thankful.

April 23 1995 brought frenetic preparations for the Summer Term. My opening days were sun-filled and almost leisurely as I settled into routine schemes. Friendships were renewed, relationships with the girls were easy-going and I was back within the internment of my friendly Portakabin.

A notebook was discovered on my desk. I was about to discard it, when I deduced that it had been left there deliberately. It lay there, open. It belonged to the young Theatre Director and I was dismayed to find that he had had a miserable time. I could only assume that he had wished to make his unease known to me. No help had been forthcoming; he had been deserted and left to his own devices. Sadly, I had been given to understand that he was superbly capable and so warranted no assistance from me before being instated. I was filled with regret and disgust that a visiting Assistant should have been stranded in such a thoughtless, selfish fashion.

Before long, the High Mistress called a Planning Meeting for the end-of-Year Production. Her Deputy, yet again clad in Strawberry-Pink-Jacket, was in attendance and wasted no time in giving her limited, derogatory opinions about the viability of the Pantomime.

The whole exercise was farcical, negative and an entire waste of my time. I was extremely angry when I recalled the considerable effort Ronnie and I had put into the project, not to speak of Kenneth Alan Taylor's expertise and generosity. What of the initial encouragement of the High Mistress? Why turn the tables?

The final and reprehensible lunge came when she announced that the Show could not go ahead because a Musical Director was unavailable! Gustav Holst would turn in his grave! No Musical Director! What of *noblesse oblige?* I was speechless - there was nothing left to say - I excused myself and repaired, despondent and furious, to the Staff Drawing Room.

Choice of Autumn play 1995 had to be agreed, so instead of requesting a further meeting I dropped a selection of scripts into the High Mistress' office. Silence reigned for a week or two until she had made a decision - no doubt in conference with the Head of English. Ronnie and I were gladdened to hear that 'The Happiest Days of Your Life' had received her blessing. Mmn...

While Ronnie spent a few days in Scarborough - essential now that Philip was no longer there to oversee - I held Auditions and also attended a MIV Parents' Evening. Such occasions were always a pleasure, for one was able to meet families and discuss Student progress in a friendly, constructive manner. It was usual for a queue to form near my desk, and although the centred dialogue was tiring, the enthusiasm shown for my Educational beliefs and practices, both past and present, registered genuine appreciation for all that I had tried to achieve.

A brief Half Term holiday in Scarborough enabled us to bring my Mother to Bowrons for a few days. She had recently been diagnosed with pernicious Anaemia and was not in the best of health. This worrying state of affairs was further exacerbated by Betty having a debilitating fall. Bowrons, in a short space of time, resembled a Sick Bay and Ronnie and I laboured under serious difficulty. Complication set in when Phyllis developed a heart defect and I came down with 'flu'. Ronnie seemed, for a short time, to be the only one to be passed A1 fit!

Such upheaval jolts one into the realisation that life can change radically in a very short passage of time...

I was awarded a breathing space. Earlier in the Term the High Mistress chose a Staff Meeting to broadcast her forthcoming plan for a Shakespeare Festival.

The whole School was to take part and all would be held in abeyance at the end of Term for this romp to be seen by the great and the good. Members of Staff were seen to muffle yawns, no doubt inwardly griping at the thought of extra work generated by this latest humbug. I was relieved of overall responsibility, but the notion of amateurish presentation and performance devoid of specialist tuition, niggled at my purist conviction. I was a perfectionist and believed that Work in Progress should be labelled as such. Unfair perhaps, for many Students would enjoy the process and, at the same time, I fully acknowledged that some Paulinas could pull rabbits out of hats regardless of who was waving the wand. Ronnie shuddered at the thought. 'I don't have to go, do I?' he pleaded.

The end of Term was approaching. It was marked by various leaving lunches and signing of VIII Year Books. It was an exercise to enjoy. Zeina Mansour, a perceptive, articulate student who, curiously, had not taken part in many Drama activities, volunteered a message of goodwill: 'Mrs. Herdman, if I was signing **your** Year Book, I would write: Carry on here, while you can. You are doing good work. They don't understand it, but you believe it, cos you are...' I took that advice and held it to my heart.

I was informed by the High Mistress that a Drama syllabus for years I to V would be drawn up by the Head of English and topics including death or anorexia should no longer be explored within the Drama lessons. All themes were to be text-based; subject matter was to be controlled. Ronnie and I mulled over methods of teaching 'Macbeth' without mentioning death. 'I suppose you could always say that Lady Macbeth was a woman of uncertain hospitality' quoth my beloved. Ronnie's ability to perceive the ludicrous was paramount.

I discovered that the Lower Vth were to study Greek Drama, which meant that I had to cover Greek History before the Chorus technique could be taught. I sought to liven things up by introducing Greek myths, Bacchus and fertility. I was crestfallen. This plan bore no resemblance to what I had set out to do. It was painful to endure. The final insensitive slight came about when the Shakespeare Festival drew to a close before dignitaries, parents and pupils. The High Mistress publicly thanked the member of Staff in charge of its overall success and introduced her as the Head of English & Drama. Stinging tears formed but did not fall until I was in the arms of the waiting Ronnie. I knew then that I was fading away....I was needed no more...

Next day, I was invited to a Staff farewell drinks party. It was held in the study of a Senior Manager. There, on the window-sill, was my missing Head of Middle School kettle! The thief was exposed...

Ronnie had a number of angina attacks during the Summer. These were often precipitated by change in temperature or being out in the wind. The attacks were unpredictable and could occur at work. Although Ronnie made light of these symptoms, I continued to brood. I had also noticed that his night-time breathing had become very irregular. I lay listening and tense while the pattern strove for normality. I would hear a pause, a terrifying silence until his lungs filled again. Within the stillness, I would be frozen with fear. Once, when the stillness had seemed endless, I leaned over Ronnie and gently shook him awake, just to ascertain he was still alive. 'Bloody hell, Alice, what are you doing?' said he, 'Do you want to **frighten** me to death!' Laughter dissolved the fear. Once disturbed, Ronnie would get up and make his way to the bathroom. If he appeared to be taking longer than usual, I would lie prostrate with anxiety, firmly believing that he had collapsed. I remained, waiting, until I could hear euphonious tones giving the best-loved rendering of 'Hey Mr. Watchacaller, what ye doin' tonight?' as the lavatory flushed and my precious made his way along the landing. 'Now what are you doing still awake?' he would hail as we attempted once more to sleep. Again, I would be his protector, watching over him; the dawn chorus would sound before exhaustion overtook me...

The recess in Scarborough was marred by ongoing family troubles. Our Mothers were presenting concerns: both were demanding for differing reasons. My own Mother, always reluctant to spend time alone, became petulant, tearful and pessimistic. When she was staying at West Bank, we found her repeated bouts of misery very trying. We were unable to pinpoint the cause of such sadness, and as a result, the house became diffused with her despair.

Louie, dealing with physical perplexity, was being referred for bowel tests. We gave assistance with these hassles, not to speak of boundless sympathy, but, ultimately, we had to rely on added help from relatives. It was demoralizing to be cognizant of the fact that our parents were not exempt from ailment and their time was growing shorter...

As August came near, I got my second wind and looked towards 'Happiest Days'. My schedule demanded an early start to the day. By 6.00 a.m. I was at my desk. All was quiet before the bustling routine began and I could work productively until the lovely Ronnie appeared with tea. Valuable progress was made which left me free to enjoy the rest of the day. This grind continued throughout the month so that when Term began, I was ready to rehearse. The planning was meticulous and impossible to accomplish midst the hurly-burly of School duties.

West Bank needed to be made ready for our departure. Our custom was to reach Bowrons with a week in hand before Term commenced. This afforded time to adjust before the foray began. This year there was added incentive for Mrs Doubtfire was to celebrate her 81st Birthday! We arranged a small party which included Betty's cousin, Hilary, Jasu, Bina (now an unbelievable sixteen with a respectable six GCSEs under her belt), Marjorie our next-door neighbour and numerous Wembley friends. I made a cake, Ronnie made everything else and the babies hovered expectantly in the hopes of an odd sandwich coming their way...

September 1995 paved the way for the beginning of Term and more unnerving attacks for Ronnie. They were now happening repeatedly, the most intimidating occurring when he was taking part in a Radio Broadcast; proceedings were brought to a halt until he had recovered.

Dr. Dancy arranged for further MIBI tests. Mystifying! By the end of the month, we learned that by-pass surgery was definite and likely to take place at the start of October. Coming to terms with such news was shattering...

In the meantime, life went on. Rehearsals for the play went ahead and, amazingly, Ronnie in virtuoso form, researched, designed and constructed a dozen school uniforms for the 'Happiest Days' chorus. Muttering 'we're on't roaaad', ad infinitum, he went on to assemble Principal's costumes and, in general, made ready 'before I go in'...

Ronnie's sister Vi, unaware of latest developments, let us know that Louie was in Hospital for observation. Ronnie and I were powerless to act. We were on the brink of a mighty shift in our lives. We were facing a monumental, life-threatening sequence of events and for once no thought could be given to anything else.

I remember attending Dr. Singh's surgery for a cursory appointment and was obliged to tell her about Ronnie's state. 'Oh no,' she cried, 'you not able to allow. Not Mr. Herdman heart - too risk'. I explained that we had absolute faith in Dr. Dancy and could only presume that he would not be advocating the operation if he was not persuaded that Ronnie would come through. 'Mmn, Mmn - Dancy good Cardiologist - Mmn - brave Mr. Herdman - Mmn'. As I left and made my way along the leafy, sari-filled Ealing Road, towards home, my eyes brimming with the tears held in check for so long, I prayed to God and the Spirit world for my darling, brave Mr. Herdman...

Daily life was observed as closely as possible. Lessons and rehearsals took up most of my waking hours. I was compelled to furnish the High Mistress with analysis of the circumstances. Hers was a sympathetic response and I was given carte blanche to come and go as status dictated. The English Department's resources would be called to account where my absence presented difficulty, but other than that, I would be leaving all in good order.

Rehearsal calls were drawn up for weeks in advance, so giving all those taking part liberal time to arrange their working life. There was to be an interlude of a fortnight for Students to learn lines and concentrate on adherence to pressing academic assignments.

A few days before this intermission, a Parent came forward at the end of a run-through. Her daughter had been cast in the play and she was there to collect her. 'Mrs. Herdman, I am Charlotte Payne's mother and I understand that Mr. Herdman is to have a serious operation. My husband is a Consultant and he would be delighted to accompany you to the Intensive Care Unit at St. Mary's Hospital where I know Mr. Herdman is to be treated. If one has not been to such a place before, the experience can be very upsetting. We are so grateful for all that you are doing for our daughter that we would like to be of help in some way'. I was quite overcome by such kindness.

Jean Payne became a force for enormous good in our lives. I have thought of her and her husband many times over the years. Guardian angels manifest themselves when they are most needed and disappear when danger has passed...

Journeys to and from School every day were consumed with agonising fear and paralysing emotion. There were occasions when, for safety's sake, I had to pull over to the roadside, for I could no longer see. Ronnie's life was in the balance and, while trying to amass courage to meet the possible outcome, I could not visualise life without him. Yet I tried to imagine and prepare for the heartbreak, the desolation.

By the time the car reached Bowrons and I could see the warm glow of our sitting-room lights and Ronnie framed in the window watching for my return, I had amassed some form of recovery. I lived in the moment, desperate to see him, love him and hold him dear. We were enfolded in fortune's embrace...

'Now, Alice, what do you think of those?' There, on the couch, spread in profusion, were crocheted coats and shawls of every shape and hue. 'Just thought I'd get my Christmas presents ready. I need to cater for a number of old ladies like you!' I knew...and Ronnie knew...words were superfluous. For the whole of my life, I have never loved as I have loved Ronnie.

Ronnie was admitted to the Lindo Wing, St. Mary's Hospital, Paddington on 6 October 1995. His surgeon, Dr. Stanbridge, was trusted. 'So handsome,' observed Ronnie. 'Wait till you see him, Alice! He must be so diverting when nurses are trying to pass him the right instruments!' It was always a constant source of amazement to me how Ronnie could notice such inconsequential detail in times of travail.

Darkness had fallen by the time I made my way to the car. Ronnie urged me to leave. 'Darling Sue, you can do nothing. Leave me to get on with it. Now you go home to those babies, they'll be looking for you. And Betty will need her morning cuppa'. I looked into Ronnie's eyes so deeply that it seemed as if my gaze would penetrate his very soul. We did not need to speak of love for its intensity was manifest; its boundary measureless, infinite.

I left him. The Hospital corridors, rooms and persons no longer existed. I was being piloted through a cloud that would not clear; a daydream detached and strange. Ronnie could die. I may not see him again. I was stricken, numb with terror. Yet, a mental opiate held me, blocked the torment and propelled me onwards through swinging doors and out, out into the rain-soaked street.

Puppet movements operated and the car slid stealthily through one-way systems, junctions and highways.

Alperton's fruit stalls and jostling Indians doing last-minute shopping were distant and dispassionate. How easy it would have been to wind the window down and shriek 'My Ronnie may die!' They would be unaffected. Impervious, they would move on with their business. My implacable agony was terminal in those chilling moments.

Charlie and Phyllis pointed the way to reason and rhyme; method, pattern, precept and habit took control. Like children, their lives revolved around a plan. I resorted to predictable, hackneyed and repetitive chores, and, in return, I received unequivocal love and dependency. Before common sense had reasserted itself, we passed that first, long night in wakeful premonition of the day to come.

'I say, my darling, I have just had my pre-med, and before I get really dopey, more so than usual, I just wanted to tell you how much I love you. Now, go and have a cup of tea and take those babies out...' Ronnie was about to have major heart surgery, yet he still looked to the familiar, the secure, loving and happy life he lived. Once more, his love held me in its peace...whatever happened, all was well...

As I remember, my behaviour was extraordinary during that anomalous, lonely morning. Yet all seemed as it had ever been. The babies were walked and as we picked our way over One-Tree Hill, I looked back over Wembley as if I expected it to be transformed before my eyes. I think my mind turned to eating. Why would I wish to eat? What would I eat? Perhaps I should, for there would be no time later...later...I would need to phone the Hospital...need to find out...surely they would tell me...

I did eat. I did feel better. Charlie and Phyllis remained near the window...the clock was moving towards the time...time to find out...

'Intensive care...yes...yes. Mr. Herdman has come through his operation. He is well. Leave it a while, then visit whenever you like, Mrs. Herdman'. The kindly voice spoke the golden words.

I visited alone. Fear followed my every step and yet I visited alone. Alone, I walked into an Intensive labyrinth. Machinery was ticking, whirring, whining and timing. Festooned in apron and mask, I was led to where my Ronnie lay. So little of the beloved Ronnie was discernible. He was obscured, covered by wires, monitors and tubes. His laughing face was still and pale. One watching Nurse, Sandra, loitered by him, checking and assessing while I looked on in disbelief.

What odd time-warp had we found ourselves within? I could only stand and stare at this stranger before me - this lifeless, environed form that was my Ronnie.

'Mrs. Herdman, Ronnie is sufficiently recovered for us to remove the ventilator. Perhaps you would like to return to the waiting area, for it can be distressing to watch the procedure'. I moved away and waited. Soon, I was recalled. Ronnie's lips curved and quivered. He was trying to smile when he heard my voice. Although heavily sedated, he knew I was there. He knew I would always be there...

When I left the Hospital, the night was dark and the street deserted. Hurriedly, I found the car. I moved off and was caught behind a truck waiting at lights. I waited...and waited. No other traffic was held in line. I edged a little further and noticed that the lights were green, but still the lorry remained stationery. In the same moment, I found myself looking at its registration plate...UBL! No sooner had I seen the letters, than the wagon moved off and my way was clear.

UBL could not have been closer to my maiden name nor its pronunciation -Uebel. In that moment, I was comforted...

Since that peculiar encounter, the identical registration has appeared at intervals in our life whenever times have been uneasy, unsettling or unnerving. It remains, to this day, a charm of hope.

I wandered through the empty rooms of home, faithfully pursued by Charlie and Phyllis. We could not settle. Again, the couch became our resting place through the lone, brooding night. The telephone took on the form of a mighty colossus as I watched and willed it not to ring. It became an instrument of dread. I could wait no longer and, in time-spans, I grasped the receiver and bedevilled my qualms. My mouth, my lips, my tongue were set as if glued or jammed as one.

'Try not to worry, Mrs. Herdman'. The voice was quiet, serene. 'Ronnie is settled. Ring whenever you wish'. Relief washed over me, a flush crept back into my cheeks and, at last, saliva flowed freely. I discovered that panic would terrify with petrifying repetition and again, I would be staring at my enemy. The telephone became a defiant antagonist until once more I was able to summon courage to seek another fix of reassurance.

The following day, Sunday, Ronnie was transferred to the High Dependency Unit where he could be monitored. He was recovering from this weighty invasion with his characteristic lion-hearted bravura.

Within a couple of days, I felt confident enough to make a short appearance at School where everyone was to send good wishes to Ronnie. I was enveloped in a mantle of affection and understanding. There was a reminder of the High Mistress' friendship when first we had been acquainted; erstwhile warmth and gentility was very evident in her message of concern, encouraging me to 'take as much time as you need'. Otherwise, it was saddening to see the change that had come about in her. I suppose there is always a reason why we behave in the way that we do. I mourned the loss of a friend for whom I had had much respect and admiration.

Before returning to St. Mary's, I spoke to our venerable Doctor in the North. I was not in quest of prediction, but was stilled with the words, 'Come on, Sue, it's downhill now...' Always, he had been our guiding light, our sage and our pundit. We were living our lives: the lives he had given back to us. It was a pilgrimage; an initiation of good or ill and we were learning...

Shortly after my arrival at the Hospital, Ronnie developed severe, terrifying arrhythmia. His heart-rate escalated, sweat poured from him and his face took on bloodless pallor. The Registrar seemed powerless to curb the catastrophic progression of symptoms. 'I can't understand why it's going so fast!' she exclaimed. Wild, I ran into the corridor. A Nurse tried to console me, 'We never know what the heart is going to do, Mrs. Herdman...' Blindly, I asked for a phone. 'Jean, please come, I think I'm going to lose him'. Jean Payne, took a taxi and was by my side in what seemed to be minutes.

Dr. Stanbridge had been on the motorway. Called for Ronnie's emergency, he took on uniform of the cavalry and on arrival, murmured evenly, 'This is always more of a nuisance than a danger' and administered intravenous Amiodarone. Ronnie's heart, once boosted, regained constancy and, as I recalled our Doctor's words 'Sue, it's all downhill', I heard Dr. Stanbridge say, 'Well, Ronnie, it's a big heart, but it's working!' Yes, it was a big heart and tears of gratitude for the saving of it, rendered me incoherent.

Jean Payne stayed with us until I urged her to return home. Before leaving, she turned to me and said, 'I know you have been treated very badly at School, but rest assured that you are held in very high regard, and Ronnie - well, he is just a wonderful man.'

Jean Payne and her husband remained in close contact throughout Ronnie's illness. Nightly phone-calls were an eternal life-line and a mark of supreme friendship. I like to think, after so many years, that their daughter's inventive, ebullient performance in 'The Happiest Days of Your Life' was a fitting reward for their benevolence. At that uncertain and fraught time, they became an unforgettable stay in our lives.

*

Bob Bottomley became a stalwart, robust friend during Ronnie's stay in the Lindo Wing.

He came to the Hospital for by-pass surgery three days after Ronnie's operation. Doctors suggested that Ronnie might be a heartening influence as Bob was asking many jittery questions. By then, my beloved was up, dressed and ministering to all and sundry, so he keenly acknowledged a call to gee-up the needy. I remember meeting Bob for the first time. He was the spit of James Robertson Justice an actor famous for the 'Doctor' films. In fact, it wouldn't have come as a surprise to hear 'What's the bleeding time?'

I happened to be visiting when Bob was grilling Dr. Stanbridge about his coming procedure. 'Now - how many times have you done this, Doctor? I'll have you know that in my opinion the medical profession is the most extensive area of undetected crime known to man!' Surely this tart assertion could have been recorded in the script annals of 'Doctor in the House'.

Bob had a very glamorous wife. It seems that she was careful to visit when his partner was not doing so. It all operated on oiled wheels. Bob lived, it transpired, very wealthily and happily with his lady. The two women in his life were as different as chalk and cheese; the macho Bob was lord. For us, he became a true, endearing friend. Long after these medical nightmares had ceased, Ronnie and I were invited to lunch. Feasting on freshly-landed lobster (transported from Newhaven that morning by Bob in his rackety old motor) and champagne, we spent a leisurely, boozy day of notable eventfulness perusing the imposing estate which extended over miles of verdant Sussex countryside. How indebted I am to Cicero: 'Memory is the treasurer and guardian of all things'.

***

PART 1

T H E N

AFTERMATH...

The Autumnal months were not free from anxiety. Once out of Hospital, Ronnie recovered slowly, but not without worrying periods of discomfort. Fatigue continued and in the early days he developed Anaemia and sleep disturbance. His chest wound showed signs of slight infection and another panic presented itself. It seemed that no sooner had we come across one handicap and overcome it, we faced yet another obstacle. St. Paul's was very patient. I would attend one day and have enforced absence the next. Throughout, my own health was not without stumbling blocks. I knocked repeatedly on Dr. Singh's door. 'Body react to shock', was her sensible summing up as she wrote out yet another prescription.

In spite of all, rehearsals for 'Happiest Days' progressed and the girls responded with their customary resilience. Nevertheless, the remorseless pressure took its toll of my lesson timetable. This culminated in weariness taking over to such an extent that I fell asleep in my Portakabin. I awakened to the sound of tentative tapping. A nervous eleven-year-old was standing in the doorway. In her shadow, I perceived the Head of English. 'We've been waiting for you in the Theatre, Mrs. Herdman. We were so worried about you, so I fetched a member of Staff to help'. I was very apologetic, but before I could say more, the teacher interrupted to explain that my Husband had been very ill and I was drained from lack of sleep. Deeply touched by their concern, I hurriedly and in some state of disarray, went to meet my class, only to find the girls in groups and working happily without supervision. Their smiles and heartfelt condolence was movingly sincere. I was grateful to the English mistress for her tactful explanation. Her understanding of the situation had been expressed in kind, thoughtful terms. Children will react appropriately if a truthful or compassionate reason is given for unusual behaviour or circumstances. They are quick to rumble excuses.

I sought a favourable time to offer my thanks. 'You must be so upset, Sue. It's the price we pay for love, isn't it?'

It was half-way through the Term before I was able to return to School without the threat of serious incident taking place. There had been disruption; another scare catapulted Ronnie into Emergency admission at Central Middlesex Hospital. Discharge the following day restored faith; once more we soldiered on through concern and commotion.

My way of life was constrained with thoughts of impending peril. Survival relied upon the capacity to deploy on differing cognitive levels. Intellectual capability fortified my time at School and the restraint of duty compelled me to apply myself to one thing at a time. Temporarily, the force of necessity relegated Ronnie's precarious constitution to the recesses of my mind. Strain, worry and increasing tension damaged carefree contemplation and, in its stead, a disconsolate melancholy began to descend and make itself plain. I concealed this sorrow. My walks with Charlie and Phyllis afforded the freedom to give vent to it; the grief, noisy and consuming, spilled on to the Park and walkway while the babies looked on in troubled alarm. I was incredibly lonely...

Ronnie strengthened over the remaining weeks of the play's preparation. Determined to alert his faculties, he took charge of the Costume Department and all was made ready for the First Night. Staff, pupils and parents were delighted to welcome him back. There he was: smiling, hospitable, ready to usher in and greet all who had befriended him. His bountiful goodness made light of the grievous ordeal he had so recently endured. He was venerated. I was overwhelmingly proud of him.

Our Christmas journey to Scarborough was joyous. We were going home! I did not permit my pensive reflection. All was well and Ronnie was well...so be it. We were meant to go. There were things to be done. We had been granted the time to do it. We had been spared. This time was precious, inestimable. Yet, I knew I would struggle; always, perpetually and for evermore I would be wary. In secret, I would be unceasingly watchful and cautious. This was my price. The reward was priceless...

'I say, darling,' said Ronnie, 'do come along to the corner shop. It's been turned into a pet store. You know, the one that used to be the Barber's. I want to show you something'. I knew that a major development was brewing. When dear Ronnie wanted to show me something, then he had a proposal. Sure enough, I was led to the birdcage section of the new pet shop on the corner of West Bank. Christmas Eve was two days away. 'Isn't he absolutely lovely. He's a show bird, but they've decided to sell him'.

I was looking at a very handsome Cockatiel and 'he' was looking rather belligerently back at me. 'Oh really, Ronnie', said I. In a matter of half an hour, we were the gauche owners of this remarkable creature and I was hot-footing it into Town to obtain a cage, birdseed and various swings and roundabouts! According to my beloved, 'he' was going to be a prolific talker and a sensational addition to our family. 'He looks like Punch,' observed Ronnie. 'Does he?' said I. 'Oh yes, I think we should call him Punch. He has two red blotches on his face, just like Punch'. So, our feathered friend took pleasure in the name of Punch, or rather 'Punchie' when Ronnie was in frivolous mood.

Punchie turned out to be the most vicious fowl I had ever come across. He had no intention of speaking, in spite of Ronnie's continued entreaties to encourage him to say 'bugger' or 'piss off'. Cleaning out his cage became an operation of military precision. Punch overlooked the whole exercise with beady, rancorous antagonism. One had all one's water on to avoid the torment of having a lump taken out of one's finger. Punchie was not heard to utter a word, but our journeys to and from the Smoke were accompanied for most of the A1 miles by ear-splitting screeching. 'He loves the movement of the car' announced Ronnie. 'Oh, I'm so glad, darling,' I nodded, 'he's been God's gift...what would we be without him!' And...all for the love of Ronnie...

The early months of 1996 brought heartbreaking bereavement. Our dearest Uncle Sandy died. We were flooded with memories of sunlit days in Hitchin and the prattle of a bantering twosome. Auntie Winnie would no more be part of that potent, boisterous and indispensable double act. Now there was one. The idiosyncratic, welcoming dwelling which had embraced us so warmly would never be the same.

Winnie lived alone for a while after Sandy's passing. It was not for long...she remained a loving part of our lives, sharing with us by letter and card, news of her day-to-day deeds. When the time came for her to join Sandy, we grieved for an enchanting bond, a link that could never be broken or forgotten. Over the years, Hoya Carnosa has been a jubilant remembrancer. A progeny now sits in a sunny corner of my home.

Then...the unthinkable happened. Betty died. We faced her death with incredulous disbelief. Our Mrs. Doubtfire had left us. The loss was insurmountable, a final and fundamental deprivation; for Ronnie, for me and perhaps most of all for Charlie and Phyllis. Betty died, unexpectedly and suddenly, during the Easter holiday when we were away. Our return to the empty house, where we had all lived so happily together, was an anguish we would not forget. The suffering of Charlie and Phyllis carried them from room to room, searching for their friend. We comforted them as we strove to comfort ourselves. We were alone...

We were plunged into a shaky series of developments. Betty's cousin and family were wanting to sell the house. All was amicable, but we fully understood that Betty's estate could not be finalised until her affairs had been put in order. I had had the foresight, after our unfortunate experience at No.20, to request, against the unlikely prospect of history repeating itself, some form of safeguard for our tenancy. Fortuitously, we kept a letter, signed by Betty's cousin, herself and us allowing six months to vacate. This would give us a breathing space before facing the upheaval of moving. It was, nevertheless, a tense turning point. Betty's solicitor asked to see the letter, drawn up some years before. After some deliberation, he concluded that it needed to be observed.

Still reeling from shock and the nebulous fortune which had come our way, we began to receive disconcerting letters from Louie. Now out of Hospital and in reasonably good health, it seems she had deemed to put pen to paper. We had assumed that all was running smoothly and, after the fright of Ronnie's illness, she was in a sympathetic state of mind.

In eccentric pattern, as was Louie's predilection, she had resolved, instead of making a Will, to divide her modest savings between Ronnie, Vi and Welsh Ken - and - distribute the money by post! We received a brown packet containing £1000! Extremely grateful, we made sure that Louie was given a plethora of thanks. She seemed well, her Hospital tests had been good, so we had no reason to believe that there was unrest. The communiqués were hurtful and pernicious. Most damaging of all, for Ronnie, was her ignominious account of the circumstances of his birth. The gist of this injurious unveiling contained details of his illegitimacy. Apparently, Louie had suspected that Winnie had divulged murky details of her past and so set out on a path of destruction. Ronnie, having more than his share of common sense, calmly ignored the whole miserable business, in spite of the fact that Louie had painted a very defamatory picture of his Father. Her description of a physically disabled, ugly man was vitriolic and hateful.

Not satisfied with piling on the agony for Ronnie, Louie had a go at me, referring to 'her tacky job in London'. We, through force of necessity, had to dismiss the attack. To become overly involved, would have harmed Ronnie's steady footing and added insult to injury. We ended up putting the whole sorry rigmarole down to a temporary (at least we hoped it was temporary!) imbalance of mind on Louie's part. I did, however, find it hard not to react in outraged fashion to this villainous tirade. We were silent and our peace, in spite of what seemed to be merciless persecution, was recouped - until the next crabbed victimisation made itself known! 'Ah well, all part of life's rich pattern', said my sagacious Ronnie.

The succeeding months were spent in feverish search for alternative accommodation. Housing associations, Brent Council and private lettings were pestered with our repeated pleas for help. How many times we blessed my fulgent presence of mind in appealing, all those years ago, for some element of security. That said, we were pitched into a turbulent set of events; they would not go away.

Bereavement brings about complete change. A way of life is mourned as well as the loss of the loved one. Betty had been intrinsic. We had never underestimated her value, love and friendship. She was a member of our impermeable kith and kin. We missed so many simple connections: shopping for Mrs. Doubtfire's Marks & Spencer ready meals, a plate of late Sunday lunch she so appreciated while watching her Songs of Praise, her cries of 'Oh, Phyllis, you **can't** want to go out again!' while she shuffled in good-natured, loving indomitability to the back door. The ground floor became a hollow, deserted shell. Cousin Hilary visited often to sort Betty's belongings. She bestowed many gifts; keepsakes for us which would become a lasting echo of Betty's rich felicity. Betty was a diamond.

All was quiet in Hartlepool. We did not ruffle any feathers, but allowed time to disperse unrest. Unable to engage in any further dialogue, we let sleeping dogs lie. In fact, life in the North became a distant affair where troubles and aggravations needed to be kept at arm's length.

Chekhov's 'Proposal' had been designated as a minor end of Summer Production and 'Pygmalion' was chosen for the end of year. Choice of play nearly always presented some consternation until a decision had been made, so it was a relief to know that at least one cause for concern had been removed.

Our search for a flat was ongoing. Would we ever find a solution? Before salvation came our way, another niggling, fractious grievance materialised. The Summer play was to be presented in the...er...Drama Studio as it was referred to in querulous tone. There was hardly room to swing a cat and in rehearsal the Company was braving a battle to avert culinary fumes from the neighbouring kitchen and Dining Hall. Windows and doors remained shut so atmosphere became a shade sweaty and close. Frustration was the order of the day. Seating capacity was minimal and we could visualise a perspiring, cramped audience. I laboured to shore up optimism and Theatrical wonderment.

In all honesty, it was impossible to use the real Theatre at this time of the year as it doubled in its duty as an examination venue. So, we made the best of the basement amenity and nothing interfered with the quality of work. In fact, a Cast of three working on such a compact play made way for an intimate, enhancing element.

Soon, life had reconciled itself into a leisurely pace. London in the Summer months can be warm and seductive. Invitation to take advantage of this ambience is tempting. Time remained of the essence, however, and the search for somewhere to live was an ever-present anomaly.

More irksome Staff Appraisal was underway and countless Managerial meetings took place with galling regularity. These were exhaustive, assiduous undertakings for many members of Staff. Grumbling and disaffection engendered a mood of protest and repetitious tedium. I was not asked to take part and so became exempt from this burden but I did remain aware. I invited the Deputy Head to appraise one of my lessons, but unfortunately she did not turn up. I continued to wait, for it was likely that a snag would unravel my symmetry.

I received word from the Deputy Head teacher. She wished to see my lesson notes! I had always kept written preparation. It was detailed, dated and summarised after each session and could be scanned by anyone worthy of the task. Yet why? Why was I being scrutinised? Why was I being policed after more than seven years of diligent, devout teaching? It was a gravely upsetting and ignominious jolt. Why was such a thing happening? Did someone wish to crib ideas and methods for the English Department? If the approach had been honest and kindly I would willingly have shared my experience. We could have worked as a team.

Eleanor Zeal, my assistant, together with Deborah Padfield - a dear young woman who visited the Drama

Department on many occasions to give lessons on Masks - were taking a leisurely break in the Staff Drawing Room and saw my distress. They could see that I found it hard to assimilate what was happening. Within a day or two, Fate dealt one of her timely cards and once more a guardian was beside me.

I received a warning. The counsel made known to me could not be mistaken. It came by way of a faithful, dependable colleague and equipped me with a means to handle such a predicament. I did not act upon it. I remained silent, knowing full well that a further request for my lesson notes would be forthcoming. Sure enough, a memo appeared on my desk, ordering contact with the Deputy and Head of English.

My close friend and fellow worker had advised that my classes were being discussed disparagingly and within earshot of others. I had no choice but to speak of this to the Deputy. I considered the matter to be unprofessional in view of the fact that a Staff Appraisal programme was in progress. I explained that, as a consequence, I preferred my lesson notes to remain exclusive.

As I made my way down the oak staircase, I thought of battles, strife and foes. It saddened me. The teaching of children should not be about plots, traps and unscrupulous, knavish dealings. I rejoiced at that moment to think of the other ethical, committed men and women of St. Paul's who, before all else, heeded the welfare of their charges and the importance of that was uppermost in comportment, perspicacity and wisdom. They would triumph...

Before the closure of the Summer Term, auditions for 'Pygmalion' and performances of 'The Proposal' were completed. We took a well-earned breather and were beginning to relax when news from the North took us by surprise. A work colleague of my Brother passed on information about a flat. A friend of a friend was moving and wished to let an apartment in Slough. (In time, we were to discover that John Betjeman had not exaggerated in his scathing attack upon the township).

With renewed vigour, we made enquiries. The young couple in question arranged to reconnoitre. We made a convoluted journey, via the problematical M4's four lanes of fast-moving traffic, to find Rochford Gardens, a modern development of houses and flats on the outskirts of the metropolis known as Slough. The home was ideal; situated in a residential area, it occupied the top floor of a block of three and was self-contained. The rent was considerably more than we were used to paying, but we were fully aware that the arrangement we had had with dear Mrs. Doubtfire had been unique, utterly convenient and generous. We were obliged to move into the real world. We learned that vacant possession of the unfurnished flat would be accessible by the end of November 1996. It seemed that the only regrettable drawback to the location was its distance from Town. We were not in a position to deny this expedient solution to our perplexing issue and settled the deal there and then. One of the most attractive facets to this removal, was the acceptance of Charlie, Phyllis and...er...Punch by our landlords. They were pet lovers, so all our dear ones were embraced within the tenancy. Phew!

We were immensely relieved to be freed from anxiety. Cousin Hilary was also immensely relieved to hear the news! She could now put plans in motion for the sale of Betty's house, and we, in the nick of time, had a new roof over our heads.

The salty air of Scarborough beckoned and, exalted with hungry expectation, we, the babies and the shrieking Punchie were 'on't roaaad' once again.

I was revitalised by my early morning walks by the sea. The babies, also sensing new breath of life, were cheekily unresponsive to command or curb. When the Spa beach was in sight, they would break into raucous barking, and once let loose, shouted all the way to the water's edge. Swimming was not on the to-do list for both seemed to view the incoming tide with noticeable fear and trembling. On a good day, Ronnie would join us and even his wheedling 'For God's sake, Phyllis, you're supposed to be a water dog..!' fell on deaf ears. We would take time to sit upon a rocky outcrop where seaweed, shells and creatures inhabiting the pools would yield indolent pastime. No leaden thoughts or leaden prompters of our other life blundered into this calm resting place.

No sooner had we drawn breath of the briny than annoyance and trouble beset us. Our respective Mothers raised cause for concern and we had to respond to the call of reliance. This burden of responsibility was not permitted to fall upon us immediately, for yet again we were faced with the dejection of bereavement.

Punchie, unsociable and ferocious for most of his stay in the Herdman household, died. He was taken ill, taken to the Vets where accident befell him and thereafter taken to his next life. The Vet had been wary and attended to Punchie wearing protective gloves. His feathered antagonist lost no time in setting about the thumb of the right hand. In so doing, his beak was damaged. Dismayed, we feared he would not survive without the use of his only weapon. In spite of reassurance, we were right and Punchie deteriorated rapidly. His death was a great sadness to us. We were affected. I remember holding him and saying, 'Oh Ronnie, this is the one and only time that he would let us touch him', and burst into tears. Encased in cotton-wool within a Doc Martens shoebox, he was buried with moving ceremony beneath a Prunus blossom shrub in the garden of West Bank. The memory of Punchie, vocally strident, rebel and challenger, stayed with us for a very long time...

***

PART 1

THEN

LOUIE AND JESSICA

My Brother had been coping with the onset of my Mother's depression. In recent months this had increased and made worrying, incessant inroads into his time and attention. When in Scarborough, we made valiant attempts to share the load. This involved bringing Mum to stay at West Bank for a couple of weeks during the Summer, at Christmas and whenever we were in situ. At the time, we found it increasingly difficult to assess Mum's unhappiness, or to find a reason for it. All we could do was our best which seemed to fall short of a real solution. Uneasiness was ongoing...

Louie did not like me. That was her prerequisite. Her hand of friendship was not proffered, but I did not stint in my wish to make constant overtures of goodwill. I hesitate to say 'love' for she did not go overboard to receive my gestures with anything other than suspicion. Bulging bags of treacle toffee and enough Mills & Boon volumes - each more racy than the other - to fill a truck, did naught to soften her bellicose bearing: I was to be kept at arm's length. My one and only trump card was the ability to drive. Accordingly, I provided the means for number one son, Ronnie, to visit. I persevered and, in spite of Louie's taxing defence mechanisms, I held fast while harbouring a faint hope of victory. The contents of her recent vociferous and repellent belle-lettres did hover in my awareness. Such thoughts were relegated to the far reaches of my subconscious. It was not within my remit to give her a trouncing.

The logistics involved for an overnight stay at Louie's sheltered housing were dependent upon monumental planning. Louie slept in the only bedroom while it was our misfortune to camp on sofa and floor. We took turns on the couch. The floor -aptly referred to as the 'dog shelf' by my Mother - was the favourite pad of Charlie and Phyllis. It became somewhat overcrowded and not designed for Ronnie's leisurely slumber. No sooner had we succumbed to a relieved kip than Louie was on the move. These nocturnal visitations to the lavatory were punctuated by grunts and 'uhh-agh, uhh-agh'. The babies would rouse and look on in disbelief as this shadowy, corpulent spectre followed a beleaguered path to the bathroom. The whole operation was winding, meandering, but each hysterical episode reduced us to smothered fits of hilarity. Yes, we could have resided in the comfort of the nearest B & B, or, taken advantage of an invitation to stay with relatives, but the invitation did not materialise. Besides, Ronnie knew that his Mother welcomed the gift of companionship. I wondered at the bond between Mother and Son, for it seemed that Ronnie had no inclination to prolong his stay and his Mother rewarded his love with scripted malice aforethought. There's now't so queer as folk...

Thereby, we spent our Summer vacation, acknowledging the fact that our energies were being dissipated by one or the other. There was momentary fraying of temper and frustrating efforts to bring back our steady placidity, but we were together and always loving. Ronnie, the comedian never known to fail, from then on backed his nightly calls of nature with 'uhh-agh uhh-agh'. Charlie and Phyllis were perturbed with scary deja-vu, as I buried my head in the bedspread. Ronnie's re-enactment of banal, risible practice was the glorious stuff of farce. To laugh with such sublime abandon was a divine blessing...

The Autumn Term of 1996 marked the beginning of text-based Drama on all levels. I dolefully anticipated

Greeks with the Lower Fifth and groaned. The repetition four times a week was just about at saturation level.

As the Portakabin bid a fond farewell to private lesson pupils and I embarked upon the planning of a belated leaving celebration for Eleanor and Deborah, my Part-time Assistants, an unexpected turn of events took place. I received a call to convene with the High Mistress.

'Were you aware that your Assistants have advertised Private Lessons for our students?' she enquired. 'Certainly not, High Mistress. Had I known, I may have advised against such a move'. This was quite true. Eleanor and Deborah had not breathed a word about their plans, knowing that I would have been placed in an awkward position if they had done so. They had left the School at the end of the summer.

The Drama Department no longer existed. They were not needed or employed there, or under any further obligation to the School, but did sympathise with girls who wished to continue with the excellent progress they were making in examinations. I presumed, therefore, that they considered themselves at liberty to offer their expertise within an independent arrangement.

Eleanor Zeal and Deborah Padfield enjoyed a very special, unforgettable commemoration of their passage at St. Paul's. It was a benevolent, well-deserved rave-up offered at the elegant home of grateful School parents. Ronnie and I were Guests-of-Honour; gaiety and good cheer echoed well into the night.

The Theatre space was requisitioned for continued classroom use. With flexible ease, I moved into another phase of my teaching life at St. Paul's. Greek lessons became a pliable, elastic undertaking, where the Myths offered excitement, mystery and scope for Theatrical craftsmanship. No filibuster would conquer ingenious creativity, frolic and fun.

The younger eleven and twelve-year-olds were at liberty to bring English texts to vibrant life. Where appropriate, themes which reflected and evoked similarity with student experience were explored and relished. My Drama lessons were not left wanting. Learning did not operate in a vacuum; we created our own freedom in defiance of restraint. Unfettered by passe jurisdiction, we flourished as before.

***

PART 1

THEN

PHYLLIS

Phyllis had not been well for some time. She was becoming lethargic and sad. Her weakening heart gradually began the pathway to its ending. Our darling Phyllis was fifteen years old and we began to prepare ourselves. We knew that Charlie could not be prepared. He would be lost. We would be lost. Every morning we rose with the hope that she would be strong again. She was not. Ronnie and I clung to each other in our moment of decision and misery. Phyllis would be protected and held while she passed from one happy life into another.

Mr. Poole, our Vet, lived in Kenton. He and his thoughtful wife had cared for our babies throughout their Alperton years. Gentle and knowing, he told us it was time. Our journey was so, so heavy...silently, Ronnie held his Phyllis, cocooned in her best-loved blanket. Her weary eyes looked up at us while Mr. Poole smoothed her life away...she was gone...

'Brothers and sisters, I bid you beware
Of giving your heart to a dog to tear'.
(Rudyard Kipling - 'The Power of the Dog')

Charlie, thereafter, was not left alone. He came everywhere with us and when Ronnie was working, I took him to School where he resided, secretly, in the Portakabin. Permission should have been sought, but I was fearful of discovery and thence, its withdrawal. His presence remained a closely-guarded mystery. Charlie was smart; he understood. His was a receptive, spellbound response to his new and very different life: an existence enriched by the beguiling contact with the girls.

St. Paul's would have welcomed him. Charlie was a stealthy concealment, but perhaps my subterfuge was unnecessary. Our domesticity was surrounded by human, kind thoughts. Yet again, I was afraid; afraid of complication and unrest. Providence was not to be tempted...

The return to Betty's each evening was steeped in heartache. So many of our loved ones were leaving us... our lives no longer took on the carefree promise of yesterday. Our thoughts were taken with the shielding of Charlie and he was diverted from searching the empty rooms for his cherished companions. Ghosts walked with us and were welcome, but the involuntary sadness which travelled with them left us three inconsolable and forlorn.

It was time for resolve. Our house move precipitated haste. We were quickened, triggered into vigour and motion. Charlie was stirred by our mood and greeted the days with vitality of barking. We were being directed, moved once more towards a new future and a restorative hand...

As October drew to a close, we were faced with major disturbance. Plans to flit coupled with intensifying Rehearsals for 'Pygmalion', exhausted our customary vitality and staying power. Ronnie's contribution to these culpabilities was two-fold. Yet again, his Costume designs were unparalleled and the girls were consumed with excitement when being fitted with such inimitable artistry. Yet he still saved time to negotiate financial terms with Removal firms and become familiar with any wheeling and dealing which seemed to run alongside such arbitration. Daily teaching rendered me ineffectual as Girl-Friday and Ronnie-boosting was relegated to the evening hours when we were both hors de combat and submitting to maximum lassitude!

Weekends were swallowed up with dummy-runs to the exotic Slough. 'Oh Sue, have you noticed,' Ronnie was heard to vociferate, 'we'll be on the Heathrow flight-path!' as screeching jets escorted our transit along the M4. Mmn..

I strove to repress my escalating euphoria. Four lanes of hell-for-leather motorway traffic was hassle enough. As a bonus, were we to be bombarded with aerial flak and crescendo at the close of each day? These airings, however, did give us some hint, some inkling as to what lay ahead. Now, it occurs to me that 'omen' might have been a more accurate maxim.

By the end of November 1996, all was ready, 'Pygmalion' was all but completed and the move was nigh. How fortunate not to be soothsayer or psychic...how scant is our knowledge...how vital it is to live our lives one step at a time. Would we ever endure if we could see what lay ahead? We were on the verge of beholding a year-long, racking sequence of happenings...a rollercoaster of unforeseen hazards while our albatross flew silently above.

***

PART 1

T H E N

ROCHFORD GARDENS, SLOUGH...

The removal from Bowrons Avenue deepened a saddening, painful ache. So many years of love and happy friendship in the warmth of our first real homes together created a lasting unbroken thread that would remain with us for the rest of our lives. Naught would rend it asunder...

Ronnie took my hand in his as the car slowly pulled away. 'Come on, Alice, get that hand back on the wheel. I'm a very precious cargo! Charlie, - in the front! Phyllis would want you to be on my knee. That motorway is a bugger and I might be frikened!' Darling Ronnie - my love, my friend and my protector...

Three flights of steps faced the removal men and there were audible sighs and groans as our belongings were hoisted to the upper reaches of the block. 'Couldn't you find a furnished, ground floor one?' wisecracked the firm's jester. Between loads, all three beasts of burden lay knackered on the upper landing.

The new lodging was compact and very well suited to our needs, although most space was devoted to the living area and kitchen, which, much to our rapture, boasted a washing-machine. No more visitations to the launderette. A large window in the sitting-room overlooked a decaying, grubby canal. The odd Tesco trolley could be seen floating near the bank. The ugly and the beautiful can exist within the same habitat; we discovered a saving grace. The waterway afforded home to a couple of Swan families. Charlie's first foray into the neighbourhood, taking in the path beside the channel, left him frozen in disbelief. He had not encountered a Swan before and cautious restraint became the order of the day. Mother Swan fixed him with a vengeful eye and much quivering went on.

Unpacking, reorganisation of our stuff, goods and chattels, all ran in tandem with Ronnie's unremitting 'Well, we're on't roaaad' and filled out most of our first Slough weekend. Needless to say, there had been ruthless paring down of possessions before we took leave of Bowrons Avenue. The man in my life had, however, found time to adapt loose covers and furnishings to fit our new household. When all was in place, we surveyed our tireless efforts with pleasure and an overpowering sense of relief. Ronnie sank into a revamped armchair and muttered 'I feel as if I've been fucked, bashed and robbed!' which I think was an approximation of how overcome he was with fatigue.

A few bothering worries had invaded my mind's eye throughout this busy, fluctuating instalment. I was concerned about Ronnie's inevitable solitary existence while I was to be absent and at work. Then, there was the encroaching alarm as 'M4 Motorway' took over my thoughts. The daily commute was stealthily giving me cold feet...four lanes of intractable, perpetual and unwavering early-morning and late-night travel. I was frightened. Would I confide in Ronnie? Of course not...

The remainder of the weekend was spent locating the nearest Supermarket. The Slough Tesco was of gargantuan proportions and in the weeks to come, it became a regular Friday evening port-of-call. Ronnie would give me strict instructions to meet him there after School for an enlivening tea-break. This assignation was to take place in the somewhat smelly cafeteria before we embarked upon the weekly shop. He would find a table and stand expectant until he saw me, whereupon he would wave ecstatically. Now, so long after, it is an image I remember with yearning and love. Whenever I am completing a lonely quest, I may pass an in-Store café and there he is once more in my daydream and insight, waving and smiling as he always did, a mirage of love and everlasting constancy. He remains...forever 'on't roaaad'...

*

Fog! Fog! I was not predisposed to the petrifying plight of an M4 bathed in its impregnable blanket of murk. It was 6.45 a.m. and the four mighty lanes were almost indistinguishable. They took on the trait of a roaring giant fully roused from sleep, all the more tumultuous, electrifying and sinister because they were not conspicuous. As I turned the car to the brink of what seemed to rear blindly before me as a bottomless depth, a Porsche Carrera slid in beside me ready to pound and pulsate its passage into the fast lane. It would not have been wise to close my eyes in panic-stricken tizzy nor to fancy my darling sitting reassuringly beside me. I did not waiver and in my hallucinatory state, Ronnie's smile spurred me onwards and upwards. Headlights blazing, I got my foot down...it had to be done. It was done. Morning after morning, I brazened it out. When I arrived unscathed at the Portakabin, lathered in a proliferous sweat, I phoned my darling 'Just to let you know I've arrived and the roads were fine!'

Splendid ruse!

So began our new life. We thrived - somehow. 'Pygmalion' was near and my daily pilgrimages to the shrine of St. Paul's ceased to become fraught with wraiths of disaster. Together as always, we took arms and tasted the field. Forged by the necessity to alter the direction of our lives, any hassle and vexation we ran into merely threw up more stumbling blocks to circumvent. The M4 giant was vanquished!

The Drama Department's 'Pygmalion' did Bernard Shaw proud. Ronnie made his customary contribution. His Costume designs were based on Thirties Erte and Aubrey Beardsley and drew gasps of audience amazement, particularly in the Ball Scene.

He complimented the performance further. His mellifluous voice, as he impersonated that of Shaw, could be heard as a link between Scenes. It was a worthy production in every sense.

As usual, the play ran for four consecutive nights. Once more, I was faced with the portentous prospect of the M4, but this time at nearly the midnight hour. As I look back, it seemed that my courage knew no bounds. Fog! Fog! A pea-souper of fog enveloped me on all crusades and its vaporous mantle became my tenacious partner. Ronnie, my intrepid, gallant fellow of esprit de corps remarked as we motored home after the First Night, 'I say, Heathrow's still on the go. It can't be that bad - oh look, I'm sure it's beginning to clear, darling. Step on the gas, Alice, I know where we can get a bag of chips!' Matchless optimism! Ronnie's manna from heaven lay concealed in a bag of chips. My spiritual nourishment lay lovingly wrapped in Ronnie's eternal gift of rose-coloured spectacles.

***

PART 1

T H E N

CHRISTMAS

Christmas 1996 plans had been drawn up well in advance. In a moment of outre largesse, we circulated invitations for family, close and extended, to join us for the Festive Season at West Bank. My Brother and his wife, Mum and for the first time, my Brother's Mother-in-law, all graciously accepted and were patently very relieved not to be confronted by turkey panoply yet again.

We rose very early on the dark Saturday morning before Christmas week. Our intention was to leave for lovely Scarborough at the crack of dawn 'in order to miss those pigging lorries' announced Ronnie with aplomb. Charlie insisted on being loaded first. He was not taking any chances. Fog! Well it was around, but not in ample measure, merely consisting of menacing wisps which hovered high above Rochford Gardens. It was cold, very cold.

I never ceased to marvel at the car's capacity for gear and impedimenta of all description. We were laden in capacious fashion both going and coming back. Why? Even more extraordinary was that we were both heard to say 'just in case' or 'oh, let's pack that'. On this occasion, we did not take on board the reality of having three flights of stone steps to surmount. Crammed to the brim, the carriage was moaning for mercy. All was ready for take-off, Charlie stared from atop a large bag labelled Father Christmas and Ronnie called 'Just fetching the sandwiches before I lock up'. It was cold, very cold.

The engine throbbed as the exhaust belched fumes...time ticked...I watched the car clock as time ticked...'Won't be a minute, Charlie'. The silent car waited as I took faltering steps towards the first stair well. I heard the heaving, panting, choking breaths before I had set foot any further.

'Ronnie! Dear God, Ronnie!' My shivering, quaking body pitched over steps, landings and railings to where my darling lay prone at the top. Ronnie was struck down with a fiendish attack of heart failure. His grey face, running with rivulets of icy sweat, took shape ghostly and luminous in its pallid expression of blind panic. 'It's alright, sweetheart, I'm going to get them...' I whispered. Crazed, I fumbled with the flat door-key, desperate to reach the telephone. Saliva was gone; vocal capacity was gone. 'Where are you?' the voice insisted. Where was I? I couldn't remember. Address and impromptu detail was sucked out of me. 'It's on its way, Mrs. Herdman...look out for him'.

I held Ronnie in my arms for a brief moment. 'My dearest darling, I must go to the door'. 'Did you find the sandwiches, Alice? I know how ravenous you get when driving...' Ronnie could hardly enunciate and yet once more he knew...I knew... Blindly, I tumbled down the stairs and leaped for the outer door of the block. Charlie watched from his Father Christmas nest. Time meant nothing to him. He was just awaiting his dawdling friends...

The blue light flickered faintly in the distance...they were coming... I felt the cold snapping at my arms...coat abandoned in the darkened car. No siren blared but I could make out our salvation. Suddenly, a blanket of cruel fog blocked my view. I ran into its midst, but as it cleared I could see the ambulance turning and pulling away, perhaps unable to find its quarry. I screamed my throes and, spurred on by a unique bogeyman, ran in the middle of the road shouting my impassioned pleas for it to return. The vehicle seemed impervious and every second moved further and further away. Then, as if hearing my impetuous cries for help, it stopped and the door opened. 'Where is he? We couldn't find you.' I had sunk to my knees on the pavement edge. 'Please, please hurry' was the only speech I could summon through my tinder mouth.

Ronnie was protected. The Paramedics lifted him gently into the safety of the ambulance. 'Where will you take my husband?' 'Wexham Park'. I was vacant, not able to comprehend. 'Don't hurry darling,' managed Ronnie, between draughts of the rescuing oxygen. 'Mrs. Herdman,' added the driver kindly, 'you can follow us, if you like'. As their engine sprang into life, I scrambled into the loaded car and looked, vainly, for reassurance from Charlie. 'I don't know where we are going, Charlie, but all I know is that we must not lose sight...I am lost here, I have no idea where the Hospital is, there is a thickening fog and it's 6.00 a.m. in the morning'. From then on, talking to myself became part of everyday life...reasoning, thinking and working out. I became my own best friend...

I could just distinguish amorphous tail-lights as I clung to the steering-wheel. We trailed through the silence and miasmic darkness. Nothing was familiar, only misshapen, unstructured fleeting glimpses of landscape were apparent. All was a somnambulistic rack. Until...the Hospital glow reached out its tentacles...we were there.

No time was wasted. Yet again, Ronnie was within the Coronary Care Unit, wired up and being taken care of by specialists. Soon, the word Frusemide was bandied about and its restorative purging was underway. Water which had flooded Ronnie's lungs because of the inefficient working of his enlarged heart, was being pumped out by way of large quantities of urine. 'You know, darling, I could pee for England,' was Ronnie's summing up once his breathing had returned to a fragment of normality. Frusemide was added to an already comprehensive list of essential medication and, in years to come, was held to account when we were in search of lavatorial stops in the countryside. Thank God my darling could pee for England. It was a small price to pay...

'I say, my sweet, you could have those sandwiches for your tea', said my bold, valorous champion helpfully.

A Doctor approached. Mr. Herdman, you are going to be with us for a while...'

'Oh, Doctor, my wife and I are going to Scarborough for Christmas...' Ronnie's pleas went unheeded as the young man continued, 'You have had a very nasty attack, Mr. Herdman, and we must make absolutely sure that you are stabilised before we can release you. I'm so sorry...'

'Bugger!' And we've bought the pigging turkey!' said Ronnie, unhelpfully...

Fervent to console the disconsolate Ronnie, I blurted 'Ronnie, nothing matters, nothing at all - only you matter and getting you well'. It was vital that I maintained my composure, that I stayed calm and resistant to these unforeseen, obdurate circumstances.

I remained beside Ronnie for the day long, only leaving his bedside to attend to poor Charlie who was now very uncomfortable on his Father Christmas bag. Before long, we had to face the inevitable. I would need to return to the flat for the night. The prospect of unpacking the burdened car was pushed to the recesses of a turbulent mind! 'Ronnie,' I felt the tears start. 'I know, darling, you have to go...Don't worry, the Nurse says you can ring in the night. Now, pop off and have those sandwiches - dear God, I seem to have got a thing about those bloody sandwiches - and I'll see you tomorrow. Sleep tight and make sure the door is locked..'

My legs seemed to be working independently as I rose from the chair. The parting was beyond words; the indescribable tearing of my own heart was almost too much to bear. I turned at the ward doorway. Ronnie was blowing countless kisses. I received every one. They warmed my frozen being all the way along the remote, dispassionate corridor before the car was reached. There, my faithful, beloved Charlie, while smothering my wet face with yet more kisses, eased the bleak aloneness.

An added attribute to our new home was the possession of a garage all to ourselves. As Charlie and I drew into the blustery, cold courtyard, I was thankful that there was shelter for the stash of belongings piled high in the car. 'We'll think about that tomorrow, Charlie'. Bundled with needs for the night, we made our way to the ghastly flight of steps where poor Ronnie had fallen. If we had been the only inhabitants on earth that night, our bereavement could not have been more aching or raw. Loud, strident noise greeted us. A Christmas party was in full swing within the opposite flat. ' Well, Charlie, that's all we pigging needed' quoth I, summoning one of Ronnie's choice oaths. Ronnie would have been satisfied to learn that the omnipresent sandwiches were consumed by Charlie and me, in bed, while being kept awake for most of the lone, long night by the excruciating clamour issuing from our neighbour's merrymaking beano.

Our unfortunate guests in the North registered dismay when news reached them of Ronnie's indisposition. Understandably so, for they were now faced with last minute Christmas provisions and not least, the housing of two elderly Mothers in a cramped Beverley apartment, instead of rejoicing in the easy setting of West Bank. Sympathy, however, overflowed for our chaotic strife.

Ronnie's recovery was slow but steady. Charlie and I spent hospitalised afternoons with our hero: me in person and Charlie patient and much more comfy in the car, now that his bumpy Father Christmas bag had been laboriously emptied, together with all the other gear, tackle and effects which had been stockpiled into the motor. I saw in my mirror a reflection resembling the Incredible Hulk after I had heaved boxes, holdalls (which didn't hold all), encumbrances - in fact, Seasonal trappings of all definition - yet again up three flights of cumbersome, perpendicular steps.

It was peculiar to find myself so insecure. Celebration and Festivities were not of prime importance. We were suspended within a panacea of precariousness waiting for others to devise a meaningful pathway for us. I had not expected to subsist alone in this strange place and pined for Ronnie. Noises were unfamiliar and I awoke at intervals in the endless nights trying to make sense of them. Charlie was my unfailing buddy...

'Well, Mr. Herdman, I think we can let you out, providing you are calm, do not go haring off to your loved Scarborough and do as your wife tells you to do!' was the Consultant's parting shot. 'I never argue with Miss Jackboots', said Ronnie delighting in renewed badinage as he gathered his pills together. He had already packed his case! 'We're bringing him home, Charlie!' was my shout as we opened doors and trussed our precious cargo into the back seat - I hasten to add that that was where Ronnie engineered most of his driving.

It was Christmas Eve and the star shone in the East. This time, I was unloading our own blessed Father Christmas and the welcoming lamps of the flat enticed.

Cosseting and chiding went on for a while until I grappled with shopping bags and headed for the maelstrom of Slough in a otiose attempt to ransack the emptying shops for eleventh hour supplies. I managed it.

Christmas Day that year was a woebegone affair. I fought to banish the dejection, for I sensed that Ronnie was downcast and sad. Filled with excitement about his Scarborough Christmas, he was now lamenting its loss. If the way had been open to him, he would have spurned advice and taken the risk. He would have travelled. He would not have been foiled or stymied.

I broached a plan of diversion; one of bountiful, rosy promise. We were a stone's throw from Windsor, Windsor Great Park, Eton and the leafy lanes of Berkshire. In the days that followed, I press-ganged Ronnie into the snug car and Charlie and I pored over routes leading to county hideaways which offered rural retreat. I was careful to include the possibility of chancing upon a village boutique which might house a stray knick-knack or two, trinkets or dubious ornament; objet trouve would not come amiss! All was accepted with grateful thanks; gratitude given for the revival of Ronnie's spirit.

Fortunately, the weather was mild and we were able to plan an initial visit to the Savill Gardens. This oasis of pleasure, rhododendron and azaleas, made room for a revered restaurant which became an added incentive to forge ahead. This diner catered for salads, sandwiches and light meals. It was an ideal resort for the recuperating patient. 'The chips, darling, are wondrous! Even better than the Fish Pan in Scarborough!' What greater accolade could there be! If energy abided, we would take a moderate stroll along the Eton High Street. There, our financial resources would show a feeble lacking and window-shopping had to suffice. We drooled over delicacies and devices of delight way beyond the bounds of possibility. Ronnie, to console himself, was heard to remark 'Revolting, Repulsive and Vulgaar', if the goodies were, in his opinion, over-priced.

So, our setback and calamity was assuaged. We were placated. We now looked forward to the next chapter of our lives. Neither voiced fears, nor did we overly anticipate further blows or snags skulking beneath the surface. The alluring Berkshire had rehabilitated us. We would seek its repose and accord again and again...

***

PART 1

T H E N

ONWARDS AND UPWARDS...

The boring, stressful repetition of M4 travel was hovering portentously in the distance. Another mental ingredient added itself to the mix. Ronnie's recent, devastating episode had shaken the foundations of hope within me. Each hideous experience chipped away at my peace of mind. Yet our lives needed to resume routine and pattern. If my Ronnie could maintain his nerve, then so could I. Our livelihood remained as critical as ever. I was the major wage-earner and our stability depended on my self-possession, cool and skills being preserved.

Ronnie's unshakeable, auspicious disposition was munificent. As I left him each morning at 6.30 a.m., he would be framed in the upper window, seemingly starkers for his Lungi was not visible, laughing and waving his encouragement. In those fleeting moments, I knew that if disaster struck, I could not return in time. I would not see him or hold him again...ever...

The car purred into life and turned the corner as I tried to swallow the choking lump in my throat...

***

PART 1

THEN

MUM

The Spring Term of 1997 was quiet. Fully occupied with timetabled Drama, I was not in ardent search for added obligations. An Autumn production was ahead, but remained distant. I awaited the calling! There, I left it.

Just as well, for I began to hear disturbing news from the North. My Brother was increasingly concerned about my Mother's health and welfare. She had become disorientated, stressed and very needy. Daily, Nick returned from work to discover with alarming repetition an excess of thirty, neurotic, fearful messages left on his answer-phone. My poor Mum could not be reassured or comforted. This was very disconcerting. There could be no doubt that we were facing the onset of a form of dementia and my Mother was no longer safe when alone in her present sheltered home. There had been accidents, falls, frantic visits to Hospital and increasing demands made on kind neighbours.

We were about to reckon with the most harrowing, perplexing decision: a judgement which went against our heartfelt instincts and presented an abomination which from times of yore had filled my Mother with dread. There was no alternative but for us to think about residential care. My Mother's housing supervisor and her Doctor both recommended such a course of action. I experienced total impotency. I felt utterly exposed in my weakness to drive these dreadful circumstances towards a happier conclusion. The facts were inescapable: I was holding down a full-time post, Ronnie was a semi-invalid and I lived over two hundred miles away. My Brother, although nearer and supported by a selfless, attentive wife, was also engaged in exhaustive occupation; his job was taxing and physically draining. This repellent development left us with an indisputable choice.

Several weeks were spent negotiating with my Brother, Social Services and commended residences. We could not even whisper the word 'home'. Eventually, Swanland House was on the radar. It was left to my Brother to initiate reconnaissance. The report which filtered through was very encouraging. Set in its own grounds and admirably appointed, the house was situated in an area my Mother knew well. It met with glowing citation and the staff proved to be solicitous, friendly and grounded.

Ronnie and I planned to drive North before the Half Term holiday in March. This time we aspired to spend a weekend with my Mother in her pensioner's flat. We sought to find a premise, a bedrock of understanding for us all, but most we needed to sway Mum gently into acceptance of a new life at Swanland House and strive to find an opportunity to ease her troubled thoughts. Ronnie rescued my Mother, me and the wretched whys and wherefores of what was to be. He talked and Mum listened. She smiled, looked at him and said, 'I know, love'. We could only hope...and love her.

We returned to London. There, plans were made and manifold telephone tasks undertaken to smooth Mum's ingress into her new life span. During our absence, my Sister-in-law, Heather, took on Trojan qualities with her distinctive, industrious and idiosyncratic polish. Perhaps her most thankless exercise was the stitching of umpteen name tags upon Mum's clothes and belongings. My boundless gratitude was inept. She had become my number two, my ambassador, when I was unable to carry out my filial, faithful and maternal bond.

Mum spent the Half Term holiday at West Bank. There we spoke of Swanland House and the safety it promised.

We talked of new friends waiting, homely surroundings, treasures around her, the constancy of our visits, holidays at Scarborough and most of all, the favourite gin 'n' tonic every evening. Nothing would be spared in loving gesture and safekeeping.

The day dawned. Mum did not resist. She acquiesced and was passive. Her tiny frame in the front seat of the car was calm as she turned, looked at me and whispered, 'I will be frightened'. I could not speak. 'How long will they make me work?' She thought she was going to the Workhouse. I will never erase the shock, misery and savage grief I felt at that moment. I felt her sense of betrayal, terror and loneliness. I longed for my Father. Ronnie, in his stead, comforted my Mother. 'Jessica, darling, we are with you. We will always be with you. Swanland House is like a lovely hotel and you are only going there for a little holiday because you've been so lonely on your own. We will not be far away and Nick will be coming to see you every day. Then, when we don't have to go to work, you will be coming to Scarborough to stay with us. Won't that be lovely?'

My dearest, dearest Ronnie...his words became the unfaltering salve of inspiration and solace. Their unguent calm gave comfort to us all. We were advised to leave my Mother. She needed time to settle and become accustomed to her surroundings. Julie, her personal carer, greeted with a hearty, warm and seductive welcome. We trusted....

After, I could not drive away. I could not speak. Within the waiting car, I clung to Ronnie and wept. The weeping was infinite, protracted and ceaseless. My darling, difficult, cantankerous, defenceless Mother had become a child...and I was guilty, guilty of an unforgettable breach of trust. She had believed that I would never, ever leave her...I knew that the sadness of what I had done would live with me forever.

In the fullness of time Mum did settle. She was deluged with cards, flowers and telephone calls. Nick visited almost daily and was continually protective of her interests and state, but he would agree that it was uncertain whether Mum ever regained her early character and temperament. She was safe but my worry for her never ceased.

***

PART 1

THEN

RONNIE AND ESTHER!

Ronnie was making good use of his Slough time. He explored at will, with the help of Charlie, the by-roads and corner shops within the community and was on good terms with many of the Asian traders. His regular canal-side ambles procured useful exercise in the wake of his recent illness.

It was while he was undertaking such a bracing, invigorating tramp, that he came upon a fellow Geordie. Esther was walking her somewhat fractious West Highland terrier, Sammy and conversation ensued. The two had a few topics in common, but Esther had a rather unfortunate hobby-horse, which seemed to rear its splenetic head whenever she gave herself the room to indulge it. 'It was the blackies that did it' she announced with guttural vocal intensity. This unpleasant reference was matched with ferocious, facial grimacing. Her strident, aggressive observations were not delivered in hushed tones and Ronnie needed to detach himself with some urgency. It seems that Esther's husband had been a man of the law and she had secreted evil thoughts of blame and unfinished business ever since his demise some years before. The luckless Asian residents took the brunt of this offensive.

It was my fatalistic and doomed mishap to be on the receiving end of an introduction to the ungracious, obnoxious Esther. Her opening device was 'Well, you see I never go out - they're dangerous!' This pernicious statement was delivered in the lowest oral register, whereupon her vocal chords reverberated with horrific force. From then on, I was blown over with desire to imitate and Ronnie was scuppered with unbridled giggling. The final straw was when my darling issued an invitation to the tart, loud-mouthed Esther to shop with us at Tescos on Saturday mornings. He was quick to inform me that he had some sympathy for Esther's isolation, in that her daughter, a Heathrow long-haul stewardess, lived next door to Esther but they were incommunicado! 'Ronnie, I wonder why!' said I.

'Well, darling, you see...' Ronnie was about to explain. 'Yes, I know Ronnie, she never goes out!! Has it occurred to you that she may not hesitate to rebuke, in offensive terms, any jinxed Tesco assistant who deigns to cross her path?'

Ronnie had the sauce to reply, 'Oh, you're just an old crosspatch!' My mouth opened to retort, only to discover that a firm kiss was being planted on it. I was thwarted by tenderness. And all for the love of Ronnie...

Some years later, when Rochford Gardens had become a distant memory, we learned that Esther had died. Hopefully, in the nick of time, before she brought the parameters of Slough to its knees!

Shortly before the Easter vacation, I had the 'calling'. The High Mistress was putting feelers out with a view to cementing the Autumn choice of play. I was told that the Music Department was to offer flights of fancy, still in embryonic form, over the coming Terms. Plans for predictable programmes from the English Department were also being tossed around. I was about to have a blessing dropped into my lap. A Senior School Production was prescribed. Perhaps this could involve a small number of students? The Theatre was to be made ready for either English or Music Departments and therefore maybe the Singing Hall would suffice for the Drama presentation in the Autumn? This did not disappoint, although juggling with the restricted space of a Concert Hall declined to put me in seventh heaven. Our recent domestic turbulence and confusion had thrown my customary long-term planning into disarray. I ushered in this unexpected release with goodly relief. This was short-lived. I had learned from experience that within this system it was usual for one academic door to shut as another slammed in one's face.

I had long nursed the idea of an Ayckbourn production. Needless to say, this could not be realistically portrayed by an all-female cast! I toyed with making overtures to St. Paul's Boys' School across the river. Ronnie's advice was sought. As so often, he came up with the goods and 'Absent Friends' was tendered as a possibility. The cast of three men, three women was ideal. I put the hypothesis to the High Mistress and the deal was soon signed, sealed and to be, in the near future, delivered. It would be an exciting enterprise and for once a breath of fresh air whistling through the feminine, feverish portals of the Paulina patch...

The second half of the Term moved slowly and yet, vacillating over this unusual detachment, was a bodeful, bothersome irritation which made indifference impossible. Naught could be done. I could not shun this awareness, this premonition, this wiring up of my aura. It could not be ignored and I was left with a restless agitation, a dubious awakening to every day.

There was much to divert. Our leisurely weekends were spent keeping pace with household chores in our modern, plush apartment and browsing the Berkshire Beeches for off-the-beaten-track eateries or pubs. This recess of time was healing and the intermission served for us to draw breath, think and make ourselves ready for the next strike, the next onus.

The last threads of the Spring Term were drawn together and again tentative cramming of the car inaugurated its readiness for take-off.

'Sue, Ronnie's having a heart attack! He was on the meadow at the top of the Park. An ambulance is on its way!' I stood in the doorway, frozen with fear as a West Bank neighbour shrieked the warning. His lips, uncoordinated and loose with fear, moved as if his marionette-strings were suddenly severed, leaving him cast within a slow motion spell.

It was the second day of the Easter vacation. Spring had arrived in Scarborough and Ronnie was eager to reach the top of Falsgrave Park. This jaunt was no mean feat for the pathway was steep, winding and far-reaching. The morning breeze had strengthened all too quickly, weakening the jubilant traveller. On reaching the summit and affected, he succumbed to searing chest pain. The distressed Charlie was beside Ronnie as he collapsed and cardiac arrest took over. His miraculous guardian angel, a very young lady and the only other dog-walker to inhabit the Park pinnacle at the time, performed artificial respiration and saved his life. It transpired that she was a Nursing Sister - in the Intensive Care Unit of Scarborough Hospital....it was not Ronnie's time....

My neighbour, who had reached the pasture as the ambulance arrived for Ronnie, took on the role of messenger and custodian of Charlie. Clarification and account came much later.

Shock accompanied me. In shock, my body resolved to reassemble its faculties. Throwing off pyjamas and the early morning contentment, I became an automaton. The house, still pervaded with the scent of toast and coffee, was renounced, eschewed and objurgated. Would I be in time?

'Darling, darling...it's alright. I'm still here...just! I say, that little girl was wonderful. She saved my life, you know. Darling, would you believe, I had been in the garden and hadn't bothered to change. I'd forgotten to clean my teeth and I think I must have smelled like a poke of devils...that poor little girl had to give me the kiss of life.. I reckon, in the circumstances, she needed it more than me!'

'Mr. Herdman, calm down, we are at present, trying to assess your state and you are wired up. The machine is going barmy...'

Ronnie survived. He was alive. How could I ever convey my thanks to his deliverer? I made my way to the loveliest florist in town and there I chose a miniature bouquet of roses and Spring flowers. The blooms were white and pure and for me symbolised a living grace, the saving of Ronnie's life. The clinical Intensive Care Unit opened its doors and there she was, Ruth. 'How can one ever thank the person who has saved your husband's life? I will be humbly grateful for the rest of mine.'

Recovery from life-threatening experience is beyond the bounds of possibility. One is laid bare, naked and in search of a rock or prop, a bulwark to sustain. That manifests itself in the restoration of your loved one...for as long as that may be...

***

PART 1

THEN

WHAT NEXT?

When Ronnie's rehabilitation was underway, it was time for me to drive the thirty miles to Swanland House. I could not contemplate this until my love was safely out of the High Dependency Unit and incarcerated on the Cardiology Ward. Once freed from wires, monitors and instruments of bondage, Ronnie strained at the leash, ready to assist Nurses, Doctors or other medical personnel. Once mobile, he hastened to pander and minister to other patients - whether they wanted to be pandered to or not! His spirited panache did not falter and, judging by the animated repartee which followed, he became a mainstay for positive thinking.

Ronnie had had a close shave. We learned that electrical impulses within his ailing heart had gone hopelessly awry. I pumped Consultants for information. There was an element of indecision. Ronnie's heart withstood a massive shock, but it was unclear whether a full-blown heart attack had resulted.

Obviously, a speedy return to London was vital. There, Ronnie had access to his own Physicians, history and previous treatment. Nevertheless, this proposal had to be held in abeyance until his health returned to a semblance of normality. I waited, anxiously, and occupied my usual position on the knife-edge. Charlie and I trod a careful path. It seemed as if we shared this wistful waiting game, hardly daring to breathe or look forward to an untroubled, insouciant hike in the Park.

'Sue, it's time you visited your Mother. She will be looking out for you and I'm in the best place, quite safe...please, darling you must.' I knew the only way to pacify Ronnie was to pursue regular activities. Order and balance was his means to rationalise; to recover. 'Sweetheart, Alice, I am much more compos mentis than I was before! Now, off you go, take little Charlie with you for company, give Jessica a big kiss and tell her to go easy on the gin!'

The ride to Swanland House was revitalising, cooling. We steadied. The countryside, full of Springtime promise, deflected. Negative thoughts were diffused, redirected and, as we drew into Swanland village, my memory of childhood days spent there, by the pond, hurling bread to the avaricious ducks, brought a stillness to my soul.

'Is it his ticker?' said Mum. I marvelled at her understanding as she reached to take my hand. 'Oh love, I am pleased to see you...it's nice here and they are looking after me very well. There's a fashion show tomorrow night...' I felt the warmth of relief wash over me. Mum was smiling, calm. She was not in the grip of loathsome fear. I was set free. In my mind's resting place, I was strengthened for the wending home...home to my Ronnie.

***

PART 1

T H E N

AND THEN....

Apprehension dogged my preparatory planning for our return to Slough and the Summer Term. A five-hour stint of driving did not fill me with joyful expectancy. The need to safeguard a seriously ill passenger - one who may brook another bout at any moment - was the added preponderance.

One would have thought that Ronnie had been discharged from Hospital with nothing more serious than the common cold. He resumed his rousing, vigorous lifestyle with habitual dash and can-do. He did not waver. 'Alice, life is for living!' was his kosher comment. Who was I to argue?

The balmy warmth of the South eased our transition into Berkshire and the sticks. While traversing borders and boundaries, Ronnie braced us with unfailing pronouncement and commentary upon the pastoral panorama. 'I ooze with rustic, masterly proficiency when it comes to agricultural science. In other words, a sylvan smartarse!' Ronnie emboldened me with his guts and stout-hearted strength of mind, nor do I fail to remember his lovingly prepared and inexhaustible supply of delectable sandwiches. These were the backbone and buttress of our travail. 'Don't eat the bloody things before you've started the car!' was the testy comeback.

Relief cushioned our safe arrival. In the coming days, before the inception of Term, urgent meetings were arranged with GP, Consultants and Specialists for the handling of the crucial development in Ronnie's sickness.

'We cannot allow this, Ronnie' stated Dr. Dancy, 'I have received word from Scarborough and it is agreed that we need the advice of a Doctor superbly qualified to deal with the heart's electricity - that's putting it mildly'. Without further ado, he arranged for Ronnie to meet Wynn Davies, a Welsh Consultant who reigned supreme in the corridors of cardiac prowess. He, it seemed, was the man when it came to dealing with the mysteries of arrhythmia, adrenaline and its effect on the intricate innards of the heart's apparatus.

Within days and coinciding with the oncoming Term, Ronnie was admitted to the Harley Street Clinic for tests and investigation. There he remained for a couple of weeks undergoing strategies geared to inducing, in controlled conditions, further attacks. Astonishingly, his tough, defiant heart refused to co-operate and stubbornly held out. Until - the dastardly adrenaline was introduced and permitted to do its worst. Wynn Davies nailed the culprit, the seizure was interrupted and a much relieved Ronnie was revived, reassured and reinstated in the luxurious surroundings of his private room. Thanks be to dear St. Paul's for the exclusive medical assistance it provided. Guardian angels come in a multitude of guises...

***

PART 1

THEN

BEHIND THE SCENES....

While Ronnie was forcibly detained, I worked to arrange our other life. Charlie's needs were uppermost. He could not be forsaken. Subterfuge became second nature as he was smuggled into the Portakabin while I, the traffiker, went about my daily duties. Quite unfazed, Charlie took on the identity of wise old retainer and behaved in highly virtuous fashion.

The daily routine began at daybreak, then breakfast for both while listening to darling Ronnie's early morning call: 'Have you got your slap on yet?' Then the car was primed for the day's consignment. 'Well, Charlie, we're on't roaaad!' was my edifying proclamation as we drew near to the M4's thunder. Brook Green became Charlie's watering hole at 7.45 a.m. every morning. Thereafter, he took up residence within my office and only emerged from concealment when calls from the Brook Green enclosure became too hard to resist.

I missed Ronnie very much. Charlie missed him very much. I drew comfort, however, from knowing that he was safe. The Hospital's prudent care brought deliverance, a balm for my troubled mind. Yes, I knew anxiety, but now unwound in the knowledge that learned, skilled experts were in the wings. After a while, it became known that Wyn Davies was deliberating at some length on the most effective course of treatment for Ronnie's flawed heart. He was kept under close surveillance while the worthy medico took a flight to America. There he was to seek further data about the efficacy of state-of-the-art implantable defibrillators. We were left in suspense. Was salvation, a lifeline and peace of mind around the corner?

I was now well into the machinations of a typical Summer Term. I cannot underrate the relief I sensed from being extricated from the obligatory end-of-Term showcase. Usually, after-School rehearsals bogged me down. Visiting Ronnie would have been very difficult. As it was, I left School promptly, drove to Slough, made sure Charlie was fed, watered, walked and ensconced before setting out along the M4 for the third time, bound for Harley Street. The whole enactment was exhausting and the days were long, but the moments spent with Ronnie at their conclusion were indispensable and precious. I learned that Wyn Davies was still reasoning, still pondering...

The ride home to the waiting Charlie was, fortunately, not in darkness. The weather was clear and as I neared noisy Heathrow, the unmitigated procession of flights roared overhead. The sky was rosy, the sun disappearing and as the car slid slowly into Rochford Gardens, I could hear Charlie's welcoming bark. He was impatient to hear my news.

'Ronnie, I'm safely back, darling, all my love...until tomorrow'. Then the phone was silent.

Here was a golden opportunity, while Ronnie rested in comfort and safety, to finish auditions for the Ayckbourn School's premiere of 'Absent Friends'. By this juncture, the more mature students were freed from the toil of examinations. Both young men and women rejoiced in the likelihood of being cast in such a sophisticated piece. I, too, gloried in the prospect of reduced numbers; it was a refreshing change from dealing with a Company the size of which rivalled a biblical multitude. The chosen few were excellent and, much to my satisfaction, had not been successful in previous School productions. This was to be their long-awaited debut.

I was also engaged in the time-consuming Report-writing exercise. I had never found this monotonous. Instead, I looked forward to reviewing each student's progress. In my experience, there was always an encouraging comment to be made, observations which complemented academic performance, but assessed abstract qualities of development: sensitivity, perception and imagination. All records were hand-written, detailed and, although I did not profess to be a grammatical grandee, syntactic.

In all, I submitted over one hundred scripts for perusal by the High Mistress. I was not accustomed to nit-picking. Erstwhile, my accounts had been acclaimed. Needless to say, on occasion, my attention had been drawn to small errors, but these were easily corrected and without fuss. Not so this time. Much to my dismay, each piece, in minutiae, had had the pencil put through it. I was left with no alternative but to re-write and obey condescending, supercilious instruction.

My labour completed, I then looked forward to finalising detail for 'Absent Friends' before Term came to an end. A matter of weeks remained, but before release, I was informed that from September 1997 onwards I would take on the duty of Year 1 Form Teacher, a liability from which I had, in the past, been exempt because of Drama Department culpability. It was becoming increasingly obvious that the remains of the Department which I had lovingly built over the last seven years, were being broken free from my grasp. I was told that in view of the fact that Drama was now being taught as a timetabled subject and under the auspices of the English Department, I would take a reduction in salary; there would be no allowance for extra responsibility. I, too, was slipping away...soon there would be nothing left...

Ronnie was not made privy to any of these disturbing and upsetting developments. I mourned in the seclusion of home, with only the loving Charlie to pay heed. All a paltry triviality, I know, when thoughts were utterly absorbed by my dearest's welfare.

Wynn Davies' return moved things on apace. Ronnie was to have an implantable defibrillator. This superlative device would act as a portable Paramedic, monitoring Ronnie's unpredictable heart, firing elan vital and a volley of monitoring beams whenever it sensed dangerous dysfunction of rhythm. 'Darling, at last I'm going to be protected...isn't it exciting!' Dearest, dearest Ronnie. This incredible gadget would restore his confidence. Once more, he would live his life to the full. The intense fear which had followed us both for so long would be challenged.

The operation was 'routine', so I was disconcerted when Wynn Davies phoned to say that Ronnie had been taken to Intensive Care. 'He's come through very well, Sue, but we are taking precautions. Please visit as usual tomorrow'. I told Charlie all about it and we tried to settle for the night. I phoned - twice. Each time I was consoled but left uneasy, distrait. I was at the ready, sleepless and alert. It was not until very much later in our life that I learned of the difficulty Mr. Davies had had in the starting of Ronnie's heart. It had stopped five times.

Ronnie lodged in the Harley Street Clinic for a further few days until his apparatus had settled, been tested and stamped with medical insignia.

The following weeks were a testing time. We imagined hearing cacophonous sounds being sent forth by this artful machine. I lay awake at night listening and on tenterhooks. We were marking time, predicting the thing to fire! Soon, our lives settled once more, largely because Ronnie was settled. Did he think about it? That I will never know, for he was compliant. Most of all, Ronnie had faith.

We were enrolled, as part of Ronnie's recovery process, in our local Hospital's Defibrillator Rehabilitation programme. There we met other 'hosts' of these puzzling, novel contraptions. Husbands and wives were gathered together to exchange experiences, notes and condolences. One garrulous elderly gentleman cottoned on to Ronnie enquiring about the probability of machines firing. 'How are you getting on, Ron?' said he. Before Ronnie could reply, he continued, 'God 'elp you if it goes off...it 'appened to me and it felt like being plugged in to the mains...I was froan from one end of the room to the uvver...mi elbow n' knees came off worst...I was black n' blue!' Tactfully, I disentangled Ronnie and directed him towards a tea break. 'Now don't start,' my beloved said, 'I'll be wearing my jock-strap from now on!'

Another marvel came about within the next few days. Stupefaction was the word to use, I think. Ronnie announced, 'You know, darling, my language is appalling'.

'Oh really, Ronnie', said I, 'you amaze me'. 'Yes, I will be trying to put a curb on it'. I was open-mouthed. 'Will I receive warning?' I enquired.

An interval of two days followed. Ronnie accidentally spilled the contents of his teacup over a clean pair of trousers. 'Twatmagoola!' he remonstrated. 'Ronnie, what did you say?' 'Oh darling, that's instead of Bollocks!' was the earnest reply. I heard several very interesting replacements for Ronnie's curses: Willy-Dilly, Dingly-Dangly, Pig-Pag-Pog, Bandjaxed and Atchicapatula to name but a few, but Twatmagoola was awarded best-loved plaudit of all time...

As far as arrangements for School were concerned, I decided that there would be no point in brooding over my fate. Ronnie was ill and peace at this time was critical. I looked towards the Summer holiday.

Governor's Day was a traditional end of Term event. Governors intermingled at lunch tables with teaching, administrative and domestic staff. This could be a very affable, pleasing time and gave an opportunity for all to become more closely acquainted. Usually, as Staff flocked together for this social congress of goodwill, Governors would be holding the final Year Meeting with the High Mistress, Bursar and other recognised officials. This year, events seemed to take an unexpected turn. The assembled host was kept waiting, immeasurably. Minutes ticked by as conversation buzzed with an attempt to deduce rationale for this wearisome delay. 'Something unexpected has taken place,' remarked a knowing colleague, 'I wonder if her contract hasn't been renewed? Perhaps she's trying to invoke an extension...' This was a revelation. As far as I was aware the High Mistress was some way off retirement. The speaker seemed conversant and in the loop.

Some time passed before the High Mistress led Chairman of the Governors and his attendant advisers to the waiting tables. It was noted by many that she was alarmingly flushed, flustered and ruffled. What had happened?

The atmosphere was tense and it took a few restorative sips of an excellent white wine to steady the buffs. Well, all comes to him who waits. We had to be satisfied with the question mark which hung over the luncheon and subsequent giving of prizes. It seems that I was not the only one who wondered what the future would bring.

I was to discover, before the afternoon was over, that the Deputy Head was to leave! What had been her transgression?

'So,' Ronnie murmured, 'the poisoned chalice has gone. As far as the High Mistress is concerned...well...who was it that said "envy not the plumage of a dying bird"?' Ronnie...so wise...

Now was the time to confide in him about the changes being made to my professional footing. He accepted all with his customary insight and shrewd, sound judgement. He knew and I knew...

The closing days of Term were nigh. It only remained for us to prepare once more for the surpassing sunshine of Scarborough. As the car pulled out of the School car-park, I viewed the Deputy Head teacher and her Strawberry-Pink-Jacket for the last time. 'How are the mighty fallen,' said Ronnie.

***

PART 1

THEN

JESSICA

Our eager expectancy of a sun-kissed holiday in Scarborough was sadly blighted by worrying news from Swanland House. I had had bulletins from my Brother, intimating that Mum was not faring well. No doubt he had been reluctant to go into detail for fear of distressing me further so soon after Ronnie's brush with disaster. I made haste to visit as soon as Ronnie was secure at West Bank, and, hopefully, as far as possible, out of the woods. I strove to resist temptation to nanny Ronnie; he could not have borne that. I needed faith. I tried to convince myself that all would be well. 'Come on, Alice, get going...Charlie and I are going in the garden. Tell Jessica I've got the cards and the gin out!'

My Brother had given Ronnie yet another very unusual present. It was a white, floppy-brimmed gardening hat. Inside the hat's crown, a small radio was concealed. Ingenious, for Ronnie was a great fan of Radio 4 when planting his seeds and he could listen while doing his horticultural best. This could foil delivery men or friends who happened to call. Ronnie would go to the door while the radio was still playing. It was an incessant mystery to the looker-on. Where was the music coming from?!

This vision and Ronnie's cheering words remained in my consciousness as I sped over hills and dales. They helped to allay the reflex sense of dread which vowed to overwhelm and browbeat me as the car pulled into the drive of Mum's final home.

My delicate, fragile Mother lay almost comatose. Her rheumy eyes flickered once in recognition as I bent to kiss her cool forehead. Her dancer's fingers were innate upon the counterpane, lifeless and without the dainty expression so creative, so entrancing. All hints of past troubles were beyond me. My only Mother, her tiny enfeebled frame so helpless and inert, was nearing the end of her days.

In spite of these predetermined events, my Mother faded then rallied throughout the Summer weeks that followed. My lonely labours left me barren, empty and desperately sad. Sometimes Mum was bedridden, sometimes livelier and bright enough to join compatriots in the lounge, but words were lost and conversation fleeting and splintered. Helpless tears would prick and I would need to hide and cover my sorrow. The tearing of emotion and tenderness so near the surface, the divided allegiance between Mum and my Ronnie, was almost unendurable. My goodbyes were breathed as if they were my last; my last sundering threads of a daughter's love.

The hollow, guilt-racked pilgrimages home were cold, distant and distracted. The absolute, entire love which greeted me there served to comprehend and gladden. 'There's no turning back, love', said Ronnie, 'all we can do is our best'.

Meanwhile, there was neither space nor inclination to seek out old friends, our dear Doctor and his family, or staunch Theatre pals. Time was swallowed with journeying, somewhat futile planning and thought-filled silences.

The approaching School Term began to take its place in our immediate consideration. Swanland House was careful to stress that my Mother's prognosis was uncertain. We were advised to resume our day-to-day lives, work and the practised commute to Yorkshire whenever possible. We would be called. The only redeeming feature in this complexity was the knowledge of my Brother's closeness and continued, dedicated visits.

We reached Rochford Gardens a few days before Term was due to begin. Soon, I would be invoked to attend Form Teachers' meetings and administrational duties. I was unfamiliar with prescriptive, dogmatic decree.

The morning after our arrival in Slough, we received the call to turn back. My Mother's state had declined and we were needed at once.

My Mother died on the evening of our return. My Brother and I were at her bedside as she slipped away. We would not have wished for her to remain. She had, in the last days of her life, slid into the blank, befuddlement of old age. She had been ready for some time. Her salad days were over.

The passing of a parent marks the termination of constancy and the sense of belonging. We are plummeted into the secluded unknown where the demand for adult self-sufficiency is achingly apparent. However possessive, controlling or dependent the parent may have been, the child feels the transcendent loss. Such mourning brings ambivalence. Before, days have been consumed with task-bearing and care. Death leaves a pit, a cavern which cannot be filled. Only time creates a handbook: this self-made manual showing the way through a veil of peculiar uncharted territory.

***

PART 1

THEN

AFTER....

My Form Teacher's workload had been allotted, temporarily, to an upright, tried 'n' tested Deputy. Sympathy was noticeably forthcoming from valued colleagues. Such wealth of understanding and empathy was heart-warming and sincere. Duty and often the trite, pedestrian routine of the School day served to mend and apply logic to my present state. It goes without saying that dear Ronnie, receptive to my restless, unhappy distraction was, as usual, a source of willpower, kindness, humour and resolve. His errant language reasserted itself in fits and starts, and, when swamped by sporadic grief, I found in its resurrection a welcome excuse to give vent to shaking laughter. In addition, 'Twatmagoola!' became a lynchpin of day-to-day living!

I had enjoyed being a Form Teacher. My eleven-year-old charges, the Middle Fourth, were delightful companions and I looked forward to Registration, tactics for raising cash for Charity and the inconsequential callings of my role. All children were individuals with distinct, arresting personalities: some dominant, some retiring, but part of a whole, a team. We were all learning.

The School day was longer than ever once rehearsals for 'Absent Friends' were underway. My worry over Ronnie's isolation did not lessen. He, needless to say, did not allow the grass to grow under his feet, and, he made daily inroads into the mystique of Slough, often partnered by the trenchant Esther who, no doubt, flagrantly armed with munitions, was ready for the fray.

I was very aware of the considerable amount of compassionate leave I had received. Eager to make this up, any extra work on the play provided me with an ideal opportunity to do so. A generous and prudent confrere reminded me that one term's after-school rehearsals on 'Pygmalion' should certainly suffice. Doubtless, the High Mistress would endorse that. Nevertheless, where such commendation and goodwill prevailed, I was forever keen to acknowledge such favour with conscientious hard work.

Sadly, over a steady period of time, life at School had changed for me. Ronnie and I realised that my halcyon days at St. Paul's were over. There is a time for everything. There had been a time all those years ago for Ronnie to encounter Mrs. Brigstocke at the BBC. Now, perhaps, I was needed elsewhere.

***

PART 1

T H E N

CHARLIE

Heartbreak was to befall us once more. Little Charlie, our dearest Charlie, became terminally ill. Our love for him knew no bounds and the prospect of his loss was plunging us into the depths of despair. In turns, we nursed and stroked our darling one. Memories of his puppy days in Oldham - backstage protection of his Phyllis when the Giant frightened - flooded our thinking and our waking small hours. Mr. Poole lulled him away while Ronnie and I wept for his passing and held him dear. We had so loved our Babies.

***

PART 1

THEN

TIME TO GO...

The days and weeks at that time were lonely and sad.

'Absent Friends' drew near and became a distinguished, superior production. I received many letters from parents in awe of such mature, accomplished performances. I created a farewell gift to the School which I had served with Educational passion and fervour.

I reminded the young actors that such succes fou was not to be underestimated! For them, a glowing telegram tribute from Alan Ayckbourn himself became their sensational triumph.

On the last day of Term, I sought permission to tell my young Middle Fourth form that I would be leaving and I asked my Deputy to be present. I attempted to speak to the girls before dismissing them for the Christmas vacation. The classroom, strewn with Festive wrapping and bathed in the scent of copious chocolate boxes, was suddenly quiet and expectant. It was an experience that I find harrowing to recall. I looked into the faces of those still, trusting children and, much to my shame, burst into dreadful tears. 'Please, Mrs. Herdman, dear Mrs. Herdman, please don't cry. Is it something we have done? Is Mr. Herdman very ill again?'

Then, the distress continued until, blindly, I managed to comfort. 'I am so sorry to leave you like this. During the holiday, I will write a long letter and perhaps one of you will read it to the class. You will know then that I did not mean to forsake or hurt you'.

That was the only goodbye I was allowed to make.

In the years to come I would spend many sombre, wakeful hours trying to make sense of the High Mistress' decisions. Perhaps she would say that all her resolutions for the future of Drama and my Department were calculated for the benefit of such a fine School and its girls. All who have a part to play within a story have their own interpretation of it. All would be different.

Silently, the car made its way through the familiar gates of the School I had loved and admired so very much. I did not look back, nor did I ever return to dear St. Paul's Girls' School. Memories of children and one's involvement in their lives are unique, a nonpareil. They have remained so, in my thoughts, unspoiled and untouchable. Those far off times enriched my life and Ronnie's. Nothing can erase them...

***

PART 1

T H E N

AFTERWARDS

Many were left, children and colleagues alike, shocked and disbelieving when the news of my departure broke. In the weeks that followed, I was deluged with farewell letters of thanks from parents and children. The young Middle Fourth form, before embarking upon their Christmas holiday, had put together individual notes to me each expressing personal feeling, some tear-stained and halting, but desperate to make sense of such sorrow. Wisely, my Deputy had encouraged a very necessary, therapeutic exercise. My parting left a devastating impact on all, not least my teaching friends.

Wise Ronnie counselled, mitigated, mollified and moderated. He led me down the path of renewal. I tried, and in the main, succeeded to build on what might have been ruins.

A senior student, in her letter of gratitude, mentioned one lasting incident. The High Mistress, when addressing the School at the beginning of the Spring Term 1997, spoke of Mrs. Herdman being 'forced' to leave. No explanation had been forthcoming and the children throughout the School had been left in bleak, despondent questioning. Most thought that Ronnie may have died or, at best, been taken more seriously ill. Many assumed that I could be terminally sick. Parents could have suspected that my sudden disappearance pointed to a serious infringement. Had I been caught with my hand in the till? All was left open to conjecture. No...all knew me too well for that...

A faithful fellow teacher forwarded a copy of the St. Paul's student Newspaper. An article, entitled 'GOODBYE MRS. HERDMAN', referring to "our delightful fairy godmother of the Portakabin", was printed for all to see. No leaving present or celebration could have equalled the sentiments expressed in the comments that followed. The student eulogy remains etched, timelessly, in recollection; a haunting and unforgettable reminiscence composed by loving children:

'Mrs. Herdman of the Drama Department left at the end of last term. There cannot be anyone at St. Paul's who does not know Mrs. Herdman. She was not only an inspired Drama teacher but was also a very special person. Some say that she alone became their mentor throughout their years at St. Paul's. She was renowned for her warm, encouraging smiles and bright, original clothes. There is not space in the whole paper let alone this one page to articulate what Mrs. Herdman meant to this school and the girls, but this is our offering.

St. Paul's is just not the same without her.

Imogen Walford, who only knew Mrs. Herdman for a term, said, "I shall really miss Mrs. Herdman because she would always appreciate any kind of enthusiasm, no matter how bad the attempt at acting".

We wish to include three more tributes to Mrs. Herdman as she makes her way to her next lucky school:

- "Mrs. Herdman put all her energy into everything she did. She had faith in all of us and will remain one of the strongest influences in my life".
(Georgina Thomas)

- was a ray of light, a fountain of good sense and throughout the dark, she was always there, for all of us".
(Catherine Baker)

- *"Mrs. Herdman saw the best there was in me and in everyone she taught."*
(*Amy Peck*)

This sublime gift, written by Natasha O'Hare and Catherine McCormack in their VIIth year, was a blessing and windfall of kindness which made recompense for my sadness. It helped me to leave St. Paul's with a song in my heart. I never looked back except to remember it with affection, huge esteem and gratitude.

Shortly after Christmas of that year, I received a packet. Inside, were the scribbled notes from my dearest Middle Fourth. They occupy a drawer in my desk. There they bide...

The High Mistress left the School two Terms later.

***

PART 1

THEN

RETIREMENT?

I had not given thought to the word 'retirement', possibly because actors abhor the prospect of a withdrawal into reclusive life. I had worked from the age of seventeen. It was second nature to me and to Ronnie. Indeed, Ronnie took great pride in telling the tale of his early days and passage through a variety of employment, from Gents Outfitter to serving chicken and chips in Lyons Corner House, not to speak of his chequered calling to catering in the Officers' Mess while completing his National Service. The thought fills one with tremor and trepidation!

The prospect of settling for indolence without a regenerative future was anathema to us. We had been used to the inexhaustible energy that fuelled our working life, not always with an aim in sight, but certainly an indefatigable attitude prevailed. Now, we lodged in an unfamiliar land. Ronnie's ill health curtailed his stamina and in turn his time-honoured Theatrical chances. I was fully aware that Scarborough was not London; what would its teaching world have to offer a highly-qualified, fifty-eight-year-old Speech & Drama specialist?

In the beginning of 1998 we were very content to settle into the gentle, commodious existence of West Bank. We enjoyed reasonable financial security - for the time being. Added benefit came from Ronnie's eligibility for the State Pension. His equilibrium was infectious and I found myself adjusting calmly to our new life with a composure that matched his. We were home at last.

Domesticity suited Ronnie. Also, I had inherited my Mother's gift of home-making; a nesting where feathers were plumped and unruffled. Hence, our loving harmony was given full reign here in our peerless kingdom. All else was put on hold...for the time being. Life was pausing.

After the turbulence of the St. Paul's years, we cruised through these opening months with no sense of urgency or pending rumpus. We allowed ourselves away-days where leisurely breakfasts were followed by no pressure to hustle, hurry or hasten. There was peace and contentment.

The blissful days found us giving way to unprecedented indulgence of time; time to garden, time to cook, time to converse about anything and everything. The evenings yielded to dubious television programmes, often rubbish, certainly equivocal, but presenting elbowroom to drop-off, giggle, or while doing so, glory in snug, homely cuddles on a sumptuous sofa. Oscillation governed this interval and the unhurried breathing space made for an excuse to loiter, dither, consider, test and speculate.

Days turned into weeks, weeks into months and before long, the proposal of returning to some gainful occupation began to assume importance. My official retirement did not kick in for a couple of years. I realised that a tiding-over job would be very useful, in fact essential if we were to remain solvent. There were few financial certainties to hang in the air.

I sent a batch of enquiring letters to various Schools, sounding out the possibility of a Speech & Drama post in Scarborough. What were my expectations? Well, I did expect acknowledgement, or at least one iota of interest, perhaps a mite of enthusiasm, but no, not a tinge of curiosity or response. I was disappointed but admitted reluctantly to myself that I had been serenely complacent. I was soon to learn that here in the frozen North, jobs akin to the Director of Drama at St. Paul's Girls' School did not drop off trees.

In the meantime, Ronnie had noticed an advertisement for Hospital Volunteers in the Evening News. 'I say, darling,' he enthused, 'they're looking for people to help in the Stroke Unit. Why don't we apply?' Dearest Ronnie who was always ready to help, to bring sunshine, to heal. 'Bugger the job, my love, we'll manage - we've got a bit in the Bank. This is much more important'. That is where it all began. The years that followed became filled with service to Stroke patients and their families. Had Ronnie's life been spared in time for him to set up this invaluable work? I believe so. 'Remember, my darling,' said he, 'there is always someone you can help'. Ronnie led and I followed. Some doors could have remained closed. Perhaps, alone, I would have held back. Ronnie led and I followed.

It would be tedious to chronicle every event which took place in the years that came after. Suffice it to say that day-to-day life was filled with Ronnie. He captured his Secret Garden and filled the greedy soil with a blaze of colour. Climbing roses - Kiftsgate and Wedding Day - rambled at will over an imposing arch which Ronnie had hijacked from an quondam Indian gentleman in Wembley. 'Can you imagine, Alice, he was throwing it out!' 'Mmn..' said I. So long after, as the perfume from every petal suffused the plot, I searched my memory for how on earth we had transported it. Oh yes, on the roof rack via a grid-locked A1.

Flowers, shrubs and miniature trees wrestled for space and, as the sun filtered through the foliage of a noble, majestic Ginkgo Biloba tree one busy wash-day morning, my gardening guru and West Bank's man of learning announced, 'You know that it is one of the oldest Chinese trees that you could come across. I got it from the oldest nursery in London; quite historical in fact, the Clifton Nursery in Maida Vale - bet you didn't know that'. 'Well, my love,' I replied, 'at this present moment that old

Chinese tree will serve as a marvellous place to hang my washing-line'.

Part-time jobs did come my way. I was invited, at long last, to offer Drama Workshops at a couple of Independent Junior Schools in the vicinity. I soon came to regret that deployment, for I found the children so badly behaved that all my careful preparation and workmanship was, initially, an utter waste of time.

Drama took a back seat, for before I could make progress, there was an urgent need for schooling in classroom etiquette and the drilling of manners. Granted, I had been trained for Secondary level teaching and consequently, was a stranger to the tenor of a younger classroom. I was horrified at the unruly, rude and tardy, undisciplined demeanour of my charges. The sessions, I came to expect, were relegated to lunchtimes and it was disappointingly obvious that Drama was being viewed as a free-for-all.

Arriving at the allocated time, my car groaning with visual aids, props and appropriate costume which had been lovingly packed by Ronnie and unpacked at the other end by myself, alone, I was dismayed to discover that the little monsters were either finishing their lunch and covered in gravy or custard, in the lavatory, or riding rough-shod over the playground. By the time they had been rounded up, by me, the lesson was due to end. I endured this demeaning pursuit until the end of Term, gave my notice and, in the wake of a surrendered invoice, looked forward to shopping on the proceeds of these irritating events. One ineffectual Headmaster's parting pleasantry was, 'I do apologise, Mrs. Herdman, I seem to have fudged a few issues'! His Bursar, equally inert and toiling with ostensible administrational shambles, came up with my wages a good three months later. 'Fuck that for a lark', echoed Ronnie.

Ronnie's main bone of contention was Alan Ayckbourn's reluctance to employ either of us. We were ignored. 'For God's sake,' exclaimed my loyal husband, 'even if he doesn't want to give me a job - I understand that, for I'm ill, and he's never forgiven me for being ill before and escaping one of his shows - he could at least have offered you a Workshop for the Theatre-in-Education project!' 'Oh, never mind Ronnie,' said I, ready to placate, 'he has many reasons, I'm sure'. From then on, however, it was not easy to persuade Ronnie to patronise the Stephen Joseph Theatre. 'I've just grown out of it, darling', he explained, 'I'd rather be at home making clothes for you!' That is precisely what he did do.

The sewing-machine purred away on the dining table as my wardrobe swelled with dress-making theatricality. Ronnie's virtuosity exhibited itself in tapestry, crochet and beadwork. He evolved at speed, without pattern or plan, his fingers weaving glitter, glitz, elegance and grace. Each remarkable item was woven with love, passion and fidelity. The intensity of his tender, holding dear poured itself into each and every thread. Aeons later, hidden within mohair or cashmere folds, I may discover a hidden bead with the words, 'I love you' inscribed; an ageless reminder of intimate love, a tender secret forever etched upon my heart...

Our life was simple, as were our tastes. Finances, manoeuvred with some frugality, made room for Ronnie's limitless yen for the nearly-new shops and lush fish 'n' chip suppers. No, it was not a lavish lifestyle. We were together and that was all that mattered.

There were many excursions to Hartlepool, often with mixed reception from the devious Louie, but the route presented varied and picturesque countryside. The bleak Moors enticed and we were content to roam. Ronnie's health remained stable and our daily existence was not punctuated by terrorising attacks or presentiment of A & E.

We were also fully engaged with our Voluntary work. The Stroke Unit Wards became a source of satisfaction for us both. Our earnestness was recognised and appreciated. We made new friends. One thing can lead to another and instead of following a planned pathway, we were lured along another avenue.

St. Catherine's Hospice in Scarborough needed more Volunteers. Before long, we were making regular visits there to present 'Drawing-Room' Poetry and Drama entertainments for terminally ill patients.

'Darling, it's always the unexpected that happens', ruminated Ronnie. Yes...indeed.

***

PART 1

T H E N

THEN ALONG CAME LUCY...

The house seemed still and watchful. Its rooms were full of activity and promise as our human bustling filled the corners, but the spaciousness put forth leeway for another occupant - a dog. The souls of Jessie, Charlie and the rather irritable Phyllis were wraiths of memory and prodded to galvanize us into doing.

The helpful, receptive RSPCA made arrangements to allocate a visit and all was set in motion for us to be vetted. Then...along came Lucy...

I was first alerted to Lucy's predicament when thrashing rain and a biting North East wind nearly blew the bathroom window off its hinges. While I fought in vain effort to tether the hook, I heard faint barking, a whimpering sounding its way across the Secret Garden. My stare followed the cries and there, in the back yard of a terraced house in the next street, coiled on the doorstep, was a puppy, a golden-haired, wretched, soaking and pitiful bundle of puppy.

Dismayed, I hurtled down the stairs. 'Ronnie, what can we do? That poor little mite has been turned out'. Ronnie, careful and cautious at such times, persuaded me to stifle the urge to be rash and wait until morning. I did. Vigilant, by the creaking bathroom casement, I kept a distant guard sleepless and unable to protect or caress, but then...within a week...along came Lucy.

Those intervening days consisted of subterfuge and secret spying as we patrolled the passage between Lucy's house and the next, vainly trying to invent ploys to relieve this rueful suffering. Reconnaissance resulted in shock and disbelief. The puppy's shameful conditions were disgraceful to behold; she tried to wag her tail amidst excrement and waste. 'Don't you cry, petal, we'll get you out of that shit!' said Ronnie purposefully.

We came up with a master plan. A letter to the heedless, unmindful owner outlined our keenness to adopt the puppy he so patently did not want. We would pay. The bait was taken and the irresolute individual demanded two hundred and fifty pounds in payment for 'this pedigree Golden Retriever'. She was beautiful.

And so...along came Lucy...

This serendipitous newcomer was deposited, complete with documents to prove her lineage and membership of the Kennel Club, at our front door within hours of the offer being settled. 'Can you credit it,' Ronnie exclaimed, as he rummaged through an Oxfam carrier-bag containing a small bag of dog biscuits and two chews which had accessorised Lucy's advent, 'he turns out a valuable dog in all weathers, but he's done the right things. Can you believe it, here are her vaccination details!' (We were to discover, a few days later, when registering Lucy with the named Vet. that remuneration was wanting and we were next in line!). Dispensation was granted on the grounds of a 'Goldie Rescue'! Yes, along came Lucy... and with her came devotion and companionship which proved, over the years, to be a wellspring of immense happiness.

Lucy was approximately five months old when she took up residence at West Bank. Apart from the fact that we knew she was a Retriever, the possibility that she was going to be rather large had not been taken on board. 'I say,' proclaimed my dearest, smiling benevolently, 'she's a big girl'. 'Mmn..' said I.

The payoff was that my beloved, once more smiling benevolently, announced, 'She'll have to go to training...'

'Mmn.. Ronnie, and I wonder who's going to take responsibility for that?' Need I say more...

Training took place on Oliver's Mount, Scarborough. This windswept parkland overlooked the Bay and even on calm, temperate Sunday afternoons, one battled a sea breeze laced with invigorating ozone. There, weekly Dog Training took place and consisted of a group of owners complete with three retired Police Dog Trainers who, rather fiercely, put us all through our paces. Lucy was ecstatic!

I was almost physically wrecked in my striving to keep her under control as she made unsolicited attempts to....er....socialise. Everyone was Lucy's friend, regardless of temperament, size or affability. We were allocated to the Beginners Class.

I hasten to add that darling Ronnie, unable to take charge of this activity because of his weak heart and unlikely possibility of the defibrillator firing if triggered by undue exertion - I decided to relegate that thought to the far innermost parts of my mind for the time being - took up his vantage point in the car. He consumed vast quantities of bullets while observing my debilitation and Lucy's cavorting. Lucy and I covered what seemed to be miles in formation with other students, which involved repetitious feats of stamina to achieve obedience in SIT, STAAAAND, **DOWN** and STAY.

When regaling friends with this latest caper, Ronnie would add gleefully, 'And that's only Sue!' Many a time, when in a Supermarket queue, I would feel an impudent pinch of my bottom accompanied by the strident instruction - 'STAAAAND!' And all, because along came Lucy....

Lucy did respond remarkably well once she had got the hang of it while learning to resist the temptation to harangue other canine learners with invitations to play. These entreaties involved rolling on her back and kicking legs in the air, grinning all the while. Our trainer, Harry, given to a rich vocabulary of profanities when things were not going to plan, would rasp 'That's it! The little bugger's 'ad it. You'll get nowt more done today. You might just as well go 'ome.' **I** was tempted, on occasion, to roll over on my back and kick my legs in the air, just in the hopes of an early release! After weeks of ten-minute practices every morning in the Park, Lucy's penny began to drop and because my pockets bulged with rewarding cheese-bites and bacon-flavoured biscuits, she reached heights of accomplishment. Our chests puffed out like pouter pigeons when her impeccable conduct did not go unnoticed at tea-parties!

Our Voluntary work increased. As time went by, we became immersed in absorbing pursuits which involved not only the Hospital Stroke Unit and Hospice, but leisure activities for Parkinson's Disease Clubs and Community Centres. On a weekly basis, Ronnie would attend the Haworth Unit at Scarborough Hospital, which specialised in support for the elderly and those struck down with terminal or ongoing, debilitating disease. There he would chat, read newspapers to the disabled, win over his listeners or ply his Theatrical stories to the entire host, Staff and patients alike.

When Lucy and I returned from a beach walk, we drove to collect our love. He would emerge replenished, smiling and only faintly weary. 'You know, **I'm** the one who feels uplifted. They know I'm a Senior Citizen and nearly kept me in this time!' Our promising lives brimmed with happiness. We were a pair, united and in tune.

This time span was not without sadness and upheaval. We faced Louie's decline in health, made repeated stopovers to the Hartlepool domain and eventually came up against the inevitable passing of Ronnie's idiosyncratic Mother. Louie's last days were spent very happily in the Manor Park Residential Home. Ronnie was relieved and glad to be trouble-free at this time. He was saved from breathless attacks which heralded his own brand of danger and was able to be the Son his irascible Mother so adored. The residual family's visits were scant, save for the faithful attention of one Niece. Ah well, all kinsfolk have issues and past outrage can be slow to fade.

Louie's funeral was well attended by members of what turned out to be a far-reaching and sizeable brood. All present for the send-off, yet all absent for the preliminaries. Dearest Ronnie coped with the tribute and I was proud of him. His remembrance, true to form, was not without an eccentric observation.

'Well, Louie's an Angel now, but....er...she wasn't always!' I suppressed a giggle when he added, 'She was, however, very generous with her Disability Allowance and there was often something in an envelope for her Grandchildren, when they remembered to visit her'. Ouch!

***

PART 1

THEN

A FINE, DEAR LIBERATOR

The death of our Doctor was hard to bear. He had been our beacon of light for so many years. We had followed where he led, listened to his wise words and recognised the karma that was ours. He had saved and brought us together. Through him, we had found redemption. His parting did not leave us denuded and empty. The rest of our lives lay before us, enriched and strengthened by an unusual, charismatic man who would never be consigned to oblivion. His was a bountiful legacy.

I was reminded of the 12th Century Poet, Omar Khayyam. Our revered Doctor had echoed his mystical writings. As I came to the closing days of my healing, I found an embossed, leather-bound collection of those transcendental verses as a gift for him.

Many years passed after my Prophet's death. In that time I did not hear the Poet's graceful, arcane words more – until, my book reached its conclusion. Then, marvellously, I sensed them being whispered again: a foretelling, a betoken of faith to hearten, remember and make strong.

'The moving finger writes and, having writ, moves on; nor all thy piety nor wit shall lure it back to cancel half a line'

OMAR KHAYYAM

**

PART 1

T H E N

SEASONS COME AND GO...

Our leisure time was given to visiting old friends, taking extended motoring excursions and loitering in Stately Homes or Gardens where we admired and acquired more collections for our own Secret one. Friends came to stay, initially for a weekend and then changed their minds - 'May we stop over for a few more days?'

West Bank rejoiced as laughter filled the night and conversation reverberated beyond the small hours. Brian and Grace from Bowrons Avenue crusaded North several times. Brian was astonished one early morning when on a trajectory, from the upper floor, to the lavatory. Unfortunately, no en suite in those days... On opening the door, he was transfixed by the sight of Ronnie sitting there intent on the business of the day. 'Oh, good morning Brian,' said he, 'how are you? I do apologise. We do not lock the lavatory door. Sue's afraid I may have a heart attack and she would be unable to reach me!' A story remembered and held dear....

Ronnie's Agent and her Sister installed themselves for short holidays away from London's jostling stampede. I made great inroads into my vestiges of cordiality. Their presence in Scarborough had been frequent over the years, long before I came on the scene and I knew that for Ronnie's sake, I should not rock the boat. Whence, I subjugated uneasiness and welcomed them. Come what may, my elephant remained in the room...

Ronnie's state of health was kept under close observation. The defibrillator was serviced regularly and this assignment necessitated a drive over the Wolds to East Yorkshire and the Castle Hill Hospital. In the course of events, Ronnie discovered that his prescription of a particular life-preserving pill was cursed with peculiar side effects, one being that he needed to be protected from the sun's damaging rays. Factor Fifty was liberally applied and when Ronnie emerged to face the powers of natural light, he was heard to elucidate thus: 'Fuck me, I look like Marley's Ghost!' A further safeguard was the addition of a large Mexican straw hat. Dazed exclamations and the odd smothered chortle from passers-by met with sanguine nonchalance.

At the opening of 2002, we were reminded by the Hospital that the generator for Ronnie's defibrillator would need to be replaced. We could hardly believe that it had been standing guard for almost five years. We were told that this would be a routine strategy and Ronnie was asked to attend Castle Hill Hospital as a day patient. I should have known from experience that nothing about Ronnie's heart was routine. It had a mind of its own.

We opted to leave Lucy at home in the care of our kind, thoughtful neighbour. 'We'll pick up a fish 'n' four on the way back,' assured the confident Ronnie, making sure, as always, that he had got his priorities right before setting off. On admittance, Ronnie was told that he would be ready for discharge later in the day, so I killed time visiting my Brother in Beverley. That time hung heavily as I waited...so much waiting...'

A Nurse was waiting. What news awaited me? 'Mrs. Herdman, things have taken longer than we expected. The Doctors have decided to keep Mr. Herdman in overnight.' 'Why?' was my strangled reply. 'Oh, just a precaution, everything's fine'. Mmn...I'd fallen foul of such a summing up on countless occasions. I reached the bedside and my somersaulting innards pitched. Ronnie was pale, very pale and his enervation very evident. ' I say, darling,...' he said in an effort to be cheery, 'they're keeping me in. Bang goes the fish 'n' four! They're keeping a beady eye on my progress!' I did not need explanation. Something had gone wrong. 'Darling, please can you have a little look at my back - it's so itchy and I can't reach it'. I uncovered Ronnie's shoulders and was horrified to discover reddish imprints on the skin. Tactfully, I also disturbed the front of his pyjama jacket, only to find similar markings on his chest. It looked as if a flat iron had been planted firmly front and back. I made no reference to this, at the same time reassuring Ronnie that I would return for the evening Visiting armed with Savlon. I knew, in dismay, that my darling had been resuscitated and those were the marks of defibrillating paddles. Poor old heart....

In the couple of hours between afternoon and evening, I drove to Scarborough to retrieve Lucy and deliver her safely to my Brother. In spite of my encroaching gloom and doom, Ronnie was brighter when I reached the Ward.

'The Doctor would like to speak to us tomorrow,' he announced, as I soothed the scorch marks with the promised Savlon and wondered why some Nurse had not thought of doing the same thing. 'You know, when they've looked me over'. The next day, I appeared at the allotted time and waited...and waited...and waited...

The Consultant eventually made an entrance - no apology forthcoming - clad in tweed coat, the collar trimmed with bottle-green velvet. I disliked him instantly.

Perception can be a damned nuisance. One sees things one does not want to see; at times, one would rather look the other way and so not perceive.

'Oh Mr. & Mrs. Herdman, I needed to see you together. We had bother with your machine yesterday and consequently there is no guarantee at this moment in time that it would fire in an emergency. When it was tested we had a little difficulty starting everything up again'. There was a sharp intake of breath from me, whereupon the cocky little shit - to use one of Ronnie's very favourite terms - continued, 'Oh yes, there were a few sweaty armpits!' How I restrained my vituperative 'Arsehole!' I will never know. 'What did Horace say, Winnie?' whispered Ronnie, quoting one of his favourite 40's radio programmes.

At that point, this profligate man of medicine must have clocked my facial reaction. He continued, 'We could of course attempt another small operation where the heart can be held in a sling...'His lips moved and voiced miracles of curative knack and know-how. 'Do you find the need to follow this plan frequently?' I enquired. 'Hardly ever...' 'And how long is it since you found it necessary to perform this operation?' 'Oh,' he scratched his nose, 'about seven or eight years...' I looked at Ronnie, who was raising his eyebrows. 'I think we need to have a little time to ourselves, Doctor' noted Ronnie. With that, the adviser turned on his heel and left the Ward. Nurses, wide-eyed and cowed by his stupendous presence, whirled in the backwash.

'Cocky little shit!' said Ronnie. 'Ronnie, you have read my mind,' was my tart reply. 'Well, my love,' continued my beloved, 'I think we'll allow God to take charge of this one. What an Arsehole! (Two minds think as one!) I'm buggered if I'm going to snuff it on his operating table, so we'll let the good Lord take me when he's ready'.

The following day, when Ronnie had given his decision and was in the process of being discharged, he asked questions. A young Doctor on the team satisfied Ronnie's curiosity. 'Yes, Mr. Herdman, we had to start your heart again and again. It was a bit touch and go, but we did it and there is every reason to believe that if the defibrillator is needed, it will do its work, so do not worry'.

I then realised why Ronnie had been moved to Intensive Care when Wynn Davies had implanted the defibrillator. He, too, had had difficulties.

We took Lucy home that evening and yes, we did detour and stop for the fish 'n' four! Ronnie was safe. Omnipotence paved the undisputed way and we were content. Our lovely life would continue for as long as it was meant to do and the all-embracing ambience of West Bank brought back our warmth and resilience. It would take more than the cocky little shit to dissipate that... Ronnie's heart proved it was a force to be reckoned with.

The disconcerting defibrillator incident left me swaying with uncertainty. In turn, this bred inexorable fear. My mind was disturbed with ephemeral, dreaded imaginings. Walks with Lucy became drifts of thought where I deemed that life without Ronnie would become a zigzagging, aimless existence without rhyme or reason. What would that reality be like? How would I contain my grief? How could I live without him? What would it be like to open the front door and meet with silence; a hollow void where whistling and his happy singing were no more. Perhaps that is why I sought solitary walks where no person could witness the heartbreak and crushing, shattering emotion. I knew the tears must fall where all was quiet, in a sparse place of purdah where they could be buried in the soft fur of Lucy's neck. Yes...then along came Lucy...

By the time we had reached home and the open garden gate, we would hear that dear whistling. As the warmth of relief flowed through my being, I would be happy once more, in time to hear, 'It's sausage and mash tonight, Alice...' resounding from the kitchen, where the laughing gentleman in a striped navy-blue apron would be brandishing a wooden spoon.

Now, when I allow my recollection of those times to surface, I accept a fuller, percipient understanding of my misery. Then, so long ago, I would topple into an unforeseen pit from which there seemed to be no escape. My innocent Ronnie could become the trigger for calamitous change of mood - a chance remark, an unwary observation would hurl me into a barren never-never land where the black dog lived. A touch, a kiss, any tangible loving would have melted away my sorrow and my sadness, but Ronnie could not break through the stony barricade. He was afraid. So, on and on I would toss, silently waiting for the shadows to pass...and in those sickening instants our binding love fought to find a chink. In time, a faltering tender touch dissolved and healed...'Darling, you are so depressed, so stressed....' my dear would dare and then the tears would spill, the never-ending thankful tears, gently washing away the hours of pain and panic.

'Ronnie, please say something funny'. 'Bollocks, twatmagoola and dingly-dangly!' would be the aphorism and, in the giggles that followed, all distress would fade into the annals of time. Now, in peaceful, wool-gathering dreaminess, I call to mind those days and know that in spite of my sharp denial, Ronnie was right. I did not know how far strain had taken me, or how heavy a burden the unknown and its fellow fearfulness had become.

**

PART 1

THEN

THE DARK DAYS

As our lives moved on and furtively crept into the months of 2003, West Bank became used to the blue lights of an ambulance. The darkness would be pierced as curtains twitched and sleep was interrupted by shuffling, hurrying figures.

Ronnie's attacks, growing in intensity, became more frequent. In turn, the Hospital stays were protracted. These hideous assaults followed a similar pattern and could occur at any time.

Often, in the small hours of the morning, I would wake to the sound of Ronnie's erratic, laboured breathing. There I lay awake, wide-eyed with fear and misgiving, listening and all the time willing the inescapable to stop; the ambush to correct itself. It did not...the wheezing respiration fought a grave battle to rout and quell, but was indolent. 'Bugger!'. Ronnie's rasping curse proclaimed the terrifying decree. 'Ronnie, darling, you're in trouble' I would whisper, my arid and shrivelled mouth barely able to enunciate. My love, sitting on the edge of the bed, his face ashen and skin glistening with cold sweat, strained to console: 'Sue, my sweet, go downstairs and make a cup of tea - by the time you get back, I'll be better...' My limbs would rally but feeling ran amok. I wrestled cups between trembling fingers, grappling for sway.

Ronnie's punishing feat to breathe could be heard from the bottom of the stairs. Relinquishing all thoughts of tea, I would lift the telephone...'They're coming, my darling, I have called an ambulance.' 'Oh dear, you shouldn't have bothered them', came the courageous reply. From then on the carpet would be worn thin as I paced from front window to the back bedroom, searching for the sign of help and willing Ronnie to hold on. Relief surged through me as the blue light, faint in the distance, promised our deliverance.

Paramedics armed with medical instruments, gear and technology, sped to Ronnie's side where the loyal and true Lucy was custodian. At once, her charge went into performance mode, all the while reassuring these messengers that he was 'Fine, I'm sure it's passing off'.

'Well, Mr. Herdman, your ECG tells us that perhaps it would be just as well to get you checked out!' Without more ado, Ronnie would fight to get into his dressing-gown and, as his breath whistled through an oxygen mask, exclaim 'Just so those nosy neighbours opposite don't see my bits!'

The subsequent process was uniform. Lucy, consumed with alarm, would fluster and need to be settled, but before I could leave the house, my body would react to the terror it had faced and I would hasten to the lavatory where vitals ruled. After, distracted and trembling, I would make my way to the rayless, darksome West Bank, where all was still, forsaken and bereft of life. I would have welcomed to-do, hurly-burly and the human stir. My fingers, numb with shock, turned the door key. I remembered the pressing need to drive carefully. I was needed. I needed to guard and watch. Despite the reflex manipulation of gears, brakes and steering, I thought of death, Ronnie's death...would I be in time? Where, in this dank silence, did I belong? Streets, houses and gardens, so well-known and ordinary in daylight hours, took on invincible, austere and singular form. My fevered, frantic motion propelled me along one-way roads and through no-go zones; reckless to reach the blurry lights of A & E.

'Darling, you're here!' would be the greeting. There, upon Hospital bed and in the antiseptic boundaries of a therapeutic cubicle, Ronnie lay enclosed within the limits imposed by appliance, apparatus and gizmos - monitors, oxygen and lines. His pallid, wan face haunted me. I was not allowed time to think. 'Now look, darling,' Ronnie boosted, 'I've told the Doctor that my lovely wife will be here soon and knows all about my history, so you're going to have to tell him what pills I take. I didn't tell him you're known as Miss Jackboots!'

In the hours that followed, I learned that Ronnie would be treated as before with intravenous Amiodarone. 'So, Alice, here we go again! I'm awash and my lungs can't cope - poor things are full of water. I'm going to be peeing for England again, so brace yourself!'

The turbulent months that lay ahead offered little interval between these sporadic knocks and poundings. Mercifully, Ronnie was able to enjoy each recess with a smattering of normality. Whether that was because Ronnie surged forward after each renewal determined to overcome this blight on his life, or whether he refused to contemplate it ending his life, I will never know. We both took on the enormity of it in secret acknowledgement. Ronnie's strength strengthened me. It has always been so, since the day that Ronnie came into my life. In my moments of sadness, stress and fear, when timorous thoughts drove me to silence and despair, Ronnie's common sense would breathe new life into me - 'Come on, Sue, this is such a waste of time...'

Thought is private, unassailable. So long ago, when in turmoil or distress, I would be driven to share each and every musing with all who were prepared to listen. I grew in 'thought stature' through the years of knowing and loving Ronnie.

I learned to be brave. I followed his gritty example and my suffering thoughts were hidden. I learned not to burden others; most of the time! I learned restraint. I will never know if Ronnie's turbulent, fearful thoughts could have been shared. I wonder if whispering our fragile, vulnerable presentiments in tenderness and love would have eased our pain. Ronnie accepted his crippling illness and its putative projection, but he must have been afraid. 'Don't tell Sue, she'll only worry', I now know he was heard to say.

In the Summer of 2004, Ronnie had a catastrophic heart attack. It is always the unexpected that happens. Where had I heard that before?

We were accustomed to the process of heart failure, the breathlessness, the incubus. This time, our emergency destination was to be Resuscitation where dearest Ronnie was revived from near unconsciousness. He was devastatingly slow to respond or return to his vigorous, saucy, plucky, and hopeful self. Consultants clad in operating garb milled around Ronnie's dormant form while scientific know-how and tackle coaxed his torpor into being. Once his lifeblood was rekindled, Ronnie returned to me with animating force, the vital spark which prompted a male Nurse to murmur softly, 'His love of life is everything to him'.

'Is that my heart up there?' enquired Ronnie. He was looking towards an X-Ray plate prominently placed upon the wall. There, his enlarged heart was clearly visible. The chest cavity could hardly contain it. 'That's the first time I've actually seen it. It's very big, isn't it?' Ronnie reflected. 'There seems to be one or two things we have to see to this time, Ronnie', understated his Specialist, who had been hurried with all haste from his Ward round. Nurses and Assistants were unusually silent and preoccupied...their absorption and immersion in dutiful tasks was disconnected, distant. Or, so it seemed to me. Nothing and no-one in those painful minutes pointed the way to triumph, gladness or jubilation. Only Ronnie picked up the pieces - 'Well, you've got it going again…poor old heart'. Poor old heart; poor old generous, warm and loving heart. As I think yet again of those far-off days, I dwell anew upon the heart as pure machinery, workings and a device. Yet, it is at the centre of our being, our soul and our essence. It is the kernel, the core of this evanescent, transitory human condition.

I knew that time was running out. Defeat was totally unacceptable. The time left was put to enabling use. Ronnie was placed upon a rehabilitation programme which involved diet - 'I'll still be able to have my fish 'n' chips once a week, won't I?' - exercise and medication.

No more would I allow my precious Ronnie to walk alone. I would drive him to the Esplanade and there Ronnie set off for his exertion around the block. In secret, I would follow in the car. I saw how his determined effort took every vestige of will power for Ronnie to proceed, yet proceed he did. Seeing him falter, hold on to a garden gate for support, my heart would break. As I pulled into the kerb, he would turn 'Oh there you are, Alice. Might have known you'd be cruising, looking for unsuspecting talent!' Then, warmly tucked into the front seat, his even-breathing once more reinstated, Ronnie would announce: 'Fish Pan for a bag of chips, or Mr. Softee ice-cream, darling. Bugger the diet!' Oh, the simple joy of sitting snugly beside my dearest love on a blustery, chilly seaside day watching the hammering waves imperil the crumbling coastline; each fleeting moment kept safe within for the rest of my life.

In October 2004 I was approaching my 65th Birthday. The weather was a conventional mix of buffeting winds and quintessential rainfall or frost. Our walks had taken on a careful, restorative and healing wandering. We roved on clement days in spite of Lucy's dogged pleading for a faster pace. Later, she was appeased with beachcombing; a trek while Ronnie rested.

Hampered by annoying health warnings from me, Ronnie was unable to set forth and forage for Birthday presents. Every year I had received an exquisite piece of jewellery to mark the occasion. In addition to brooch, necklace or ring, there would be a richly-ornamented crochet coat or jacket, enhanced with a thousand and one beads lovingly amassed from the purloining of antique booths or car boot counters. This year, Ronnie began to design a full-length mohair coat. The wool was a manifold fusion of hue. 'This is to be your Christmas present' he added. 'Bit early', I said. 'You know me, I often look ahead where you're involved. I don't like being caught out!' Again, Ronnie seemed determined to extend my wardrobe and spent many hours at the sewing-machine, creating outfit after outfit. Numerous fittings took place and West Bank turned into a minor cottage industry.

As my Birthday dawned and not to be discouraged, daunted or dissuaded by unpredictable form or fitness, Ronnie suggested a shopping splurge at Tescos. As I brought packing to a close and man-handled a creaking trolley, Ronnie appeared. He was barely visible beneath a monumental bouquet of Stargazer lilies. 'For my darling on your Birthday' said the beaming Ronnie while spectators smiled and cooed 'Ah...' 'You see,' explained Ronnie, 'I remembered that in the language of flowers, Susan means Lily'. I will never be able to count the number of times that a lump has formed in my throat when faced with Ronnie's great love. At such times, I could not speak, but only make muffled, choking sounds....

On the morning of my Day, I received an unusual Birthday Card from Ronnie. I say unusual, for in the past his cards may have been rude in the extreme, often with an accompanying verse or caption expressing vulgar, rough-hewn sentiments or unflattering remarks about one's physique. This time, my card displayed a very beautiful picture of a ballerina: delicate, refined and ethereal. 'I thought of your Mother, Jessica, when I chose it,' Ronnie explained. Inside, dear Ronnie had inscribed: '**Happy Birthday, my Darling. Loved you then, love you now and always will**'. Little did I know as I wept over the loving words that they would prove to be so lasting, enduring and timeless...

Six weeks later, my darling Ronnie braved his worst, most petrifying attack. The procedure was not unfamiliar in any way, but the outcome was virulent, lethal. By the time I reached the Coronary Care Unit, Ronnie was in extreme danger, although I was unaware of this at the time. I was advised to wait in an ante room.

This compartment housed out-of-date magazines and well-thumbed editions of 'Hello'. At the dead of night, this waiting cavity or dungeon elicited fantasies of condemnation, then imprisonment within one's thoughts. Those thoughts ran riot as my breath came in rapid inhalations striving to keep tempo with my racing heart.

'Mrs. Herdman, you can see your husband now'. The Night Sister, standing in the doorway of my crypt, beckoned. I followed. 'The Doctor will have to do something about his medication...' were the agitated, nervous words. I could feel the icy clutching of my fingers. Ronnie was sitting, but breathless and still fighting to control his blighted body. I was deeply shocked. I had grown to recognise the pallid, weak aftermath of previous heart failure seizures. I was not, however, steeled for the havoc that this pitiless aggression had had on Ronnie. He was laid waste. His bloodless, waxen features were sickly and vapid save for two crimson patches on his cheeks, a harlequin memory of his ordeal.

Ronnie knew. I knew. All else was superfluous. I remained by his side, holding him, until some peace returned.

I was ushered to one side, urged to go home, to rest...Ronnie's eyes stared, implored. 'Go darling, Lucy needs you...leave them to it....they know what to do'. I suppose I surrendered to flimsy reassurance when I agreed to leave my darling. I longed for peace, for sanctuary, a place where someone would tell me that all would be well.

Lucy lay beside me that night. She knew and I knew. Sleepless, we tossed and turned until the telephone bell jolted and clashed us into wakeful fear. 'Mrs. 'erdman, the Doctor ask me to let you know' the Filipino voice explained, Mr. 'erdman has had another do. You can come?' I could not move. 'Mrs. 'erdman, are you there?' 'Yes, I'm coming...'

Now, I cannot remember the journey. Somehow, I must have driven to the Hospital. Somehow, I must have settled Lucy and then dressed myself. I cannot recall the dull, self-propelling actions. I had become a robot, a mechanical thing presided over by unknown, esoteric forces. The Physician awaited me. I knew him. Ronnie knew him. He was the husband of our Volunteer Organiser and principal Consultant for the Stroke Unit. 'Come this way, Sue'. He directed me back, back to the functionary, dispassionate ante-room. Before he could forecast or predict, I whispered the words, 'He's dying, isn't he?' Then came the uncompromising, candid answer: 'He is'.

From deep within my being came a cry, a wail, an animalistic outpouring. It ruptured the silence. It rent me null, wanting and in a place of senseless oblivion. All was still, slack and lifeless. 'How long?' Who was this speaking? Me? Some borrowed agency had become my mouthpiece. The terrible answer seared into my sensibility. 'Perhaps he will have the weekend'. It was Friday. 'Does he know?' I pleaded. 'No'. He shifted uncomfortably. 'Come, Sue, you will have to pretend that you are on stage...' I stared, unable to discern, grasp or perceive. My unseeing gape fixated. The silent human being before me was a stranger, an unwelcome messenger. Listlessly, my leaden, insensate and frozen limbs found life again. I groped my way towards the open door. Ronnie, my dearest love, I am coming...

Caught in a whirlpool of disbelief and disorientation, I found my way to the bedside. Ronnie was slipping in and out of awareness, but he knew I was there. I took his hand and willed my energy and spiritual resilience to infiltrate, to permeate his weariness. 'Darling', he breathed and succumbed to fitful sleep. Silently, I stroked his still hands. Ronnie's fingers were never still. They coaxed plants into life or entwined wool. They worked ceaselessly to create and fashion. How untidy, how illusory the world had become in just a few short hours. Nurses, Doctors, helpers with tea-trolleys went about their business. Did they not know my love was dying? Did they not know I was clinging to his life, inwardly imploring for it to endure, to last, to stay...just for a little while. I would not be greedy with time...but...just for a little while longer. I would never leave him.

'Mrs. Herdman, can we call someone for you?' came the softly-spoken words. A Nurse with outstretched hand was guiding mine to the upholding tea-cup. The sweet sips broke through the sealant lips. 'Please would you direct me to a phone?' My Brother's busy voice answered. He was at work. 'Sue I cannot leave the shop'.

I felt the colour drain from my cheeks. 'Please Nick, Lucy is alone and I cannot leave Ronnie. The Doctor...' the words strangled, 'the Doctor says Ronnie may not survive. It may only be the weekend'. I sensed the shock. An intense silence filled the air before comprehension sunk in. 'I'll be there as soon as I can'. Then the quaking voice was gone. The mist descended once more. I fumbled, scrabbled my way through the daze and muddle, knowing all at once the dread of blindness: the fiend which intimidates, frightens, isolates and, at first, depicts perfect impotence. Ronnie was awake. 'I say, is Holby City on tonight?' Denial's cloak wrapped its folds around us; we lived in the moment...

Ronnie survived. The weekend came and went. Ronnie remained in the Coronary Care Unit where he was nursed by dedicated Doctors and Nurses. He was gravely ill, but...he remained. Ronnie rallied, slipped back, revived and slipped back. His willpower drove him on while I watched and prepared; primed myself to look certainty in the eye. There, by his bedside, I kept my vigil. When my darling's trial planed, I made short-lived visits to West Bank where Lucy was comforted and walked. These short intervals allowed enough time for my Brother to pick up the threads of his business, before returning to help. When he came back, Coronary Care made provision for me to stay overnight. A side room was made ready for Ronnie and me.

Throughout the week, Ronnie clung to his life. During his brighter moments, television revived his morale. He and I watched 'Strictly Come Dancing' and, implausibly, 'Holby City' and 'Casualty'. 'You know, darling,' he said, 'I must be the only person they've nursed here who watches Hospital programmes when in Hospital!'

Ronnie's Nursing Sister arranged for a large television set to be brought to the Unit when it was learned that 'Four Weddings & A Funeral' was to be transmitted. All Nursing Staff, Doctors and any patients who could marshal might and main, were invited to watch Ronnie in his role as First Vicar! As the camera homed in on Ronnie's one and only close-up, there was a burst of cheering and foot-stamping. Surrounded by his friends who offered so much love, admiration and regard, my uncanny, remarkable and fantastic Husband said, 'Well, now I am Queen of all I survey!!' He looked at me and winked. Hmn... thought I.

Ronnie remained, lived on and defied predictions. We did not speak of the precipice which towered before us. We knew. We protected each other from the truth. I was Ronnie's accomplice and he trusted me. He would live until he died. I accepted.

Ronnie was sleeping in snatches. A senior Nurse approached and drew me aside. 'What are we going to do about Ronnie's defibrillator?' I gawped vacantly. 'Sue, if Ronnie was to go into cardiac arrest, the machine would continue to fire, trying to re-start his heart. He would suffer very much indeed'. I stared in panic. 'No, that cannot be allowed to happen. What can you do?' Gently, he replied, 'I am carrying a magnet around in my pocket in case of an emergency. It would deactivate the defibrillator'. 'That solution is not certain,' I continued, 'we must arrange for it to be switched off, but my husband is not to know, for he would refuse permission anyway. It would take away his hope'.

The following day, a technician, under the auspices of servicing Ronnie's defibrillator, turned it off. I was desolate. I had made a decision that was not mine to make. Had we been counselled when the machine was implanted, we would have learned of the possible end-of-life consequences. We would have made the judgement together. I wept in secret - in secret despair.

Circumstances took a different turn with the advent of visiting Heart Failure Specialist, Miriam Johnson, who spoke at length to Ronnie and me. 'How would you feel about going into the Hospice, Ronnie?' she queried. 'Oh, I'd be delighted,' replied Ronnie, 'it would be like going home'. Miriam became a beacon of light.

It was arranged that Ronnie would be transported to the Hospice as soon as a bed became vacant. In the transitional period, he would be admitted to a general Hospital Ward for the weekend. We were informed of arrangements when the Coronary Nursing Sister declared, perhaps with some insensitivity, 'Ronnie we must move you, for this is a high-dependency Unit with a limited number of beds and we cannot save your life'. I did not look at Ronnie, for I fervently hoped he had not absorbed the significance of her statement. He did not comment and in the hush that followed, I tidied and fussed with bedclothes, belongings and books. The Sister's summing up was thoughtless and crude, but she was not an unfeeling woman, just one who was caught up in form-filling, schedules and criteria.

The least said the better regarding Ronnie's two-night stay on the routine Ward. By now, he was wired up to a morphine driver. The Doctor on duty forgot to 'write it up' and, as a consequence, Ronnie was left without relief. This culminated in me threatening to call Coronary Care myself unless steps were taken to rectify this worrying situation. Action was taken immediately. I was given overnight Hospital accommodation, on the other side of the campus, by the League of Friends and spent a desolate, sleepless early hours waiting for dawn. My staying nearby, did not alter the fact that Ronnie spent the uncomfortable night badgered by morphine-induced terrors in near isolation, until morning broke when I could console, bathe him and do my best to accelerate his passage to the Hospice. It was a miserable, frightening time. Monday morning brought an ambulance. In spite of my loving, encouraging endearments, Ronnie could not be cheered with expectation of the Hospice's warmth. He was weak and despondent. He was also displaying symptoms of paranoia and anxiety, which I put down to side effects of medication. I was greatly relieved to hold his hands as the ambulance pulled away from the place which had rescued, and then, inadvertently, condemned us to two whole days of heartache and constraint. Yes indeed, Ronnie, the Hospice would be like going home.

***

PART 1

THEN

ST CATHERINE'S HOSPICE

Rooms in St. Catherine's Hospice were named after familiar North Yorkshire settings. Ronnie was to find himself in Staintondale. The luxurious bedroom was equipped with en-suite facilities, telephone, a television and comfortable chairs which could be adapted to lounging or an upright position. French windows allowed fresh air and sunshine to flood the light, hopeful place; not, however, on this frosty December morning. Poor Ronnie was too poorly, too drained and pinched to imbibe of such indulgence. The Hospital Ward had depleted and almost annihilated his flicker of expectancy or will.

Step by feeble step, Nurses gently tended Ronnie. They allowed him to lie in peace. I sat by his side as the afternoon faded and dusk began to form. Stillness, calm and repose were his boon companions. Benign and compassionate, they emboldened and braced. As I felt the faint squeezing of my hand in his, I took hope to my sad heart. Just a little while longer, it seemed to beat...

I lingered on, and on...and on...all the while knowing that sooner or later I must leave. Lucy needed me.

Nurses were watching over Ronnie as I made my way home that evening. He was safe. I had been urged to rest and return in the morning. It was sound advice. The haven of home, the joyful walls of the house where we spent so many happy hours, seemed to heal, repair and mend my frayed soul. Again, Lucy slept by my side until morning light stirred us; made us ready for whatever the day may bring.

Ronnie had had a restless, distraught night. Bedevilled by morphine nightmares, he fought to disentangle his senses. Miriam Johnson, beside him when I arrived, was explaining carefully and with keen sensitivity the reason for his troubled distress. 'We left you in peace last night, Ronnie - gave you time to settle in. Now we're going to do something to help you unscramble your head. We'll re-jig your tablets, make sure that you're spot on with them. I think you'll soon feel a lot better. Much more like your old, cheeky self!' Ronnie heeded. He was engaged and ready to fight once again.

I followed Miriam from the room. I spoke as she was heading off along the corridor. 'Doctor, I am so very worried about Ronnie. I want to be with him all the time...' Hurriedly, off-balance and disrupted, I spoke of Lucy and about not being able to leave her indefinitely. 'Sue, you must do what your heart tells you to do'. She knew the answer, before the words had formed. 'Sue, bring her here. Let her live with you both...here'.

Lucy came to the Hospice that night. She slept on her duvet between Ronnie's bed and mine. I had been invited to sleep on a folding camp-bed. We were together...the three of us... swaddled in a world of unabated caring. Lucy knew; just as I knew. She did not bark or disturb, but only lifted her head protectively when Nurses came in the middle of the night to turn her Ronnie.

It was the beginning of December 2004. The winds blew and snow flurries wafted across the windows of Staintondale. In those early detached and disconnected days, our life was conveyed to a jumbled land where past, present and future merged into a fathomless, vague, remote and rapt daydream. The past was a pocket of enticing, captivating reverie where laughter, dear love and safety lodged. The present was jailed within the daily round of medicine, drugs, uneaten tempting food and silence. A silence pierced only by the desultory drone of puerile television down the passage. It was a pretending time. There in the present, we pretended that everything was going to be all right; all the time knowing that it was not going to be all right. The future was out of bounds, one did not go there... there was nowhere to go...

Caring for a desperately ill loved one is a lonely existence. I lived in a secretive world; a world of protection where malady becomes an invisible burden one can never put down. Again and again, as Ronnie slept, I would find myself trying to imagine the end. I remembered that years ago I had heard a Radio interview where a widow spoke of her Husband's failing heart and how she had watched and listened to him choking to death. Gripped with unimaginable fear, I confided this to a young student Doctor. She was so very young: a novice with so much to learn about dying. 'We would never allow that to happen to Ronnie, Mrs. Herdman. You can trust us'. Her compassion was all the more palpable because she was so young.

Hospitals are often sad and confused places, and when we, or our loved ones are sick, our state of mind makes sensible decision-making impossible. So, for us, St. Catherine's Hospice became a dissimilar sanctum, a place of aspiration. It's serene shield became a cradle where we could rest. As Lucy and I stayed at Ronnie's bedside, my thoughts travelled far.

Sadly, the word 'Hospice', to many, is synonymous with death. There is grief, there is sadness, but therein lies the opportunity for many things. In the quiet of reflection, of meditation, one can try to prepare. It is a privilege to accompany a loved one towards their other life.

Our Hospice room was a hallowed, inviolable and lustrous private place reserved for protection. Medication becomes someone else's responsibility; the visions, terrors which can partner morphine and the gut-wrenching nausea are treated with Specialist Palliative knowledge, patience and sympathy. Domestic affairs are distant. They reside in some far-off reality. Where else but in this travellers' house of rest could one relinquish worry and exchange it for peace? Fear is diminished, and, in spite of the agony of watching an unrelenting process, safety and healing replace the dread. Ronnie could put his utmost faith in help being just around the corner. I recall that my uppermost thought was for anguish, confusion and fright to be taken away from Ronnie. While I prayed for this to happen, Nurses, a Chaplain and the ever-vigilant Doctors reassured me.

One has the scope to behave in strange fashion. Everyone understands. I remember trying to capture Ronnie's smell, the personal scent that was so individual. I buried my face in his neck while he slept, attempting to fill my nostrils in the hope of retaining the essence of what was so familiar, intimate and unique. A Nurse happened to call while this was happening. She understood at once. No explanation was needed. A definitive moment remains forever.

In a Hospice, we meet kindred spirits: tea ladies, receptionists, gardeners, caterers and many more who are there to comfort. Often, your experience echoes theirs. You become part of an irreplaceable alliance where time is suspended. Time is so important when someone is dying. No one must intrude, as loved ones cannot help but do at home. You do not have to make excuses; the Hospice makes them for you. I learned to begin the grieving process; the waiting, the loneliness, dejection and despair when we are left with the approaching end to life.

And so...the days turned into weeks...we waited and we waited...relatives came and went...friends came...were helpless and distraught.

Ronnie and I had been due to give a Christmas entertainment in the Day Hospice. I remember mentioning to Ronnie that I would not leave him. Suddenly, he was wide awake. 'Sue,' he tried so hard to speak clearly, 'you cannot let all those ladies and gentlemen down. Now go home, put on one of the dresses I made for you, and go and do it!' Somehow, I did do it. I performed with only one thought in my head - Ronnie and my transcendent love for him. When I returned to Staintondale, Ronnie was sleeping. 'I did it Ronnie', I whispered and for a moment his eyes flickered. He smiled. He had heard me.

As Christmas came into view, Miriam broke the silence. 'Sue, dear Sue, he will not be with us for very much longer. Try to think of this as if you are waiting on the platform for a train that is coming, but it is late...he will do it his way'. Christmas Day dawned and my darling awoke for a while, then drifted off to sleep...awoke, then once more drifted...

The quiet sedation pervaded all; I emotionally sedated and Ronnie medically so, yet he could still hear me, and smile.

Ronnie was extremely agitated the day before he died. It was the most distressing thing I have ever lived through. All at once, a Nurse guided me to another room as others assured me that Ronnie would be helped and cared for. That wonderful Nurse did not speak, but held me while I endured what I can only describe as paroxysms of grief. Her strength restored me. Her total empathy was healing and I have never forgotten those desolate moments. The unsolicited, plain, certain solace of a little known person is somehow so nurturing because it is entirely unconditional.

Lucy and I stayed beside our darling until the early hours of the following day. Then, an extraordinary thing happened. I moved to my bed and Lucy to hers. We fell asleep. A Nurse had called later and was astonished at the sight. I was told that she had spoken to a colleague saying: 'That is almost as if Ronnie knew how much strength they would come to need. He helped them and they are all fast asleep'.

Ronnie, my dearest love, Ronnie died at 7.30 a.m. on New Year's Eve morning. I had awoken ten minutes earlier and as I held his hand in mine, he was gone...in that incredible moment he had left me.

In one transitory second he had gone. The vital, crucial entity of Ronnie was gone. He was on his way to that other land and I was happy for him. His suffering was no more and his pain a distant memory. The bleak, barren devastation was mine only; the sense of loss was perennial, final and absolute.

One hears the phrase 'dying with dignity'. It means different things to different people. Ronnie died with dignity, in an environment where dignity was supreme; where dying bodies were upheld, blessed and prepared. Ronnie died well, with courage, humility and generosity of spirit.

We struggle to understand the nature of our animating force, but when you look at the still, lifeless face of someone you have loved so much, you know for certain that something so manifest, so salient has vanished. Ronnie's soul, his personality, his being had gone. Indeed, we are puzzling, mystical and impenetrable; moving, breathing and paradoxical creatures.

I learned much from Ronnie's illness. It changed our lives. I do not, however, regret a moment of it. I would go through it all again - for him. In the years that followed I was to miss him unbearably, dreadfully, but loving him and living through that ghastly time with him was to make a contribution to who I am today...

I did not wait beside Ronnie's body. He was not there. He was gone and the proof of his existence lay on a Hospice bed. All that was left behind resembled a suit of clothes. Empty and so terribly alone, I left the room. Mechanical phone calls were made. When I returned, Ronnie's body had been prepared. Oh, but they had combed out his grey curls! Why had I not thought to remind them? Unharmed by illness and pain, those curls had remained as vibrant as ever, an intrinsic evocation of the Ronnie who had left me. So often I had turned those curls in my fingers; so often hearing the beloved voice 'Give over Alice, leave a man alone!'

Those beginning moments were intangible. I was snared in a web of ceaseless, pitiless keening. I pined for my Ronnie, yearned to call for him, cry for him to turn back, to wait for me...as if he was just a few steps ahead of me in the street. He was gone, gone away in the murky, dim and misty spheres of an unknown tract. I was saved by one thought. He was safe.

As I drift back in memory, I think of how peculiar my behaviour must have seemed to the bystander. Perhaps I appeared to be callous, indifferent or crass. Why was I not weeping beside the remains of my dear husband, unwilling in my paralysis of grief to be torn away from my dead love? Within my drained and helpless frailty, I knew that to prolong was useless. Ronnie was not there. The room was empty once more.

My Brother and Sister-in-Law came and words of comfort abounded. Praxis took charge as doors were opened and cars sprung into life. I knew where I wanted to be. I longed to be at West Bank with my Lucy. I longed to be alone there. There, I knew safety, kindness and the cooling walls of home. I knew I could be alone there. How strange to be so deeply lonely and yet crave to be alone. How foolish to expect others to understand. No, they think, I suppose she should not be left alone. In the tumult of grief one finds oneself straining to accommodate the feelings of others. How sad it is when those who are close try so hard to offer support and cheer. They fail and they know they fail. They can do nothing to assuage, commiserate or gladden. All is blank.

Practicalities rush in to fill the gap. 'Perhaps we can have fish 'n' chips tonight' I say, trying to be natural; trying to be sane. No shops are open. Had I forgotten that alas, it is New Year's Eve 2004? It is the day my Ronnie died.

Later, the ritual of bedtime...time to dull the senses, to slip exhausted into soporific dreamless sleep. As Lucy lay near me, I felt the deadening anaesthetic of nothingness folding its blanket of forgetfulness around me; until the morning when the harsh Winter sun would flood the room and my hungry, outstretched arms would reach for my darling. I could not think of waking.

I persuaded my Brother and his wife to leave for home the following day. I was ready for the testing, the questioning, the agonising separation from Ronnie and the thinking.

Ronnie had not wished to talk about Funerals - his nor anyone else's. I could only glean flimsy suggestions after he had attended those of friends and had later remarked on this or that. Some years before, we had heard a rendition of 'Thine Be The Glory' played on a lone trumpet at the Memorial Service of a close Theatre Designer friend who had died very suddenly. Ronnie had not forgotten the power of that music. **'I'd** like that', he had said.

Our tastes were spiritual and simple. Overt religion was not for us. We had a very strong belief in an Afterlife but patent religious encumbrance and its trappings did not trammel or clog our basic, vital faith. As I had kept the vigil beside Ronnie's bed, my wandering, pensive thoughts idled on words and music for I knew the creation of a Funeral Service would be the task assigned to me. It would be a triumphant, shining and brilliant Remembrance of a fine man.

How would I do it? What would I choose? Before those questions resolved themselves, I was helped yet again. Chance, fortune took hold once more.

I had taken Lucy for her walk in the Hospice gardens. When I returned, the Chaplain was deep in conversation with Ronnie. ' I was confiding in Ronnie,' she explained, 'a gentleman along the way is about to plan his Funeral. I thought that was very sensible, but he didn't know what to choose for the Service. Ronnie has come up with some splendid ideas'.

'Yes,' added my Ronnie, 'do you remember that trumpet, Sue? I think that would be wonderful, get them all in the right mood! **And**..' he went on, 'Sue, I would like you to say a few words - that's if you could keep your head, when all those about you are losing theirs!' He knew! I almost heard him say, 'There's no flies on me, petal!'

So all was planned. The Chaplain, Catherine Jackson, arranged for Ronnie's Celebration to take place at her own Church, St. Columba's in Scarborough. The ancient, ornamental and embellished Church was so in keeping with Ronnie's love of elegance, ceremony and Theatricality. 'Camp as Chloe!' would have been his exuberant summing-up. I do so hope that Ronnie was there on his Day. There to see his friends and all who loved him seeking a place where they could enjoy his presence and remember him with love. The Church was overflowing.

Dear friends came to read. Humour threaded its way through crevice and cranny; laughter filled the vast expanse of vault and arch as reminiscences or recollections of Ronnie's antics, escapades and scrapes - some happening long before I met him - banished all trace of sadness.

I chose Vaughan Williams' 'Lark Ascending', for its strains reminded me evermore of Ronnie in his treasured garden. 'Lakme' was his favourite opera and the Service would not have been complete without its 'Flower Duet'. The notes soared and resounded around pillars, pulpit and chancel.

I did speak. I spoke of our meeting, our fun and the joy of sharing my life with Ronnie. I wore the full-length mohair coat, spangled and glowing with love-beads that Ronnie had been determined to finish. My final gift to him formed the lump in my throat and the tears so ready to fall as I looked down on the sheaf of Stargazer Lilies where he lay. I echoed his own words, the ones which had been written so tenderly on my Birthday card and upon my heart: 'Loved you then, love you now and always will'...

Then, never to be forgotten, was the sound of the glorious sole trumpet, applause and fervent, rapturous singing as the Service came to a close. Yes, the Glory was Ronnie's on that memorable day.

Friends came to the house. Friends were there. Family was there. Then...the house vibrated with silence. And yet...West Bank was never silent. Its walls rang with laughter, barking of dogs and voices. Now, it was silent. The table, where curling sandwiches marked the passage of time, waited to be cleared. Its opulent centrepiece, a touching flower array from St. Paul's Girls' School carrying its card and heartfelt message 'St. Paul's owes much to Ronnie', shone with memory and gratitude. He would have been very touched.

The last guests left the house. My Brother and his wife remained for a further night. I was utterly unable to function with any vestige of regularity, routine or reason. I wept as though demented. There was no end to it. I was nerveless, unfit to curb or quell the wash of tears: to slake or stifle my grief. The lament and heartache was all prevailing: it devoured. To the alarm of the onlooker, I must have appeared to be unstable, deranged and lost. I was so. All hope seemed gone and in its place resided a sickness; a homesickness, a homesickness for none other but my Ronnie. He was my home. My delirium was crazed until tiredness left me empty and feeble.

Lucy had stayed with my Brother in the upstairs sitting-room that evening. Now, as I stared, spent, through the black, vacuous density of the conservatory window, she came to lean heavily against my armchair. I looked into the face of one so faithful, so unwavering in her trust. There, in the midst of darkness, I saw the return of belief, of faith. 'Ready to go into the garden, Lucy?' I said and knew that Ronnie had not left me. He was there just as he had always been there, filling the house with love and hope. Yes, we would long for him, but step by aching step we would look to build another life; a life that our darling would wish for us and one that he would help us to live.

From that moment, I picked up the jagged, shattered pieces of my broken heart.

***

PART 1

THEN

LOSS

In those early days of parting and loss, walking Lucy became the most true, prudent part of each day. Morning and evening we trudged together over our best-loved trails. In rain, mist and often snowfall we would mark each pathway with dedication and purposeful pleasure. As Lucy ran and leapt for her ball, my thoughts strayed; off at a tangent, or, listlessly, they would float and roam to the place of secreted memories where tokens and keepsakes of Ronnie were stored. Then, again, the agony would begin. It rose from the very centre of my senses, my existence, and teemed tears that ravaged and tore until Lucy found me.

There was a grassy bank overlooking the sea. A memorial bench inscribed with the words 'In memory of Elsie Stanhope who loved Scarborough' rested there. Lucy rested there too. She would climb up and wait for me to sit beside her. Then I would be leaned upon, until my arm encircled her, hugging, while we both looked out - out over the white-horse waves - as far as the eye could see, lost in our dreamy worlds where a craving, a hunger for Ronnie and the life we had lost, clawed at every sinew. Perhaps Elsie reposed in the selfsame spot remembering. I wondered, wondered if she too had cried out for a lost love and come to her windswept cliff to awaken an eternal reminder. My thoughts were not perpetually lugubrious or given to brooding sadness. At times, I could feel Ronnie's nearness; be mindful of his buoyant, potent discerning of the zany and farcical. His boyish revelling in the daft, the silly and the absurd bubbled over into my consciousness, bringing him close until I could hear his voice, not in the expression of words, but as a sensation in my head, in my mind. Riotous cachinnation would attract the attention of casual passers-by, so, in daylight hours, my odd behaviour needed disguise or my appearance would seem even more eccentric, even weird, as peals of laughter radiated through the chilly morning air...a lone, strange woman and her dog...laughing, alone and strange.

*

I had grown used to the beep of an answer-phone message. Friends were attentive, dear and unfailing in their bid to lend a hand. One message had been partly obliterated, but the tape played on and the voice was Ronnie's. 'Darling, how are...things...I'm here...oh, I thought I was getting better, but....'. The tones were shaken, drugged and weak. All at once, I was reduced to bottomless, twisting, ringing grief as I sank to my knees. Ronnie had tried to ring me, tried to speak in the way he always did in the past, tried to reassure and comfort...even though...even though...he was dying, dying. The message had been lost, unheard until now. I had missed him. I had missed him when he needed me. It was a twist of fate.

Some time before he died, Ronnie had recorded our answer-phone missive. I listened, and listened. I could not elude his lovely voice. I kept it. To this day, I can hear his words again and again when I fail to pick up the receiver in time. I keep him there. For some time, I could not bear to listen to Tapes of the many Radio programmes he had made. Now, they heal and bring his distinctive, mellow voice near to me...a soft, gentle memory.

I imagined returning from a walk with Lucy. I imagined Ronnie standing in the kitchen clad in his striped butcher's apron, just as he always was. Would he still be there? Would I open the door and see him? Had he really gone away? Yet, I knew...knew that the kitchen would now be empty, lifeless, motionless...save for a warmth, a presence that loitered...a faint whistling wafting through the air.

***

PART 1
T H E N

LIFE?

So, a new existence began. Should I say 'life'? I would prefer to speak of living, of vitality, animation and energy. I existed, trying to realise those qualities, but for a while, all was nebulous, intangible and unreal. My life was planned, yes, determined and deliberate, but without its life-blood, its essence, its vital spark.

I could never give way, slump or crumple. Ronnie's endowment spurred me on, drove and gave me the impetus to build again from scratch. I knew I would not surrender to the intensity and magnitude of bereavement. I only wished for Ronnie to be proud of me. So...I imagined his joy, his thrill, his gladness at my achievement. This became my mainspring, the why and wherefore.

West Bank needed me. I cleaned, gardened, shopped and strove to eat well! Oh, how I missed Ronnie's cooking, the delicious fragrance of spice, casserole and roast. I decided that in order to advance my culinary skills, such as they were, and tempt my flagging appetite, I needed to have goals. I needed to entertain! Friends and neighbours were invited to afternoon tea-parties and lunches which were wholesome, but not unduly ambitious in choice of menu! It is true to say, however, that I achieved...and improved. Ronnie would be proud.

Ronnie's garden gave in to my amateurish husbandry, and, in that forlorn first year of 2005, the Spring Snowdrops brought more hope and beauty. I could hear Ronnie's dear exclamation, 'Darling, have you noticed...' as I perceived my handiwork, remembering him marvelling at the miracle of his planting. His blessedness, his pleasure and contentment were infectious and warmed me as I worked. He would have been proud.

In the months that followed, I tried to be busy. The house and its demands kept me busy. Lucy kept me busy. Lucy knew all my turns of mood, my desperate sobbing and my forsaken, secluded misery. Three steps led from the hall passageway and down into the kitchen and that was our place. When days and moments were wild and disconsolate, I remember crouching down there, down until I came to huddle upon the uppermost step, arms clasped around my knees. The tears flowed on and on until I was dry, expended and wiped out. Lucy would climb to the second step and shuffle closely to me. There she leaned. I would feel my arms about her, her warmth holding me still until the shaking had eased. Yes, along came Lucy...

Aggravating tests of patience presented themselves. Television sets broke down and gas fires refused to work. Appalling curses, expletives and language to rival Ronnie's colourful vernacular coursed round room and staircase. I resorted to long conversations with either myself or Lucy, all the while attempting to solve these maddening practical setbacks. I came to the conclusion that screaming obscenities was useless. I had no one other than Lucy with whom I could pick a fight, and anyhow, there was no one else to listen. Also, I had to admit that had Ronnie been on hand, he too would have been at a loss. He had, however, on occasion dealt with electrical malfunctions. Alarm was written on the faces of all present when switches were switched and plugs popped and smoked. No, now these irritations had to be overcome by me - me and only me.

During my stay at the Hospice, I had made a new friend. Angela was to become a lasting companion. Her Husband lay terminally ill in the room next to Ronnie's. Angela had heard Lucy bark and came along to investigate. She and I had much in common and became close friends. Ian, Angela's Husband, died two months after Ronnie left me.

It was Angela who offered sensible advice. She thought it would be a very good idea to accept all invitations to go out and about, whether we wished to accept them or not. So, we found ourselves trying to enjoy Theatre visits, Restaurants and Concerts together. It was never the same for either of us, but our determination to be independent, resilient and positive in heart-sickening change began to win through. We found some motivation to laugh, to exchange ideas and to criticise. Grumpy old women, did someone say - ah well, I wonder. We never see ourselves as others see us.

Angela has seen me through some of my most saddening, worrying and barren times and I owe her much. Well-meaning folk speak of 'moving on', and 'getting over it', but little do they know. 'It' never leaves you. 'It' becomes the immortal traveller who sits on the shoulder; the perpetual, persistent passenger who reminds us of hurt. The kindness of time softens the load and we can carry the consort more easily, but 'it' prods and punctuates every fibre of our being for evermore.

I was not in fine fettle. Until now, there had been no time or inclination to consider my own salubrity. Issues, if there were any, had been rebuffed or shrugged off. In the moments between frenzied activity and sleep, I found myself raising alarm at what, in the past, would have been trivial, paltry niggles.

Suddenly, without warning, the motion of my heart seemed to make its presence felt. Its fluttering invaded my chest. Perhaps I should hold my breath awhile, thought I. Was it racing? Was that a missed beat? If I stirred in the night I would peer into the dark, listening to the silence, yet so sure that I could hear my heart thudding, throbbing on its irregular flow. Panic would drive me to the edge of the bed, where, petrified and drenched in glacial sweat, I would tremble until the spasm passed.

Back and forth, back and forth with a notional portmanteau crammed with ailments, I traipsed to the Doctor. My doldrums were met with patience and an insight born of appreciation; a comprehension. Tests: bloods, investigations, assessments and analysis surrendered proof of my being hale and hearty. Yet still my mind remained scourged with doubt...

'Sue, you need some help, some advice...an ordeal and anguish can take its physical effect' the gentle Hospice voice tentatively proposed. I had received several enquiries and biddings over the months since Ronnie died. I rejected them all, firmly in the belief that I could manage without Bereavement Counselling. At last, miserable and frightened, I took notice.

My gifted, humane helper led me along a way of healing, of remembrance and huge distress. Here, I found permission to place my sorrow on another's shoulders. The trammelling was harboured, lulled and eased. I spoke of Ronnie and me and our love. I spoke of the time before illness and strife tried to destroy our happiness; a time before our love-making became a life-threatening dread. 'Sue, I am so sorry, so sorry that you and Ronnie were never able to recapture that early contentment'. 'No...'.

I wept until there was nothing left. It was time to begin again...a time to mend and get ready. I was alone, but never lonely...for a fleeting glimpse, a faraway voice carried me to a place of renewal, promise and perhaps...dreams. Life would never find that sure, true oneness ever again.

As the close of 2005 drew near, I was invited to attend the opening of a refurbished Stroke Unit at Scarborough Hospital. Alan Ayckbourn was to do the honours and, as Ronnie, while weathering repeated and lasting life-saving treatment there had come to regard this facility as his second home, I suppose it was fitting for me to be included on the guest list. The experience was a painful one, but in the course of that afternoon I began to be steered in a very unexpected direction.

'Have you considered consulting a medium?' The enquiry came from a pleasant, outgoing young woman who was secretary to the Unit Physician. I had not met her before. She continued, 'My Father died at the same time as Ronnie. I have seen a very special woman. I don't really believe in them, but she helped me a great deal. Do go and see her'. A name, address and telephone number was thrust into my hand. Then, this mysterious confidante disappeared into the afternoon-tea crush. I do not recall meeting her again.

The contact details for this stranger were shoved into a sideboard drawer and forgotten.

Events overtook me again and I was beset with nagging symptoms of Carpal Tunnel Syndrome. 'What the fuck's that?' I could hear my beloved saying.

An operation was immediate and for some weeks Lucy was walked by a semi-invalid who nursed a sore, heavily bandaged and immobile arm. These walks were time for ruminating - Ronnie was a great believer in ruminating. My thoughts were often disjointed and sometimes worrying. A solitary life can trigger the temptation to get things out of proportion or perspective. One can become fixated on the attitude or behaviour of others and ridiculous questioning begins. Did she mean that? Why would he say that? One is alone, alone in this odd world, a wilderness: starved of a chance to share, to love and be loved, to just...be...together. Here, there is danger, for one may visualise dreamy, seductive or engaging qualities in others. In our searching loneliness, we are impervious to flaws. We project a desire to see them as we want to see them, so desperate are we to find a home. It is only much later that we know the truth. Thoughts no longer play tricks upon us and our sight is plain. We harness reality and think on our narrow escape.

'Come on, Alice, get a grip!' The joyous words would flash into my senses. Nullifying gloom would be no more. Lucy and I then laughed all the way home, when he was there.

The 20th September was our Wedding Anniversary. A few days before, I was rummaging in the drawer where the name and address had been stowed. The appointment was made.

The Tarot cards lay on the polished pine table before me. I was asked to choose twenty-one cards and take my time shuffling them. I glanced at the smiling, jolly face. It was a young face. Its open expression coaxed this nervous, sceptical listener. Before the cards were consulted, there was a pause. 'A gentleman is here, a very determined gentleman and he is bringing an overwhelming love to you. It is overwhelming me. I am told he has passed with a heart condition. You will know that, he says.' There was another pause. The messenger resumed 'This spiritual connection is rare. I have not experienced such a compelling, fundamental and sublime bond, an affinity, between two souls for a very long time. It is a special, great love'. 'Yes', I whispered, 'a great love'.

'He is still here. He will always be here. Talk to him. He listens. I am being told, and now I am not sure if it is he who is speaking, to ask if you are a writer. There is to be a book. You must get on with that, for it will help others. Readers will learn more about this gentleman - and about you. It is important'. Another pause. 'How long ago did this gentleman pass?' When I answered, my envoy exclaimed, 'I am astonished. He is very persistent, strong-minded. It is often a long time before they make themselves known'. Then came my laughter. Only Ronnie could be that positive, that clear. Nothing would stand in his way. 'Yes, he has an unflinching resolution', I agreed.

I did not doubt these revelations. Ronnie and I had embraced such beliefs throughout our time together. My meeting with this gentle, compassionate seer had only strengthened the sentiments I already held. As I made my way home, on this my Wedding Day, I was filled with hope for the years that my future may hold. Years which may be many without my Ronnie. Yet, for how long that may be, I knew in my heart that he would be there.

*

The book? What about the book? That idea seemed too absurd, too extravagant to contemplate. A writer? No, how could an Actress and teacher of Drama become a writer? Nonsense...

The card dropped from my bedside table. I stooped to pick it up. Every evening I had read the cherished tidings....'Happy Birthday, my Darling. Loved you **then**, love you **now** and **allways** will', complete with spelling mistake!

In that moment, I knew that those three words would form the fabric of the book. It would be a story, a story of a marriage. A story of our life together. I did not question this remarkable turning point, for I pinned my faith, my trust, on a singular guide. I would be helped.

But - where would I begin? The answer was instantaneous - 'On the day we met'.

My trembling fingers hovered over the computer keys. Panic! What was I doing? Where were the words? Would they come from this baffling blank? Was I about to embark upon a fool's errand? No. All was immediate.

The opening sentence formed. The hesitation, the dread of stepping into the unknown vanished. Anecdotes, recollections, reflections and recall surged forward and flooded on to the page. I was off!

No biting of the metaphorical pen, or probing the mental diaries which, in the colourful past, it had not occurred to me to keep. The book became a new calling; a plucky mission which was beginning to fill the lonely hours. I say 'lonely' and yet this was not so, for, as I told of our adventures, I was at one with my beloved Ronnie. Whenever I sensed a hiatus in my thinking, I was aware of mindful nudging. The elusive word would jab into my senses. Unbelieving, I would thumb through the thesaurus, searching for confirmation. Yes! It was there! It was right! I travelled far on this bookish passage.

Fleeting thoughts for the future intruded upon these changed, unwitting happenings. The upkeep of West Bank, a huge Edwardian terraced house, was about to eat into my very small purse. Lucy and I rattled around the many rooms where the seemingly inefficient central heating system found difficulty in permeating the draughty corners. Gradually, the idea, or rather the necessity, of moving began to dawn. The realisation was upsetting. There was so much to leave behind.

Well, I thought, it would do no harm to invite valuations on our dearest house. I contacted a number of Estate Agents and all offered favourable details. Then, yet again, another guardian angel came into my life. A trusted friend recommended a very reputable Agent. So, the number was dialled and a message left.

'Mrs. Herdman, I'm ringing in reply to your enquiry. Brett Thornton, of our company Thornton-Holbrough - we are new to Scarborough - could call on you tomorrow, if that is convenient'. Puzzling! This was not the business I had phoned! Had I confused the number? I explained. 'Not to worry, Mrs. Herdman. I quite understand. I do hope you will be able to reach the firm you wanted'. The young lady was about to ring off. Without hesitation, I asked her to arrange a meeting with the mysterious, unknown representative. Some things are meant to be.

I had become accustomed to the unexpected and more often than not, my 'helpers' turned out to be equally unpredictable, surprising - but always fortuitous! I opened the door to a young, personable and winning Estate Agent. I hasten to add that he also proved to be professional, honest and reliable in his summing up of West Bank. Mr. Thornton got the job! Little did I know then that his friendship would steady me through the tense, taxing times ahead and bring back confidence to the heart of a widow who was doing her best to be a Merry one!

Ronnie had made sure I was not wanting for couturier outfits. I came to realise how much he had given loving thought to providing for me after he had gone. During devitalising weeks between spells of weakening illness, he had remained seated at the dining-table guiding the sewing-machine through feats of mastery. Each and every rig-out was worn with pride, enjoyment and a tiny rebirth of belief. Not once did I allow apathy or indifference to influence my thinking or my preparedness to face this strange, new reality. What? Let myself go? Never! But...how I missed Ronnie's gags, his appreciation and his genial approbation:

'Well, Alice, that's a wonderful piece of schmutter!' I did not, however, lack notice.

It was Brett Thornton who filled a space. Not only was he doing his best to sell West Bank, he was solicitous in accompanying me to view. I was to down-size and the prospect was alarming. On one such occasion, Brett remarked,

'Mrs. Herdman, you always look so elegant'. Pause. 'In fact,' he continued, 'if I may be so bold, quite a funky chick!' Of course I laughed but, for the first time in some considerable time, I found myself dithering, partly because I wasn't quite certain what 'funky' really meant and also, because I was so taken aback by his esteem. After all, I was sixty-five! Silly old bugger! 'Oh, you're not old!' Who said that?

I remember mentioning this to a friend: ' I say, would you think that "funky chick" was a compliment?' Her reply, 'For God's sake Sue, I would say so!' From then on, fear of trips to view or provisions to move became diluted by an unusual, light-hearted friendship.

Brett sold West Bank within six months and was by my side when I decided upon my new home. A short while before, panic had set in when dear West Bank was completed and I was facing the prospect of homelessness. Where was Ronnie?

No doubt he was searching. Soon, a small advertisement tucked into the corner of the Evening News Property page appeared. It caught my attention: a new-build, end-of-terrace tiny house on the outskirts of Scarborough. Brett and I looked at it and concluded: 'A funky doll's house for a funky chick!' Mmn...

Ronnie had found my home; a complete, perfect little home in all aspects. It sat in the middle of a contemporary cluster of dwellings, surrounded by fields and overlooking, at a distance, the Bay of Scarborough. The South-facing garden was a blank canvas, devoid of plants or identity. Well, thought I, I'll think about that tomorrow...

Lucy and I moved into our doll's house on 29th September 2006. The process was a tribulation, a harassing baptism of fire, but at last we had overcome the packing and the safe transportation of boxes filled with treasures. There was a tear when leaving West Bank, a place of lasting happiness and a garden full of precious retrospection and reminder. I had scattered a sprinkling of Ronnie's ashes beneath the Wedding Day rambling rose which crept over the arbour. Part of him would remain forever within the beauty of his Secret Garden. Now, alone, I would create another Garden and hope that he would wander through it, at peace and with us always...

After the frenzied brouhaha and pandemonium had died down, Winter was upon us and there were adjustments to be made within the new house. Friends were unflagging in their willingness to help. Some decorated, some built and assembled built-in cupboards, bookcases and shelves and some were just there. At first there was jumble, a welter and tangle of belongings to wade through, but the shape began to emerge and after Christmas of that year it was time to look to the Garden...

I had read about gardens. I looked at other people's gardens and then looked at mine. I began to realise that the terrain before me was none other than grassland and cold sweat formed upon my brow. I needed Ronnie's help more than ever before. I did not envisage a Garden of Eden, but instead a plot that could be easily managed, beautiful yet practical and something of a refuge, a personal paradise.

I did not have to wait long. I read of Beth Chatto's Mediterranean Garden in the South and marvelled at how she had created a landscape of loveliness within expanses of gravel and rough, parched land. Again, I scaled an unexplored region, a patch of scrubland that one day would become a 'thing of beauty and a joy forever'.

A neighbourly friend recommended a builder, a trusty craftsman and expert in the laying of hard-core. Hard-core? What the fuck was that? I was soon to find out. In no time at all, the foundations of my small Secret Garden were laid and I was looking out on gravel, gleaming in the sunlight. 'A garden should be wall-papered, Sue - you know, trellis...' Ronnie's words floated through the air, 'then you will have a sure fixture for climbers'. So, he couldn't resist it. He was there.

I had noticed his presence in the house. I wrapped its walls around me, knowing I would find a kind of happiness, a contentment there. I would be coming home again.

In the Spring of 2007 the garden was planned. Paved paths wound in and out of gravel, driftwood and terracotta pots. Once the trellis was ready, David Austin's Rose business blossomed under the growth of my orders for climbers: Gertrude Jekyll, The Generous Gardener (yes, really!), Handel (Betty's favourite) and Crown Princess Margareta ('I should have a Queen' Ronnie would say!). The Will Shakespeare floribunda rose, lugged all the way from West Bank, flourished in a large planter beside the wrought iron bench which had graced the rear yard. It kept company with the two huge, antique Garden Gnomes (from Uncle Sandy) standing guard on either side of the back door.

I had read about a Weeping Pear tree. It was to take its place in a far corner of the patch and when in illustrious Spring bloom, its silver leaves attached to sweeping, flowing branches, I may see Blackbirds or Ronnie's Robin perch there. A weeping Cherry Blossom on the other side formed natural symmetry. Alpines, grasses, bulbs filled every gap until the shining stones provided only a framework for vibrant colour. The soil beneath, although nutritious, was heavy. I was, however, encouraged by the sight of worms and spiders. If they could thrive, then so would my precious plants. Some well-meaning neighbours, seeing me toil from morning till night, chipped in with dour remarks: 'Terrible soil, you could be wasting your time...' Ah, little did they know that I had done (wait for it, Ronnie!) a soil test! My challenging clay, my loam was ideal for Azaleas, Camellias and Ceanothus! And...all flourished!

The open plot at the front of the house was devoted to ground cover firs and roses, together with small shrubs such as myrtle or heathers. All was complemented by Summer hanging baskets bursting with pansies, lobelia, begonias and geraniums; not forgetting a standard Canary Bird Rose.

On fine Spring and Summer days, Lucy and I would garden together. She would sit beside me as I weeded, leaning heavily as was her wont, until my arm drew her close. We would pause awhile and think...ruminate.

One can lose oneself in a garden. I knew I had missed so much over the years. This lovely pastime, this fond hope had come late. Often, I would sense a fleeting movement, something in the corner of my eye. I would turn...nothing there...but amity.

Brett made sporadic visits. I enjoyed his stories of house-selling and buying; his horror tales of 'minging' bathrooms and the like. This strange vocabulary of the young was refreshing, funny and easy. He marvelled at the garden, drank liberal glasses of water rather than coffee or tea, and one day announced that he would be tying up the business in Scarborough and plying trade in Newcastle, his home town. I knew that the time had come to say farewell to another guardian angel.

On 19 October 2007, my darling Lucy died. When the time came for me to write about this chapter in my life, I firmly believed that I would be riven, utterly defenceless and unable to do so. Now, she has taken her place in my heart and I think of her with great love and gratitude. Photographs of her fill the little house, some with Ronnie, some in the garden and from some she gazes out into my very spirit.

She had been poorly for several weeks. The faithful Matthew, her Vet., gave deeply shocking news after further tests had been completed. Lucy was gravely ill, so ill that I knew I could not keep her for my own sake.

She was staying in the Veterinary Hospital. I had told Matthew what was to be done. I remember standing in the consulting room waiting for her to be brought to me. The door opened and - along came Lucy. She was joyous, she was happy and for a moment I could not believe that anything was wrong. She was ready to come home. I held her in my arms and spoke of her Ronnie and that he would be waiting and she gently left me forever. I thought my heart would break. My darling Lucy, my stay, my loving friend who had seen me grieve, ache, long for and sigh...

My life was never the same. Walks were never the same. I tried to follow the tracks, sit on the same benches, but it was never the same. I saw Lucy around every corner and glimpsed her lolloping over our special outcrop of rock in search of her ball. I looked for her everywhere and in the long Winter evenings, my hand would drop down by the side of the chair waiting to stroke the soft head, imagining I could see melting brown eyes staring back at me.

Yes, along came Lucy...

The following times were taken up with the daily round, often stimulating, but often empty and without purpose. Not for long...

Australian Doug once said to me 'Life's not a bowl of cherries, love. Believe me, if you can grow up like me, a poof, in the Australian outback, then you're not afraid of anything!'

Doug and Ronnie had worked together many years ago at Lincoln Repertory Company. I first met him on my Wedding Day when he had taken a mild fancy to Reg! He and Ronnie had extended telephone conversations which rocked West Bank with peals of laughter. After Ronnie's death, Doug and I became phone friends. We spent many hours talking. Doug was wise, Doug was very funny and Doug blessed me with the comfort I needed.

The in-between years were not filled with incident, but were comfortable, somewhat predictable and certainly ordinary. The days and months came and went and my time was spent in the management of things that were necessary: washing, cooking, ironing, not to mention repeated visits to the Garden Centre. I loved my home. It was a pleasure to care for it, to regard all the lovely ornaments and pictures around me; to remember from whence they came and who gave them to us.

I became acquainted with neighbours. I had learned much from Ronnie. He was forever outgoing, friendly and eager to draw people to him. My overtures were rewarded as his had been. My Voluntary work for the Hospice and Stroke Unit continued and I was invited to give Poetry Readings and entertainments for various gatherings in the area. I was busy.

I learned much from those years. I learned to be alone. I learned to be independent and positive. There was neither room nor time for self-pity or misery. Some moments caught me unaware and then there was sorrow. There was weeping and there was loneliness. I learned to keep those moments in a private place. I learned patience and perseverance as I endeavoured to change plugs and lift the bonnet of the car. I also learned to be proud of myself.

My book became my best friend. I would look forward to mastering the baffling perplexities of the confounded computer. All with the help of guardian angels. Neighbour Steve and his wife Tracey and Rob, an electrician, became dear friends who guided me through the technological minefield of word processing wizardry. All played their part in my painstaking, agonising growth, my need to forge ahead.

I would talk to Ronnie. I never doubted his presence or influence. It filled the house and garden. I looked upon the hardships, the illnesses and worries as milestones. All I asked for was the strength to live through them, to make the best of grievances when adversity seemed to take the upper hand. I lived the life we would have lived together. It was a simple life, the only difference being that the tangible presence of Ronnie was no more.

I did not write every day. Often I was tired but more often I would quibble, or prevaricate. Excuses for not getting-down-to-it would cause delay. The real culprit was timidity. Would the words come? Would I be able to do it? I was a beginner...how?...'Come on, Alice, get a move on!'

Then, Ronnie and I would be as one and travelling the road once more. Laughter, tears and love fashioned the faltering words and through the mists of time we were together again. 'We were on't roaaad!'

*

In 2010, Miriam Johnson came into my life again. Headway had manifested itself in both our lives. She was now Professor Miriam Johnson, Specialist in Heart Failure and Honorary Consultant at St. Catherine's Hospice.

'Sue, I'm organising a Medical Conference to be held at the Spa, here in Scarborough. It will be in March of next year and I would like to invite you to give a presentation.'

Miriam went on to explain. At first, I had difficulty in absorbing the full implication of what she was saying. I was wholly taken aback. This was to be an unnerving undertaking.

'Sue, just speak about your life with Ronnie. Talk about the enormity of breathlessness, its restraints and the toll it took on your lives. Talk to us about the life of a carer, you, and how you coped with it. We Doctors need to know what it's like to be on the chalk face of such actuality. Talk about endurance and survival'.

Ronnie, it seems, had not been idle! Somehow, somewhere, I was convinced that he had been a party to bringing this about. Fanciful perhaps, but once again a visionary happening; too much of a coincidence, too uncanny to dismiss without credibility.

I realised that my eligibility for this new role depended on my particular skills. As actress and teacher, my aptitudes were useful in this fresh, yet somewhat disarming communication. I was scared stiff. To speak before the great and the good of the Medical world, was a force to be reckoned with. This time, **I** muttered the time-honoured words, 'Come on, Alice...'

On March 31 2011, I faced nearly two hundred delegates. I had been asked to speak for forty minutes and Miriam, knowing that I entertained Hospice patients with readings, asked me to include appropriate Poetry. For help, I turned to my Brother, Nicholas Uebel, a writer. His poem, 'Fear' began my presentation. I include it here for it encompasses all. An attack of Heart Failure at night is traumatic both for the sufferer and the one who looks on.

My Brother captured the core of that experience:

Half awake and still dreamy, a background sound
Suddenly alert, that wretched noise, familiar ground
Gasping, wheezing, clawing for breath
My darling is ashen, is it now, is it death?

Fumbling fingers, tapping the phone
Oh for God's sake, answer it, I feel so alone
They're coming, thank God, they're on their way
Deep in my heart I beg, please not today...

Later, the Doctor says he'll be OK
You did the right thing, you called straight away
I shudder, steal a look at my dear
Inside I'm like jelly held together with fear.

Each new day - a trial, as we journey on
I must hold it together until it is gone.
Fear travels with me wherever we go
A horrible memory I'll always know.

A part of me dies with each episode

Stress fills my heart with a piercing cold.
I must carry on for the sake of my dear
Two separate lives, one of hope...one of fear...

Copies of this poem, intense and poignant in its simplicity, were requested by many Doctors. It was to augment training sessions for Students who wished to specialise in Heart Failure.

I spoke to people from specific Medical domains, provinces and functions: Cardiologists, Macmillan Nurses, Palliative Care Specialists and General Practitioners. I shared with them our Hospice repose, our thoughts and our life. In a most unforeseen, arcane way, I had brought Ronnie and those who suffer as he had done to cardinal experts; people powerful enough to encourage greater awareness, knowledge and discernment when in pursuit of helping others who could not help themselves.

I, too, had been helped.

Towards the end of 2011, Miriam contacted me again. This time, I was invited to speak at the National Conference in London, due to take place in March 2012. It was being arranged by the British Heart Foundation in conjunction with the Council for Palliative Care. The content of my presentation was to be different. The Conference, entitled 'Beating the Barriers', was to concentrate on the needs of people with Heart Failure at the end of life.

I addressed nearly three hundred delegates. The group was made up of Heart Failure Specialists, Palliative Care professionals and Consultants who operated in settings working with people approaching the end of life - those in Primary Care, Hospital, Social Care, Housing and beyond.

I spoke in detail of our end-of-life pilgrimage, so protected by the Hospice. Ours was a fact and a truth; a test and a trial that we went through together.

Not until I reached my Brother's final few lines 'New Beginnings' did my calm leave me and I was, once more, sitting at Ronnie's bedside with his hand held in mine...

Ronnie came so full of anguish, fear and fret
But found tranquillity - and yet
A place of hope, he was not adrift
Its bold reality a vital lift.

An embrace of understanding held him tight
Banished that all-pervading fright.
Safe at last, he could be
His old self - Ronnie - free...

Such things, such feelings can only be expressed in wondrous simplicity. Before leaving for London, I remember a dear friend and colleague from my St. Paul's days, Nicholas Dakin, saying to me 'Good Luck, dear Sue. I'm sure Ronnie will be there on the front row, no doubt clutching a box of matinee chocolates and cheering you on...' What a glorious image...an image of a time when life was in sunshine and not half shadows...

***

PART 2

N O W

Now, it is nearly ten years since Ronnie died.

Now, it seems like only yesterday or five minutes before.

Now, I have made a life. A life that I hope Ronnie would have me enjoy. He was my torchbearer and my guide, without ever knowing it was so.

Now, as I come closer to the end of my own life, I am thankful for its riches; thankful for my years with Ronnie.

Now, as I choose a title for this book – 'Happy Birthday, my Darling', I know it is a testament to the beginning of my true life. Ronnie brought renewal and a sea change, adventure, courage, laughter - so much laughter - and realisation. When I met him on that far-off day in the Theatre Wardrobe Department, I had no idea that that day was to be a birth day. Every aspect of my life was to be transfigured.

Now, as I think of long ago, I marvel at Ronnie's fortitude, his strength of mind and stout-heartedness. He showed me how to be brave; how to withstand hurt, unfairness and pain. There was no room in Ronnie's life for selfishness. He knew that time spent in argument or unrest was wasteful. Time was precious, more precious to us than we could ever know.

Now, I have time to think and time to ruminate! I have a greater depth of understanding. I can remember and perceive the paradox surrounding our early coming together. At the time, I did not realise how puzzling it must have been, how contrary, how discordant it must have seemed to others, when Ronnie and I fell in love. Yet most of all, I think of Ronnie's fearlessness, trust and loving kindness.

'Ronnie', I said one day, 'do you think you would have changed your life if you had not met me?'

'Sue, I knew I loved you very deeply. Nothing else mattered except being with you. That's why I changed my life. It was for the love of you'.

Now, I know that love transcends all. It surpasses, eclipses and remains everlasting and for evermore....

***

PART 3

A L W A Y S

A great love is a rare, fine gift; a ceaseless, limitless bestowal. One day, I know that Ronnie and I will share it perfectly, in another time...

'We are not human beings on a Spiritual journey.
We are Spiritual beings on a human journey.'

PIERRE TEIL HARD DE CHARDIN
French Visionary

***